The Price Guide to
to

COLLECTABLE ANTIQUES

by James Mackay

Published by

THE CHANCERY HOUSE PUBLISHING CO.,
5 CHURCH STREET,
WOODBRIDGE,
SUFFOLK.

Published 1975
by Chancery House Publishing Co.,
5 New Bridge Street, London, E.C.4.
for the Antique Collectors' Club

ISBN 0 902028 08 1

Printed in England by
Baron Publishing, Woodbridge, Suffolk.

To Evelyn and Andrew Mathieson

FOREWORD

The Antique Collectors' Club

The Antique Collectors' Club, formed in 1966, pioneered the provision of information on prices for collectors. The Club's monthly magazine *Antique Collecting* was the first to tackle the complex problems of describing to collectors the various features which can influence prices. In response to the enormous demand for this type of information the *Price Guide Series* was introduced in 1968 with **The Price Guide to Antique Furniture**, a book which broke new ground by illustrating the more common types of antique furniture, the sort that collectors could buy in shops and at auctions, rather than the rare museum pieces which had previously been used (and still to a large extent are used) to make up the limited amount of illustrations in books published by commercial publishers. Fourteen other price guides followed, all copiously illustrated, and greatly appreciated by collectors for the valuable information they contain, quite apart from prices. This, the fifteenth price guide, is the first general one to be produced. It combines a range and depth of detail which marks a further step forward in providing information on the values of antiques.

Club membership, which is open to all private collectors, costs £6.95 per annum. Members receive free of charge *Antique Collecting* the Club's monthly magazine, which contains well-illustrated articles dealing with the practical aspects of collecting not normally dealt with by magazines. Prices, features of value, investment potential, fakes and forgeries are all given prominence in the magazine.

In addition members buy and sell among themselves; the Club charges a nominal fee for introductions but takes no commission. Since the Club started nine years ago many thousands of antiques have been offered for sale privately. No other publication contains anything to match the long list of items for sale privately which appears monthly.

The presentation of useful information and the facility to buy and sell privately without the middle man's profit would alone have assured the success of the Club but perhaps the feature most valued by members is the ability to make contact with other collectors living nearby. Not only do members learn about the other branches of collecting but they make interesting friendships.

As its motto implies, the Club is an amateur organisation designed to help private individuals get the most out of collecting; it is informal and friendly and gives enormous enjoyment to all concerned.

The Antique Collectors' Club

Clopton, Woodbridge,

Suffolk.

For Collectors – By Collectors – About Collecting

PRICE REVIEW

1st December annually

(The first review will be published in 1976)

The usefulness of a book containing prices rapidly diminishes as market values change, for prices can fall as well as rise.

In order to keep the prices in this book up-dated, a price review will be issued on 1st December each year. This review will record the major price changes in the values of the items covered under the various headings in the book.

To ensure that you receive the Price Review yearly, complete a banker's order form and send it to the address given below.

The Price Review costs £1.75 a year by banker's order or £1.95 cash, from:–

**THE CHANCERY HOUSE PUBLISHING CO.,
at 5 CHURCH STREET, WOODBRIDGE, SUFFOLK.**

ACKNOWLEDGEMENTS

I would like to acknowledge the help and assistance provided by the following experts who gave me invaluable information which I have been grateful to include in my text.

Elizabeth Aldridge
John Andrews
Janet Arnold
Sarah Battie of Sotheby's,
    Belgravia
Dr. C.F.C. Beeson
Denys Bellerby
A.E. Boothroyd
M. Broadbent of Christie's
Cynthia Brown
Simon Bull of Christie's
Ron Dale
Gordon Dando
N.K. Davey of Sotheby's
Tom Frost
Phillipe Garner
J. Harris
Peter Hawkins of Christie's
Philip Hewat-Jaboor of Sotheby's,
    Belgravia
Peggy Hickman
Edward Holmes of Christie's
Anne Clark Hutchison
Peter Johnson of Phillips
Tom Lawson
A.Leslie

H. Linecar of Spink & Son
Susan Mayor of Christie's
Cecil A. Meadows
Mary Middleton
Christopher Minns
J.E. Minns
P. Mould
Sally Mount
H. Otten of Weller & Dufty Ltd.
David Paterson of
    Stanley Gibbons Currency Ltd.
Primrose Peacock
Ian Pickford
Dr. E.R. Roberts
George Savage
James Storm
Christopher Sykes
W. Tilley
Paul Viney of Phillips
Tony Voss
Roland Ward
Graham Webb
Graham Wells of Sotheby's
Jeanette White
J.B. Winter of Sotheby's
Christopher Wood of Christie's

I would like to thank the following individuals and organisations who have allowed me to reproduce some of the photographs used in this book and those who have had them specially taken for me. For their help I am most grateful.

Charles Allix
Boardman & Oliver
Charles Boardman & Son
British Industrial Plastics Ltd.
The Director, Chemical Research Establishment, Porton Down (gas masks).
Christie's
Christie's, South Kensington
Constance Chiswell Antiques
Delomosne & Son
Dennis Neal
Dreweatt Watson & Barton
King & Chasemore
Knight Frank & Rutley
Locke & England
Maggs Bros. Ltd.
Sylvia Mann
Messenger May Baverstock
Mitchell Museum
Parsons Welch & Cowell
Phillips
Science Museum
The Shuttleworth Collection
Sotheby's
Sotheby's Belgravia
Henry Spencer & Sons
Spink & Sons Ltd.
Stanley Gibbons Currency Ltd.
Christopher Sykes Antiques
The Victoria & Albert Museum
Wallis & Wallis
Weller & Dufty
Whitton & Laing

James Mackay

CONTENTS

Aeronautica 1
Apostle Spoons 6
Apple Corers 8
Autographs 10
Badges 16
Barometers 22
Books 27
Boot and Shoe Trees 37
Bosun's Pipes 39
Bottles 41
Britannia Metal 54
Buckles 56
Buttons 59
Caddy Spoons 71
Cameras 73
Candlesticks 77
Card Cases 81
Carriage Clocks 86
China Fairings 92
Christmas Cards 97
Cigarette and Trade Cards 100
Commemorative Medals 104
Commemorative Pottery 111
Copper and Brass 117
Corkscrews 122
Costume 128
Cow Creamers 137
Decanters 143
Dining Chairs 150
Dolls 166
Enamelled Boxes 176
Fans 182
Fireside Objects 188
Flatware 196
French Art Glass 204
Gas-Masks 211
Goss China 215

Gramophones 218
Hatpins 222
Helmets and Headgear 226
Horsebrasses and Harness 232
Inro 238
Jelly Moulds 242
Jetons 246
Knives 250
Lace 253
Lace Bobbins 257
Locomotive Models 261
Mauchline Ware 266
Medals and Decorations 271
Microscopes 277
Militaria and Navalia 281
Mirrors 286
Model Soldiers 292
Money-Boxes 297
Musical Boxes 300
Music Covers 310
Musical Instruments 317
Netsuke 329
Nutmeg Graters 334
Oil Lamps 338
Ormolu 344
Paper Money 348
Paperweights 357
Papier Mâché 364
Patchwork 368
Pewter 370
Photographs 375
Picture Postcards 384
Pipe Stoppers 391
Plastiques 395
Playing Cards 402
Propelling Pencils 407
Pottery and Porcelain Cottages 411
Powder Flasks and Horns 416
Railway Relics 423
Rolling Pins 434
Safety Lamps 436
Scales and Balances 438
Scent Bottles 444

Scientific Instruments 447
Screens 452
Sextants 456
Signs 458
Silhouettes 466
Snuffboxes 472
Spoons 478
Stools 482
Sundials 486
Tea Caddies and Chests 492
Telescopes 497
Thimbles 500
Tie Pins 506
Tiles 510
Tins 517
Toby Jugs 520
Tongs 524
Treen 528
Tsuba 534
Tunbridge Ware 539
Typewriters 543
Valentines 547
Vesta Boxes 550
Vinaigrettes 554
Walking Sticks 557
Watch Stands 563
Weapons: Bayonets 568
           Daggers 571
           Swords 575
           Tipstaves and Truncheons 581
Wine Labels 584
General Reading List 589

INTRODUCTION

This book is a compendium of minor collectables, some long established, others of comparatively recent interest, and is intended to give some guidance as to current market values, together with a survey of the points which enhance an object's value and the pitfalls which the collector may be likely to encounter.

Over a hundred major categories of collectable objects are given in alphabetical order by subject. Within these groups, however, many larger and more general subjects are sub-divided into more specific categories. The more important (or more fashionable) aspects of militaria or scientific instruments, for example, are treated separately, while the lesser collectables are discussed under the generic headings of Militaria and Scientific instruments. In a similar way, a large number of minor items are dealt with under such headings as Aeronautica, Fireside Objects and Railway Relics.

When I started to prepare for this book the problem I faced was that of exclusion rather than inclusion, for without exertion, I was able to put together a list of 600 items. Closer examination showed that while it would have been possible to include them all (in several volumes) some subjects present either a very wide range of variations or are extremely complex. The former category is exemplified by Pot-lids, a subject which would require a large number of pages of illustrations for the titles are not always self-explanatory. To include them would have taken up one volume, and, as there is already a Price Guide to Pot-lids, it would seem sensible to exclude them. The second category can be typified by Antique Watches. To give detailed assistance would require a great deal of explanation for comments such as "Stackfreed generally start at £4,000" would not be particularly helpful without a detailed technical description and photograph. This again would require a complete volume and so was excluded from the list.

A third basis for exclusion is cost. If one is going to collect marquetry clocks or Fabergé eggs, one needs detailed help and assistance outside the range of any book, let alone a general price guide. Accordingly, the scope of the book was, in general, confined to the less valuable antiques (obviously early or very special examples of any subject can be expensive) where at least some examples can be acquired without huge expense.

Even so, this left a list of entries which could easily have doubled the size of this present volume, and it is hoped therefore to produce a supplemental volume at some future date. By that time no doubt the ever-spreading net of the collector will have embraced many subjects whose collectability has scarcely been considered as yet!

Why are the items in each photograph not valued? Both the publishers and myself feel strongly that a general price guide based simply, or even partly, on photographs with a price attached, can be misleading if not dangerous. What is important is why a piece is worth £100, not the fact that one isolated example is worth that much. To make sense of priced photographs, one would need to have long explanatory captions under each photograph to make the reasons for the value clear. As these explanations are already given in the text, I have decided to use the photographs to illustrate type, date or some other feature which is helpful.

The usual arrangement of this book is a very brief introduction to the subject, followed by a concise summary of the development of the subject by date. Where convenient, pricing is included in the **Date-lines,** but in certain cases this is discussed separately. This is followed by **Points to look for**, drawing attention to the features which tend to enhance value, and the **Pitfalls** which detract from value, or against which the collector should constantly be on guard. In some cases where dating is immaterial or of much lesser importance, other criteria have been adopted. These include the grouping of objects according to the materials, method of construction or actual types.

While many of the more traditional antiques are discussed, emphasis here is laid on collectables which, while now having a fairly well-established market, are mainly of more recent interest to collectors. These newer interests tend to be a reflection of the times in which we live. The significant rise in interest in all aspects of militaria for example, (one of the largest growth areas in collecting over the past decade), may reflect the attention of a generation which never knew National Service, far less the Second World War. Similarly the significant increase in railwayana is in inverse proportion to the number of viable lines now operated by British Rail. Of course nostalgia or a hankering for the objects of a bygone age has always been one of the root causes of collecting. The rapid changes in our modern way of life, and the cult of built-in obsolescence, may well mean that many functional everyday objects in current use will have an antiquarian value in ten years' time.

There were many other minor collectables which I was tempted to include, but by limitations of space I felt constrained to omit them on this occasion for various reasons. One of these reasons in some cases was the absence of an established market with a recognisable scale of values. Herein lies a dilemma, since some guidance to these very items is what is probably needed most.

I make no apologies for the brevity of the introductory remarks in each subject. There is now an abundance of general dictionaries and encyclopaedias which cover the ground perfectly adequately, and these books are given in the general Reading List. More specific guidance to further reading, however, is given at the end of each entry, where detailed handbooks and monographs are listed. My own experience has been that, if you cannot actually handle objects to learn about them, the next best thing is to study them in museum collections. For this reason I have considered it very important to give lists of museums appropriate to each subject. Auctions too are a good place to learn.

As this is, in essence, a Price Guide, it follows that the most important aspect of the book is its attempt at pricing the various grades and types of objects. This has been the most exacting and challenging aspect of the work, and one which was fraught with innumerable problems. In some cases there might be as many as a dozen criteria governing the value of an object: age, material, type of construction, quality of craftsmanship, artistic or aesthetic considerations, unusual technical or decorative features, the provenance of personal association, the presence or absence of makers' marks, full hallmarks, dates, inscriptions and so forth. These and other criteria vary in importance from one object to another, and may even vary within the range of a single category, at different periods or in certain circumstances. So far as is humanly possible I have tried to assess these factors, giving reasons for the rarity or desirability of certain features at some times and their comparative unimportance at others, but the reader must form his or her own assessment of the worth of an object in the light of all the factors concerned. For this reason values are invariably expressed as a range of prices rather than a single sum. In many cases the price bracket may be fairly narrow, with not much differential between the upper and lower ends of the price scale; in other cases the value of an object may literally run from £2 to £2,000, though in such extreme cases I have broken the price range down into more manageable portions.

Where the price range remains wide, it is fair to say that the bulk of the items the collector is likely to come across will be towards the bottom of the price range simply because they *are* the most frequently found and hence do not have the scarcity which, together with quality of production, tends to command a price premium. Of course one can be lucky and this is part of the charm of collecting.

In setting the prices in this book, it has been assumed that all the pieces discussed are in reasonable condition. Reasonable condition of course, depends on the object and the degree to which damage and repairs are accepted by specialist collectors and dealers. A very fine early panelled chair might well have a replacement to the last two inches of a back leg and if well done this would have practically no effect on the price. On the other hand, a run of the mill lacquer object scratched and crudely repainted would be almost valueless. The general rule is that where a piece is interesting and few collectors have one in their collection, a much damaged example will fetch a surprisingly good price. This often happens with early examples from important factories, whereas a common jug, missing a handle, will be virtually worthless. The failure to appreciate the effects on value of poor condition, which of course includes lack of patination, loss of original surface, fading etc., etc., is one of the most common causes of the misunderstanding of quoted prices. 'But it must be worth at least £20, it says so in the book' uttered by some woebegone individual clutching a broken pot missing its lid, must have annoyed many a dealer whose stock includes six perfect examples he cannot sell at the eminently fair price of £25. Once, however, the collector gets past the limited mentality approach, pandered to by publishers who simply quote prices under ancient auction photographs or crude sketches, then price guides of this nature can be of considerable value.

The price ranges also take into account the imponderables of where, when and how an article comes on to the market. Even now there is still a wide disparity in the sum which identical objects may fetch in a major or minor London saleroom, in a provincial auction or a country house sale. The individual vagaries or obsessiveness of two or more wealthy collectors may grossly affect the auction price of certain objects on a particular occasion, while absolutely identical objects can (and sometimes do) fetch half these sums at other times in other places. Moreover, there is both a greater disparity between prevailing auction realisations and dealers' retail prices in general, and between the prices of one dealer and another — not always miles apart! Unfortunately the collector cannot do as the housewife ought in these inflationary times, and shop around before making a purchase. The price ranges quoted in this book are considered to represent the sort of prices which would not be unreasonable to pay when purchasing articles. There are still many bargains to be picked up; but all too often one finds that objects are outrageously over-priced in general antique or junk shops. Contrary to popular belief, I have found that the best bargains are still to be had in the London area; conversely some of the most atrocious over-pricing has been observed in Edinburgh and Glasgow. I must qualify this statement by adding that there is no clearly definable regional pattern of pricing in the United Kingdom; this is something which each collector has to explore for himself.

AERONAUTICA

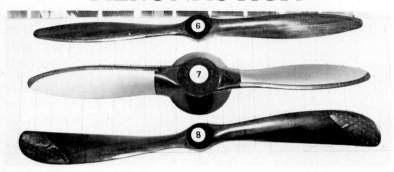

6 - 100 h.p. Mono Gnome. 7 - Bristol Bulldog. 8 - 80 h.p. Renault suitable for all Avro 504.

Anything collectable pertaining to the history and development of civil or military aviation. Although man's pre-occupation with flight is as old as mankind itself, the practical expressions of this date from the 16th century and the writings of Leonardo da Vinci. Collectable items, however, date only from the late 18th century when ballooning (or 'aerostation' as it was then known) became a craze in western Europe. This manifested itself in the use of balloons or ballooning motifs as a form of decoration on furniture, fan-leaves, watch-cases, porcelain dishes and engraved glass. Thereafter aeronautics developed in many directions, and produced a number of categories of collectable items which are discussed separately below.

Ballooning Subjects

These date mainly from 1783 to 1830, the period in which man-made balloon flights were still regarded as a novelty. Balloons provided a colourful and highly topical motif of decoration in many media. They may be found engraved on the lids of snuff-boxes and vinaigrettes, painted on fan-leaves, enamelled on glassware or the insides of watch-cases, in underglaze polychrome decoration on pottery and porcelain (principally plates and plaques, but also less commonly on tankards and bowls). The most highly prized form of balloon decoration is inlaid boulle or marquetry on boxes, chests and commodes. The presence of a ballooning motif on any of these objects enhances their value by 50%, or up to 60% if the balloon is identified by a quasi-commemorative inscription. Other articles of this period which are highly prized are books, pamphlets, prints and broadsheets relating to Pilâtre de Rozier, J.A.C. Charles, Vincent Lunardi,

1

Montgolfier or other early pioneers of ballooning. Among the early ephemera may be mentioned posters, tickets of admission to exhibitions of balloons and balloon ascents at the Cremorne and Vauxhall Gardens, etc. Later ballooning memorabilia, though actually scarcer, is not so highly regarded. Among items belonging to the period 1850-1900 are printed handkerchiefs and scarves showing balloon ascents mainly in connection with American fairs and exhibitions. Stevengraphs and other woven silk pictures featuring balloons were popular from 1860 to 1890. Similar subjects may be found on embroidered bookmarkers of the same period. Particularly desirable are flown letters, envelopes, miniature newspapers, commemorative medals and other ephemera connected with the Siege of Paris Balloon Post, 1870-71 (£5 – £70). Flown flimsies from the Siege of Metz are exceedingly rare (£100 – £250).

Model Aircraft

Experiments into the problem of heavier-than-air machines began in the late 18th century and models of various aircraft were constructed between 1796 and the advent of the first powered flights in 1903. Authentic models by Cayley, Stringfellow, Penaud, Henson, Manly, Langley and others are very rare and difficult to value. Commercially produced model gliders, however, date from about 1880. Box kites date from the mid-19th century, but are difficult to date accurately. Toy aircraft became very popular in the decade before the First World War. The majority are ungainly and out of scale, often incorporating features taken from mythology or ornithology. Accurate scale model gliders and elastic-operated aircraft began to develop about 1910, but authentic early examples are rare. 'Dinky toy' models between the wars range from £2 to £10 depending on condition and rarity. Wooden Second World War models to about £5.

Souvenirs of Aviation Meetings

There was a resurgence of the ballooning craze in the 1890s, and this developed in the years immediately before the First World War into the fashion for aviation meetings. Various aspects of this may be considered separately. Apart from the free balloons, there was the development of dirigibles by Parseval and Zeppelin, the prototypes of the airships of the First World War. Souvenirs connected with these early flights include special postcards, pop-up cards, labels, posters, postmarks and semi-official stamps, commemorative medals and medalets, badges and pins, publicising or commemorating air displays, pioneer flights and aviation meetings. Examples of these souvenirs exist from most western European countries, but principally France, Germany, Britain and Italy.

Royal Flying Corps Christmas card.

Royal Flying Corps boots.

They may also be found from the United States and more rarely, from Russia and Japan. Original posters are from £5 – £50; postcards unused £2 – £10, £5 – £50 if actually flown; other mementoes vary considerably in value, but generally from £2.

Early Aircraft Equipment

Fragments of aircraft, pieces of fabric (where the provenance can be authenticated), primitive flying instruments, control columns, bombsights, etc. were popular souvenirs of the First World War. Their value depends very largely on the degree of inherent interest, or the association with some famous ace or spectacular event. As with militaria (q.v.), components of military aircraft usually bear official markings and serial numbers which aid identification and dating.

Propellors from aircraft of First World War vintage have certain aesthetic qualities – polished laminated wood surfaces, polished brass leading edges and centre. £50 – £100. Later propellers of wood, with fabric covering, are less desirable. £35 – £60. All metal propellers (duralumin or aluminium), are less decorative but often have unusual technical features. Pre-Second World War up to £50. Second World War and later up to £30.

Early helmets, goggles, flying suits and insignia, uniforms of the Royal Flying Corps and other air services, are in great demand. First World War goggles range from £2 to £5, leather and cork helmets from £5 to £15 and uniforms from £25 to £50.

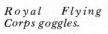
Royal Flying Corps goggles.

Later Aviation Souvenirs

In this category come memorabilia of the inter-war period when flying was still in its infancy and the commercial airlines were born. Aircraft captured the popular imagination in the same way as the earlier balloons, though to a much lesser extent. Small decorative objects with an aircraft motif include desk sets, ash-trays, tins and boxes, embossed metal plaques, porcelain and pottery mugs and plates. Miniature aircraft cast in bronze, white metal, aluminium, brass or spelter are highly collectable if dated before 1940. Second World War items in cast aluminium are still fairly plentiful (mostly Spitfires and Hurricanes) and range from £2 to £12 according to type and quality.

Airmail

This is a vast subject in itself, ranging from the Ballons Montes and Papillons de Metz of the Franco-Prussian War, to the latest air letter sheets and first flight souvenir envelopes and cards. Semi-official airmail

Royal Flying Corps gloves.

Royal Flying Corps leather helmet.

4

stamps date from 1877 and official issues from 1917 and form an important branch of philately. Another major aspect consists of aerial propaganda leaflets, mostly relating to the two world wars, but also including items dropped in other campaigns from 1920 onwards, and also publicity leaflets dropped from aircraft to advertise fairs, exhibitions or even to disseminate government policies. Leaflets of this sort from £1 to £15.

Museums
British Museum, London.
Science Museum, London.
Royal Air Force Museum, London.
Transport Museum, Glasgow.
Shuttleworth Collection, Biggleswade.

Reading List
Dallas, Brett, R. History of British Aviation. 2 vols. 1908-1914 and 1913-1914.
Duval. G.R. British Flying-boats and Amphibians, 1909-1952. London, 1953.
Funderburk, Thomas R. The Fighters: the Men and Machines of the First Air War. London, 1966.
Green, William. Famous Fighters of the Second World War. London, 1962. World Guide to Combat Planes. London, 1966. The World's Fighting Planes. London, 1964.
Hatton, Turner. Astra Castra. 1865.
Hodgson, J.E. The History of Aeronautics in Britain, 1924.
Jackson, A.J. British Civil Aircraft. 2 vols. 1959. British Naval Aircraft, 1958. Aircraft of the Fighting Period. Vols. 1-7. World War Two and after.
Janes All The World's Aircraft — published annually.
Mackay, James A. Airmails, 1870-1970. London, 1971.
MacMillan, Norman. Great Aircraft. London, 1960.
Nowarra, Heinz J. and Duval, G.R. Russian Civil and Military Aircraft, 1884-1969. London, 1970.
Smith, Charles H. Gibbs. The Aeroplane. London, 1960. A History of Flying. London, 1953.
Swanborough, F.C. Combat Aircraft of the World. London, 1962.
Taylor, John W.R. Aircraft. London, 1964. Warplanes of the World. London, 1967.
Taylor, J.W.R. and Munison, K. History of Aviation. 1972.
Warring, R.H. Aeromodelling. London, 1965.

APOSTLE SPOONS

Spoons made in Europe from the 15th to mid-17th centuries, usually in silver but occasionally found in pewter or brass. These spoons were a popular christening present and given in sets of thirteen (composing Christ and His Apostles), though the less well-endowed might receive a half-set of six. Complete sets are of the utmost rarity and are virtually unknown outside museum collections. From the number of individual spoons found, especially those portraying Apostles with names such as James or John, it is assumed that in humbler circumstances it was quite acceptable to give a child a single spoon representing his saint's name. The bowl and stem of Apostle spoons conform to the style and construction of other silver spoons (q.v.) of the comparable period.

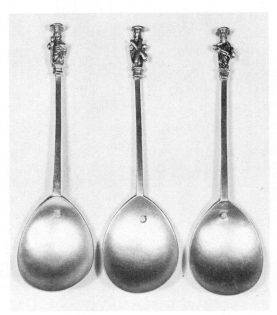

Typical London made Apostle spoons of the early 17th century. All in fine condition. Left to right: St. James the Greater (pilgrim's staff); St. Andrew (saltire) rare; St. Philip (Latin cross).

Date-lines

15th century — 1570	Very rare. £400 — £1,500.
1570-1600	£350 — £1,200.
1600-1630	£250 — £1,000.
1630-1650	£200 — £750.

The earlier spoons are characterised by finely modelled figures. Later spoons have coarser modelling, as the moulds became worn with constant use. Apostle spoons were revived in the 19th century (£10 – £25) but should present no problem in identification.

Condition affects values and London examples are normally more expensive than provincial.

Points to look for

Spoons featuring Christ (the master spoon) are relatively scarce. Because of the demand in Scotland (whose patron saint he is), St. Andrew is much in demand. The Apostles can be identified by means of the symbol or emblem (e.g. Peter and his key, Andrew and the saltire cross). Occasionally saints other than the Apostles may be encountered and these are worth a good premium, as are Mary and Edward VI spoons. Spoons up to about 1565 normally have a pierced nimbus; later spoons usually have an Esprit nimbus, with a solid disc featuring a dove.

Pitfalls

Pierced nimbi of early spoons are liable to damage or loss. Beware of replacements or substitutions. The same remark applies to the saint's emblems which were cast separately and soldered into position. Beware of examples with the emblem missing or re-equipped with a modern copy, also spoons in which the Seal top has been filed down and an Apostle figure soldered on, or where the seal top has been completely removed and replaced by an Apostle. Look for tell-tale signs of solder lines. Watch out for repaired splits in the bowl, new or partially replaced bowls. The most dangerous fakes are castings from original spoons.

Museums and **Reading List** — see **Spoons**.

Rear view of James I Apostle Spoon, London 1610, maker's mark crescent enclosing W. Notice V notch join of figure to the top of the stem. Notice also the small triangular section at junction of stem and bowl.

APPLE CORERS

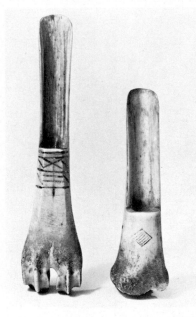

Implements for removing the core from apples and other fruit. They appear to have come into use about 1680, attained their peak in the 18th century and went out of fashion about 1830. They have a short cylindrical handle attached to a length of metal like a tube cut in half, and terminate in a rounded scoop. In its earliest form the apple corer was little more than a metal tube, with part of the surface cut away to form a scoop. More sophisticated examples were made in two parts, with the handle containing a storage compartment for spices. Although the earliest corers were made of base metal (brass, tinned copper, steel) the most collectable were made of silver, either wholly or partially. The great majority of 18th century corers were made of silver, though examples in Old Sheffield plate were produced around 1800. Later corers often had handles of wood, bone or ivory.

Bone objects often referred to as apple corers but which could equally well have been used as cheese scoops or for other suitable domestic activities.

Date-lines

1680-1703 Silver corers of a simple design, without spice compartment. £70 – £100.
Similar corers, but with a spice compartment. £120 – £150.

1703-1750 Corers with spice compartment, full hallmarks. £40 – £80.
Similar corers with maker's punch mark only. £30 – £60.

1750-1792 Scoop attached to handle by a screw thread, so that the blade could be reversed and screwed into the handle when not in use. £30 – £60.

1792-1830	Fully hallmarked corers, with silver handle, large-sized. £30 – £60.
	As above, but small-sized. £20 – £35.
1810-1830	Silver scoop attached to handle of ivory, bone or wood. £20 – £50.
c.1800	Corers in Old Sheffield plate. £25 – £45.
	Corers with splits and repairs where scoop and handle join are worth 50% less. Those with bad dents on cylindrical handles where the interior cannot be reached 25%-50% less.

Points to look for

Full hallmarks on corers before 1792 are relatively scarce, while the appearance of a full set of marks on late 17th century corers is so unusual as to double the value. The silver handles are usually relatively plain; examples with ornate chasing or engraving are highly desirable. Most corers were made in London or Birmingham; those with hallmarks of other centres are worth a good premium.

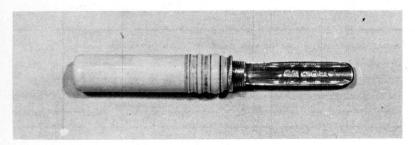

Example of a silver apple corer, hallmark - Birmingham.

Example of an ivory apple corer.

AUTOGRAPHS

Anything literally in the handwriting of a particular person comes under this heading, but it is important to distinguish the various forms of autograph, since their value depends on the category far more than on the signature or the prestige of the person signing it. In its simplest form an autograph may be no more than the signature of a person, and in its rudimentary form this is what is regarded as an autograph by the layman. It cannot be over-emphasised that there is very little value in the autograph signature *per se*. The bulk of the value lies in its association with the rest of the document. The hobby of autograph-collecting developed in the early 19th century when the practice began of getting the famous and not so famous to inscribe their signatures in an album. Victorian autograph albums of this type do possess some value in themselves, but this may range from £2 to £2,000 and will depend on the extensiveness of the collection and the degree of importance attached to the people concerned. Outstanding features, such as the inclusion of lines of verse by a famous poet, lightning sketches by famous artists and aphorisms or maxims (preferably hitherto unpublished) from the pen of famous literary figures, statesmen or contemporary celebrities, will increase the value.

The majority of Victorian albums, however, consist of larger volumes wherein are pasted the fronts of old letters, prior to 1840 when the franking privilege of peers of the realm and members of parliament was abolished. Before the adoption of Uniform Penny Postage in 1840 holders of the franking privilege had to endorse the lower left-hand corner of the front of the letter or envelope with their signature. It follows that such pre-1840 letters were avidly collected on account of the signatures found on them. Unfortunately countless thousands of such letters were subsequently vandalised by the collectors who merely cut out the front of the letter and pasted it into their albums. Until relatively recently these 'fronts', or whole albums containing them, had little value. They are now keenly sought after, not so much on account of the autographs, but because of the various franks and other forms of postal markings found on them. Individual fronts of this type are currently worth from 30p to £2 each, depending more on the postal marking than the signature. Complete albums are now comparatively scarce, as many of them have been broken up for their individual franks. £10+

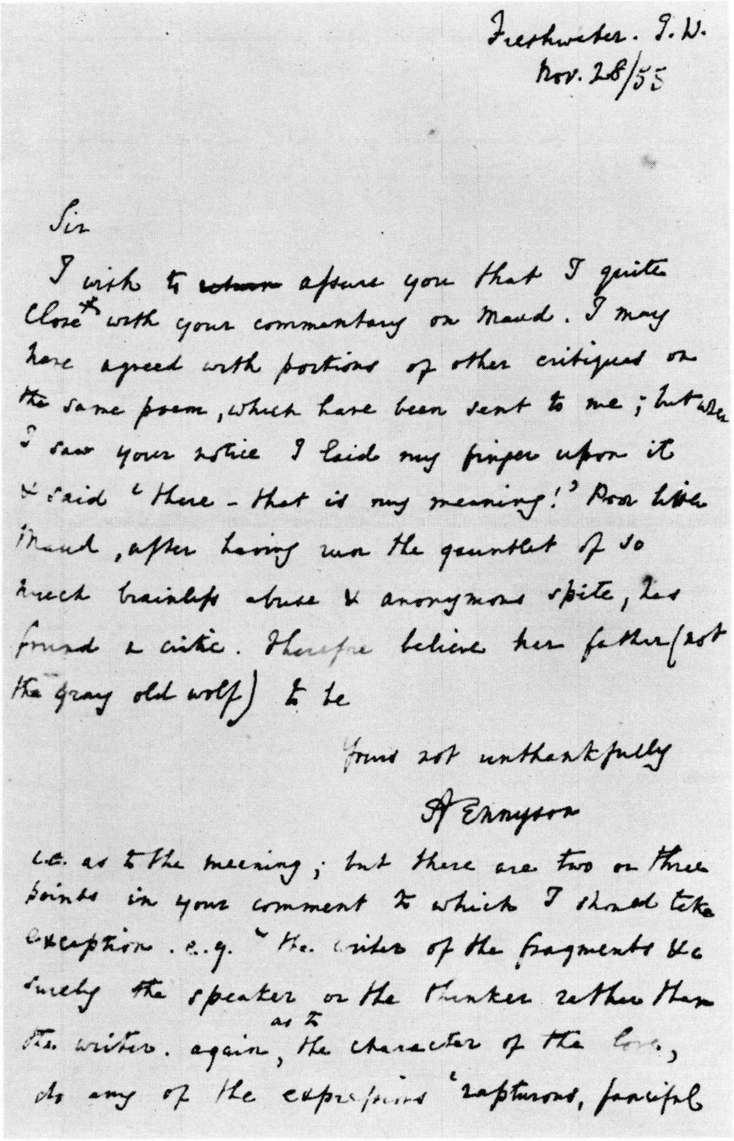

Freshwater. I.W.
Nov. 28/55

Sir

I wish to ~~whom~~ assure you that I quite
close* with your commentary on Maud. I may
have agreed with portions of other critiques on
the same poem, which have been sent to me; but when
I saw your notice I laid my finger upon it
& said "there - that is my meaning!" Poor little
Maud, after having run the gauntlet of so
much brainless abuse & anonymous spite, has
found a critic. Therefore believe her father (not
the "gray old wolf) to be

Yours not unthankfully

A Tennyson

i.e. as to the meaning; but there are two or three
points in your comment to which I should take
exception . e.g. "the writer of the fragments &c
surely the speaker or the thinker rather than
                        as to
the writer. again, the character of the love,
do any of the expressions "rapturous, fanciful

*Alfred Lord Tennyson. 28th November 1855. Autograph letter signed
to an unnamed critic who had written a sympathetic notice of
Tennyson's dramatic poem Maud which had just been published.*

11

Types of Autograph

Autographed Ephemera consists mainly of signatures on cheques, receipts, bills and similar small documents. Much will depend on the specific document and the circumstances in which it was signed, as well as the signature itself. From £2 upwards.

Signed copies of books fall into two categories: those autographed by the author and those inscribed by persons other than the author. It is difficult to generalise on the value of author-signed copies, which may be worth little more than unsigned first editions if the author or his works are relatively obscure. Moreover certain authors were more prone to sign copies of their books than others, and much also depends on the nature of the inscription – whether to a relative or intimate friend or whether to a mere member of the book-buying public. In the second category the presence of a signature on the fly-leaf may merely serve to establish the provenance of ownership; or it may greatly enhance an otherwise undistinguished book because of its association with some famous person.

Charles Dickens.

Charles I 1634.

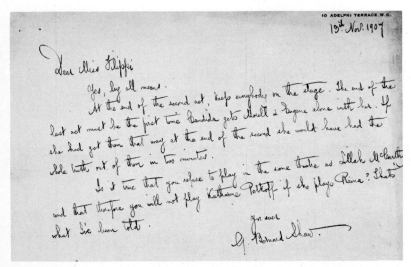

George Bernard Shaw. 13th November, 1907. Autograph letter, signed, to the actress Rosina Filippi.

Autographed Letter signed (A.L.s.) is the most desirable form of autograph normally encountered by the collector. The value of such a letter, written entirely in the hand of the person concerned, depends very largely on the person, the length of the letter and the nature of its contents. These factors assume greater or lesser importance taken in conjunction. Thus a brief, formal note in the handwriting of a very important historical figure may not be as valuable as a letter from a person of much lesser historical significance to a person of relative obscurity, but containing material of great sociological or historical importance.

Letter, signed (L.s.) denotes a letter with the signature alone in the hand of the writer. Many extant letters by Queen Elizabeth I, for example, are written by her secretaries, and the signature alone may be in her own hand. Occasionally a short phrase or endorsement may also be in the hand of the writer. The value of such letters depends on the age of the letter, the identity of the signature, the length and content of the letter. Obviously letters in this category are worth much less than comparable letters which are completely in the hand of the writer.

Autograph Document, signed (A. Doc.s.) denotes manuscripts other than letters which are in the handwriting of the author and bear his or her signature. Orders and ordinances of state in this category are extremely rare, whereas wills and other semi-legal documents are more commonly met with.

Document, signed (Doc.s.) denotes a document which bears the signature of the author but is otherwise written in another hand. The vast majority of state documents are in this group.

Typewritten Letter, signed (T.L.s.), increasingly common since 1900, though a few examples are known from about 1870 onwards. Very early T.L.s. are, of course, interesting and of some value on that account alone, but the majority of them are classed in the same price range as L.s.

Autographed Photographs, Cartes de Visite, Postcards date from the late 19th century. The bulk of these items relate to actors and actresses (as well as Society beauties of the Edwardian era) and are of relatively little value. Signed photographs of celebrities in other walks of life are much more desirable.

Autograph Manuscripts also vary considerably in the amount of personal association. At one extreme are manuscripts of books, plays, stories, poems, etc. which are entirely handwritten. Lower down the scale are similar manuscripts in the hand of a secretary or amanuensis, with autograph corrections by the author. In a similar category, and more common since 1900, are manuscripts in typewriting, with autograph corrections by the author. With these literary autographs may be grouped galley or page proofs with manuscript corrections by the author. The value of any of these types of literary manuscript depends on the degree of personal participation by the author evident. Here again it is impossible to make any general assessment of values. The original manuscript of a sonnet on the back of a used envelope by a poet with a wide international reputation will often be more valuable than the entire autograph manuscript of a lengthy book by a writer of lesser standing.

Rupert Brooke

Robert Browning

14

Points to look for

Entire letters pre-1840 are worth much more than letters which are in every other respect similar but which lack the outer part of the sheet bearing the address, superscription and postal markings. Unfortunately it was an old-established practice, when filing letters, to detach the address portion (usually half of the folded sheet). The presence of rare or unusual postmarks may greatly boost the value of an otherwise undistinguished letter by a complete nonentity. The recent growth in postal history collecting has vastly altered the sister hobby of autograph collecting, to the extent that any letter of 1800-1840, regardless of content, is now worth £2 minimum, while those from 1750 to 1800 are in the price range £5 – £20, and those from 1700 to 1750 may be from £10 to upwards of £100, depending on their postal markings alone.

Pitfalls

The authenticity of autographs is often problematical, even when the handwriting of historical personages is well documented. Letters written by Lord Nelson before and after he lost his arm, or by Guy Fawkes before and after judicial torture in 1605 are well-known examples of the way in which a person's handwriting may alter dramatically in a short space of time. Illness and advancing years are more common factors, but subtle changes in personality may also affect a person's calligraphy to a marked degree and cast doubt on the authenticity of autograph letters.

This is a field in which forgeries abound and it is advisable to study one's subject thoroughly before making a purchase (except from one of the reputable dealers in autographs). A knowledge of paper and watermarks can often be useful in detecting the more careless forgeries.

Museums

British Museum (Department of Manuscripts), London.
Public Record Office, London.
Register House, Edinburgh.
County and regional libraries and archives, the archives and muniments rooms of the universities and many of the great landed families contain material which is an invaluable yardstick for checking the authenticity of autographs.

Reading List

Benjamin, Mary A. Autographs: A Key to Collecting. New York, 1946.
Broadley, A.M. Chats on Autographs. London, 1910.
Charnwood, Lady. An Autograph Collection. London, 1930.
Munby, A.N.L. The Cult of the Autograph Letter in England. London, 1962.

BADGES

Insignia embroidered on cloth or struck in metal and worn to denote membership of an organisation, ranging from military formations to schools, societies and clubs. The disparate nature of badges requires that they be classified to some extent. From the collector's viewpoint, badges are grouped into military and naval badges, badges and emblems of police, fire brigades and para-military forces, badges of clubs and societies, badges of commercial organisations, and badges associated with schools and colleges. These groups are given in their descending order of popularity.

Military Badges

Badges formed a minor part of the uniform distinguishing opposing military forces from the middle of the 18th century and are now found in every army, navy and air force throughout the world. The scope of this book does not permit a detailed account of these badges and the following remarks are confined mainly to those in Britain. Military badges are more sought after than other badges, because they tie in with the interests of military collectors, and such collectors require the badges to be in first-class condition. Those bent or damaged, or plated badges with much of the gilt or silver worn away, will be of little or no interest. Good condition is paramount.

Date-lines

1751-1790	Prior to 1751 regiments were identified by the name of their commanding officer, but regimental numbers were then introduced. The earliest badges consisted of large numerals embroidered on the tall mitre caps and other headgear. Gradually regimental names and emblems (often derived from the arms of the regiment's colonel) were added. These embroidered numbers, names and devices formed an integral part of the headgear (q.v.).
1790-1810	Numbers, stamped on thin metal plates, sometimes also incorporating the name. Usually in brass or copper. £10 — £30.
1800-1820	More elaborate badge plates incorporating armorial designs and mottoes; embellished with cast ornament or engraved. Other ranks' in brass, £20 — £40; officers' badges in silver, £40 — £70.
1815-1830	Large badge plates designed to fit the stovepipe shako

then in use. Other ranks', stamped in brass, often very ornate, £25 – £40. Officers' badges in silver, usually rather smaller, £50 – £80.

1830-1855   Star-pattern badge adopted with the bell-topped shako, with regimental devices mounted on a star. Relatively large sized. Other ranks', £15 – £30; officers', £25 – £40.

a. Officers' shako plate. Royal Artillery 1812-16 pattern. b. Shako plate Royal Artillery 1812-16 pattern, other ranks. c. Officers' shako badge. The Scottish Borderers Militia. d. Officers' shako Plate. 21st Regiment of Foot 1812-16 pattern. e. Officers' shako plate. 57th Regiment of Foot 1812-16 pattern. f. Officers' gilt shako badge. 51st Regiment of Foot 1844 pattern.

1855-1879   Lower-crowned shako required a much smaller badge; still star-pattern, but much smaller. Other ranks', £10 – £25; officers', £20 – £40.

1879-1881   Large star-pattern re-introduced for use with the blue cloth helmet; prices as 1830-1855, though some rare badges used by regiments formed since 1855 may be up to £85 (other ranks) or £120 (officers).

1881-1901   Regiments re-organised and numbers dropped in favour of names (largely county). Large star-pattern badges as before but new designs. Other ranks', £10 – £20; officers', £25 – £45.

1901-1910   As before, but 'queen's crown' replaced by 'king's crown' emblem in those badges incorporating a crown. Other ranks', £5 – £10; officers', £15 – £30.

1910-1953   Smaller badges with a metal clip introduced for use with the service dress cap. Smaller variants adopted for berets (first used briefly in the First World War and revived in the Second World War). Wide variation in styles and materials (brass, white metal for other ranks; silver and silver-gilt for officers). Some Second World War badges in plastic. Prices for cap badges of this period range from 50p to £3 (other ranks), £2 to £7 (officers), depending on date and materials. Badges of obsolete or short-lived formations rate a premium if original.

1953-1960   Elizabethan crown replaced king's crown and this pattern still in use. The more collectable badges are those of regiments and formations which disappeared in the amalgamations which took place from 1960 onwards.

In addition to the above, there are ancillary badges, ranging from plaid belt badges of Highland regiments (£30 — £50 for other ranks; £45 — £85 for officers), collar badges — modified and miniaturised versions of the cap badges, best collected in pairs, sporran badges of Highland regiments, epaulette badges (usually bearing the name or initials of the regiment only, except in Guards regiments), small cap badges designed for wear with the Glengarry bonnet (common to many English as well as Scottish regiments from 1874 onwards) or for mounting on the puggaree of tropical helmets.

Cloth badges

The horse-shoe motif embroidered on the caps of army farriers in the mid-18th century is thought to be the earliest instance of a trade badge. This practice developed in the early 19th century when badges were embroidered in wire of various metals. Badges woven in silk or cotton thread and worn on the sleeve developed in the late 19th century following the introduction of service dress. To this day wire thread and cotton thread are used respectively on ceremonial dress and battledress. There is relatively little interest in the cloth badges which refer mainly to trades and specialist qualifications, and do not vary to any extent from regiment to regiment. Conversely there is great interest in the cloth badges worn by units of the German armed forces of the Second World War. These are known as bevo badges and are usually made of metal wire on a cloth backing. Prices for these badges range from £1.50 to £5, depending on the unit or formation concerned.

The cloth badges bearing the insignia of squadrons of the R.A.F. are only now beginning to attract the interest of collectors. As these armorial badges are of comparatively recent origin (post-Second World War), they do not have any fixed market value as yet.

Here, again, condition is the first consideration. It should be fairly obvious that such badges made of silver and gilt wire or woven in silk or cotton have but little appeal or value if they are tatty. Certain circumstances can vary this, however. If one obtained such a badge whose provenance can be established back to a person of great importance, its condition would become of secondary consideration.

Badges of other armies

In Britain collector interest centres on three main areas, outside the United Kingdom. The chief interest lies in the badges of regiments and units of the British Commonwealth, dating from the colonial volunteer units raised during the Boer War in support of the mother country. In many cases these regiments are 'twinned' with a British regiment. For this reason the badges of the army units of Canada, Australia, New Zealand and South Africa to the present day are of prime interest. Similarly the badges of the former Indian Army (to 1947) are collected because of their long connection with the British Empire. The majority of these badges date from 1900 and pricing is comparable with British badges of the same period.

Selection of British regimental badges: Top Row: All white metal. Scottish infantry. Second Row: White metal and bronze, mainly English County regiments. Third Row: All brass Scottish yeomanry (1st and 5th). Bottom Row: All brass king's crown pattern. Pioneer Corps (2nd) silver officer's king's crown pattern. Rifle Corps (4th).

Since the Second World War there has been a great deal of interest in the badges of the Third Reich. The German army did not have distinctive cap badges on British lines, but this is compensated for by the wealth of insignia worn on the tunic. As well as bevo badges, mentioned above, there are collar badges and numbers and a vast array of breast badges worn over the pocket. Many of these denote specialist units, while others refer to specific campaigns and are comparable to British campaign medals. Prices of German badges of this type range from £3 to £15, depending on the campaign or unit concerned.

The third area of interest is of more recent origin. Since 1960 collectors have taken a growing interest in American badges, which may be divided into two categories. The more decorative of these are the small enamelled insignia worn on the forage cap in walking-out uniform. These vary from unit to unit and afford considerable scope (£1 – £3). The older-established badges consist of gilt metal or brass lapel badges indicating the arm of the service (infantry, artillery, engineers, chemical corps, medical corps, etc.). This is a comparatively limited field, although there are differences in the patterns worn by officers, warrant officers, non-commissioned officers and enlisted men, as well as variations between First and Second World War. Prices seem to vary from £1 to £5, depending on date and the particular arm of the services.

Non-Military Badges

This is a relatively small side-line associated with militaria and no hard and fast market exists as yet. This is an area which offers considerable scope to the new collector, and for that reason it is growing rapidly. The most popular of these groups is police badges which date from the mid-19th century and consist of belt-buckles, helmet plates and cap badges, collar insignia, epaulette numbers and buttons. Many of these badges have been rendered obsolete by the various county and regional amalgamations. The value of these badges depends largely on local interest. Because of the enormous variety in their size, style and design, American police badges, both metal and cloth, have become very popular in recent years, but there is relatively little interest in police badges from other parts of the world.

To a lesser extent, badges of fire brigades, prison guards, ambulance brigades and youth movements are also collected, but no fixed market yet exists.

Clubs and Societies

The oldest badges in this category belong to the political clubs of the 18th century. These badges are collectable, not so much as badges *per se,* but because of their aesthetic appeal and historic interest. An important group consists of the badges containing glass paste cameos or sulphide profiles of political leaders (Wilkes, Fox, Pitt, etc.), mounted in silver and often engraved with the name of the club and the date. The gilt-with-cameo badges of the Pitt Club are in demand by members of the London Pitt Club, which still meets. Glass paste cameo badges of this type, belonging to the period 1760-1820, are generally in the price range £40 — £120, depending on materials, date, decorative features and particular historical importance. Provincial club badges take various forms, mainly that of a silver or silver-plated medal, up to about 2 inches in diameter, enclosed between watch glasses and provided with a ring for suspension. Some of these pieces are exceedingly rare and rarity would command a premium. Once again, condition is paramount. A provincial Pitt Club badge, still enclosed in its silver ring and with its original watch glass, is a rarity.

Museums — see under **Militaria**

Reading List

Almack, Edward. Regimental Badges Worn in the British Army One Hundred Years Ago. London, 1900; reprinted 1970.

Bloomer, W.H. and K.D. Scottish Regimental Badges 1793-1971. London, 1973.

Chichester, H.M. and Burgess-Short, G. Records and Badges of the British Army. London, 1970.

Cole, H.N. Badges on Battledress. Aldershot, 1953.

Cole, H.N. Heraldry in War. Aldershot, 1953.

Edwards, T.J. Regimental Badges. Aldershot, 1966.

Farmer, J.S. Regimental Records. London, 1901.

Parkyn, H.G. Shoulder-belt Plates and Buttons. Aldershot, 1956.

Wilkinson, Frederick. Badges of the British Army 1820-1960. London, 1971.

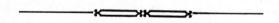

BAROMETERS

Scientific instruments for measuring atmospheric pressure. In Britain, a country notorious for its changeable weather, barometers developed into an important article of domestic furniture and the styles of casing reflect the fashions in clocks of the corresponding period. The theory of measuring atmospheric pressure using a column of mercury was propounded by Torricelli in 1643, but it was in the post-Restoration period that barometers first developed as domestic furniture. The barometer attracted the attention of English instrument makers, such as Quare, Tompion and Henry Jones, who produced barometers from 1670 onwards. Barometers may be classified chronologically by their technical features, and also by the kind of wood used for the casing.

Date-lines
1670-1830

Stick barometers, with a relatively simple columnar case and readings indicated by a graduated card behind the mercury column. The earliest mounts were made of walnut, but subsequently mahogany, pearwood, satin-wood, rosewood, maple and ebony were used (the last-named being very rare). Lacquering was used on barometers from about 1710 to 1740. Late Georgian and Regency examples were often intricately cross-banded with contrasting woods and inlaid with brass and mother-of-pearl. Late-18th century examples have more ornate tops, often with a broken pediment design. Stick barometers range from £100 to £500 for the simpler varieties. Those with lacquering or marquetry decoration range from £150 to £600. Very early stick barometers or those with ebony cases are from £400 to £1,200.

A portable walnut stick barometer by one of the top makers, Daniel Quare, c.1700.

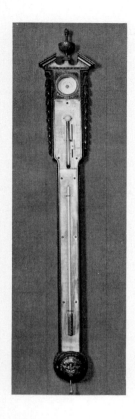

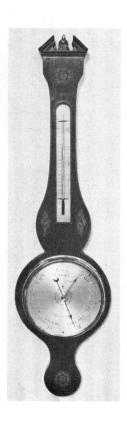

Left: A carved mahogany stick barometer of the third quarter of the 18th century by H. Pyefinch, London.

Centre: An unusual form of combined barometer and thermometer in a gilt frame, early 18th century.

Right: A Sheraton mahogany 'banjo' shaped barometer. Note the shell and round inlays which give it the Sheraton character. This type was made between 1780-1820. The maker Fiora was recorded as working in Nottingham in 1815.

1695-1720   Portable barometers, patented by Quare. As above, but supported on an elegant stand of three or four legs. Now £1,500 − £2,000.

1720-1750	Diagonal barometer patented by Sir Samuel Morland. £800 – £1,200.
1750-1830	Pediment barometers. As stick barometers, but with more elaborate housing at the top. The simplest varieties are worth from £100 to £250, but the more elaborate types, incorporating thermometers, hygrometers and other instruments, range from £400 to £1,200.
1770-1880	Wheel barometer, designed by Robert Hooke in the 17th century, but not marketed commercially till a century later. The height of the mercury column was shown on a needle and dial indicator mounted near the foot of the barometer. This led to a change in the design of the case, which swells out at the lower end to accommodate the dial, hence the alternative name 'banjo barometer'. The styling of barometer cases varies considerably and prices fluctuate accordingly. In general, the most common sizes are the 8 to 10 inch (measured across the face of the barometer). The proportions of these are often very good, with the result that they can be the most pleasing. Nevertheless, because they are the most common, the price of an 8 inch is about £150 while that of a 10 inch, £150 – £200. The width used and the decoration are important. Kingwood banding, for example, on a nicely proportioned piece would increase the price to the upper end of the range. The shape of the bottom is also significant the round bottom being more desirable than the square one. Least common are the 5 to 6 inch size, which fetch between £150 and £225 but satinwood examples would cost more. Very desirable are the 12 to 14 inch size, which start at £300. Elaborate decoration on early Victorian examples and the inclusion of other instruments enhances the value.
1844-1900	Early aneroid barometers, first patented in 1844, using a metal drum instead of a mercury column. Aneroid barometers did not become popular till the turn of the century and thus early examples are scarce. The more expensive ones have a case not unlike a wheel barometer, but are shorter and more squat. Others have a completely circular shape, either with a bracket for wall suspension, or mounted on a plinth, like a clock, for use on a mantelpiece or table. This group is currently undervalued. £15 – £45.

Left: An example of a good standard, well-designed, mahogany 'banjo' shaped barometer from the very early part of the 19th century. Note the shape is balanced by the various dials.

Right: A fine quality early 19th century mahogany 'banjo' shaped barometer, by G. Bianchi of Ipswich who was working during the first decade, cross-banded in a variety of woods, with large dial and the important addition of a clock and pillars.

1881-1920   Early 'Fitzroy' barometers, named after Admiral Fitzroy. A development of the stick barometer, with a circular card bearing comments about the weather and a patent storm glass. This is the type of wall barometer still in production. Prices are from £20 to £50 and depend on age, decorative features and the inclusion of other instruments.

Points to look for

Most barometers, especially the early ones, bear the maker's name or mark, and often include dates and registration numbers when applicable. Barometers produced by Sheraton, Chippendale and the other leading cabinet-makers rate a handsome premium, but a large number of barometers were produced by other craftsmen emulating their styles. Barometers manufactured for a special purpose, e.g. ships' barometers, are worth much more than their contemporaries designed for purely domestic usage. Regency ships' barometers, for example, are in the price range £250 – £400.

Pitfalls

Prices quoted are for barometers in perfect working order. The commonest type of damage consists of broken mercury columns due to careless handling. A number of firms, mainly in the London area, undertake repairs and restoration. When purchasing barometers, examine the column very closely with a magnifier to see if there are any air bubbles on the surface. If these are present it is not a true vacuum and this may be due to flaws in the glass or impurities in the mercury. The meniscus (top of the mercury level in the tube) should be noticeably convex; if not, the column is faulty. Another tell-tale sign to watch for is cloudiness on the wall of the tube, caused by mercury of a poor quality tending to 'gum'.

Museums

National Maritime Museum, London
Science Museum, London
Victoria and Albert Museum, London
Wallace Collection, London
Waddesdon Manor, Aylesbury
City Museum and Art Gallery, Birmingham
National Museum of Wales, Cardiff
Royal Scottish Museum, Edinburgh
Museum and Art Gallery, Glasgow
City Museum, Gloucester
Hampton Court Palace
Museum and Art Gallery, Leicester
History of Science Museum, Oxford
Salisbury and South Wiltshire Museum, Salisbury
County Museum, Stafford
Windsor Castle, Windsor

Reading List

Bell, C.H. and E.F. Old English Barometers. Winchester, 1970.
Goodison, Nicholas. English Barometers, 1680-1860. London, 1969.
Fiddleton, W.E. Knowles. The History of the Barometer. Baltimore, 1964.

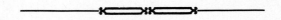

BOOKS (Victorian)

Apart from the wide range of books which are collected on account of their edition, their literary merit or the popularity of their authors — a vast subject which is beyond the scope of this book — there are many kinds of 19th century books which are collectable according to their type or physical appearance. Books are also collected for their subject matter and a collection can be assembled on thematic lines: e.g. theological, philosophical, topographical or historical works. We are here concerned only with books collected according to their technical features, regardless of their content. A convenient starting point would be the introduction of trade binding in the early 19th century. Hitherto the majority of books were issued to the public in unbound sheets which could then be bound up to the individual requirements of the customer. A transitional stage was the use, in the latter part of the 18th century, of paper boards which could be discarded when the volumes were properly bound in vellum or leather.

Date-lines

1800-1860	Books, mainly novels, issued in parts or volumes bound in paper. Usually these paper bindings were discarded when the parts were bound together. Consequently unbound parts of novels with paper wrappers are relatively scarce. Prices for such paper bindings vary considerably according to the popularity of the author. Thus unbound parts of Dickens's novels may be from £50 upwards for a single part. As a rule, paper-bound parts or volumes of novelists of lesser rank are in the price range £5 – £20.
1800-1820	Works of non-fiction bound in paper as above, usually in a single volume for shorter works, but occasionally in two to five slim volumes in the same manner as novels. Generally of lesser interest than the novels of the more famous contemporary authors (e.g. Scott, Dickens), but their value is governed by the degree of interest shown in the subject. Theological treatises of this type are comparatively overlooked and are worth from £2 to £5; whereas early travel books, or works on natural history and sporting subjects may be from £20 to £50.
1820-1830	Non-fiction bound in glazed calico. Relatively rare. From £10 upwards.

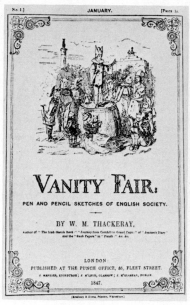

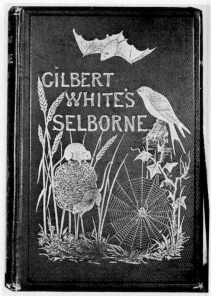

Left: The outside wrapper of Part I of Thackeray's 'Vanity Fair' 1847-48, originally published in 20 parts Right: A good example of the lavish cloth-gilt bindings beloved in the Victorian period.

1830-1840	Non-fiction bound in cloth, with lettering on paper labels affixed to the front cover and the spine. £3 — £10.
1840-1860	Development of machinery capable of a wide range of blind-tooling (raised or recessed areas in albino), simulating the hand-tooling of the 17th and 18th centuries. Gilding confined to the lettering on the spine.
1860-1910	Increasingly elaborate gold-tooling on cloth bindings using metal dies. Trade bindings of this type become more desirable as the size and intricacy of the decoration increases. The most sought after are examples combining both gold and silver tooling, and those with elaborate vignettes which reproduce one of the plates (often the frontispiece) inside the book. The most elaborate motifs were used for books on travel, topography and natural history which are immensely popular subjects *per se.* £5 — £25.
1880-1920	Pictorial bindings die-stamped in black and one or more colours. This style of binding ornament was much

favoured for light fiction and also children's prize books (usually moral tales). There is a very wide range of styles, from the bold vignettes in the manner of the Beggarstaff

Pictorial trade bindings, c.1890-1910. Romantic fiction and moral tales; topography and natural history, popular biography.

Die-struck pictorial bindings, 1860-1900. Mainly travel and natural history. The Stamp Collector's Handbook (1874), with motifs from contemporary stamps, is a highly prized rarity from the early period of philately.

Brothers, found on early editions of Henty's adventure stories, to the floral Art Nouveau motifs of late 19th century novelettes. Prize books are in the price range 50p – £2; adventure stories, £1 – £3; light romances, 50p – £2; non-fiction from £1 upwards, depending on subject.

1920-1940   Pictorial bindings were superseded by plain cloth bindings, covered by decorative paper dust jackets. This period has been disregarded up till recently, although the growing interest in the graphics of the inter-war period means that unusual dust jackets in good condition are now being snapped up. No established market for the majority of books of this period and still likely to turn up in jumble sales at 10p – 50p. The more desirable books are those with letterpress or lithographed jackets in the prevailing poster styles. Jackets with half tone pictorial decoration are relatively disregarded, though undeniably scarce in fine condition.

Points to look for

A major plus factor in any 19th century book is good illustration and plenty of it. Steel or copper engravings printed by the intaglio or taille douce process (detected by very fine ridging in the paper) are a highly desirable feature, mainly confined to the earlier period. Less expensive books from 1800 to 1900 were illustrated with wood-block engravings, reproduced by the letterpress or surface-printed method. Copper stereotypes or clichés were used as a cheap substitute increasingly from 1850 onwards and were less liable to wear. The value of books depends to some extent on the quality of the illustrations, and works illustrated by such artists as Hablot Browne, Tenniel and Doré, are now keenly sought after.

Lithography was used to some extent for book illustration from 1870 onwards, often with the detail in black against a toned background. Lithographic illustrations are not as desirable as line engravings, and were largely superseded by 1890 by half tone photographic illustrations. Relatively few books from 1860 to 1890 were illustrated by actual photographs, mounted on separate plates, and these are now much in demand for their photographic content. Half tone photographic illustration was confined at the turn of the century to non-fiction works, and was generally of a poor quality. Illustrations to watch out for, however, are those by the collotype process, a form of lithography which gave a very high quality of reproduction without the tell-tale screening of half tones. Photogravure was used for book illustration from about 1895 and is comparatively rare. It may be recognised by the very fine screening and the high quality of calendered, chalk-surfaced paper needed to give effective results. As a rule some guidance to the method of illustration is given in the title page or printer's colophon, while the more elaborate illustrations often have brief details of the artist, engraver and printing process in the plate margin. Chromolithographed plates (usually confined to the frontispiece) became common in the late 19th century. Earlier examples are highly desirable.

Armorial or pictorial book-plates, especially those designed for a specific bibliophile, have long been of interest, but the highly ornamental prize labels which became fashionable about 1885 are also worth looking for. They attained their artistic peak about 1905, with a late flowering of Art Nouveau lettering and borders, and became more prosaic from 1915 onwards.

A selection of Victorian 'goody' books, most of them dating from the 1880s. Some of them have inscriptions inside showing that they were given as school or Sunday School prizes for 'good conduct', 'regularity' and so on.

BOOKS (Miniature)

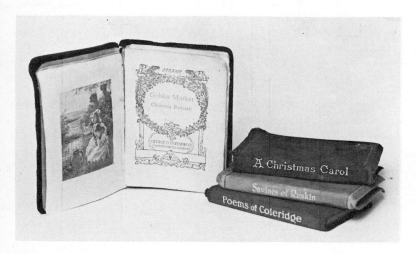

*Examples of late miniature series books all bound in yapped calf.
'Goblin Market', one of 31 titles in the Sesame series booklets;
'Christmas Carol' and 'Sayings of Ruskin', two of a series of 50
published by Seigle; 'Poems of Coleridge', one of 24 titles published by
Nimmo, Hay and Mitchell. 3½ x 2½ins.*

Books with overall dimensions of less than three by two inches are
regarded as miniature books, and have attracted the serious attention of
collectors, regardless of any other criteria. The earliest miniature books
were bibles, prayer books and books of hours or other devotional
exercises and they were designed to be carried around in the pocket.
Although miniature printed books date from the late 15th century, and
manuscript miniature books are even older, the majority of collectable
examples date from the beginning of the 18th century.

The best known type of miniature books were almanacs and
ephemerides, containing calendars, tide tables, tables of important dates
and events, political data and commercial information. Many of these
miniature almanacs were printed from special type, using non-clogging
ink and specially prepared paper. Titles to look for include *The London
Almanack, Victoria Miniature Almanack* and the *English Bijou
Almanack* which are among the more decorative of the miniatures, with
finely tooled morocco bindings or even tortoiseshell covers.

The majority of miniature almanacs date from between 1773 and 1874. Almanacs of this period are usually finely engraved, and the inclusion of tiny pictures is a major plus factor. £5 – £50. After 1874 almanacs were illustrated by line blocks, produced by the letterpress method and these are less desirable. £2 – £5.

Among the other categories of 19th century miniature books may be mentioned minuscule history books (culminating in Goode's *Miniature History of England*, 1903), volumes of poetry, from individual works to the complete sonnets of Shakespeare, miniature atlases, ready reckoners and, most common of all, miniature dictionaries, many of which are produced to this day. £1 – £10.

Miniature children's books had their origins in the pocket-books and chap-books published by John Harris (1756-1846) and John Newbery (1713-1767). Newbery began in 1744 with his *Little Pretty Pocket-Book,* originally retailing for sixpence, but now worth from £20 to £50 (though an excellent facsimile was published in recent years). Newbery produced some 35 children's titles as miniature books, including *Alphabet Royal* (1750), *The Spelling Dictionary* (1755) and *Wonders of Art and Nature.* £12 – £40.

John Harris took over the Newbery business at the beginning of the 19th century and greatly extended the range of titles, including many books of purely entertainment value as well as the older established run of didactic books. The best-known of the Harris titles include *Old Mother Hubbard* (1805 and many subsequent editions), *The Butterfly's Ball and The Grasshopper's Feast* (1807), *The Peacock 'At Home'* and *Dame Wiggins of Lea* (1823). The value of these books depends on the edition and also on whether the illustrations are plain or coloured. £10 – £100.

S. and J. Fuller published a series of miniature doll books from 1810 onwards. These tiny books were sold with a board slip-case secured by a silk ribbon to keep the cut-out doll figures in place. The books contained poems, hand-coloured illustrations, paper dolls and dolls' outfits. Titles include *Little Henry* (1810), *Little Fanny* (1811), *Ellen* (1811), *Phoebe* (1811) and *Cinderella* (1814), all of which ran to several editions. These books were comparatively expensive at the time of publication (5 shillings) and today complete examples are of the greatest rarity. Examples which are partially intact range from £70 to £150.

There are many other miniature children's books of the 19th century. Up to 1835 the illustrations were hand-coloured. Examples of these books are in the price range £30 – £80, depending on the title, edition and the quality of colouring (which varies considerably).

After 1835 chromolithography was used for coloured illustrations. The best of these were produced by George Baxter, while the Kronheims produced illustrations of rather poorer quality. Books in the period 1835-1860 are generally in the range £20 – £50. After 1860 colour illustration became more garish. Run-of-the-mill children's titles of the period 1860-1890 are often rare but have been comparatively overlooked. £10 – £20.

During the same period, however, there was a revival of good quality line engravings without colouring in children's books. Books of this type depend on the illustrator and those which are highly regarded include Tenniel, Millais, Arthur Hughes, Keene and Birket Foster. A very wide range of values, depending on the title and edition. £10 – £200.

Later illustrators whose work is also highly prized include Richard Doyle, George Cruikshank, Gordon Browne. Of the early 20th century illustrators Arthur Rackham is the most in demand. £5 – £30.

Routledge published a series of sixpenny toy-books, 1866-1876, illustrated by Walter Crane. Altogether some 38 titles were produced in this series, mostly in the form of illustrated alphabets. £50 – £150.

Later titles illustrated by Crane include *The Baby's Opera, The Baby's Bouquet,* and *The Baby's Own Aesop.* These were much more substantial and illustrated by the xylographic (woodblock) process. £90 – £300.

Books published by Marcus Ward and illustrated by Crane after 1885 were sold for half-a-crown. The illustrations were chromolithographed and much more garish than the earlier books. They are much less desirable and generally more plentiful. £5 – £20.

Books published by MacMillan from 1875 onwards, with illustrations by Randolph Caldecott engraved by J.D. Cooper, include *Old Christmas* and *Bracebridge Hall.* £100 – £200.

Later works by Caldecott, published by Evans, include many of the most popular children's classics: *John Gilpin, The House that Jack Built, Hey Diddle Diddle* and *Jackanapes.* Some 16 titles were produced between 1879 and 1886 and subsequently ran to numerous editions, using the original boxwood blocks until fairly recently. Prices therefore range widely, from £2 – £5 for early 20th century editions, to 100 times as much for first editions of the early 1880s.

From 1878 to 1895 Kate Greenaway produced a large number of illustrated books, published by Routledge, beginning with *Under the Window.* Other early titles now much sought after include *Marigold Garden, A Day in a Child's Life, Mother Goose, Little Ann* and *The Language of Flowers* (1878-1884). £30 – £120.

From 1883 to 1895 she also produced an annual series of little *Almanacks*. £10 – £40.

Among the other late 19th century children's books worth looking for are works by Thomas Crane (elder brother of Walter), published by Marcus Ward, including *At Home* (1881), *Abroad* (1882) and *London Town* (1883). £10 – £30.

Harrison Weir specialised in books illustrating humanised animals and birds and his works were published by Routledge, including *The Cats' Tea Party, History of the Robins* (1869) and *Animal Stories* (1885).

Points to look for

Any small children's picture books with the imprint of Cundall, Evans, Marcus Ward or Routledge are worth collecting. Hitherto little interest has been shown by collectors in the works of other publishers (noticeably Frederick Warne, who produced the Beatrix Potter story books), but this is an area which is now worth considering, as these books are still relatively cheap.

Pitfalls

As many of these children's books were frequently reprinted over a long period, it is important to emphasise that only the very early editions are worth real money. Editions after 1900 are still of little interest or value.

Museums

British Museum, London.
Victoria and Albert Museum, London.
Museum of Childhood, Edinburgh.

Reading List

Carter, John. The ABC of Book Collecting. London, 1964.
Crane, Walter. An Artist's Reminiscences. London, 1907.
Konody, P.G. The Art of Walter Crane. London, 1902.
McLean, R. The Reminiscences of Edmund Evans. Oxford, 1967.
Muir, Percy. English Children's Books. London, 1954.
Spielman, M.H. and Layard, G.S. Kate Greenaway. London, 1905.
Spielman, P.E. Catalogue of the Library of Miniature Books. London, 1961.

BOOT AND SHOE TREES

Wooden implements for stretching leather boots and shoes and for keeping them in shape. Boot stretchers are of considerable antiquity and examples have been recorded from the Middle Ages, carved to resemble the shape of the ankle and calf and often segmented to facilitate insertion into the legs of boots. As a rule these boot stretchers have turned wooden handles set in the top. Boot trees of this type remained in use, with variations, up to the end of the 19th century and a modified version is used to this day for riding boots. As men's boots became lower in the 19th century, progressing from top-boots to low-boots and then from ankle-boots to shoes, the shape of the trees varied accordingly. Daintier versions of shoe trees, for the use of ladies, became more common from about 1850 onwards when uppers began to be made of leather instead of brocades and satins.

Boot and shoe trees were generally made of beechwood, sometimes polished, occasionally varnished, and sometimes left in the white. They often bear the names and addresses of cobblers and shoe manufacturers

A pair of Peals' "S.P." trees can be seen above left, and Watt's adjustable patent on the right.

and this adds considerably to their interest and value. The simplest types consist of pieces of wood carved to the shape of a foot and ankle, with a turned handle at the top. The more elaborate versions have jointed sections and the most desirable examples have a screw fitment which allows them to be expanded and adjusted to the shape of boots and shoes within a certain range of sizes. Additional refinements were corn and bunion pieces, which seem to have been optional extras. Skeletal types became popular at the beginning of this century and consisted of wooden toe-pieces with a stout wire or metal handle. A later development was the toe-wedge attached to a springy piece of metal terminating in a wooden ball which fitted snugly inside the heel. The curved metal could then be used as a carrying handle. This type has remained in use to the present day, though more recent versions have substituted plastics for wood.

Price Range

There is no established market for boot and shoe trees, although this overlooked aspect of treen is now attracting the serious attention of collectors. 20th century skeletal types are usually available for less than £1; ladies' shoe stretchers from 1850 to 1900 are in the range from £2 to £5 depending on quality, mechanical features and inscriptions. Men's shoe trees of the same period are probably worth slightly more. Earlier examples of boot trees may be from £3 to £10. Matched pairs pre-1900 rate three times the price of singles.

BOSUN'S PIPES

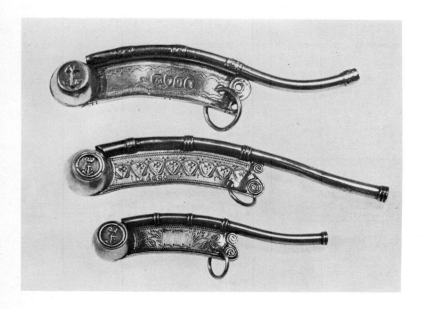

From top to bottom: Mary Chawner, London 1829. $4\frac{7}{8}$ins. long. Hilliard and Thomason, Birmingham, 1886, 5ins. long. Hilliard and Thomason, Birmingham, 1875, 3¾ins. long. Notice the stamped anchor on the buoy of the two Victorian examples.

Very high pitched whistles used in the Royal Navy for transmitting orders which could be heard above the noise of the sea. Pipes of this type seem to have been used from the mid-17th century, the earlier ones being made of brass, copper or tinware, either painted or silvered to prevent corrosion from the salt sea atmosphere. Silver pipes date from about 1750, though they are rare till the end of the 18th century. Bosun's pipes were (and still are) of a standard shape, with three main components, known as the keel (the broad underblade), the gun or cannon (the slightly curved pipe) and the buoy (the barrel shaped finial).

Date-lines

1750-1800	Usually much larger and longer (up to 8ins.) than the later ones. Base metal pipes £30 – £50; silver pipes £150 – £200.
1800-1830	Smaller (about 4¾ins.) and usually more ornate, with full hallmarks £100 – £150.
1830-1900	The most plentiful period for silver pipes. Larger (up to 4¾ins.) £60 – £100; smaller pipes (3¼-4ins.) £40 – £70.
1900-1920	Fewer pipes in silver and those are usually less decorative than the 19th century examples. £20 – £40. Electro-plated pipes £5 – £10.

Points to look for

The value of bosun's pipes is largely governed by the decorative features – engraving, chasing, bright-cutting and piercing – on the keel. The ends of the buoy are usually ornamented with the anchor emblem of the Royal Navy; more ornate motifs enhance the value considerably. Particularly sought after are pipes engraved with the names of individual ships. or of naval establishments in other parts of the world (e.g. Malta, Mauritius, Cape of Good Hope, Aden, Hong Kong). Condition is a very important factor in price variation.

Pitfalls

Many of the earlier silver pipes are either unmarked, or bear only the maker's initials. It is important to distinguish these rare pipes from silver-plated or Old Sheffield plate pipes of the same period which are worth very much less. Pipes by famous makers such as Paul Storr command a premium.

BOTTLES
(Glass)

From the inception of the British bottle industry in the early 17th century, the bulk of the output was wine bottles. From 1623 to 1860 it was illegal to sell wine *by the bottle* in Britain, and because of heavy taxation on glass, bottles were expensive to buy.

The more affluent members of society were compelled to order wine by the barrel from the wine merchant, but also owned a private stock of bottles which were filled from the barrel by the merchant. For ease of identification the wine bottles were personalised by the addition of a glass disc or seal which was applied to the bottle, and which was embossed with the owner's name, initials or crest, as on his letter seal, and these have become known as seal bottles. Although illegal, some tavern keepers did sell wine in bottles which had no seals, and the value of these unadorned bottles is considerably less than their sealed counterparts.

Shapes and Values of Early English Wine Bottles, 1620-1870

1620-1660   Specimens so early are unlikely to be encountered by

Seal bottle bearing the name Anne Eilhering and the date 1708.

A seal bottle with the initials C.P. 1686, the neck severely contracted.

Seal bottle, c.1645-1660, with spherical body and a tall thin neck, a rim near the top enabling a cork to be tied down. The initials G.M.W. surround a crude figure of a bird on the seal. Due to long incarceration in the soil the glass has started to decay.

Left: Maraschino liqueur bottles with applied glass seals, showing the Austro-Hungarian Imperial eagle. Made in Zara, now in Yugoslavia, 1900-1914. Rare. Right: Half-egg shape mineral water bottles used during the transitional period, moving towards the completely upright 'pop' bottle. 1890-1905. left: Small Splitlet bottle with blob-top for cork stopper; right: full-sized bottle with flat-sided lip, threaded for internal screw stopper.

the collector outside museums. In this period, they had a round bulbous body with a very long neck, and are known as 'shaft and globe' bottles. Height about 9½ins. to 9¾ins. by 1650. Extremely rare with or without seals. Price — by negotiation.

1650-1680   Angle of the shoulder now more acute, with the body more tapering from the base, with a narrow indentation or 'kick' in base. String-rim for securing cork has a knife-edge. Height lessened to 6¼ins. by 1680. With seal, £100 — £200; without seal, £40 — £60.

1675-1715   Squat onion-shaped bottles, now very popular with collectors. Dumpy body, shoulders very tapered, with a short neck. String-rim now with rounded edge. Height rising gradually from 6¼ins. to 7ins. With seal, £100 — £150; without seal, £30 — £50.

1715-1745   The body now more square, producing the famous mallet-shaped bottle by mid-century. From about 1730,

Bottle with seal show-ing the name Walter Maclal, Glasgow 176(3?).

Codd-Hamilton hybrid bottle, combining the lay-down shape of the Hamilton with the dimpled neck and glass ball stopper of the Codd bottle. Rare. c.1880-1900.

Soda water or aerated water bottles, c.1890, from the Royal German Spa, Brighton. Left: round-bottomed cylinder; right: torpedo-shaped Hamilton.

bottles made by moulds and more cylindrical and slightly taller. Heights of dated specimens: 1720 — 7½ins., 1750 — 8ins., 1767 — 9¼ins. With seal, £60 — £100; without seal, £25 — £40.

1740-1800   By 1750 the mallet-shaped bottles becoming slightly taller and with a narrower body. Around this time, wine laid down in bins for maturing, necessitating a more elongated, cylindrical bottle. By the 1760s, diameter down to 5ins. with a deeper 'kick' in base. Giant-sized bottles also known for champagne and gin. With seal, £50 — £80; without seal, £15 — £30.

1800-about 1870   By the early 1800s, diameter of bottles reduced further to 3½ins. Lips now have a tapered outline. Height increased to 10ins. by 1840, and after this date many shapes and sizes introduced, following no dating pattern. With seal, £30 — £50; without seal, £5 — £10.

Note: The above values appertain only to bottles in good condition. The range of values is dependent on the details portrayed on the seals. Dated specimens are of higher value.

Foreign Seal Bottles 1880-1914

Maraschino Liqueur
 Elongated square or round bottles of small diameter and in several sizes in sea-green glass. Seal depicts the Austro-Hungarian eagle, and producer's name: F. Drioli, Zara. (Once capital city of Dalmatia and now part of Yugoslavia). £15 – £25.

Vieux Cognac
 French bottle in dark glass, champagne shape. £10 – £12.

Other French Wines
 and champagne bottles, sometimes dated 1903, 1905, etc. £8 – £15.

(Mineral Water 1840-1920)

Most common colour for bottles of this period is aqua, which is practically clear colour, faintly tinged with green. Dark green and brown was used towards the end of the 19th century only.

Turn-of-the-century 'pop' bottles, now cylindrical in shape. 1900-1910. Left: dark green normal shape with flat vulcanite screw-stopper; right: richly embossed aqua-coloured bottle with shoulders, and the Riley patent chisel *screw-stopper.*

Codd bottle with bulb neck. The bulbs, being on both sides of the neck, hold back the marble, and allow the liquid to be poured or drunk from either side of the bottle. c.1900-1910.

Codd or marble-stoppered bottle. Also depicted: wooden plunger for pushing down the marble to allow escape of gas holding it in place.

Black glass beer bottles with pictorial trademarks in high relief are most attractive. The above specimens have internal screw-stoppers, c.1900-1910.

Case gin bottle in dark glass, embossed with the name of the Dutch distiller, J.T. Beukers, Schiedam. Embossed types are comparatively rare, with unembossed bottles more common.

The Torpedo or 'Hamilton' Bottle

First used by chemist Jacob Schweppe in the late 1790s when he introduced the first commercial medicinal soda water. As gas escaped via the cork stoppers of upright bottles, Schweppe used a pointed bottle which had to be laid on its side. The gaseous soda water was thus in permanent contact with the cork, making it swollen and therefore airtight. Although in use earlier, most specimens date from about 1840-1905, with the majority coming from the last twenty years of this period.

Very early Hamilton, short rounded end, crude, and unembossed, c.1830-40 (rare), £8 – £10.

Embossed Hamilton, 1870-1905, aqua colour, £2 – £3.

Unembossed Hamilton, 1870-1905, aqua colour, £1 – £1.50.

Embossed Hamilton in dark green glass (rare), £25 – £30.

Embossed Hamilton in dark cobalt blue (very rare), £60 – £70.

Codd-Hamilton Hybrid (a combination of the torpedo-shaped bottle, fitted with the marble stopper neck of the Codd), £15 – £25.

Brown salt-glazed stoneware Hamilton, name incised (very rare), £50 – £60.

Other early types of lay-down bottles, cucumber shape, £20 – £30.

The Codd or Marble Bottle, 1875-1930

The popular lemonade or ginger ale bottle, with imprisoned glass ball acting as internal stopper when filled with gas. Most existing specimens from the period 1900-1920, when at its peak of popularity.

Normal Codd bottle in aqua glass, £1.50 — £2.50, according to design.

Normal Codd in amber or brown glass, £15 — £20.

Normal Codd in dark green glass, £20 — £28.

Normal Codd in dark cobalt blue (very rare), £60 — £70.

Known to exist also in brown stoneware (extremely rare), £80 — £100.

Other similar type internal stopper bottles, e.g. bullet stoppers, similar to Codd, without neck cavities, £1.50 — £2.50.

Unusual Codd type patents, ball cavity at base, etc. Many different types known. £3 — £15.

Codd bottles with coloured lips, blue, brown, red, green, £12 — £18.

Codd bottles with coloured glass marbles, £5 — £8. (Caution: some modern Indian bottles have black or blue marbles.)

Other Types of Mineral Water Bottles, 1880-1920

Various types of stoppers, swing stoppers, internal screw stoppers,

Left: Poison bottles in cobalt blue and bright green, 1890-1920, hand-applied lips and embossed. Right: Warner's Safe Cure bottle in brown glass, c.1900. These desirable bottles are embossed with a safe on the front and are known in various sizes, medicine names, and in both brown and green glass.

The most popular types of ink bottles, 1880-1920. All have unfinished or jagged tops as it was not considered necessary to apply smooth lips to ink bottles. Left to right: boat-shape with pen-rests; square with pen-rests and ridges for pen-nibs; octagonal shape, most popular for easy gripping; bell-shape with flared base, to prevent tipping.

Two rarer types of ink bottle: cottage ink shows roof tiles door and window embossings, very rare, c.1870-1880; umbrella ink, c.1880-1890.

cork stoppers etc. Various colours — aqua, black, brown, dark green. 75p — £1.50.

Crown cork bottles, 1905 onwards only. 50p — 75p.

Beer Bottles 1880-1920

Embossed with name only, green, brown or black glass. 75p — £1.50.

Embossed with name and pictorial trademark, brown or green. £1 — £2.

Embossed with name and pictorial trademark, black glass. £2 — £6.

Poison Bottles for Household Use 1880-1920

Various shapes and sizes, octagonal, triangular, hexagonal, etc. Embossed NOT TO BE TAKEN. From 1in. to about 9ins. Bright green, 25p — £1.50; cobalt blue, 30p — £2.

As above, but with POISON or POISONOUS embossed in addition or in lieu of. Bright green, 30p — £2; cobalt blue 50p — £3.

Poison Bottles used by Chemists

Embossed with ridges or wording, and with ground glass stoppers. According to size: clear glass, £1 – £3; green glass, £1 – £4; cobalt blue, £2 – £8.

Unembossed bottles, about half the above values.

Note   Poison bottles in brown, green and blue were still made until about 1940, but were machine-made; the seams coming up to the extreme top of the bottle. On early types, seams stop below the lip.

Medicine Bottles

The range of patent medicine bottles is so great that it is impossible to list all known types Rarities are usually those which are very early, or those which have an attractive pictorial embossing on dark glass.

Types common, 1880-1910. (Manufacturer's name and commodity only)

Veno's Cough Cure, Elliman's Embrocation, Woodward's Gripe Water, Lamplough's Saline, etc. 50p – £1.

Some Special Rarer Types (Pictorial Embossing)

Radam's Microbe Killer: dark glass rectangular bottle with

Common types of bottles for various household liquids, 1890 to 1920. Left to right: walnut ketchup; Eiffel Tower lemonade crystals; Shieldhall; C.W.S. coffee; game sauce; Bovril; small sauce bottle.

Left: Spa water bottle in brown stoneware for natural waters imported from the German springs, c.1880-1914. Also used for Dutch gin until recently. Right: Brown salt glazed stoneware bottles in common use 1850-1920. Left to right: ink bottle with pourer lip; wide-mouthed blacking bottle; round-shouldered mercury bottle; ginger-beer bottle incised with bottler's name.

embossing of a skeleton hitting a man on the head with a club. £40 – £50.

Warner's Safe Cures: many varieties in dark green or brown flat bottles, with rounded shoulders, and heavily embossed with a picture of a safe. Known in half pint, pint and two pint sizes. £10 – £25, according to type. Two pint size, £40 – £50.

Early medicines, embossed with names only, 1800-1870, e.g. Daffy's Elixir, Dr. Steer's Opodeldoc, Turlington's Balsam of Life, etc. £15 – £20.

Hop Bitters bottles: usually tall rectangular bottles in brown glass. Sometimes in shape of log cabin, or Dr. Soule's Hop Bitters, embossed with hops. £10 – £18.

Glass Ink Bottles, 1850-1920

Most types have unfinished, jagged lip known as 'burst-top'. Hundreds of types known. The following are a representative selection:—

Octagonal, with sloping shoulders, aqua colour. 50p – 75p

Octagonal, dark green colour. £1.50 – £2.

Octagonal, amber colour. £3 – £4.

Octagonal, cobalt blue colour. £3 – £4.

Rectangular, boat-shape type, with two pen-rests on top side, values as above.

Square, with pen ridges on top, and with grooves for pen-nibs on some sides, values as above.

Unusual designs, tent-shape, igloo, umbrella, etc. £2 – £5.

Rare figural shapes, cottage, bird-cage, chicken, tea-kettle, spinning top. £10 – £15.

In all cases, increase value for dark colours, blue, brown, green.

Domestic Glass Bottles, 1880-1920

Many common types known, too numerous to list. As a general guide, most are small, unattractive bottles, embossed only with names, but are ideal for beginner-collectors.

Beef extracts: Bovril, Oxo, Valentine's Meat Juice, Bi-Win, Borthwick's Bouillon, Oxvil and other brown glass bottles. 50p – £1.

Coffee bottles, sauce bottles, etc. 50p.

Small rectangular bottles for lemonade and other crystals, e.g. Eiffel Tower, Bird's, Chivers', etc. 50p.

Rarer type Eiffel Tower bottles: with tower embossed on side, £3 – £6; in shape of Eiffel Tower, £8 – £12 (considerably more if dark coloured glass).

Gin, Whisky and Rum Bottles
Public House Spirit Flasks 1880-1914

Flat, pocket-sized flasks, in a variety of shapes, either embossed or etched with name of public house and/or landlord.

Embossed with names, rectangular, ovoid or pumpkin seed shape. £1 – £1.50.

As above, but names etched on glass. 75p – £1.

Case Gin Bottles

Dark green or dark brown glass, rectangular body, tapering from shoulders, virtually no neck. Named due to the shape being adopted for ease of transport as Dutch gin exported widely.

Earliest types, late 18th century, early 19th century (very crude manufacture, crude thick lip, rough base). £20 – £30.

Later types, 1880-1914

Unembossed. Sometimes marks on base, such as letters, circles nodules, crosses. £1.

Embossed with distiller's name. £3 – £5.

White milk glass, embossed with distiller's name (very rare). £25 – £30.

Glass Whisky Bottles 1880-1914

Aqua glass, with name only embossed. £1.50 – £2.

Dark glass, with name only embossed. £2 – £3.

Aqua glass, with name and pictorial trademark. £2 – £3.

Dark glass, with name and pictorial trademark. £3 – £6.

(Pottery whisky jugs also sometimes found, with handle, and transfer-printed with names and pictures, e.g Mitchell's Irish, £15 – £25).

(Stoneware)

Bellarmine Bottles or Jugs

Large brown stoneware bottles often with handles, made in England after the original Continental bottles, used for drinking ale. Early types bear the mask or face of Cardinal Bellarmine on the neck, and often a device or seal on the body. First English examples made by John Dwight at the Fulham Pottery in the late 17th century, but only a few authenticated specimens existing in museums. Their manufacture continued into the 19th century, and need expert examination to date them correctly.

18th and 19th century Bellarmines with mask, and perhaps seal. £50 – £100.

19th century types, with no mask or seal. According to size, £15 – £30.

Note   Crude reproductions exist in a variety of sizes.

Figural Spirit Flasks

Flat bodied flasks in brown stoneware, sometimes two-tone, brown and stone colour. Originally made in 17th and 18th centuries at Fulham. The flasks bear caricature figures in relief on front of bottles and earlier specimens extremely rare. Most encountered are 19th century, usually the Reform Flasks of the 1820s to 1840s.

Left: Stoneware ginger-beer bottles with transfer-printed labelling, c.1905-1910.

Right: Scotch whisky bottle in stoneware with transfer-printed label, c.1900-1910.

With relief figures of Royalty, lords, politicians, etc. £30 – £45.

In shapes of fish, powder horns, clocks, barrels, etc. £18 – £40.

Plain, non-figural flasks, 1850-1900, with or without incised name of public house or merchant. Various sizes. £3 – £10.

Ginger Beer Bottles 1860-1939

1860-1920	Single colour, brown salt-glazed, often with incised name of bottler and/or pottery manufacturer. 50p – 75p.
1895-1900	Earliest type of transfer-printed specimens, made by Doulton, and date printed in full, on brown glaze. £3 – £5.
1900-1939	The most popular type of ginger beer bottle. Transfer-printed with name and often pictorial trade-mark on two-tone brown and stone colour liquid glaze. Pictorial more desirable. According to design, £1.50 – £5.
	As above, but with unusual colour to top, e.g. blue top, green top. £5 – £8.
	Miniature transfer-printed bottle, two-tone. £4 – £6.
	Bulk ginger beers, with or without handles and taps. Transfer-printed, from 1 gallon to 5 gallons. £2 – £8.

Various Household Stoneware Bottles, 1860-1920

Spa Water or Dutch gin, (this bottle used for both liquids). Tall, cylindrical, often with small handle, no neck, and usually incised with names. Various sizes from miniatures to 15ins. £1 – £2.

Blacking Bottles, for boot and harness blacking. Wide-necked bottles. Three sizes. 50p – £1.

Squat Ink Bottles, approximately 1½ins. high. 50p – 75p.

Bulk Ink Bottles, with spout. Many sizes. Some used up to 1950. 30p – £1.

Small brown stoneware bottles for everyday commodities, 1880-1915. Left to right: squat ink; conical glue; larger type desk ink; cylindrical blueing bottle.

Small Blueing Bottles, for wash blueing. Narrow cylindrical, no neck, about 4ins. high. 30p – 50p.

Larger Blueing Bottles. Incised GIESSEN BLUE. 50p – 75p.

Mercury Bottles, round-shouldered, bulbous at top, narrow at base. Height 4ins.-8ins. £1 – £2.

Pitfalls
Condition of Bottles

Glass bottles, which have been buried for many years, are often affected by what is known as 'glass sickness'. This turns the glass opaque and is detected as a grey or white film on the glass, which, when rubbed, may flake away. 'Glass sickness' is caused by the continual action of water draining through the soil, and occurs most heavily on waterlogged land. Once a bottle is affected, there is no known cure. Bottles in this condition are not normally collected, unless rare. Some collectors have a liking for bottles which are very badly affected and which acquire an opalescent sheen, reflecting the spectrum of the colours of the rainbow. In the case of common bottles, however, they have little commercial value.

When purchasing bottles, especially if valuable, hold up to the light to check for cracks and 'sickness'. Run the fingers around the outside and inside edges of the lip, and around the base of the bottle. Even the slightest chip or crack considerably reduces the desirability and value of a bottle.

Museums

British Museum, London.
Pharmaceutical Society Museum London.
Victoria and Albert Museum, London.
Art Gallery and Museum, Brighton.
National Museum of Wales, Cardiff.
Royal Scottish Museum, Edinburgh.
City Museum, Gloucester.
City Museum, Hereford.
Central Museum and Art Gallery, Northampton.
Pilkington Glass Museum, St. Helens.
Salisbury and South Wiltshire Museum, Salisbury.
City Museum, Sheffield.
City Museum and Art Gallery, Worcester.

Reading List

Bedford, John. Bristol and Other Coloured Glass. London, 1964.
Davis, Derek C. English Bottles and Decanters, 1650-1900. London, 1972.
Fletcher, Edward. Bottle Collecting. London, 1972.
Midland Antiques Ltd. British Bottle Price Guide. Burton-on-Trent, 1975.
Revi, Albert C. American Pressed Glass and Figure Bottles. London, New York, 1964.

BRITANNIA METAL

An alloy of tin, antimony and copper used in the manufacture of hollow ware in the late 18th and early 19th centuries. Superficially Britannia metal often resembles pewter, but has a hard, bluish sheen, unlike the soft, silvery-yellow tone of pewter. Britannia metal is often known as hard metal or white metal. Its more versatile properties than those of pewter enabled it to be spun rather than cast, and this made it a more commercial substitute. It was popularly used as a cheap substitute for Sheffield plate and was eventually electroplated. Examples of the latter bear the mark E.P.B.M.

Britannia Metal tea, coffee and chocolate pots.

Top row: 3rd left, fluted tea pot by Vickers, other tea and coffee pots by James Dixon c. 1825-1840.

Second row: Extreme right, early example by J. Wolstenholme; second left, chocolate pot by Ratcliffe; others are later Victorian examples.

Third row: Extreme right, early chocolate or coffee pot by Wolstenholme; second right, early Victorian pot by Sturgess.

Bottom row: Small early examples; third left by James Vickers; fourth left very early hand-made pot by Kitching.

Date-lines

1769-1800 Earliest wares known as white metal and produced originally by James Vickers of Sheffield. Towards the end of the 18th century it was also manufactured by Kirby, Smith & Co. and by Matthew Boulton of Birmingham. Used primarily for teapots which can be dated by size and style. Early pots were small (seldom larger than half-pint), and had wooden handles with a Georgian thumb-piece. Pricing usually goes according to weight, even though the smaller pots are earlier and more desirable. Teapots or coffee pots of this period are in the price range £10 – £20.

1800-1830 Pots becoming larger, with patent non-conducting handles. Styles still relatively simple, with plain round bases. £15 – £35.

1830-1850 Larger pots as before, but becoming increasingly elaborate, with cast, scrolled feet and elaborate decoration. £8 – £12.

Points to look for

James Dixon and Sons made the finest Britannia metalwares and their name enhances the value of an item. Other names to look for, however, include James Vickers, Kirby, Smith & Co., William Holdsworth, J. Wolstenholme and Matthew Boulton. Small sized pots and those with unusual shapes (especially tall, elegant flagon shapes) are the most desirable.

Pitfalls

Beware of damaged or dented pots, since the cost of repair by an expert tinsmith will outweigh the value of the piece in most instances. Poor quality Britannia metal by lesser makers tends to warp with age, so check that the lid fits firmly and easily.

BUCKLES

Metal fasteners for clothing and footwear, widely used in western Europe from the 16th century and fashionable in Britain from about 1660 onwards. The most collectable forms are belt and shoe buckles, which are discussed separately on account of their distinct history and development. Other buckles which are collectable include the small buckles of garters, arm-bands, suspenders and braces which, in the mid to late 19th century, were often die-struck in fancy shapes and silver-plated. These small dress buckles may be found in human or animal form, inanimate objects such as barred gates, hearts or horse-shoes, floral designs or geometric patterns. The price range of these 19th century baubles is from 50p to £2.

Belt Buckles

Found in various base metals (brass, steel, wrought iron, spelter, bronze). Silver belt buckles are relatively uncommon, and in those cases usually only the rims were made of precious metal, over a steel base with base metal prongs or locking bar. The most desirable are silver buckles and those bearing hallmarks prior to 1790 are now very expensive. £50 – £100.

Later silver belt buckles are more frequently met with and may be divided into several categories. Military belt buckles may be found in two types, intended for the waist belt and the cross belt respectively. Officers' buckles in silver, complete with regimental insignia, belong mainly to the 19th and early 20th centuries and range from £25 to £80, depending on age and the intricacy of the insignia.

Highland belt buckles became fashionable in silver about 1820 and were an important feature of the Highland dress worn by the Scottish upper classes. The more elaborate examples were extravagantly decorated with Celtic tracery and thistles, and often encrusted with cairngorm semi-precious stones. By the end of the 19th century these very heavy cast silver buckles were superseded by lighter and simpler buckles of silver sheet, with decorative motifs chased or engraved. £20 – £120.

Silver belt buckles, set with semi-precious stones, glass paste jewels, or gold inlay were fashionable in the late 18th and early 19th centuries. £15 – £60.

Base metal belt buckles paralleled the silver buckles in style and ornament but extend to the present day and provide a much wider range. The most collectable forms are military buckles and belt plates decorated with regimental insignia. £2 – £25.

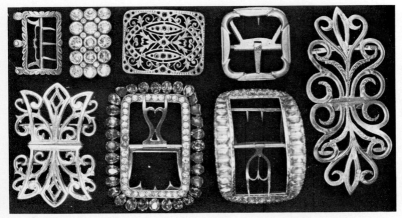

Top row, left to right: Georgian belt buckle; large paste Regency or Victorian buckle; cut steel shoe buckle, Georgian; unusual early Georgian, single spiked, belt buckle.

Bottom row, left to right: A particularly desirable item, mainly due to its wide use nowadays. It is used as a nurse's buckle and dates from the early 20th century (slightly crude cut, but interesting design); unusual Georgian paste shoe buckle, could be either French or English, if it were not for the fact that a few brilliants were missing it would be more valuable; French paste shoe buckle with large set square brilliants and inlaid.

Far right: Late 19th century nurse's buckle, good standard Victorian design.

Uniform belt buckles, in brass or bronze, nickel-plated iron or German silver, date from the mid-19th century and are collected according to subject: e.g. youth movements, security organisations, police, fire brigades. Of these, the most collectable are the highly decorative belt buckles worn by mail-coach guards, especially the Wells Fargo Company, of which there are numerous varieties. Many of these are embellished with pictorial vignettes embossed or cast in relief, and of these the most sought after are those commemorating topical events, such as the Centennial Exposition, 1876, or the Columbian Exposition of 1893. £1 – £20.

Brass buckles set with stones. £5 – £20.

Nurses' buckles, ranging from simply worked silver to an Art Nouveau style. £14 – £30.

Shoe Buckles

Fashionable from 1660 (when they superseded shoe strings) until 1800, when straps and laces came back into fashion. Thereafter shoe buckles continued fitfully on ladies' shoes and on Highland brogues. For this reason a high proportion of 19th century silver shoe buckles will be found with Scottish hallmarks. The vast majority of silver shoe buckles belong to the 18th century, though they are very seldom hallmarked before about 1773, or bear the maker's mark only. Buckles which can definitely be assigned to the late 17th century are very rare. £40 – £70, singles; £100 – £250, pairs.

Small shoe buckles of the early 18th century are more plentiful and their value depends mainly on decorative features, cutting, engraving and embossed ornament, or the inclusion of gemstones or glass paste. £20 – £80.

Very large and heavy buckles (known as Artois buckles, after the Comte d'Artois) were briefly fashionable about 1750, and weighed up to 8oz. £50 – £120.

Later 18th century buckles became smaller again. Elaborate decoration was combined with various patent devices, such as spring mechanism and unusual prongs and catches. A wide variety of styles, with prices ranging from £10 to £60.

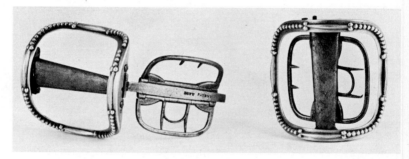

Pair of George III shoe spring buckles, London 1792.

Ladies' shoe buckles of the 19th century were generally much smaller, though many different decorative styles were employed. £5 – £30.

It is important to note that while the rims and prong bars were made of silver, the working mechanism was invariably in brass or steel. Examples which have become badly rusted or whose springs are broken, are worth very much less than perfect specimens (deduct 50-70%). Prices quoted are for single buckles, but matched pairs are usually more desirable and are priced at 2½-3 times that of singles.

Large bow-shaped buckles may also be found with rims in other materials – ivory, stone, tortoiseshell. £10 – £15.

Smaller or Victorian buckles in these materials. 50p – £5.

Museums
Kenwood House (Lady Maufe Collection).

58

BUTTONS

Small discs used as dress fasteners have been recorded since early civilisation. Examples in a variety of materials have been found in various Middle Eastern archaeological sites, but it is possible that some of the early button-like objects were used for purposes other than fastenings. Buttons as fastenings are known from 6th century Persia onwards, as this was the first period when tight clothing was worn. Button-making was established as an industry in France by the 13th century and became organised in other European countries, including England, by the 16th century. Buttons, up to and including the early 18th century were regarded as an integral part of dress ornamentation, being richly decorated and, in accordance with the costumes of the day, largely a male accessory. With the exception of utilitarian articles for underwear and household linens, buttons for female apparel did not become decorative until the 19th century. Age in itself therefore is not

Read across rows, left to right: a hunt button, four railway buttons, a bank button and eight livery buttons.

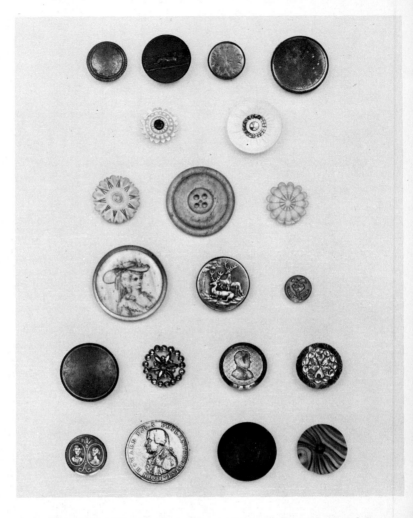

the most important criterion when assessing value, but the following date-lines give an indication of the varieties of button a collector is most likely to encounter.

Date-lines

1700-1750   The majority of fine buttons from this period were made in France and may be of marcasite, fine enamel, pearl, silver, gold and jewels. British examples include those made from brass, copper, pearl shell, tortoiseshell and

PRE 1850

Read across rows, left to right: early 18th century pewter type button, chased design, probably English; bronze finished sporting button by Firmin & Sons, Strand; reputed 17th century metal button; 18th century metal button, this type more usually found in copper or brass and known in America as a 'colonial'; two 18th century decorated pearl buttons; early 19th century carved ivory button; turned bone button c.1825, this type is often dyed brown and is usually smaller; early 19th century carved ivory button; hand-painted portrait under glass, Continental, late 18th century; sporting button marked 'Trebel standard extra rich', c.1810; Victorian gilt c.1840; japanned wooden button inscribed 'Clay, Japanner to His Majesty' (Geo. IV); riveted steel in the style of Matthew Boulton, c.1830-40; two-piece brass button depicting Daniel O'Connell – The Liberator – inscribed 'Repeal' on front and 'Treble rich standard' on rear (Hipwood & Steeple die) c.1843; Victorian gilt (Golden Age) marked 'Extra rich, gold surface, Warranted', from a die by H & S Birmingham c.1840; button to commemorate the marriage of Queen Victoria and Prince Albert, 1840, marked 'Piggott and Co's fast shank' (H & S die); button made from trade token, depicts John Howard F.R.S., philanthropist, on face and inscribed 'Portsmouth and Chichester Halfpenny 1794' on rear; pressed black horn button showing the crowned harp of Hibernia and inscribed 'God Save the Queen, Repeal 1844' (one of many political buttons made for Irish repealists); late 18th/early 19th century English glass button with pinhead shank, possibly made in the Nailsea area.

bone. The engraved copper and brass types are referred to as 'colonials' in America. All buttons from this period are now rare.

1750-1800   A continuation of earlier types and also passementerie (embroidered fabric over a mould) together with the cut steel borders popularised by Matthew Boulton, the centres being Wedgwood jasper discs, hand-painted porcelains or carved shells. On the Continent many fine 'under glass' buttons were produced showing intricate scenes, paintings, feather work, etc..

1800-1850   The advent of the Birmingham button industry and, due to many changes in dress, a completely new approach to button-making which gradually moved from the decorative to the utilitarian for men's wear and vice-versa for ladies. 1802 saw the invention of the Florentine button, a fabric-covered male accessory which gradually replaced decorated gilt-plated brass buttons, referred to now by collectors as the 'Golden Age'. Men's buttons were much reduced in size (from the size of a half-crown to that of a two pence piece), but some ladies' buttons became large and ornate, a trend which continued to the end of the century. Steel, (without the insets) pearl shell, hardstone and glass became popular, and many fine brass buttons depicting sporting designs were produced. Black and natural-coloured horn was used from 1830 for a variety of designs.

1850-1875 Due to the industrial revolution and the invention of button-making machinery shown at the 1851 Exhibition, a somewhat traumatic period with machines taking over the work of outworkers in Dorset and Macclesfield and revolutionising the industry in major button-making centres both in Great Britain and on the Continent. Mechanical processes resulted in 'small chinas' (originally invented in England, but quickly transferred to France), the pressing of steel, brass, wood, horn and the introduction of 'vegetable ivory' (dum or corozo nut) to replace bone.

1875-1900 By this time men's buttons other than military and sporting were almost entirely utilitarian although at the end of the period the vogue for fancy waistcoat buttons returned. Ladies' buttons became highly decorative, but failed to recapture the beauty of the 18th century or the degree of craftsmanship. Machines were used all over the world to mass-produce metal, glass, shell, horn, vegetable ivory, hardstone, etc.. The long period of Queen Victoria's mourning created a fashion for imitation jet buttons made of black glass, some of which were silver-lacquered to imitate steel, now out of fashion. Her interest in Scotland resulted in the popularity of

1850-1875
Read across rows, left to right: carved pearl button, English or Continental; horn button inlaid with pearl and brass, c.1850; pressed horn, undyed; "vegetable ivory" Corozo nut button, c.1875; carved pearl button with riveted steel trim; Scottish agate mounted in silver plate; brass bound agate button with pinhead shank; Scottish agate mounted in silver plate with pinhead shank; agate button with pinhead shank; pressed steel button Tricot type; early type of black glass button prior to more sophisticated pressing techniques, c.1855; small china (Calicoes) made by pressing dry clay dust by Richard Prosser patent method, c.1855; sporting button in two-piece brass, c.1860; small china, c.1855; livery button, silver plate on copper by Firmin & Sons Ltd; vegetable ivory Corozo nut button, c.1875; Dorset thread button, c.1850; painted pearl; livery button, silver plate on copper by Firmin & Sons Ltd.

Scottish pebble, celtic designs in silver and other metals. Children's wear was frequently adorned with small glass and hardstone buttons. Thousands of buttons emanating from this interesting period are easily obtainable for the average collector.

1900-1915 A period of change in dress and the introduction of Art Nouveau designs, which produced many fine buttons in silver, enamel, horn, tortoise-shell and other materials. Many were limited productions from small makers and some rather fragile and impractical. Austria, Bohemia and Germany were now leading producers and French productions tended to be limited to the more superior articles for the couturier trade. Many Birmingham makers closed during this era.

1915-1930 The First World War virtually terminated the production of fine buttons as military items became predominant.

1875-1900. *This period is noted for buttons made in deliberate imitation of 18th century types. Collectors are warned!*

Read across rows, left to right: Moses in the bullrushes, typical three-piece metal button c.1890; probably German; two-piece pressed metal, c.1890, probably German; gilt plated brass hunting button, probably German or Austrian 1895; one-piece brass button from Zodiac series, c.1895; two pressed black glass buttons with silver lustre trim; pressed black glass, known as imitation jet; two-piece brass button, known as a 'picture' in America; French brass button c.1895, marked 'Paris' on rear, known as 'small picture' or 'Paris back' in America; milk glass in steel mount, made to imitate 18th century, British 1900; black glass with lustre trim; pressed clear glass button with gold painted backing, known as Lacy glass in America, made in Bohemia, rare in this shape; cloisonné in gilt mount c.1890, Japanese made for export; brass mounted waistcoat button; a glass apple-shaped button; small glass button; paperweight type button; two small glass buttons; late 19th century French enamel with cloisonné border and hand-painted centre; transfer-printed porcelain, probably British c.1900; satsuma pottery button c.1895, Japanese made for export to West; French 'jewel' button, made in imitation of 18th century type; enamel, pearl and steel button, fine quality, probably French in imitation of 18th century type; early celluloid type made to imitate earlier steel button; late 19th century imitation of 18th century under-glass button, with illustration from French nursery story printed on paper; alloy and brass button with steel riveted trim, probably French 1890.

1930-1940	Due to the revival of fitted clothes and the influence of Art Deco designs there was a brief resurgence in buttons. Heavy wooden and celluloid buttons predominated and painted tin, perspex and early plastics were also in vogue.
1940 onwards	Buttons during the Second World War were almost entirely military and subsequently became mass-produced utilitarian items made of plastics, glass and metals. Recently a few enterprising firms have produced limited numbers of quality buttons and some of the older houses are re-striking from 19th century sporting dies.

Categories of Buttons

Apart from the materials and techniques outlined above, buttons can be classified according to the purpose for which they were made. Dress buttons for both sexes depend on their aesthetic appeal for collectability, whereas uniform buttons are of interest on account of the organisation for which they were made. Metal buttons were worn by schools and colleges, shipping lines and railway companies, fire

brigades, police forces, municipal and government employees and the armed services. Each of these groups has its following, though the buttons of the last group (Army, Navy and Air Force) are in the greatest demand. Military buttons are a vast subject in themselves and their value depends on a number of factors which can be summarised in date order.

Early 18th century Officers' buttons of thin gilt or silver metal, rims turned over a bone or wooden base, the two sections cemented together.

1767	Regimental numbering introduced on buttons; continued to 1871 (other ranks) and 1881 (officers).
1790	Buttons flat with a long shank.
1800	Buttons becoming convex; by 1820 the convexity was filled in.
1800	Manufacturers' names stamped on the back; addresses and trademarks added by 1850.
1830	Regular regiments changed from silver to gold buttons; thereafter only militia regiments wore silver buttons.

1855	Brass buttons introduced for other ranks (previously pewter having been used). Tunic buttons superseded coatee buttons (larger and rimmed).
1871	General Service buttons (with the Royal coat of arms) superseded regimental buttons for other ranks, though in some regiments N.C.O.'s continued to wear regimental buttons.
1881	Regimental numbers replaced by county names and insignia.
1900	Large number of 19th century buttons re-struck for collectors; these can be identified by the inscription 'Special Made' in place of the makers' names on the backs.
1920	Brass regimental buttons re-introduced for private soldiers.
1940	Black or brown plastic replaced brass for buttons as a temporary wartime measure.
1950	Anodised aluminium replaced brass (other ranks) and gilt-metal (officers).
1953	Queen's crown replaced King's crown on insignia.

In addition changes in the pattern of buttons occurred within certain regiments, insignia was altered, and amalgamations of regiments took place at certain times. All of these changes affected the buttons which can be dated accordingly.

1900-1915

Read across rows, left to right: painted metal, with glass imitation moonstone centre, Continental c.1915; later type of Satsuma, blue border, Japanese c.1912; pearl and brass button, French 1910; French enamel, hand-painted centre, c.1910; milk glass button in gilt mount with painted decor to imitate brocade, probably French in imitation of earlier type; pressed brown glass with Art Nouveau design; milk glass Art Nouveau head with gold trim; French brass nursery button, Paris back; German glass and tin button made to imitate earlier style; small enamel button, probably English; black glass in purple painted tin surround, German 1910; three-piece metal with pearl centre, Bohemian in imitation of earlier type, 1905-1910; three French brass buttons depicting actresses of the day; pressed brass with steel trim, probably German; two pressed brass buttons, peacocks were in vogue 1900-1910; Chinese silver and enamel, Shanghai 1910; grey pearl in metal mount, French c.1905; gilt decorated alloy button with Egyptian design, c.1905; hallmarked silver, Birmingham R. & W. 1902; hallmarked silver and enamel, Birmingham 1901; foil and cloisonné in gilt mount, quality Japanese export button, 1900.

From the foregoing it will be seen that certain types of button had a relatively short life and these are the ones mostly highly prized today. They include brass regimental buttons of 1855-71. More recently, the transition from brass to anodised aluminium, combined with the change of crowns, gives rise to two scarce groups: brass with the Queen's crown pattern and anodised aluminium with the King's crown pattern.

Price Range

Prices are for individual buttons in perfect condition. A set of buttons is not worth more than ten times the individual price. Condition is vital, a damaged or scratched button, unless 18th century, is never worth more than a few pence. 18th century damaged about a quarter perfect value.

Military buttons are often collected singly, though sets showing the various sizes in each pattern are in the price range £3 − £10 for late 19th century specimens. Individual buttons from 1830 to 1955 range from 10p to 75p; 1900 re-strikes are worth 10 − 25p each at most. Naval and Air Force buttons are comparable in price. Police and Fire Brigade are usually worth about 25 − 50% less than military or naval buttons, though the minimum price in each case is around 10p. Brass, pewter or white metal buttons of the old railway companies of the pre-grouping era (prior to 1923) are a good buy. Currently undervalued compared with military buttons they are often much rarer, and the growth of interest in railway relics (q.v.) will inevitably rectify this.

The following prices are for single specimens.

Underglass 18th century, unsigned £5 − £10; signed from £10.

18th century enamels/steel mounted etc., £5 − £8.

'Colonials', pearls, etc., from £1.

Early 19th century

Gilts (decorated 'Golden Age'), 50p.

Sporting, 50p − £1.

Riveted steel, from 25p − £1.

Mid 19th century

Decorated pressed horn, from 25p − £2.

Decorated pearl shell, from 25p − £2.

Black glass, from 10p.

Hardstone, 25p − £1.

Late 19th century

Satsuma (Japanese pottery), 50p − £5.

Decorative metals, one piece 25p − 75p; multi-piece construction 50p − £1; 'Paris backs' 25p − £2.

POST 1915

Read across rows, left to right: two celluloid Bohemian buttons, 1920s; two-piece painted tin, Bohemian, 1920s; quality Art Deco button in composition and pearl; celluloid 1920s button, Bohemian; English pottery button, 1930s; perspex, German, 1935; beaded button, English, 1936; two laminated plastic buttons, 1938; button made from 1934 farthing; plaster of Paris 'utility' button, 1945; 'Habitat' button, wood mount with seeds under perspex cover, 1948 (this type originated in the 18th century); one-piece painted tin button, Czech, 1950s; celluloid 1920s button, Bohemian; English Glass Company button, Leicester, 1948; coronation button 1953, made by Cash's of Coventry; modern glass, Czech, 1960s; 1950s glass painted German button; hand-painted glass, made in London 1972; 1974 Union Jack pattern, Italian made for American market.

Black glass, from 10p.
Lustre glass, from 20p.
'Lacy' (clear pressed glass with backing), 50p – £1.
Hardstone, waistcoat or ball, 25p; larger, 50p.
Vegetable ivory, large well decorated, 25p.
Small fancy coloured glass, waistcoat etc., 25p.
Large fancy glass (flat), 50p.

Early 20th century
Art Nouveau, silver, hallmarked, 50p – £2; enamel/silver, £1 – £2; other materials, from 25p – £1.
French Edwardian enamels, 50p.
Decorative metals, as earlier period.
Small metals, 'Austrian tinies', 5p.
Quality French porcelains etc., from £1 – £3.

Post 1st World War
No button of this period made for general sale is worth more than a few pence.

Museums
British Museum, London.
Guildhall Museum, London.
London Museum, London.
Victoria and Albert Museum, London.
Imperial War Museum, London.
National Army Museum, London.
National Maritime Museum, London.
Waddesdon Manor, Aylesbury.
City Museum and Art Gallery, Birmingham.
National Museum of Wales, Cardiff.
Dorset County Museum, Dorchester.
Royal Scottish Museum, Edinburgh.
Somerset County Museum, Taunton.
National Museum of Transport, York.
Most civic museums and every regimental museum include buttons in their exhibits.

Reading List
Albert, Lilian Smith and Kent, Cathryn. The Complete Button Book. London, 1952.
Luscomb, Sally C. The Collector's Encyclopedia of Buttons. New York, 1967.
Peacock, Primrose. Buttons for the Collector. Newton Abbot, 1972.
Squire, Gwen. Buttons: A Guide for Collectors. London, 1972.

CADDY SPOONS

Small spoons used for ladling tea out of the caddy, characterised by a comparatively large and shallow bowl and a short handle. There is considerable variety in the shapes of bowls, from the scalloped shell (an allusion to the actual shells used in the 17th century), to leaf-, scoop-, shovel- or pear-shaped, fluted or circular. Handles range from the slim and elegant of up to three inches in length, to the short and stubby which are little more than thumb plates attached direct to the bowl. The styling of caddy spoons usually reflects the period of manufacture. Silver was used in the earlier period, reflecting the fact that tea-drinking was confined to the upper classes. As the price of tea dropped drastically in the 19th century, and with the advent of electroplate in the 1840s, caddy spoons of cheaper construction became common. Novelty and crested caddy spoons were a popular manifestation of the late 19th century tourist industry and their variety compensates for the generally cheap and shoddy construction.

Date-lines

1740-1770	Shaped like miniature ladles, with handles up to six inches; relatively simple designs, but very rare. £50 — £90.
1770-1800	Short-handled, wide-bowled spoons with handles decorated in contemporary styles. £20 — £40.
1770-1800	Short-handled spoons with novelty shapes in handles and bowls (e.g. eagles, jockeys' caps, hands, foxes, Chinamen, leaves and vine-stalks). £50 — £130.
1800-1820	Regency styling. £15 — £30.
1800-1820	Novelty forms as above. £20 — £50.
1820-1900	Silver caddy spoons, usually more stereotyped in design. £15-£30.
1840-1900	Electroplated spoons in contemporary styles. £1 — £5.
1890-1940	Crested spoons, usually electroplated, occasionally in brass. £1 — £8.

Points to look for

The hallmarks of the more important London and Birmingham silversmiths are important plus factors, as are good examples of caddy spoons with provincial hallmarks. As caddy spoons vary enormously in quality, check that they are solid to the touch (flick the bowl with the finger to see whether it rings true or feels tinny). The marks should be clear. Beware of mends or soldering at the joint of stem and bowl, especially on slender handled spoons (which may well have been salt spoons converted).

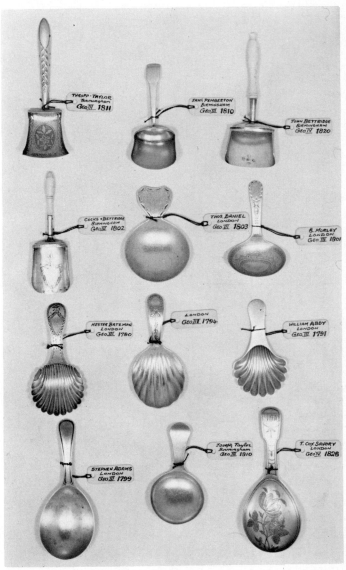

Silver caddy spoons from 1790 to 1828.

CAMERAS

Devices for taking photographs have become eminently collectable in recent years. The principles of photography were discovered by Nicephore Niepce, who achieved the first fixed photographic image in 1816. Between that date and 1840 experiments were carried out in France, Britain and other countries leading to the development of practical cameras which could be reproduced commercially. The pioneer cameras of Niepce, Fox-Talbot and others are virtually unique and largely confined to museum collections. Commercially produced cameras began in 1839, when Louis-Jacques Daguerre patented his Daguerreotype process and manufactured a simple box camera which was subsequently put on the market. Collectable cameras date from 1840 to about 1940, though there are many post-war cameras which, on account of their technical features, are worth considering now as collectables of the future.

Date-lines

Up to 1816   The "camera obscura". This precedes the actual photographic camera. In its simplest form it consists of a box with a lens in front and a screen to receive the image

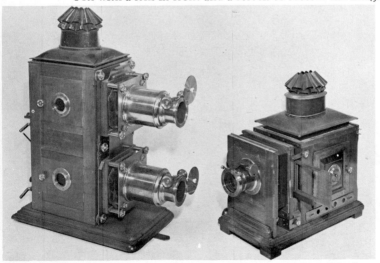

Left: A double oxy-hydrogen biunial lime light lantern in original case, 3¼ins. Right: A mahogany and brass 3¼ins. lantern in original case, converted to electricity.

Left: Half-plate Sands Hunter Imperial Double Extension camera c.1880.
Right: 5 x 4in. Sanderson de Luxe camera.

at the back. Early examples are worth hundreds of pounds dependent on workmanship, date and technical features.

1816-1840　The cameras of this period are museum pieces and should one reach the market, it would be worth several thousand pounds.

1840-1880　The 'wet-plate' period. Cameras were large, cumbersome affairs, housed in wooden boxes. Technical features were very simple. The earliest models consisted of two wooden boxes, one sliding within the other. Later versions had leather bellows with squared corners. The earliest all-wooden cameras are often beautiful examples of the cabinet-maker's art. £200 − £1,000.

Early bellows cameras are less desirable, though often quite rare. £60 − £150.

1880-1920　The 'dry-plate' period, introduced by George Eastman, inventor of the Kodak dry - plates in 1879. This technique revolutionised photography, greatly extending its popularity and stimulating the growth of a major industry in the production of cameras. Numerous different types of dry-plate camera were produced in this period. From 1880 to 1895 technical features were still simple and the value of cameras depends largely on appearance: mahogany casing, brass mountings and Russian leather bellows are desirable features. £50 − £150.

1888-1901　The first camera to take rolls of film was invented by George Eastman and patented as the "Kodak". Some are

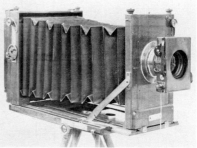

Left: Whole plate camera by Newton & Co. c.1880. Right: Sands and Hunter's "Imperial" half-plate camera of 1888. Note the boxed roller blind shutter (somewhat later than the camera) mounted on the front of the lens.

	fitted with a brass engraved counter. These cameras took up to 100 shots. £40 – £220.
1895-1920	Bellows with 'cut-off' corners; first accurate camera shutters. Greater attention to technical detail; casings more functional. £30 – £100.
1896	Folding pocket Kodak cameras first appeared. Patent dates are found inside on the back. In good condition, £30.
1921-1940	The hey-day of the early Rollei, Leica, Zeiss and Contax cameras. Prices of cameras of this period vary enormously as this was the period of greatest technical developments. Technical features now more important than the appearance of cameras. £20 – £200 or more, depending on model.

Points to look for

Any wet-plate camera is now highly desirable and it is important to be able to distinguish wet-plate from dry-plate. Inside the plate carrier at the back of the camera there should be a short insert of silver wire (for the plate wet with silver nitrate to rest on). This feature is absent in the dry-plate cameras. Many of the earlier cameras had elaborately engraved metal plates mounted on the woodwork giving the manufacturer's name and address. Patent numbers and dates are often a useful guide to dating. The cameras prior to the First World War incorporated the crafts of cabinet-maker, instrument-maker and optician; thus its value will be based both on the stage of technological development and on the quality of the craftsmanship.

Pitfalls

The cut of the bellows is not always an infallible guide to date, since 'cut-off' bellows may have been fitted to a pre-1895 camera at some much later date when the original bellows became worn. Such modifications tend to detract from the value of a camera. Other modifications include changes in the first model Rollei, which originally took a six-exposure film but was often modified subsequently to take a larger film. Unmodified Rolleis are now rare and would be worth £150 — £200 in mint condition.

Folding Poᵣᴋet Kodak, model E.4.

W. Watson and Son Plate camera c.1900.

Museums

Science Museum, London.
Kodak Museum, Hemel Hempstead.

Reading List

Holmes, Edward. An Age of Cameras. Kings Langley, 1974.

76

CANDLESTICKS (Brass)

Although made in many parts of central and western Europe from the Middle Ages onwards brass candlesticks for the collector practically date from the mid-17th century. The pricket candlestick, characterised by its conical spike on which the candle was impaled, gave way to the socket candlestick during the 17th century and examples in brass are of considerable rarity. Socket candlesticks, though in existence from about 1500, did not become fashionable until 1650. Thereafter candlesticks in brass became increasingly popular and a wide variety of types was produced in the 18th and 19th centuries. From about 1840 onwards, however, styles became mixed and eclectic, and there is a considerable vogue at the present day for 'period reproductions'. Candlesticks today have taken on ornamental, as opposed to actual, functions and the situation is further confused by the unfortunate practice of converting genuine candlesticks to take electric light, and by the cannibalisation of pieces from different candlesticks, sometimes of widely varying periods.

Date-lines

Antique brass candlesticks can be classified by types which fall into fairly well-defined periods. The earliest types have a wide grease-pan half-way up the stick and a flat, spool- or trumpet-shaped base, with some evidence of bobbin-turning on the stem. A shorter form was

C.1650, height 5ins.

Octagonal base candlestick c.1710, height 5¼ins.

Left: Hexagonal high domed base c.1715-20, height 6ins.

Right: c.1735, showing the development in the design of hollowed angles on square bases, height 7½ins.

popular in the late 17th century and had the grease-pan mounted on a tall circular base. A characteristic feature of this type was the rectangular slot in the side of the socket, so that the candle-stubs could be easily removed. Solid brass was used for the stem, which was either screwed to the base or hammered on to it.

The Huguenots introduced a new method of construction some time after 1685 and this had superseded the solid-stem construction by 1700. The stems were hollow-cast in two halves and joined together by brazing. Such sticks have two thin seam lines diagonally opposite each other and running vertically up the stem. Relatively plain octagonal bases were fashionable in the early 1700s, but by 1720 faceting had become popular. Hexagonal, and later square, bases were in vogue in the 1720s and 1730s. The grease-pan disappeared at the end of the 17th century, as a result of the improved composition of candles, and was replaced by an enlarged socket rim. From this evolved the sconce, a detachable rim for catching the wax drips, which came into use in the 1720s. Later sticks can be dated by the shape of their bases which become more elaborate as the 18th century wore on. Square bases with chamfered corners (1725-35) were followed by scalloped or petalled bases (1735-50) which are more or less circular in form. In the corresponding period the baluster stems also become more elaborate, and the number of knops increases.

A comparatively rare type of candlestick has a single seam, indicating that it was made from sheet brass. This type has a broad lip at the top where the sheet metal is folded under. A distinctive feature of the sheet brass stick is the sliding rod in the stem by which the height of the candle could be adjusted and the stub ejected.

About 1770 sticks became taller and more elegant, though a more positive guide to date is the technique of die core casting evolved in Birmingham which permitted the production of stems in one piece. Candlesticks from this date onwards have no seams. The neo-classical brass sticks of 1790-1830 may be recognised by their square or octagonal bases, relatively high, with tall, slender, slightly tapered stems characterised by fluting and gadrooning. Later 19th century sticks imitated earlier styles and it is thought that the controversial candlesticks bearing the name 'Grove' on the underside come into this category. The later sticks have little antiquarian interest or value at present, an exception being the Aesthetic candlesticks of the late 19th century designed by Philip Webb and made by W.H. Haseler of Birmingham for Liberty's; these sticks have a simple stem, broad drip-pan and high circular base, consciously modelled on the late medieval style.

Points to look for

The presence of single or double seam, or its absence when considered in conjunction with other features, is a useful guide to dating. This feature is more important than the shape of bases or the styling of stems since both were copied indiscriminately in the later 19th century sticks. The quality of the brass is also important, new techniques in casting about 1690 producing brass of a better colour and surface texture. By 1760 poor quality sticks were being made for the cheaper end of the market; such sticks can be recognised by the use of bases of brass sheet roughly beaten over a template with the minimum of decoration provided by a few incised lines.

Left: Tapered stick, c.1780, with beaded decoration and tapered fluted stem.

Victorian candlestick c.1850. The bold, heavy cotton reel stem is inelegant.

Pitfalls

Because the market in brass candlesticks is relatively modern and antique varieties of little value until recent years, the collector had only to contend with late 19th century imitations which differed radically in production techniques from the originals. Now, however, early 18th century sticks retail at over £100 and it has become profitable to forge them. So far these forgeries have been fairly crude. Apart from the fact that they are generally heavier (having been cast solid) these imitations differ markedly in the finishing off underneath. In genuine sticks the rough metal and casting marks were removed on a lathe using a chisel. This produces the tell-tale pattern of fine concentric circles. In many cases the corners of bases with a square or petalled form were finished off by means of a chisel. Furthermore, genuine sticks have a rich black patina on the underside which it is impossible to simulate. Forgeries of recent date are crudely finished off, if at all, and lack the deep patina of age.

Price Range	Singles	Pairs
1650-1690	£120-150	£300-500
1690-1710	£ 30- 70	£150-200
1710-1720	£ 20- 40	£100-200
1715-1730	£ 20- 40	£100-200
1730-1740	£ 20- 40	£100-150
1740-1760	£ 15- 25	£ 65- 90
1760-1830	£ 10- 30	£ 25- 80
1830-1890	£ 5- 10	£ 12- 25

Prices tend to drop with the appearance of the classical revival square base and column, circa 1760. These sticks vary in quality more than the earlier ones and they do not have the gold colour of earlier examples.

Other Metals

Pewter was used as a cheaper substitute for brass in the 17th century but declined in popularity about 1700. It enjoyed a brief revival in the early 19th century but had gone out of fashion by 1850. Gun-metal bronze was used occasionally from about 1760 but was never widely popular. Though these metals are much rarer than brass, there is no premium on their value at present. However, should a pair of pewter sticks of the first quarter of the 18th century turn up they would keenly be sought after by the candlestick collector.

Reading List

Grove, John R. Antique Brass Candlesticks, 1450-1750 Queen Anne, Md 1967, London, 1968.

Michaelis, Ronald. Base Metal Candlesticks, Woodbridge, 1976.

Wills, Geoffrey. Candlesticks. Newton Abbot, 1974.

CARD CASES

Small flat containers for visiting cards, dating from the beginning of the 19th century up to the outbreak of the Second World War. Prior to about 1780 people used playing cards, endorsed in manuscript, as visiting cards, but from then onwards specially printed cards were used. At first all visiting cards were of roughly the same format as playing cards, but by the middle of the 19th century those used by gentlemen were greatly reduced in size, 3 x 2¼ins. being the usual size. By the end of the century, however, gentlemen's cards had become slightly shorter and much narrower, a format retained to this day. Ladies' cards also became much smaller after about 1900, and these changes of format are reflected in the sizes of the card cases produced at various times over the 135 years in which they were in use. The earliest card cases were made of silver or silver-gilt and this continued to be a popular material throughout their career. By the middle of the 19th century, however, other materials were becoming fashionable, including mother-of-pearl, tortoiseshell, ivory, bone, wood, leather, papier mâché or even cloth-covered card. The date-lines that follow apply only to silver card cases; those in other materials belong to the period 1850-1910 and are discussed separately, according to materials and decorative techniques.

Filigree case c.1825.

Silver 'Castle Top' case 'Windsor', a good early example by Nathaniel Mills.

Mother-of-pearl case decorated with diamonds of dark and light pearl, the light pearl being engraved with more diamonds and a feathered edge.

Date-lines

1800-1830	Filigree boxes in silver or silver-gilt; seldom hallmarked. Tops separate and slide over a long bezel. Very sharp corners. £15 – £30.
1830-1840	Heavier cases, with filigree, but tending towards intricate pierced design; hallmarking more common. £15 (unmarked) to £120 (with marks of famous smiths).
1833-1840	Early 'Castle Top'; sharp angles as before, scenes and landmarks (especially castles) in plain rectangular setting with pierced foliate ornament above and below, £90 – £250.
1840-1860	Later 'Castle Tops'; more elaborate styles, with ornament following the outline of the building. Rounded corners and scrolled outlines. £75 – £350.
1840-1870	Rounded corners, hinged top, and scrolled outline with pierced floral decoration surrounding rectangular or circular plaque engraved with name or initials. Cases lighter in construction. £40 – £75.
1835-1870	As above, but pierced floral decoration replaced by guilloche or engine-turned ornament. £25 – £50.
1825-1850	Gentleman's card case smaller in size (3¼ x 2½ins.); often curved to fit the pocket. £20 – £40.
1850-1910	Later styles of gentleman's card cases; usually less ornate than the earlier styles. £7 – £15.
1870-1930	Later 'Castle Tops'; smaller and lighter than earlier types; post-1900 examples usually bear an inscription identifying the building. £25 – £60.
1860-1910	Lighter cases with engraved rococo decoration. £15 – £35.
1890-1910	Cases with engraved or repoussé Art Nouveau motifs. £15 – £35.
1900-1914	Smaller cases fitted with chains and a suspensory finger ring. £15 – £25.
1900-1930	Novelty forms, resembling slim purses (sometimes fitted

	with satin compartments); book type (opening out like a book); cases incorporating a patent stamp holder. £15 – £30.
1920-1935	Return to earlier angular format; cubist or Art Deco motifs; decoration usually engine-turned, but also incorporating enamelling. £6 – £15. Good Art Deco examples. £50+.

Other Materials

Card cases in materials other than silver were mainly produced in the second half of the 19th century. The exception to this is mother-of-pearl, which was popular between 1830 and 1850, and remained sporadically fashionable till the end of the century. The earliest mother-of-pearl cases were often inlaid with silver on tortoiseshell (piqué) or with silver or gold directly on mother-of-pearl. £10 – £25.

Later cases were produced in mother-of-pearl alone, the decorative effect being achieved by using squares or diamonds of the material cut or decorated in contrasting patterns. They may also be found with cameo carving or fretted ornament. £10 – £20.

Piqué card cases, with silver or gold inlaid on tortoiseshell; often book-shaped with small matching pencil attached to the spine. £15 – £30.

Ivory cases with delicate pierced decoration are rare. £25 – £40.

More frequently ivory is inlaid on sandalwood in chinoiserie motifs. £15 – £30.

From 1850 onwards there was a vogue for wooden cases with Scottish tartan decoration applied in paper which was then varnished or lacquered. £8 – £15.

Papier mâché cases with floral painting or mother-of-pearl inlay. £8 – £20.

Card cases in cloth over card: £2 – £5 for plain satin; £5 – £10 for embroidered examples, with a premium for those incorporating fine beadwork.

Electroplate cases supplied the cheaper end of the market from 1850 onwards. £6 – £15.

Points to look for

With the exception of the early filigree cases, silver cases should be fully marked, in the earlier period on the bases and later on the bezel. As a rule the lids are only partially marked (with the lion and year letter). Names to watch for are the Birmingham silversmiths Nathaniel Mills II, Edward Smith, Taylor & Perry, George Unite, Joseph Willmore

Collection of silver card cases, the centre example being a 'Castle Top' 'Scott Memorial'.

and Yapp & Woodward. Condition is very important, and the value of cases showing signs of wear, extensive rubbing, dents or damage may be halved. Damaged and worn hinges can reduce value by 25-50%. In filigree cases check that every detail of the ornament is intact. In repoussé cases (especially early 'Castle Tops') examine the high points of the relief, as these are the first areas to show cracks where the silver is thinnest. Dents in the sides, especially of curved cases, are a serious drawback, as it is virtually impossible to hammer them out. The value of 'Castle Tops' is greatly affected by the rarity of the scene, e.g. Birmingham-made Scott memorial £75 – £125,   Wellington Monument £350.

Museums
London Museum, London.
Victoria and Albert Museum, London.
Royal Scottish Museum, Edinburgh.
City Museum, Hereford.
Museum and Art Gallery, Leicester.
Central Museum and Art Gallery, Northampton.

Harris Museum and Art Gallery, Preston.
Salisbury and South Wiltshire Museum, Salisbury.
City Museum, Sheffield.
Museum and Art Gallery, Tunbridge Wells.
City Museum and Art Gallery, Worcester.

Reading List
Delieb, Eric. Silver Boxes. London, 1968.
Harris, Ian. The Price Guide to Victorian Silver. Woodbridge, 1971.
Hughes, Therle. Small Antiques for the Collector. London, 1964.

CARRIAGE CLOCKS

Travelling timepieces developed in France in the 18th century and produced down to the early 20th century. Carriage clocks evolved out of the portable clocks of the 16th and 17th century, provided with an outer casing and carrying handle. Clocks in this group included the sedan clock, designed to be hung in sedan chairs. These resembled outsize watches and were often circular, though occasionally square or polygonal and fitted with a wooden or metal casing. Sedan clocks were produced between 1750 and 1800. Small square travelling clocks in brass or gilt metal were devised about 1770 mainly for the use of military officers, though the name *pendule d'officier* was not actually coined by Abraham-Louis Breguet till 1800, and then described a model specifically designed for the use of officers in the Napoleonic armies. *Pendules d'officier* invariably had a circular dial and a curved top, often with elaborate moulding, handles and feet. For these reasons these clocks were regarded as decorative rather than functional, though occasionally unusual technical features will be found. *Pendules d'officier* of the period 1770-1820 are still relatively undervalued and are in the price range from £400 to £1,000. Similar French clocks with square tops and circular dials, made from c.1780-1820 and known as *Capucines*, are much closer to the carriage clock in appearance, although they are usually surmounted by the striking bell. £250 – £600.

Carriage clocks themselves developed during the same period, and may be distinguished by their rectangular gilt cases, glass panels, rectangular face and comparatively large carrying handle. Unlike the *pendule d'officier*, early carriage clocks were bereft of ornament apart from restrained fluting on the sides or occasional baluster pillars on the sides and handles.

Date-lines

Carriage clocks were made between 1770 and 1910. Prior to about 1820 they were made almost exclusively in France, but thereafter they were also produced in Britain, Austria and the United States. Dates, however, are not of major importance compared with other criteria – the combination of various styles and the number of technical features.

Types of Carriage Clock

Carriage clocks may be broadly categorised according to size. Of these, miniatures are the most desirable (3-4 inches in height). Clocks in

Top, left to right: A gilt metal-cased repeating carriage clock — 8 day movement, 6ins. high; a gilt metal and bevelled glass-cased carriage timepiece, 4¼ins. high; a gilt metal-cased repeating alarm carriage clock, 8 day movement, 5¼ins. high. Bottom, left to right: a miniature, gilt-cased alarm carriage timepiece, 3ins. high; a carriage miniature timepiece in gilt metal case, 3ins. high.

the 4½-5½ inches range are worth half as much, all other points being equal, and larger clocks (6-12 inches) are worth about 20% less than miniatures. Exceptionally large clocks are worth £60 — £250 more, depending on other features.

Since the principal value of carriage clocks lies in their technical features, the price rises steeply in the case of clocks that incorporate striking and repeating mechanisms. In ascending order of value are clocks with hour striking, hour striking and repeating, quarter striking and repeating, grande sonnerie (with the hour repeated every quarter), and minute repeating. For larger clocks possessing these features, the value is about 25% greater than for the smaller clocks.

Technical features

The inclusion of an alarm adds about £25 — £30 to the value of a carriage clock, irrespective of type, except for miniatures (add £40 — £50) and minute repeating clocks (add £60 — £75).

Clocks with an engraved case and masked dial command a hefty premium, doubling the value of miniatures and ordinary timepieces and adding £150 — £200 to the value of the striking and repeating varieties.

An oval case adds about £80 — £100 to the value of all types of clocks, from miniatures to hour striking and repeating types, but from £150 to £300 in the case of the more complex types.

Calendar work on ordinary timepieces virtually doubles their value, and is a most desirable feature on the striking and repeating varieties, though it decreases in importance in relation to the more valuable types. Thus, for hour striking and repeating clocks add 50% for calendar work, whereas minute repeating clocks add about 30%.

Porcelain or enamel panelling is the most important decorative feature, and automatically adds £200 — £300 to the value of most clocks, and from £400 to £600 in the case of grande sonnerie and minute repeating clocks.

The presence of a duplex escapement adds £100 — £120 to the value of a clock; but spring-detent or chaff-cutter escapements add twice as much.

English Carriage Clocks

The foregoing remarks apply mainly to French clocks. English clocks, characterised by the fusee and chain drive, are more difficult to assess. The simplest timepieces are now in the price range £300 — £500, but outstanding examples, by the more reputable makers, may be in the range from £2,000 to £4,000 and upwards.

A 19th century English brass carriage clock, the enamelled dial signed Dent, 13 Cockspur Street, London, 8ins. high.

A fine French carriage clock, the movement contained in a gorge case inset with porcelain dial and side panels.

This table provides a general guide to average values for those French carriage clocks most usually found. The left-hand figure column is the base figure.

Type	Size		Alarm	Engraved Case and Masked Dial	Oval Case	Porcelain/ enamel Panels	Early Example	Calendar Work
	4½-5½in.	6½+in.						
Miniatures c. 3in.	£130		+£35	+£100	+£80	+£200	v. rare	—
Timepieces	£55	+£35	+£25	+£70	+£70	+£150	+£30	+£50
Hour Striking	£150	+£20	+£20	+£80	+£70	+£150	+£30	+£60
Hour Striking/Repeating	£180+	+£30	+£20	+£100	+£80	+£150	+£30	+£80
Quarter Striking/Repeating	£350	+£35	+£20	+£120	+£120	+£180	+£50	+£100
Grande Sonnerie	£500+	+£50	+£20	+£150	+£200	+£300	+£100	+£150
Minute Repeating	£1500	+£200	+£50	+£150	+£250	+£450	v. rare	+£400

Points to look for

Because they were used while travelling, carriage clocks invariably show some signs of wear. Exceptionally fine examples in very good condition are scarce and are worth about 30% more than good average specimens. The presence of original gilding, carrying case and key are highly desirable features which enhance the value.

Pitfalls

Modern carriage clocks of Continental manufacture have been produced in recent years but may easily be distinguished from 18th and 19th century examples. The chief problem, however, concerns antique carriage clocks decorated with enamelled panels of 20th century Viennese manufacture. Caution should be exercised in the purchase of any clock with enamelled panels.

METEOR STROLLER SENTINEL

A selection of typical American carriage clocks.

CONDUCTOR COMPANION WANDERER

Museums
British Museum, London.
Guildhall Museum, London (Clockmakers' Company collection).
London Museum, London.
Science Museum, London.
Victoria and Albert Museum, London.
Wallace Collection, London.
Waddesdon Manor, Aylesbury.
City Museum and Art Gallery, Birmingham.
Art Gallery and Museum, Brighton.
Royal Pavilion, Brighton.
Gershom-Parkington Collection, Bury St. Edmunds.
National Museum of Wales, Cardiff.
Minories Art Gallery, Colchester.
National Museum of Antiquities, Edinburgh.
Royal Scottish Museum, Edinburgh.
City Museum, Hereford.
Temple Newsam House, Leeds.
Newark House Museum, Leicester.
Wernher Collection, Luton Hoo.
Central Museum and Art Gallery, Northampton.
Museum of the History of Science, Oxford.
Scone Palace, Perth.
Salisbury and South Wiltshire Museum, Salisbury.
City Museum, Sheffield.
City Museum and Art Gallery, Stoke-on-Trent.
Windsor Castle, Windsor.
Snowshill Manor, Broadway, Worcestershire.

Reading List

Allix, Charles and Bonnert, Peter. Carriage Clocks. Their History and Development. Woodbridge, 1974.
Bruton, Eric. Clocks and Watches. London, 1968. Clocks and Watches, 1400-1900. London, 1967.
Edey, Winthrop. French Clocks. London, 1967.
Goaman, Muriel. English Clocks. London, 1967.
Lloyd, H. Alan. The Collector's Dictionary of Clocks. London, 1969. Old Clocks. London, 1970.
Salomons, Sir David. Breguet. London, 1921.
Tait, Hugh. Clocks in the British Museum. London, 1968.
Tyler, E.J. European Clocks. London, 1968.

CHINA FAIRINGS

Porcelain figure groups, produced as fairground gifts and souvenirs, and popular in Britain between 1860 and the end of the 19th century. The majority of these groups stand about four inches high. They are characterised by a heavy body and relatively simple form. High temperature polychrome colours were used for the figures but bases and much of the surrounding decor were left white. Captions, often amusing, whimsical or slightly risqué, appear in copperplate script along the front of the base. The vast majority of fairings, and certainly the more collectable ones, were produced by one firm, Conta and Boehme of Possneck in Saxony, but though Germanic in origin they were intended almost exclusively for the British market and never seem to have been popular in Germany itself. The subjects are those that would have appealed to a British public. One might go so far as to say that they were the German answer to Staffordshire pottery figures. Like Staffordshire figures they have a certain naïve charm and many of them were modelled on contemporary pictorial music covers (q.v.) which were also a source of inspiration for Staffordshire figures.

Date-lines

c.1860-1865	The earliest fairings are unmarked.
1865-1880	Bases have incised numerals running serially from 2850 to 2899 and from 3301 to 3385.
1880-1891	Serial numbers are impressed, and fairings also bear the Conta and Boehme mark — a shield containing an arm and dagger.
1891-1900	Later fairings bear the mark 'Made in Germany' (to comply with the American McKinley Tariff Act of 1891).
1890-1914	Many fairings made by other factories. These are usually unmarked, of inferior quality and have hollow bases whereas all Conta and Boehme fairings had solid ones. Of these later imitations the only ones to excite interest are the Welsh tea party groups, which emanated from Japan.

Points to look for

Early unmarked fairings generally show much finer quality in moulding. The later fairings have a heavier, more blurred outline, since

'It's only Mustache', show-ing a girl stroking a cat as her mother enters the room and a lover hides under the table.

the moulds were used over and over again and inevitably showed signs of wear. As fairings were made from up to twenty moulds, the arrangement of components may vary considerably. The presence of unusual features in otherwise common fairings would greatly enhance their value. Thus the fairing 'Last in bed to put out the light', which is worth £8 – £10, is worth three times as much if the bed-head is quilted.

Price Range

Apart from desirable features on otherwise common fairings, prices are largely governed by the subject. The rapid growth of interest in fairings since 1965 is reflected in the rise in prices for the more popular or unusual subjects, some of which have increased in value 30 times in a decade. At the other extreme, however, the commonest fairings ('Last in bed') have merely doubled in price, from £3 – £4 in 1965 to £6 – £10 in 1975. Prices rose very sharply in 1973 when the £1,000 mark was passed, and reached their peak in early 1974 when the top price (for a hitherto unrecorded example) became £1,470. Prices have now stabilised, however, and it is unlikely that any fairing will pass four figures again in the foreseeable future.

Below is given a selection of fairings, grouped by subject, with their approximate current values.

Bicycles:

To Epsom.	£400
To the Derby.	£300
Beware of a collision.	£200

Every vehicle driven by a horse.   £200
Other bicycling subjects   £200
Political:
Ĺ English Neutrality, 1870.   £125
Free and independent elector.   £175
At Chancery.   £120
Children:
Attack and Defeat (pair).   £75
Tug of War and Spoils of War (pair).   £75
Pluck and the decided smash (pair).   £75
Lovers:
It's only Mustache.   £250
If old age could.   £150
Cupid's watching.   £175
Two different views.   £90
An awkward interruption.   £90
Kiss me quick.   £25
The power of love.   £35
Everyday Scenes:
Out by jingo.   £250
A long pull and a strong pull (pair).   £120
How's business and Slack (pair).   £240
The organ boy.   £150
Well! what are you looking at?   £250

Beware of a collision.

English neutrality 1870/1 attending the sick.

Well! What are you looking at?   *The Orphans.*

Cancan (various).	£200
Lor three legs.	£60
God save the Queen.	£50

Animals:

The Orphans.	£50
Hark Tom somebody is coming.	£60
Oh do leave me a drop.	£50
Good Templars.	£45
My Lord and Milady.	£40

Historical:

The Death of Nelson.	£100

Marriage Difficulties:

Happy father what two?	£30
When a man is married.	£15
Did you call sir?	£40
Twelve months after marriage.	£12
The wedding night.	£20
Last in bed to put out the light.	£10
Shall we sleep first or how?	£10

Later fairings (1885-1900) by Conta and Boehme or anonymous factories, with subjects redolent of the Naughty Nineties, are in a class of their own, and some of these are now comparatively expensive.

The first pair.	£40
Now they will blame me for this.	£45
Morning prayer and Evening prayer (pair).	£25

Hollow-based fairings imitating Conta and Boehme subjects are of little value, £2 – £5.

Shall we sleep first or how?

The last in bed to put out the light.

Museums
Victoria and Albert Museum, London.
Central Museum and Art Gallery, Northampton.
City Museum and Art Gallery, Stoke-on-Trent.
Beamish Museum, Chester-le-Street.
Elizabethan House, Totnes.

Reading List
Bristowe, W.S. Victorian China Fairings. London, 1971.
Godden, Geoffrey. Antique China and Glass under £5. London, 1965
(still useful, although fairings are no longer the unconsidered trifles they
were when the book was published).

CHRISTMAS CARDS

The custom of exchanging seasonal greetings by letter at Christmas received new impetus in 1843 when Henry Cole and John Horsley devised the first Christmas card. Retailing at a shilling it depicted a middle class Victorian family round a table groaning with festive fare. The custom was slow to catch on, and examples dating from the 1840s are of the greatest rarity. By 1850, however, it was becoming established among the upper classes of society, but did not become universally popular till after the advent of the printed paper and postcard rates of postage in 1870. Thereafter cards became increasingly stereotyped and mass-produced, though certain categories (animated cards and patriot cards of the Boer and First World Wars) are highly desirable. From 1920 onwards Christmas cards have become highly commercialised and quality has suffered as a consequence. The more collectable cards are those whose subject, rather than production techniques, merits special interest.

Date-lines

1843-1850   Earliest cards published by Felix Summerly's Home Treasury (run by Cole). Line engraved and hand-coloured. Different designs used each season and all now very rare. £50 – £100 (without envelopes).

Examples with their original envelopes and contemporary postmarks are extremely rare. £300 – £500 would not be an exaggerated sum, should any examples of this period turn up.

The first Christmas card designed and executed in 1843 by John Horsley.

1850-1870	Christmas cards decorated with lacy embossed borders and collages, similar to the Valentines (q.v.) of the period. Centres decorated with chromolithographed scraps. £10 − £20.
	Similar cards, but decorated with lace, feathers, jewels, sea shells. £15 − £30.
1870-1900	Embossed or cut card work, decorated with scraps. £5 − £8.
	Similar cards, but with more elaborate motifs stuck on. £7 − £15.
	Printed and embossed cards, without scraps or other additions. £2 − £4.
1900-1920	Fold-over cards, with embossed and chromolithographed decoration. £1 − £3.
	Postcards with Christmas greetings or seasonal motifs. 50p − £2.
	First World War or Boer War patriotic cards. £2 − £5.
	First World War embroidered silk postcards with Christmas motifs. £5 − £10.
1920-1940	Commercially printed cards; value depends on subject matter. 20p − £2.

Points to look for

Among Victorian cards the following types are scarce and highly desirable: cards with a complicated folding arrangement, including concertina cards, padded cards incorporating sachets of scent, embossed cards with irregular shapes, pop-up or other mechanical cards. Christmas cards of these types were popular from 1860 to 1890 and are generally in the price range £10 − £20, depending on the particular gimmick employed. Such cards should be intact and in perfect working condition.

Cards reflecting contemporary crazes in the applied and decorative arts are worth a handsome premium. In this group come cards decorated with Japonaiserie (1875-1890), Art Nouveau motifs (1895-1910), and the Aesthetic Movement (1870-1890). Cards designed by such artists as Kate Greenaway, Randolph Caldecott and Walter Crane; or early cards bearing the imprints of Valentine, Raphael Tuck or Marcus Ward, are highly collectable.

Among the more modern cards, the most desirable are those containing fine etchings, lithographs or engravings in limited editions, or incorporating hand-painted decoration.

Pitfalls

The number of serious collectors of Christmas cards is still relatively

Christmas and New Year card showing the interior of The Great Exhibition.

small and the market consequently restricted, so it is a subject which has not as yet attracted the attention of fakers and forgers. The only point to watch is the authenticity of the various embellishments found on 'collage' type cards of the second half of the 19th century.

Museums
British Museum, London.
London Museum, London.
Victoria and Albert Museum, London.
City Museum and Art Gallery, Birmingham.
Blaise Castle Folk Museum, Bristol.
Beamish Museum, Chester le Street.
National Museum of Wales, Cardiff.
City Museum, Hereford.
Museum and Art Gallery, Leicester.
City Museum, Sheffield.
Elizabethan House, Totnes.
Royal Tunbridge Wells Museum and Art Gallery.
City Museum and Art Gallery, Worcester.
Castle Museum, York.

Reading List
Buday, George. The History of the Christmas Card. London, 1965.
Chase, E.D. The Romance of Greetings Cards. Cambridge, Mass., 1926.

See also **Picture Postcards, Valentines.**

CIGARETTE AND TRADE CARDS

Pictorial cards issued with various foodstuffs and cigarettes date from 1879 when cigarettes were sold in paper packs with a small card inserted as a stiffener. The earliest cards carried on the tradition of the earlier trade cards, i.e. small pieces of cardboard bearing tradesmen's names, addresses and advertisements. The emphasis was on various styles of fancy lettering and the pictorial element was minimal. Cards were usually printed in monochrome letterpress. Although they are extremely rare they are comparatively undervalued. Individual cards may be worth from £3 to £20. The idea of producing sets of cards developed very gradually and the cigarette card in its modern form dates only from 1885 when chromolithography was first applied to the pictures.

Date-lines

1885-1902   The golden age of British cigarette cards, when countless small companies produced their own brands of cigarettes and began issuing pictorial cards usually in sets of 50 developing a particular subject. It has been estimated that over 10,000 different sets were published in Britain alone in this period. The value of cards depends on the numbers available; it follows therefore that the most desirable are those produced by the smallest companies. Sets published by Macdonald of Glasgow and the London firms of Alberge and Bromet, and Taddy, and Ainsworth of Harrogate are among those most keenly sought after. These sets are now in the price range £150 − £300. Cards of this early period had a picture on one side and the manufacturer's advertisement on the reverse. Pre-1902 subjects which are in greatest demand include sports, ships, kings and queens, soldiers of the world, military heroes (especially of the Boer War), contemporary celebrities and heraldry. Prices are generally from £10 to £50 a set; individual cards range from 50p to £2.

Cigarette cards, all from British series. Left to right: Queens, cricketers and soldiers.

1902-1918   Attempts by the American Tobacco Company to capture the British market led to the formation of the Imperial Tobacco Company by many of the independent firms, while those absorbed by the Americans formed the British American Tobacco Company. At the turn of the century, extending up to the time of the First World War, these giants were engaged in a trade war waged largely on their respective cigarette cards. Cards attained the peak of technical perfection in this period, including the use of gilding and multicolour processes. During this period also, cards became more informative, with pieces of explanatory text superseding the advertisements on the reverse. The names of the larger companies within the Imperial and BAT groupings were retained, although the inscriptions invariably include a reference to 'A Branch of the Imperial Tobacco Co.'. Among the finest cards of this period are those produced by Ogden's (including the celebrated 'Guinea Gold' series), Wills, Carreras, Gallahers, Churchman and Players. £5 − £10 (sets). 30p − £1 (individual cards depending on subject).

101

1918-1940   The interwar period saw the extension of cigarette cards on a grand scale and as many as 70 million sets of a particular issue might be produced. The range of subjects covered was infinite and the volume of information purveyed was encyclopaedic. From about 1930 cards were issued with adhesive over the reverse side, so that they could be stuck in small albums, sold for a penny. The albums contained matching texts alongside the spaces for the pictures.

Many of the post-1930 sets are still available for £1 or less, many of them being post-war reprints from the original blocks. The value of cards in this period depends mainly on subject. Technical subjects, such as transport and the armed forces, were frequently updated and thus afford the greatest scope. Sets of this type are in the price range £2 – £5. Other sets with a particularly topical slant of the Twenties and Thirties, £1.50 – £3. Silks, bearing pictures of flags or heraldry, £3 – £15.

Individual cards of this period are virtually worthless and can be picked up in miscellaneous lots for a pound or two for several hundreds, or individually from 2p to 5p.

Points to look for

The more collectable cards are those produced by the American or British companies. European or Asian cards are quite plentiful, but there is very little interest shown in them at present. Many European countries had a tobacco monopoly and therefore did not feel the need to issue cigarette cards as there was no competition to be faced. Many sets remained in use for long periods, or were periodically revived. Different editions can be dated by subtle changes in style of lettering or in the subject matter. Particularly desirable are the 1937 Coronation cards bearing portraits of, or references to, Edward VIII, who abdicated

40. The gout, Sir, just you marry a widder as has got a good loud woice, and you'll never have the gout agin.

Dickens Gallery No. 49 of a series of 50.

in December 1936. These cards had to be suppressed and replaced by others referring to King George VI. Sets should be complete and in crisp condition. Sets mounted in their matching albums usually rate a small premium.

Other Types of Card

Although fitful attempts have been made since the Second World War to revive cigarette cards (the most notable British examples are those produced by Allman's in the early 1950s), costs of card and printing restricted them severely. Carreras attempted to print pictures directly on to the cardboard insert in their packets, the collector being required to cut out the pictorial portion, but this never caught on with cartophilists. In more recent years competition between the cigarette manufacturers has led to the inclusion of gift vouchers or trading stamps and there is thus little chance of the traditional cigarette card being revived.

On the other hand new media have been found for pictorial cards. In actual fact trade cards of this nature have been in existence since the late 19th century, the best known being the large pictorial cards which were given away with beef extract and other foodstuffs marketed by the Liebig Company. These cards may be found with captions in various European languages. Though never as popular as the more ubiquitous cigarette cards they are quite elusive and sets now range from £5 to £15.

Trade cards were given with cereal breakfast foods, confectionary, tea and other foodstuffs in the United States, Canada, Australia, New Zealand and South Africa in the 1930s but this idea did not catch on in the United Kingdom until the 1950s when it was taken up by the tea companies, notably Brooke Bond and Twinings. Trade cards of this type are now also given with bubble gum, sweets and other consumer goods aimed at children (judging by the subject matter of the cards), in an attempt to revive the pre-war schoolboy craze for cigarette cards, but this does not seem to have become popular to any extent. Various attempts at using trade cards for other products such as petrol have only been sporadic. It remains to be seen to what extent modern trade cards will ever attain the same degree of cartophilic interest as the pre-war cigarette cards. At present they are available at under £1 a set.

Reading List
Bagnall, Dorothy. Collecting Cigarette Cards. London, 1965. Catalogue of British Cigarette Cards, 1888-1949. London, 1975.

COMMEMORATIVE MEDALS

Elizabeth I, defeat of the Armada medal.

Medals, medallions or medalets produced to commemorate events and personalities can trace their origins from the quasi-commemorative coins of Greece and Rome. Many of the so-called 'large brass' coins of the Roman Empire were commemorative in nature and never intended to circulate as money. This idea fell into abeyance in the 5th century and was revived in the late Middle Ages in the form of commemorative ducats and thalers. At the same time, however, the medal as a distinct art form was also developed. The earliest authenticated medal was that cast in bronze by Antonio Pisano to commemorate the visit of the Byzantine Emperor John VIII Palaeologus to Italy in 1438. Medals were generally larger than coins, and the much higher relief enabled the sculptor much greater scope in portraiture and allegorical composition.

Date-lines

1450-1500 Earliest medals cast in bronze using *cire perdue* process. Portrait of a person on the obverse and his or her *impresa* (personal emblem, often punning on their name) on the reverse. Wide range of value, from £100 to £2,000. Value depends on the person depicted, the date

Attempts to recover the treasure off Hispaniola.

of the medal, the name of the medallist, Pisano, Boldu, Enzola, Niccola Fiorentino, Guacciolotti, Guidizani, Lixignolo, Melioli and Pollaiuolo being the most sought after.

1500-1600   Very large medals continued to be cast, but smaller medals (crown-sized) now being struck. Outstanding medallists include Pastorini, Foppa, Cellini, Leoni, Primavera, Jacopo da Trezza and Francia. Large cast medals range from £300 to £1,000; struck medals from £50 to £500.

1490-1550   Earliest French medals, under influence of Italian medallists Laurana and Pietro da Milano. From 1500, French medallists developed their own 'Gothic style'. Many medals of this period executed by Italians. £200 − £600.

1550-1650   Large cast and chased medals on a very large module distinctive to France. Medallists include Pilon, Dupré (very prolific) and Claude and Jean Warin. £50 − £250.

1520-1600   Earliest Dutch medals, cast by Metsys, Second, Bloc and others. Not of such a high quality as the Italian or French, but vigorous, rugged portraits. The Dutch developed the pictorial reverse, paving the way for the later propaganda medals. £150 − £400.

1600-1700   Later Dutch medals mainly political in nature and covering a wide range of subjects at home and abroad. Most medals now struck. Enormous historical interest compensates for lack of sensitivity in engraving. £50 −

£300.

1500-1650   German medals carved from boxwood or stone from which casts were taken, hence the clear-cut lines and precise quality making for stark realism in portraiture. Many medals of a political nature. £150 – £750.

1650-1750   Later German medals by Italian immigrants (the Abondios, Melon and de Pomis), pale imitations of Italian Renaissance style, more flattering portaits. £30 – £150.

1540-1600   Earliest English medals sculpted by foreign artists, (including Holbein, da Trezzo, Primavera and Jonghelinck). Notable exception is Hilliard's Armada Medal of 1588. Earliest medals cast in bronze or lead; later struck in bronze or silver. £100 – £600.

1600-1720   Later British medals mostly political in nature, culminating in a spate of propaganda medals in 1680-1715 reflecting the turbulent political and religious state of the country. Medals struck in bronze, pewter, brass, or silver. Value of these medals depends largely on the event commemorated. £30 – £250.

1700-1800   Quality of design and execution dropped everywhere. Medals now invariably struck from dies in the same manner as coins; lower relief,-stereotyped portraits and conventional allegory. Some medals were struck in gold, but these are very rare indeed. Development of newspapers after 1760 led to a decline in the political propaganda medal. £25 – £150.

1800-1900   Nadir of commemorative medals. Majority struck for trivial events and sold commercially as souvenirs. Vast

British Colonisation.

Captain Vernon and his attack on Porto Bello.

majority struck in brass, bronze, pewter, white metal. Local event medals now being sought by students of local history. Base metal medals from £1 to £10; silver, £5 – £20.

1900-1920 Revival of propaganda medals (during Boer War and First World War), mostly of European origin. Invariably struck in base metal. Commonest is the British forgery of the alleged German 'Lusitania' medal (£1 – £3); war satirical medals (£2 – £10); patriotic medals, portraying war leaders and allegory of victory or justice £1 – £5).

1900-1950 Local event medals, struck in base metal, from 50p to £3; in silver £4 – £8.

Points to look for

The above give a rough guide to prices according to the major periods and areas of commemorative medals. There was a sporadic revival of cast portrait medals in the mid-19th and early 20th centuries and this continues intermittently to this day. These medals are cast in bronze or silver and their value depends on the identity of the sitter and the artist who modelled them. Most of these early limited editions are in the price range £25 – £100. They are generally larger in flan and bolder in relief than the commercially produced souvenir medals of the period and, of course, exhibit the characteristics of hand-casting as opposed to machine-striking.

The subject matter of medals is an important factor. Apart from the political propaganda medals the most popular group are those commemorating coronations, jubilees and other royal events, preference being for official issues, though private and commercial issues are also of interest.

William Pitt.

Series and sets of medals date from the 1720s when Jean Dassier produced his set of 72 rulers of France, followed by 24 portraits of religious reformers. Other 18th century sets include the series of 30 portraying British rulers, a set of 60 Roman emperors and a series of Geneva theologians. British sets of this period include the Royal family, contemporary politicians, Thomason's scientific series, the medallic Bible (60 medals), battles of the Napoleonic War, the War of 1812-14 (27 American medals), Otley's Cambridge Chancellors, the cathedrals of England and Caque's episodes in French history. Very many sets were issued in base metals such as in damascene copper; silver and gilt also exist. They were usually offered in a book-form case which soon broke up under the weight of its contents. Sometimes an additional explanatory volume went with the set of medals. To obtain both a set of medals in the book-form case and the explanatory volume is now quite a rarity. The fashion for these lengthy sets, many of which were very popular and even issued by subscription, died out about 1870, but has been revived within the past decade, mainly as a medium for investing in silver or gold. It remains to be seen whether these expensive series will retain an antiquarian value much in excess of their bullion value.

Pitfalls

Italian Renaissance portrait medals have been so extensively forged, new casts being taken from the originals, as to be suspect without a professional opinion, and even then they may differ. Recasts are rather smaller than the originals so accurate measurement and comparison with the known dimensions of the original are a useful guide. Interest in later commemorative medals is too recent for fakes to have become a worthwhile proposition. The value of medals depends on condition and prices quoted are for specimens in *fleur de coin* condition with original lustre. Worn or damaged specimens should be heavily discounted unless their subject is of outstanding interest.

Museums
British Museum, London.
London Museum, London.
Guildhall Museum, London.
National Maritime Museum, London.
Victoria and Albert Museum, London.
Wallace Collection, London.
City Museum and Art Gallery, Birmingham.
Fitzwilliam Museum, Cambridge.
National Museum of Wales, Cardiff.
National Museum of Antiquities, Edinburgh.
Royal Scottish Museum, Edinburgh.
Art Gallery and Museum, Glasgow.
Ashmolean Museum, Oxford.
Quite small provincial museums can often produce some surprising possessions.

Reading List
Babelon, Jean. Great Coins and Medals. London, 1959.
Baker, W.S. Medallic Portraits of Washington. New York, 1965.
Blanchet, A. and Dieudonne, A. Manual de Numismatique Française. Paris, 1930.
Brooke, G.C. and Hill, G.F. Guide to the Exhibition of Historical Medals in the British Museum. London, 1924.

Restoration of Alnwick Castle.

Archbishop Sandcroft and the Seven Bishops

Brown, M.D. Catalogue of Medals relating to Transport. London, 1968.

Forrer, Leonard. Biographical Dictionary of Medallists. London, 1904-30, reprinted U.S.A. 1974.

Grant, M.H. Catalogue of British Medals since 1760. London, 1936-41.

Hawkins, E., Franks, A.W. and Grueber, H.A. Medallic Illustrations of the History of Great Britain and Ireland. 1885, reprinted London, 1969.

Hill, Sir George F. Portrait Medals of the Italian Renaissance. London, 1912. The Commemorative Medal in the Service of Germany. London, 1920. Corpus of Italian Medals of the Renaissance (2 volumes). London, 1930. The Medal, its Place in Art. London, 1941.

Linecar, Howard W.A. The Commemorative Medal. Newton Abbot, 1974.

Loubat, J.F. The Medallic History of the United States of America, 1776-1876. New York, 1967.

Mackay, James A. Commemorative Medals. London, 1970.

Milford Haven, Marquess of. British Naval Medals. London, 1919. Naval Medals of Foreign Countries. London, 1921-28.

Mira, W.J.D. James Cook, his Coins and Medals. London, 1970.

Parkes Weber, R. Medals and Medallions of the 19th Century relating to England by Foreign Artists. London, 1894.

Rochette, E.C. The Medallic Portraits of John F. Kennedy. New York, 1966.

Sandwich, Earl of. British and Foreign Medals relating to Naval and Maritime Affairs. London pre-1914, reprinted (no plates) London, 1950.

Whiting, J.R.S. Commemorative Medals: A Medallic History of Britain from Tudor Times to the Present Day. Newton Abbot, 1972.

COMMEMORATIVE POTTERY

The following notes apply mainly to pottery and porcelain of British origin, although the practice of commemorating persons and events in this manner was by no means confined to the United Kingdom. The earliest commemorative wares, the celebrated blue dash chargers of the late 17th century, were modelled closely on the *istoriato* maiolica dishes and jars of Italy and Spain, many of which were decorated with the portraits of historic personalities. The majority of the Continental maiolica pieces featured people and events of the distant past, classical Greece and Rome, the Bible and mythology being fertile sources of inspiration. English delftware, however, had plenty of contemporary figures and the dishes of the late 17th century were largely of a political nature. Until the beginning of this century, in fact, there has always been a strong political slant in British commemorative wares.

Date-lines

1670-1702	Delftware chargers depicting the monarchs Charles I, Charles II, James II, William III and Mary. In many cases the monarch is identified by the Royal cypher; in some equestrian motifs, however, the identity is not specified, so that either James II or William of Orange could be inferred, depending on one's political persuasion. £600 − £1,200.
	Rather scarcer are similar chargers depicting generals and politicians of the period, such as the Duke of Marlborough or the Duke of Ormonde, but they are of lesser interest than the Royal portraits. £800 − £1,000.
1702-1730	Later delftware (Lambeth or Bristol) dishes portraying Queen Anne or George I. These are much rarer than the earlier chargers. Portraits of Anne are particularly

Left to right: King of Prussia, Wolfe, George II, (all c.1757-60).

111

George III (1810 bowl).

desirable. £1,000 – £1,800.

George I, £750 – £1,200.

1750-1760   Electioneering plates in Bristol and delftware. These plates bear the names of candidates in elections, mainly for constituencies in the west of England. These plates were short-lived and are consequently scarce. £200 – £400.

1750-1780   Liverpool delftware plates with nautical subjects, often commemorating specific warships and naval heroes. £600 – £800.

1750-1830   Pottery (and later porcelain) plates and mugs bearing the names of individuals and dates. Domestic commemorative wares celebrated births, christenings, betrothals, marriages and coming of age. They may be found in delftware (Lambeth, Bristol, Liverpool, Delftfield) or porcelain (Lowestoft). £100 – £150.

Slipware posset pots with initials and dates. £500 – £800.

1760-1790   Commemorative dishes, mugs with a pronounced political bias. The most desirable are those alluding to John Wilkes and Liberty:

Mugs and dishes, £100 – £150.

Bowls and teapots, £150 – £400.

Other commemorative items of this period feature the young George III, Frederick the Great, naval and military heroes of the Seven Years' War (1756-63) and

*Left to right: Caroline (1820); George IV (1830 death); Caroline/
Leopold (1815).*

the American War of Independence (1776-1783).
Delftware dishes and mugs, £100 – £250.
Prattware dishes and plaques, £50 – £200.
Salt-glazed stoneware teapots of Frederick the Great.
£400 – £600.

1775-1830   Commemorative pottery with religious, sporting or literary allusions. A wide range of wares may be found honouring the Wesley Brothers, and includes dishes, mugs and busts in creamware, Staffordshire pottery. £50 – £100.

Sporting items, mainly transfer-printed creamware portraying famous pugilists, horses and jockeys are always in great demand. £200 – £300.

1790-1820   Pottery and porcelain commemorating naval and military heroes of the Napoleonic War period: Nelson, Wellington, Howe, Duncan, Moore, etc. Dishes and mugs, £30 – £80.

1800-1860   Pottery commemorating industrial events. Among the commonest are dishes, mugs and jugs celebrating the Sunderland Bridge or the Iron Bridge at Coalbrookdale; but both motifs were used over a long period. The most desirable items are those which can be dated to the first decade of the 19th century. £50 – £100.

Later examples, £30 – £50.

Jugs and mugs with early railway scenes, commemorating the opening of railway lines. Most desirable are those in the period 1825-1830. £200 – £500.

Later examples of railway and canal commemorative pottery. £120 – £200.

1809-1837	Pottery commemorating Royal events: Jubilee of George III, coronations of George IV (1821), William IV (1831) and Victoria (1838), Royal weddings. £40 – £75.
1838-1902	Later royal commemoratives: wedding of Victoria and Albert, births of the Princess Royal and Prince Albert Edward, the Golden and Diamond Jubilees, Royal weddings, coronation of Edward VII (1902), mourning items for Queen Victoria (1901). Early Victorian commemoratives are scarce but not so desirable as the Jubilee items, of which there is an enormous range of plates, plaques, mugs and jugs. £15 – £40.
1854-1902	Popular patriotic items, ranging from the Crimean War (1853-56) to the Boer War (1899-1902). Commonest type are rack-plates portraying individual heroes. Regimental plates bearing battle honours and dates, are also worth looking for. £25 – £75.
	Porcelain figures ('A Gentleman in Khaki', 'The Volunteer', etc.). £120 – £250.
1840-1902	Staffordshire pottery flatback figures. Early examples (1840-45) are small and individually potted, mainly of Victoria, Albert and the Royal children. Poor likenesses but vigorous colouring. £30 – £40.
	After 1845 most figures produced from moulds. Colouring still excellent. Certain figures predominate in different periods. Thus Florence Nightingale and heroes of the Crimean War (1854-1860), the political and moral issues of the American Civil War (1858-65), the Franco-Prussian War and the struggle between Gladstone and Disraeli (1865-1880) are the outstanding features.

Left to right: Victoria wedding (1839); Universal plate (1897); Victoria Coronation mug (1838).

Left to right: William IV (1831); William IV (1831); Prince Consort (1861).

Figures of British and foreign royalty perennially popular in this period. £30 – £100.

Celebrities of the period 1850-1880: stage, sporting, religious, literary figures, criminals and their victims. These include the more ephemeral items, which are consequently expensive today. £100 – £300.

Matched pairs of figures, £240 – £500.

After 1880 the colouring became more cursory, and by 1900 figures were mainly white, with some gilding and no more than vestigial colouring. Best items of this period are General Gordon, Lord Roberts and the heroes of the Boer Wars (1881 and 1899). £40 – £80.

1910-1940   Decline of popular interest in commemorative pottery which, in this period, was mainly confined to Royal events: death of Edward VII, coronations of George V and George VI, Silver Jubilee of George V. Mugs, beakers, cups and saucers, and dishes. £5 – £20.

Coronation items prepared for Edward VIII, but suppressed on account of his abdication, are worth a small premium only.

A few plates were produced in the period 1910-20 with the themes of women's suffrage, the controversial social welfare budget of 1909 and Irish home rule. These are scarce, but of relatively little interest. £20 – £40.

Points to look for

Prices quoted above are for items in good condition, but this is a relative term. Delftware is seldom found in perfect condition and the rarity of the subject is of much greater importance. On the other hand Royal commemorative wares from 1887 onwards are reasonably plentiful and should only be collected in perfect condition.

	decorative handles; small brass bird-cages; copper warming-pans with wooden handles and fairly plain covers; small beaten copper panels with Art Nouveau motifs.
£20-£30	Brass warming-pans (19th century), braziers, brass heaters and small stoves; Bidri ware (Indian inlaid brassware of the 19th century); large copper kettles; plate warmers.
£30-£50	Copper urns and stock-pots; copper coffee pots of the 18th century; large copper or brass gongs; most ships' bells (though decorative features or association with a well-known ship may boost the value considerably).
£50-£100	Brass footmen of the late 18th century; ship's compass binnacles; 18th century brewer's yeast vessels; brass ship's gun tompions with raised crests and decoration; late 18th century Continental brass plates; brass furniture (magazine racks, music stands, etc.).
£100-£200	Brass or copper warming-pans, with ornate piercing on the cover. Plus factors are straight sides and flat lids (pre-1790), dates and sets of initials. Curved sides and slightly domed lids (fashionable from about 1780

Right: A brass oil lamp, the wick coming out of the spout, complete with hook to hang and chain attached to the lid; probably late 19th century.

Below: Saucepan in copper with wooden handle.

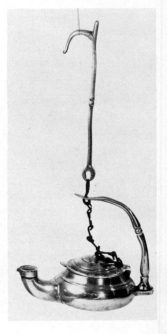

Left: Copper warming pan of the late 18th century with turned wooden handle.

Right: 17th century brass warming-pan with engraved pattern on the lid and the usual type of flat steel handle.

onwards) are of less value. Piercing was discontinued in the late 18th century as canisters of hot water replaced the earlier hot ember method. Late 17th and early 18th century Continental brass plates. Copper divers' helmets of the 19th and early 20th centuries.

£200+ Large brass plates of the Nuremberg type pre-1650. Very fine brass warming-pans with names, dates and brass turning half way up the handle.

Points to look for

Copper and brass ware given as wedding presents were often dated and inscribed with the initials of the bridal couple. This charming custom seems to have died out by 1750. Examples of pots, pans, warming-pans, kettles and jugs with dated ornament on handles, rims or

Late 19th century copper skimmer for removing unwanted objects from the top of the milk or other liquid.

119

sides are highly desirable. Examples with dates before about 1620 are of considerable rarity and would be worth from £500 upwards. Brass utensils with mottoes on handles and rims are much sought after and would be in the price range £100-£250.

Pitfalls

The fashion for copper and brass domestic objects of yesteryear in modern interior decor has created a major industry in reproductions. These can be distinguished from genuine wares by their much thinner, lighter quality. Check seams and rivets which are invariably (though slightly) uneven in handmade articles. Modern wares are machine-made and possess a much too even appearance. Genuine brass and copper should have a more solid appearance, minute surface pitting, flaws and impurities. Patination is not always an infallible test, since it is possible to fake this on modern metalwares by chemical processes. Much more difficult to fake, however, is the soft, rounded feel of brass or copper which has been polished for generations.

Museums

London Museum, London.
Victoria and Albert Museum, London.
Borough Museum, Berwick-on-Tweed.
City Museum and Art Gallery, Birmingham.
Art Gallery and Museum, Brighton.
Blaise Castle Folk Museum, Bristol.

Graduated range of copper saucepans with lids, and bearing owner's monogram.

A brass dish of the 19th century with heraldic motif.

Attractive late Victorian brass trivet on which to stand teapot or kettle close to the fire to keep them warm.

City Museum and Art Gallery, Bristol.
Beamish Museum, Chester le Street.
Royal Scottish Museum, Edinburgh.
Museum and Art Gallery, Glasgow.
City Museum, Hereford.
Central Museum and Art Gallery, Northampton.
Museum of English Country Life, Reading.
Salisbury and South Wiltshire Museum, Salisbury.
City Museum, Sheffield.
Elizabethan House, Totnes.
Ashworth Museum, Turton.
City Museum and Art Gallery, Worcester.
Castle Museum, York.

Reading List

Burgess, F.W. Chats on Old Copper and Brass. London, 1954.
Haedecke, Hans-Ulrich. Metalwork. London, 1970.
Lindsay, J. Seymour. Iron and Brass Implements of the English and American Home. London, 1964.
Wills, Geoffrey. The Book of Copper and Brass. Feltham, 1969.
Collecting Copper and Brass. London, 1962.

See also *Fireside Objects, Horse Brasses, Oil Lamps, Pipe Stoppers, Scales and Balances.*

CORKSCREWS

Devices for extracting the corks from wine bottles. The basic form is a steel screw attached at right angles to a handle. Variation lies in the styling and composition of the handle, and in the numerous patent attachments for making the job simpler or more efficient. 'Bottle-scrues' probably date back as far as corks were used to seal bottles but examples prior to the mid-18th century are of the greatest rarity. Early corkscrews were relatively cumbersome and were obviously designed for use in the dining-room or butler's pantry. Date is less important than type, since the same type with variations have been in use since the mid-18th century. The variable factors which govern value are materials used and form of decoration as well as patent gimmicks incorporated in the corkscrew itself.

Travelling Corkscrews were developed from about 1750 and were doubtless indispensable to young gentlemen making the Grand Tour. The fashion for picnics, which developed about 1790, further stimulated the popularity of this handy pocket type of corkscrew. The most basic form consists of a screw with a ring on the end fitting into a protecting cylindrical cover which serves the double purpose of a handle for the screw when in use. Variations include a double-ended cylinder, unscrewing in the centre to reveal the screw, hinged from the centre. Other types include those with two hinged handles with the screw in the centre, examples with the handle in the form of a pin which lodges neatly within the encircling screw, and the German early 20th century type with hinged casing whose side joints pull apart and rise to form the handle.

Travelling corkscrews in plain steel range from £2 to £10, depending on styling and age. They were often produced in more decorative forms, with ornamental handles of silver, porcelain, ivory, mother-of-pearl or hardwood. For obvious reasons of durability these corkscrews are never found with handles entirely of silver, although the casings may often be in this metal. As a rule silver-mounted corkscrews incorporate other materials in the handle. These ornamental screws appear to have been produced mainly between 1780 and 1840. In ascending order of scarcity they are:

Ordinary ivory handles £25 – £50.
Decorated ivory handles £35 – £70.
Mother-of-pearl handles £60 – £100.
Porcelain handles £70 – £120.

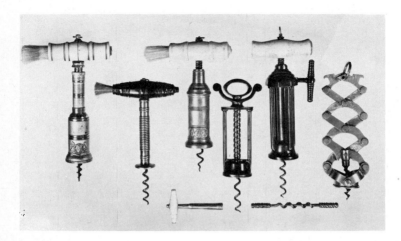

Left to right:

1. A patent brass corkscrew of unusual design, with elongated bell-shaped barrel and extended neck, with coat of arms and supporters, fine bone handle and brush and unusual tapered steel screw.

2. A double thread corkscrew of rare design with long slender turned brass barrel, steel helix thread, turned ebony handle and brush.

3. A Henshall's patent double action double thread corkscrew, with enclosed brass barrel, patent tablet and supporters, bone handle and brush, with short irregular helix screw.

4. A ladies' travelling corkscrew with mother-of-pearl handle and silver sheath − length 3in.

5. An all-steel double thread corkscrew of rare design, the inner helix thread with finger ring and wing nut to raise cork, supported by two columns, and inscribed with makers' name: G. Nazer, 51 Royal Exchange.

6. A steel corkscrew with central shaft and four supporting rods, with bone handle, raised by smaller horizontal steel ratchet handle. Fine long helix thread.

7. A small travelling corkscrew, the handle being interlocked within encircling helix thread.

8. A patent concertina corkscrew of steel with four sets of hinges, neck ring and steel screw.

Ladies' Corkscrews are small corkscrews of elegant design with upright handles of bone, ivory, mother-of-pearl or silver. Too small for drawing the corks from wine bottles, they were probably intended for opening scent bottles or cosmetic jars, and were usually produced *en suite* with travelling dressing-cases. They were popular from about 1880 to 1910. The prices for these relatively rare corkscrews are only slightly lower than those for silver-mounted travelling corkscrews.

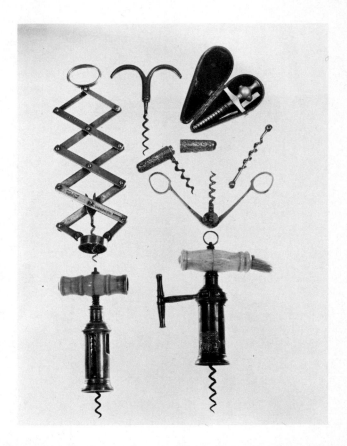

1. *A metal concertina corkscrew, Weir's Patent, maker J. Heeley &*
Sons, eight steel hinges, wire screw, neck ring and ring pull.
2. *Patent double action, double thread, open panelled brass barrel, bone*
handle, brush cavity.
3. *A steel corkscrew, mid-19th century, broad wire thread, simple*
arched-eyebrow handle.
4. *A metal screw tap in leather, velvet-lined case, for broaching casks in*
private cellars.
5. *A travelling corkscrew, handle overlaid in silver, chased with flowers*
and foliage, two-part screw-on barrel containing screw.
6. *A travelling corkscrew, steel, the handle in the form of a pin lodged*
within the encircling screw.
7. *A folding corkscrew, polished steel, with scissor-like handles.*
8. *Dray's Patent, 1847, steel regular helix screw, brass shank, double*
screw, bone handle and brush, steel ratchet handle, based on Henshall's
'King's Screw', with plate 'Registered May 14, 1847/W. Dray/Patent/
London Bridge'.

Left: A steel corkscrew with neck ring and central shaft supported by two rods, helix screw and turned bone handle, brush and ring.

Right: Patent double action double thread corkscrew, with copper barrel chased with grapes, vine leaves and other fruit, brass raising thread, short steel helix screw, turned bone handle and brush cavities.

Mechanical Corkscrews form the largest and most varied category and incorporate an enormous range of mechanical gadgets and accessories. Henshall's Patent King's Screw, patented in 1795, was the first of a long line of mechanical screws. It had double thread and double action and was housed in a brass cylinder. The handle, usually of bone, often incorporated a small brush. Later Henshall screws were made of steel with an all-steel casing. Prices from £70 (steel) to £120 (brass).

There are numerous other mechanical corkscrews of which the following are typical:

Edward Thomason, steel and brass with continuous screw, open-sided barrel-shaped handle of wood with matching brush. £50 – £80.

Dowler's patent, double thread, double action, brass barrel with plate, broad helix screw, turned bone handle with brush, horizontal steel ratchet with bone handle. £70 – £130.

Farrow and Jackson brass screw with open-sided barrel, single screw and wing-nut. £80 – £120.

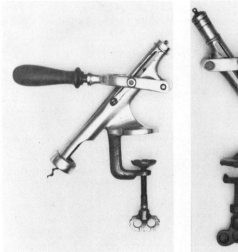

Left: "The Don" heavy brass cylinder angled bar corkscrew with counter clamp, wooden lever handle and two-stroke lever action, which draws cork and removes from screw. Cylinder length 11½ins.

Right: "The Merritt" heavy brass cylinder angled bar corkscrew with counter clamp, wooden lever handle and two-stroke lever action, which draws cork and removes from screw. Cylinder length 16ins.

Plant's patent wulfrun screw, all steel with continuous long double screw, open barrel and unusual locking device in handle. £40 – £80.

James Heeley and Sons 'A1' double lever corkscrew. £75 – £120.

Weir's 1894 patent concertina screw, steel hinges, wire screw, neck ring pull. £70 – £120.

Plus factors are decorative features on the casing, such as family coats of arms or regimental insignia (add 15%). Defective or broken screws and working parts reduce values by about 20%.

Bar Corkscrews are invariably of much heavier construction and include some form of clamp for attachment to the bar counter. They also incorporate a lever action cork extractor. These indispensable tools of the publican's trade were patented from about 1860 and there are many types in current production. The more collectable varieties include the following:

'The Don' heavy brass cylinder angled bar corkscrew with counter clamp, two-stroke lever action which draws cork and removes it from screw. £60 – £120.

126

'Original Safety' steel vertical bar, chromium plated, neck vice, single lever action, comparatively decorative handle and shaft, with wooden knob terminal. £50 – £90.

'Merritt' heavy brass cylinder, wooden lever handle, two-stroke lever action. £50 – £90.

Trade Corkscrews are screws of fairly functional design whose interest lies in the inscription on them. Medicine corkscrews were supplied by pharmacists and druggists with medicine bottles and will be found bearing the names of patent medicines. These are the most ephemeral of corkscrews and many of them must have been thrown away. Consequently they are now decidedly scarce and because of their interest to collectors of medical antiques they are highly desirable in proportion to their intrinsic worth. The more elaborate types include a small medicine spoon in the handle. £10 – £40.

Wine merchants, brewers and distillers often gave away corkscrews advertising their wares. Again, the screws themselves are of little intrinsic value, but are generally of robust, simple design and bear the names of companies and their brands. £5 – £30.

Oddities and Novelties are a vast field, mostly dating from the end of the 19th century and continuing to the present day. It is impossible to give a guide to value since the range is so wide. Types to watch for are those which incorporate other gadgets, such as the 'All Purpose' (early 1900s) which combined a corkscrew, glass cutter, inch scale, tin-opener and other improbable devices. Conversely corkscrews may be found incorporated in other articles, such as walking sticks, cane-handles or umbrellas. One of the most grotesque forms was the Vigneron Special whose handle consisted of a generous length of vine root, all twisted and gnarled. Corkscrews with staghorn handles are relatively common. Novelty types belong mainly to the cocktail era of the Twenties and Thirties and exhibit all the characteristics of Art Deco. At best they are very attractive, at worst they typify the banality and kitsch for which the period was notorious. Handles incorporate negro heads, dancing girls, drunken revellers, etc., and make it very difficult to get a straight clean pull. Highly desirable are the corkscrews produced by Monart (also known as Vasart) of Perth, with millefiori glass handles.

COSTUME

Although articles of textiles, clothing and accessories have survived from antiquity in Egyptian tombs and from the Bronze Age in bog burials, very few of early date ever come on to the market, and then the price is beyond the reach of the average collector. The majority of items up to the beginning of the 18th century are now in museum collections. In many cases these rare specimens were in private collections and have only recently been acquired by museums. Although sometimes the owner kept careful records of purchases and

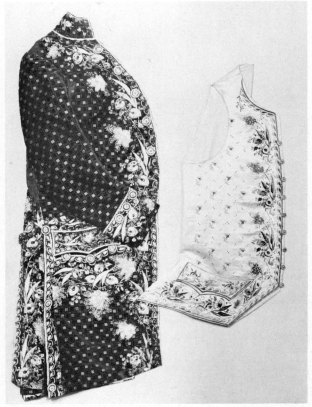

A good example of the full-skirted coat, often of velvet, with rich embroidery on the fronts and on the cuffs and pocket flaps. The waistcoat is heavily embroidered and often each button had a tiny motif on it.

gifts, more usually there are no clues to the provenance of each object. In this way much irretrievable information has been lost. All costume collections, however small, need a system of records. The larger the collection the more vital it is to keep consistent and complete records of each item, which should be passed on if an object is sold, retaining a duplicate card for reference. It is wise to start a card index system when the first object is acquired. Each card should record the provenance (country of origin, gift, donor's name, shop or sale room purchase and price paid etc.) and type of garment. The date should be clearly marked at the top of the card, with Male, Female or Child, for quick reference. A description of the material is needed (with the measurement of the width from selvedge to selvedge if possible), and then a full description of the garment and the methods of construction, by hand or machine (lock stitch or chain stitch), type of fastening (buttons, hooks, zip fastener etc.). While looking at a garment in this way to gather information for the card, anyone who is a beginner at collecting costume will start to learn a great deal.

The care of a collection

There are many reasons for starting a costume and textile collection, but one point should be made — it is unwise to collect as a hedge against inflation. Costumes are the most fragile of all objects and they are difficult to store without causing damage and take up a lot of space. Dust, light, damp, moths and mildew can reduce the value of an object very easily, so good storage conditions are essential. For a small collector this is relatively easy. Florist's boxes lined with white acid-free tissue paper or drawers in an old chest may be used. Crumpled tissue paper should be placed carefully between the folds in a costume if it is being stored flat, to avoid hard folds being pressed into it. If there is not enough space to store the costume flat and it is strong enough to be hung up (beaded dresses of the 1920s should never be left for very long on a hanger), a wooden coat hanger, padded and with a cotton cover, should be used. Wire coat hangers with sharp ends should never be used. Very fine muslin covers opening at the side and bottom, which can be laundered, or very lightweight polythene bags, which do not set up too much static electricity and attract dust, split open at one side, should be hung over the costume. The open sides can be fastened with plastic paper clips. The polythene can be wiped with an anti-static fluid before use and should not be allowed to get dirty before being replaced. Clothes should never be completely sealed in polythene bags, because moulds will grow. No costumes should ever be hung in the light as they can easily fade, and the fabric will soon disintegrate. A lightweight dust sheet should be hung over the rail. About 65°-68° is a reasonable temperature at which to store clothes and the air should not get too dry. This does not mean that it should be damp enough to grow moulds, but a hot dry atmosphere will make silks brittle. A few paradichlorobenzine crystals should be placed in a tin with a perforated lid to prevent moths.

Conservation should only be undertaken by the amateur after watching professional methods and practising on scrap material. Every specimen presents a new set of problems and a great deal of damage can be done by incorrect treatment. It is important to remember that in some cases the information provided by a slightly grubby costume is invaluable and irreplaceable. If conservation is carried out, all this may be lost. Fragile trimmings, filthy though they may be, could be the only surviving specimens of a particular type of 18th century fabric. Tiny tufts of thread and little holes may denote an earlier line showing the original shape of the garment. Often it is better to leave the costume alone, or spot clean it, rather than destroy valuable evidence. A linen ruff which has survived from the early 17th century is the record of the work of a laundress as well as a seamstress. The drops of wax holding the pleats in shape are still in position. Cleaning would have destroyed this evidence.

Theatrical costumes are a specialised field and not to be confused with examples of ordinary clothing. Some are made of cheap materials with decorations stuck on with glue, or have been treated with bleach, various spray dyes and French enamel varnish. They were never intended to have a long life and quite often cleaning and repair are almost impossible from an economic point of view. This costume from the BBC Television series, 'Elizabeth R', was made of good quality materials and would stand a better chance of survival.

A rare, early to mid-18th century tailor's sample of a dress coat, 7ins. high.

Original stitching should never be removed from a dress. If for any reason it is absolutely necessary, full notes should be made and close-up photographs taken before the stitches are removed.

Building a collection and the pitfalls

It is wise to visit displays in several of the museums listed below to see as much costume of the period which you intend to collect as possible. Some people collect examples of a particular type of garment, regardless of country of origin or period. Waistcoats are a good example of this sort of group, collected for their attractive embroidery; they are also easy to store. Other groups include children's costume, babies' christening robes, men's clothing, women's costume, which can be subdivided into day or evening wear and into short periods of twenty years, underwear or dress accessories such as hats, shoes and gloves.

The value of the clothes depends not so much on age as the materials used, the colours, the presence of the original decorations and fastenings, the quality of the workmanship and — above all else, the condition. It is for this reason that such great care must be taken in looking after them. Costumes should not be worn as fancy dress etc. If it is necessary to photograph a costume on a living model, care should be taken to see that the garment is not marked with perspiration.

Other factors can influence the value of the costume. The value of a dress in poor condition can be enhanced if the identity of the original wearer can be proved, with an accompanying photograph showing the dress, particularly if it is a famous — or notorious — person. In this case the personal factor may outweigh the intrinsic value of the clothing itself. A dress in perfect condition with all the accompanying accessories (for example, a wedding dress, veil, orange-blossom head-dress, shoes, stockings, gloves and prayer book) will increase in value, and a collector should never allow the items to be separated in a sale. Certain colours were particularly fashionable at different periods, but this is not an infallible guide to dating a costume; all the other features must be taken into consideration, particularly the quality, design and weight of the fabric. It may be that the dress has been made from an unpicked dress of an earlier period. There are quite a few dresses of the 19th century in museum collections, which are well made and in the latest fashion, but the fabric on close examination reveals the tiny holes of previous stitch marks, and faint creases from former pleats. Usually the fabric is very similar in design and weight to the fashionable materials of the later period and has been used for the second time without looking unfashionable. This should not detract from the value of a dress; indeed in some people's eyes it gives an added interest to the costume. Some dresses have been adapted for theatrical use or fancy dress parties in the 19th century and may drop in value if this has been badly done; others are original theatrical costumes and high prices may be asked for a costume worn by Nijinsky in a Diaghilev ballet. Dresses originally made for a fancy dress ball by a couturier can also be quite expensive.

The presence of a couturier's label in a dress inevitably boosts the value of a dress, but collectors should be warned that labels have been removed from many couture dresses, sometimes to avoid customs duty and sometimes because the original wearer did not want the label. A trained eye will be able to detect an unlabelled Worth, Vionnet, Balenciaga or Dior. It is also possible to find dresses which are not of couture quality with labels stitched in. This has been done to raise the value. One of the earliest recorded labelled specimens of c.1861-3, which is French, has the dressmaker's address stamped in gold on the white silk bodice lining. Printed or woven labelled petersham or ribbon waistbands appear from the mid-1870s onwards. Large shops and local

Early bustle petticoat of c.1869 made of watchspring inside tape casings. The steels spring out at the back to support the light draperies of the 1870s bustle dresses.

The textile from which a dress is made can be as interesting to a collector as the style. This is a beautiful example of a fine wool, printed à disposition, in a dress of c.1856 from the Red House Museum, Christchurch.

dressmakers used them, as well as the court dressmakers and the top couture houses. It is unlikely that a label would be faked, but the collector should try to determine if the label has been stitched in at a later date.

From the collector's viewpoint, bright, unfaded colours are the most desirable. Black is relatively unpopular, probably because it is difficult to see the details on it. There is a great deal of clothing in this colour from the mid-19th century onwards as part of the widespread ritual of mourning; it is generally worth 50-70% of the value of comparable items in other colours. Fading, particularly where it is in large irregular patches, will lower the value of a dress, however good its condition otherwise.

In some cases costumes have been modified or slightly altered to keep them in fashion. Hems were raised and lowered as they are today. Although the unaltered dress is the more sought after, one that has been altered well and retains a look of fashion, should be of interest to

Chemises, corset-covers, frilled bodices and spencers, £3 – £10.
Brassieres, 1912-1930, £3 – £5.

Museums
The Museum of Costume, Bath.
Blaise Castle Folk Museum, Henbury, Bristol.
Welsh Folk Museum, Cardiff.
The Royal Scottish Museum, Edinburgh.
Royal Albert Memorial Museum, Exeter.
Art Gallery and Museum, Glasgow.
Folk Life and Regimental Museum, Gloucester.
Worcestershire County Museum, Kidderminster.
Churchill Gardens Museum, Hereford.
Lotherton Hall, Leeds.
Wygston's House, Leicester.
City of Liverpool Museum, Liverpool.
Victoria and Albert Museum, London.
The Museum of London, London.
Museum and Art Gallery, Luton.
Gallery of English Costume, Manchester.
Central Museum and Art Gallery, Northampton.
Strangers' Hall Museum, Norwich.
Salisbury and South Wiltshire Museum Salisbury.

A Page of Honour's uniform as worn at the 1911 Coronation.

Reading List
Adburgham, A. Shops and Shopping, 1800-1914. London, 1964.
Arnold, J. A Handbook of Costume. London, 1973.
Arnold, J. Patterns of Fashion 1 and 2. London, 1972.
Costume, The Journal of the Costume Society. 1965.
Davenport, J. The Book of Costume. New York, 1948.
Gibbs-Smith, C.H. The Fashionable Lady in the Nineteenth Century. H.M.S.O.
Laver, J. Taste and Fashion. London, 1945.
Leene, J.E. (Ed.) Textile Conservation. London, 1972.
Lynam, R. (Ed.) Pan's Fashion. London, 1972.
Waugh, N. The Cut of Men's Clothes, 1600-1900. London, 1964.
Corsets and Crinolines. London, 1954.

COW CREAMERS

Milk or cream jugs in the form of a cow, introduced to England about 1775 by Johann or John Schuppe, a Dutch silversmith resident in London. European silver creamers in cow form date from the early 18th century and may be found in a variety of sizes, invariably free-standing and with a small hinged lid in the back, usually decorated on the top with a bee. Silver creamers were made sporadically down to the end of the 18th century and are in the price range £40 – £150, depending on size, maker and unusual decorative features. The vast majority of creamers, however, were made in pottery and range in quality from the sensitively modelled cows produced by Thomas Whieldon in the 1760s to the relatively crude productions of unnamed potters in Scotland and Yorkshire. Cow creamers were widely produced in the period from 1770 to 1870 in many parts of Britain, in a wide variety of distinctive local styles and decorative glazes. Date-lines are not as important as makes and decorative styles, though 18th century creamers are scarce and include the more expensive examples. At the other end of the time scale are early 20th century creamers of a somewhat stereotyped form, and the modern reproductions made to

Left: A Whieldon creamer with calf, sponged in brown and grey, the stopper with floral finial, 6ins. Desirable because of the bold decoration, the suckling calf and the original rectangular stopper. Right: A Staffordshire creamer, boldly decorated with splashes of dark brown and manganese, 6¼ins. Desirable features are the seated milkmaid, the bold patches of colour and the crisp cutting of the neatly modelled base.

cater to the growing demand from collectors. Cow creamers are listed below according to makes and styles, in broadly chronological order.

Astbury-Whieldon. It seems unlikely that any creamers were actually made by Thomas Astbury, since the bulk of his output pre-dates the

A rare Leeds yellow creamer, sponged in brown and with a calf.

A fine Yorkshire piece, desirable for its very stiffness and naïvety Note the crisp cutting of the base, and the blue-ringed eyes, both plus points.

silver creamers; but examples are known in the distinctive marbled clays and glazes associated with this potter. Creamers ascribed to Thomas Whieldon are more probable, since examples are known with the characteristic sponged or splashed 'tortoiseshell' effect or with the distinctive streaky glazes associated with this potter. Bases are flat, usually waisted and chamfered at the corners. The modelling of the cows is good, the beasts being elegant and well-proportioned. Less commonly Whieldon-type cows may be found with a brown stippled decoration between horizontal green and ochre stripes. £150 – £350.

Prattware. Felix Pratt of Fenton began making cow creamers about 1770 and his cows are also well modelled, often with some attempt to reproduce the natural brown and white markings of the Hereford breed. Other examples have splashed, stippled or daubed pigments, in the high-temperature underglaze colours associated with him – brown, orange, ochre, a distinctive bright warm yellow, dark olive green and blue. £150 – £250.

Yorkshire. The Don Pottery at Swinton and the St. Anthony Pottery, Sunderland, produced creamers from about 1780 to 1830. Attribution to these Yorkshire potteries is uncertain, but they have been credited with the production of the rare creamers incorporating a milkmaid.

£250 – £400. The bases of Yorkshire creamers have chamfered corners and are waisted in the middle. Another idiosyncrasy of Yorkshire creamers is the outline of the eyes in blue (though this is not always present). £150 – £280.

The St. Anthony factory continued in operation till 1878 and cow creamers were made intermittently throughout that period. The later examples have thicker bases, rounded at the edges, but lacking the characteristic waisting of the earlier creamers. Later decoration was more colourful and often regardless of breed, vertical stripes being a popular device. £80 – £200.

A few creamers were made at the Leeds pottery in the late 18th century, and can be recognised by their distinctive canary yellow colour on a creamware body. These creamers have a brown glaze sponged over the yellow, and often have a disproportionately small calf nestling underneath. £200 – £270.

In the early 19th century, the Brameld pottery in Swinton produced rather clumsily modelled cow creamers decorated with a dark brown translucent 'treacle' glaze. Brameld cows were made throughout the 19th century and rank among the commoner types. £25 – £40.

Scotland. The small potteries of Portobello and other east coast towns produced creamers in the late 18th and early 19th centuries, with modelling similar to the Yorkshire cows but much cruder in execution and with a naive style of decoration in a wide range of colours. The name 'dabbies' given to this kind of pottery succinctly describes it. Scottish creamers are relatively scarce and prices are on par with Yorkshire. £100 – £200.

Sunderland. Late 18th and early 19th century cow creamers were decorated with lustre (usually pink or lilac), either in random daubs combined with iron-red, blue or green, or arranged in floral patterns. £70 – £120.

Wales. Early Welsh creamers were decorated with lustre in the same manner as the Sunderland creamers and are comparable in value. Later Welsh cows, however, are noted for their transfer-printed decoration. Willow pattern motifs may be found in blue or black on the cow's sides and on the stopper. The bases are elliptical with an excrescence in the centre. In the more clearly modelled forms this appears as a daisy, but in later examples it is nondescript. Transfer-printed creamers may also be found with simple floral or shell motifs of local inspiration. The modelling is often relatively poor, particularly in late 19th century examples, and this is reflected in the pricing. Welsh creamers of the early period, with lustre, are in the range £70 – £120; transfer-printed creamers range from £45 to £90, depending on quality and local associations.

greatly enhance a cow creamer and raise its value correspondingly, as will bold decoration or finely coloured glazes and enamels. The emerald green glazes of Whieldon are particularly desirable, as are the canary yellows of Leeds. In general the earlier the example the more desirable, as quality declined so much in the 19th century, and the earlier pieces are of course rarer.

Pitfalls

Beware of cows with broken or repaired horns. Examples with missing horns are only too common and should be heavily discounted. Unfortunately new horns have been grafted on to such specimens and the mend cleverly disguised by an excess of gilding. Be on your guard against cows whose horns have an excessively bright or glossy appearance. Creamers with their stoppers missing should also be heavily discounted. Check that the stopper is in fact original to the creamer and fits perfectly, since replacements are sometimes added to complete an otherwise defective jug. Cow creamers are very seldom marked in any way, and can only be identified by their glazes and characteristics. Care should be exercised in purchasing creamers reputed to be one of the rarities, since attribution is often tentative at best. Because of the interest in cow creamers some of the commoner types have been the subject of recent reproduction. This seems to apply particularly to Jackfield creamers. Creamers without a base are late 19th, early 20th century imitations and are of little value, though often passed off as Welsh.

Museums

London Museum, London.
Victoria and Albert Museum, London.
National Museum of Wales, Cardiff.
Littlecote House, Hungerford.
City Museum, Sheffield.
City Museum and Art Gallery, Stoke-on-Trent.

Reading List

Hughes, Therle. More Small Decorative Antiques. London, 1962.
Mount, Sally. The Price Guide to 18th Century English Pottery. Woodbridge, 1972.

DECANTERS

Otherwise known as serving bottles or jugs, these vessels were introduced into Britain in the third quarter of the 17th century. Hitherto wine was served direct from its own bottle at the table. The earliest decanters were fitted with handles but otherwise closely resembled the contemporary wine bottles (q.v.) These so-called decanter-jugs were straight-sided, round-shouldered vessels with funnel-shaped, spouted neck carrying a loose-fitting stopper. Virtually all of the 17th century examples of these decanter-jugs are now in museum collections. For all practical purposes the decanters available to the collector commence with the early 18th century. It is important to note that where a decanter is to be used small decanters are less desirable than bottle sizes while larger ones such as magnums and upwards are very desirable.

Date-lines

1710-1730	Straight octagonal sides, rounded shoulders and a tall neck, often tapering slightly towards the mouth pouring lip. Handles often found in the earlier examples, but these are rare. £200 – £500. Octagonal body minus pouring lip and handle; variations include gadrooning and fluting. £150 – £200.
1720-1745	Deeply indented bodies of various forms, broadly designated as cruciform. The idea was to permit the maximum surface area of glass to be exposed to the ice in the wine cooler. Plus factors are decoration on the tall necks and collars. £150 – £350.
1730-1745	As above, but with cut glass ornament, mostly confined to the neck. £250 – £350.

An early cut glass decanter which dates from about 1730.

143

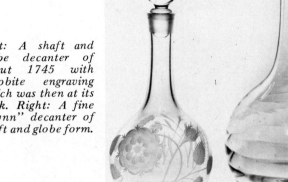

Left: A shaft and globe decanter of about 1745 with Jacobite engraving which was then at its peak. Right: A fine "Lynn" decanter of shaft and globe form.

1745-1765	The so-called shaft and globe decanters: bodies spherical with elegant slim long necks. Entirely plain decanters of this type, £100 – £150.
	As above, but the body ringed with regular indented lines – so-called Lynn moulding. £150 – £300.
	Shaft and globe decanters with engraved surfaces vary considerably in decoration and value. Those with the name of the wine engraved range from £150 to £300 depending on the rarity or obscurity of the wine.
	Those with pictorial scenes may range from £200 to £500, with up to £1,000 for fine, genuine examples of Jacobite or Williamite motifs.
	As above, but with overall cutting and faceting, £300 – £700.
1755-1770	Shouldered decanters, so-called because they are widest at the shoulders, tapering slightly towards the base. Early examples have a 'spire' stopper; later examples have a flat disc stopper with flat, faceted borders. Names of wines engraved on the side become increasingly common with this type. £120 – £300.
	Engraved decanters with floral or scenic motifs. £200 – £500.
	Shouldered decanters with enamelled ornaments by the Beilbys. £3,500 – £6,000.

As above but in coloured glass with gilding and enamelling by James Giles. £2,000 – £4,000.

Opaque white decanters decorated by Giles are of the greatest rarity. £4,000 – £6,000.

(These very high prices for work of the Beilbys and Giles apply only to examples where the condition of the enamelling or gilding is still very good).

1765-1775 So-called mallet decanters, with a wide base, sides rising and tapering slightly towards the shoulders and a relatively short neck, giving the vessel the shape of a stonemason's mallet. Decanters of this shape coincided with the richest and most prolific period of manufacture. Styles of decoration vary enormously.

Relatively plain examples with minimal engraving. £75 – £150.

Engraved decanters with very fine floral or armorial decoration. £250 – £400.

As above but incorporating dates and/or inscriptions. £300 – £500.

Coloured glass with overall faceting if of top quality. £500 – £800.

Clear glass with combined cutting and engraving. £250 – £400.

Mallet decanters with enamelled decoration (these may be decorated by Giles). £2,000 – £6,000.

Three nice mallets of about 1775.

1765-1790	'Indian club' decanters. Early examples (1765-1770) have names of wines engraved on them. £150 – £350.
	Later examples have engraved motifs on their sides often combined with faceting on the neck and stopper. £100 – £300.
1780-1800	Tapered decanters of a form which continued to be used in the 19th century. The majority are plain, or very lightly engraved or occasionally cut. Among the earlier examples, names of wines are very occasionally found. £150 – £300. Clear colourless glass is the most plentiful of the plain types. £30 – £50.

Indian club shaped decanter which might date from as early as 1765.

Coloured glass, in ascending order of rarity: green or blue, £50 – £150; amethyst, £150 – £350. (If gilded add 50% to the above prices.)

Coloured decanters were often produced in pairs or sets of three. Usually these had gilded wine labels and are often in stands. For pairs, prices should be about three times that of singles: for sets of three about five times that of a single.

1780-1840 Mould-blown decanters often of Irish origin. Names and sometimes even the addresses of the manufacturers may be found on the base. This technique coincided with the fashion for elaborate collars and neck rings, horizontal disc stoppers and elaborate overall cutting. Prices depend on the maker's mark. Unmarked specimens in colourless glass with minimal decoration, £40 – £70.

Elaborately decorated examples, but no maker's name, £70 – £120.

Marked specimens range from £100 – £150 for the Cork Glass Co. (the most common name) to £250 – £350 for examples bearing the marks of Penrose, Waterloo, Edwards of Belfast, Francis Collins, C.M. (Charles Mulvaney), Armstrong, or Ayckbown of Dublin.

Heavily cut Irish decanter from the end of the 18th century.

1800-1830	Diamond moulding in an overall pattern in flint glass (Irish). £75 – £100.
	As above, but in soda glass (usually Scottish or Northern English), crudely engraved, gaudily painted in cold enamels or gilded. Little interest in this type and currently undervalued at £40 – £60.
1810-1840	Heavy cut glass decanters; the deeper the cut and thicker the glass the later the decanter. Deep mitre cutting and ponderous, bulbous shapes with elaborate collars and stoppers. £30 – £50.
1830-1850	Vertical form with pillar cutting and fluting. £25 – £40.
1850-1900	'Gothic' style characterised by deep cutting with pointed arches. £20 – £35.
1865-1890	Globular decanters cut with rows of shallow depressions, with or without wheel engraving. £30 – £80.
1870-1900	Decanters of coloured glass overlaid on coloured glass, with cutting to reveal the colourless glass underneath. Amber, green, blue, cranberry glass. £45 – £100.
1875-1900	Decanters in the Arts and Crafts style, some elaborately decorated with inlays of semi-precious stones, classical coins, silver mounts and handles. Very rare and difficult to value since they were made individually to specific commissions. Much of the Arts and Crafts movement was a move towards simplicity as a reaction against heavy cutting.
1895-1910	Decanters with moulded or pressed ornament in the Art Nouveau style. £45 – £90.
1900-1930	Decanters with rectangular or cuboid form. Return of wheel-engraving. Value depends largely on the fineness and intricacy of the ornament. £30 – £80.
1920-1940	Clear, colourless glass in geometric forms, Art Deco 'cocktail' style. £50 – £70.

Points to look for

The majority of the decanters discussed above can be clearly dated according to their form, and values are in most cases well-established. The greatest scope, however, lies in the so-called classical Georgian style decanters with a 'Prussian' body, which remained the most popular type throughout the 19th century and continued into the 20th. Desirable features are three rings on a relatively short neck, a flat disc stopper, or a stopper in mushroom form with radial cutting. The commonest form of body decoration consists of vertical fluting extending half way up the body, but points to look for include unusual neck rings — the milled neck ring grained like the edge of a coin, the feathered neck ring tooled in the centre to give a feathered effect, or the blade neck ring which has a triangular section.

The diamond cutting which was so prevalent in the 19th century, ranges from the simple, overall cross-cutting to chequered diamonds in which the points are delicately notched. Other, more desirable forms of cutting to look for include hob-nail cutting and strawberry cutting, in which the tops are cut away into tiny pyramids simulating the surface of a strawberry. Pillar cutting, with alternate bands of strawberry cutting, is a major plus factor.

Pitfalls

Prices quoted are for specimens in excellent condition. Minute cracks, sometimes found in bases, are caused by stress while the glass is being annealed and are not regarded as a serious blemish. They should not be confused, however, with cracks due to impact and careless handling which detract gravely from the value. A crack clearly visible next to a good piece of engraving would be very detrimental. Chips on neck or base are a serious blemish which adversely affects value. Beware of examples which have been re-ground to remove or minimise such blemishes; this process usually results in asymmetrical or uneven surfaces. This 'restoration' usually removes all normal traces of wear at the same time, so the unnaturally high sheen produced by the polishing wheel should be immediately suspect. However, asymmetry should not be taken as a rule of thumb, since it may arise just because the object is handmade. Beware also of plain examples which have been cut or engraved at some subsequent date. Fortunately the style of engraving is usually a sufficient indication. Be particularly wary of dated specimens and items engraved with Jacobite emblems. A further factor which reduces the value of decanters is if they are stained on the inside. The most frequent is a whitish bloom due mostly to failure to dry out the decanter properly after washing. This rarely can be removed by domestic detergents but generally needs acid treatments or polishing out with a wheel.

Museums

British Museum, London.
London Museum, London.
Victoria and Albert Museum, London.
Royal Pavilion, Brighton.
Art Gallery and Museum, Brighton.
Royal Scottish Museum, Edinburgh.
Museum and Art Gallery, Glasgow.
City Museum, Hereford.
Pilkington Glass Museum, St. Helens.
City Museum, Sheffield.
City Museum and Art Gallery, Stoke-on-Trent.
Windsor Castle, Windsor.
City Museum and Art Gallery, Worcester.

Reading List

Ash, Douglas, How to Identify English Drinking Glasses and Decanters (1680-1830). London, 1961.
Davis, Derek C., English and Irish Antique Glass. London, 1965. English Bottles and Decanters. London, 1972.
Elville, E.J., English and Irish Cut Glass. London, 1953. English Table Glass. London, 1961.
Hughes, G. Bernard, English, Scottish and Irish Table Glass. London, 1956.
Lloyd, Ward, Investing in Georgian Glass. London, 1969.
Wakefield, Hugh, Nineteenth Century English Glass. London, 1961.
Wills, Geoffrey, Antique Glass for Pleasure and Investment. London, 1971. English and Irish Glass. London, 1968.

DINING CHAIRS

Originally made in sets, many of which have now been split up, they are eminently collectable in 'harlequin' sets of roughly similar types.

Chairs of one form or another have been used by man from the earliest times but as far as the collector is concerned, the earliest available type dates from the early 17th century. Panelled back chairs with solid backs and seats made with mortice and tenon joints and panels were in vogue until the middle of the 17th century and continued to be made in country districts into the 18th century. The back was often decorated with carving on several panels. The legs were usually part turned with four stretchers joining the legs just above the floor. These chairs were made for the head of the house, the rest of the

Good quality late 17th century panelled arm chair. The quality is evident both in the carved back and the configuration of the top rail.

A high-backed elbow or arm chair with typical decorated front stretcher, the top rail having winged cherub and thin panel of carving.

A walnut dining-chair of very good quality with ball and claw feet, the shells on the top of the legs hipped into the seat rail, c.1725.

A primitive but rugged country interpretation in oak of the Queen Anne/George I style. It is stiff and lacks movement but the top rail is unmistakable.

people round the long thin refectory table would sit on joint stools or log benches. Many made in oak and not made in sets. The main developments can be defined as follows:

Date-lines

c.1620-1660   Square-shaped upholstered chairs with or without arms with backing having a gap just above the seat and higher up. The rectangular, or sometimes square, area formed by the uprights and the square top rail covered in either upholstery, leather or just plain slats of wood attached sometimes with large round brass-headed nails to the woodwork. When without the typical square-shaped arms they are sometimes called 'farthingale chairs' after their suitability in accommodating the large dresses

151

worn. There is an open-backed variety with vertical column of turning often of 'bobbin' form, and another late variety with a cane back. Though mainly in oak some were walnut. A number of designs including Yorkshire and Lancashire.

1665-1700 Chairs of this period tend to have richly carved high backs. The front stretcher was also adorned with a thick band of carved decoration often based on an elongated S scroll and frequently incorporating cherubs and crowns, symbols of the restoration of the Stuart monarchy to the English throne. The back was however the main centre of decoration often with vertical runs of carved or part fretted panels separated by thin vertical panels of cane-work. The front legs too moved away from the

Walnut chair, c.1740, of the pre-Chippendale type of reasonable quality.

A lack of pegs through the mortise and tenon joints and a certain bandiness about the legs make what purports to be c.1725 more like Victorian, and thus to be avoided if you want a period chair.

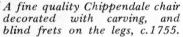

A fine quality Chippendale chair decorated with carving, and blind frets on the legs, c.1755.

This Hepplewhite shield-back design shows a more restrained use of decoration.

square shape. Apart from the carving (which is not always present) the other distinguishing feature of the period is the very high back. Where examples have arms they are no longer square in shape but rounded in section, sweeping out and often terminating in a scroll or similar design. The main woods used were walnut or if it was painted black (ebonized), beech. A common type are the simply made ones with no arms and moulded slats forming the back.

c.1705-1750 Another design resulting from Continental influence was the cabriole leg chair which originated in Holland. At first the carved ornamentation of the previous type continued but soon shape became more important than decoration which disappeared. These chairs are among the finest ever made in this country. They are comfortable, the base of the splat supporting the small of the back. They have hardly a straight line in their design, apart from the seat rail. The cabriole legs, which are difficult to make, are usually well shaped and the back is shaped both from back to front and side to side,

A fine Sheraton chair, c.1790. Compare the lightness of design and sparing use of decoration with the heavy carving of the Chippendale rococo.

A solidly made square-shaped Sheraton type dining-chair of the last decade of the 18th century, with turned legs.

usually made in walnut. They provide a marked contrast to the square shapes of the previous period's chairs, only the back legs remaining reminiscent of the previous period.

At first these chairs had a curved stretcher but on less sophisticated examples there were two turned lengths with square sections where the wood was jointed. By about 1715-1720 the seat rails had become thicker, the seat had started to broaden and the front projecting knee of the cabriole legs were not so near the top; the stretchers too had gone. The back became less high and shaped, and the cabriole more of a standard design.

By the late 1730s a dark heavy dense Spanish (San Domingo is another name) mahogany was imported and used to make chairs of roughly the same design. Carved decoration (shells and acanthus leaves were a favourite) which had previously been used only on the knee of the cabriole legs during the walnut period, now blossomed with a scroll on the back, this mahogany being ideal for the carver who was able to produce clear engravings which would last much better than on walnut. The cabriole leg was still popular right up to the late 1750s and featured in Chippendale's designs first published in 1754. By the end of the decade it fell from favour to return nearly a hundred years later in an attractive but distinctly Victorian form.

1750-1775   Although many of the rich Chippendale chairs feature the cabriole leg it is the square-legged chair with which his name is mainly associated, for these are by far the most common. The main feature of these chairs is, however, the highly decorated splat which usually takes the form of a series of curves. By the inclusion of various minor decorative motifs they are categorised. Thus pointed arches make a chair *Gothic*, interlaced ribbons with a hanging tassel a *'ribbon back'* while the *Chinese taste* is provided by lattice work in which is incorporated a pagoda-shaped motif. The legs may also carry a lattice design called a blind fret, because it looks like fretwork yet does not go right through. A high degree of ornamentation and scrolled carving is known as rococo. While these types are interesting the large majority of chairs that the collector will find have a single vertical splat fretted into a simple design. The country-made chairs may be very simple, perhaps a little stiff and upright, but have an attraction of their own.

1775-1800   In the latter part of the 18th century designers played a much more important role than previously and a wide variety of forms are used including refined cabrioles as well as square turned legs. Names are important and are used to describe various figures all under the broad heading of Neo-Classical; ideally a return to a more simple use of naturalistic ornamentation — a reaction to the heavy and detailed carving of the rococo. The Neo-Classical furniture-makers used lyres, honeysuckle decoration, foliage husks, wheat ears and shells and generally moved away from the splat as the focal point of the back. It is the overall design of chair that matters and decoration is now of secondary importance often being glued on or 'applied'. Moreover furniture was often designed to fit into a particular setting by architects like Adam. Hepplewhite who published a guide in 1788 made use of curved backs in a variety of designs, among them shields or oval backs. He also advocated a scroll foot and aimed at a chair of elegant appearance and lightness of design. For the collector the influence of the designs which Sheraton noted in his guide will be slight, for in all but the fine examples merely the outline is copied. The designs that Sheraton notes at first in his Drawing Book of 1791 and later in the 1800s represent a move towards a squarer form of chair. The back is lower with the arms higher and set forward, almost on top of the leg at times, rather than the swept-back form often used by Hepplewhite. The 'Prince of Wales feathers' which Hepplewhite used, continued, often with a rose and swags of drapery finely

A fine example of a high quality Hepplewhite chair, c.1795, the arms and the back making a continuous curve which gives it both comfort and elegance. It has all the elegance of this late period.

A late Regency dining-chair of somewhat heavy design with the top rail overhanging the uprights; the brass inlay makes it a desirable chair.

Right: A fine Regency chair, c.1820, with drop-in seat on to cane base, brass inlay and rope twist back.

Below left: the start of the evolution of the balloon-back chair. The cabrioles have not yet arrived but the top rail is moving towards a new form. c.1835.

Below right: William IV mahogany dining-chair with heavy top rail and turned and reeded legs, c.1830.

carved in the vertical splats which formed the backs of these chairs, from which the concept of a formal splat has now completely disappeared. Painted chairs also became more popular, the use of paint to provide detail being an easier and brighter medium and fitting in with the concept of an overall design for a room.

The first decade of the 19th century produced some well-proportioned chairs. The 'Egyptian' style and sabre legs and a more heavy rounded-back approach took over from the lightness of the Neo-Classical. Decoration increased and the use of brass inlay and impressed designs became common on good examples. The Egyptian designs of Thomas Hope first published in 1807 gradually made their impression on taste (perhaps Nelson's victories in the Mediterranean helped) and as a result designs gave way to a heavier form. The William IV period is generally credited with the enlargement of

A further one towards the balloon back. Here the cabrioles have returned and the whole design looks lighter.

This fully developed balloon-back chair presents a good clean functional design which it would be hard to better. c.1850.

the legs, often by decoration with reeding, and a generally more solid appearance. A major feature of this style is the thick back rail overhanging the two uprights. Fortunately, Hope's ideas never caught on to any great extent outside the fashionable few and Sheraton's simpler style, therefore, continued to be the main inspiration, with the result that there are many pleasant chairs from this period which can be bought, even though the general trend was to thicken up the design.

1840-1880 The natural reaction against the straight thick back rail was to make it thin and curved. By the 1840s it had started to emerge as an oval-shaped back fully integrating the top rail and the two uprights into a single curve. These chairs can be faulted by a connoisseur of 18th century furniture on the grounds that the cabriole legs are bandy and that there is too much of a curve at the bottom of the leg. Nevertheless they are most collectable and a mixed set would give as much pleasure in comparison as would be gained from a similar 18th century chair. Inevitably the design coarsened as the need to produce more for less increased, due to the affluence of the lower paid members of the industrial society. The balloon back was waisted, straightened on the front surface, grooved and decorated. By the 1880s there was an even greater multiplicity of designs than previously, the final designs of the balloon (which of course was still available to order and many were ordered) was a square- or turned-legged upright chair with a single cross splat and an arched top rail. There are hundreds of variations of this design.

An interesting feature of this period was the reproduction of designs from earlier periods. Today's position had been reached where cabinet makers, or increasingly factories, made for stock rather than to specific order. As wide a range of stocks as possible was made to cater for all possible requirements.

Chairs were produced to Victorian standards of workmanship which were excellent but were often pinched and mean, lacking the free flow of the original. Everything was reproduced but with no intention of deception and most would not fool anyone who has bothered to study the original. Large quantities of these 'Vicky Repros' or 'half age' chairs are exported. Once at their destination they become real Chippendale or Sheraton.

A reaction against the production of indifferently designed mass-produced objects (not just furniture) came from the Art & Crafts movement of which William Morris was the moving force. They wanted a return to the simple 'Ye Joynted Oake Furniture' in fumed oak. By the 1890s they were copied commercially and these chairs, by such designers as Mackmurdo, Voysey and MacIntosh make an interesting subject for the 'dining-chair collector'.

Pitfalls

Panelled Chairs. The late Victorians loved old oak and made up pieces to look like early examples. They covered them with carvings but they are easy to identify. Less easy to detect are the ones which incorporate original panels or bits of old carved rails. You can spend some time trying to tell what is original, what is Victorian.

Hepplewhite design but not period. The back is too large, flat and stiff-looking and despite the carefully executed carving, does not fit in with the chair.

A genuine 17th century chair with a decorated top scroll added in Victorian times. Look at the leaves dripping down in a manner not used until the early 18th century.

Simple yet elegant 19th century country version of Sheraton's design.

A country Chippendale chair in oak, stiffer without decoration, nevertheless an attractive and very collectable chair.

Mid-17th century

The high back type chairs, many of which were made in walnut to which woodworm are very partial. Live woodworm is no problem, but if they have already eaten the structure of wood so that it has the appearance of being dry and powdery then a considerable amount of restoration (often more than the chair justifies) has to be undertaken.

Some of these chairs can be very uncomfortable but occasionally this can be remedied by the use of a squab cushion. Where cane is used it can be replaced. Test how soon the chair tips over backwards when pushed, the angle of tolerance can be very slight.

Queen Anne and onwards

Check that the chairs are really old. Lots of fakes made in the 1880-1940 period now look old but the state of the unpolished surfaces usually give them away. The designs can be very good and the workmanship very

161

realistic, yet they often look too thin or stiff which is the result of attempting to economise in wood. The mid-18th century chairs have a boldness and fine square quality about the back legs which is usually missing in the reproductions.

Price Range
Panel Backs
Finely carved Elizabethan panel back chairs. £1,250 – £2,000.
Good mid-17th century examples. £500 – £750.
Simple 17th century. £170 – £300.
Without arms, considerably less e.g. late simple one. £80 – £150

The Victorians enjoyed the unusual, especially if it was ornate, so there are quite a few 'one off' designs to be picked up.

From the 1880s, a return to the square easier-to-produce style where the limited stylised ornamentation is cut in by machine.

Two strongly contrasting styles in oak chairs. Both, however, are decorative. On the left a good example of a Derbyshire-type oak chair c.1660, on the right a commercial copy of the style devised by the Arts & Crafts Movement in an attempt to return to the simplicity of medievalism. The inset copper plaque bearing sinuous curves is typical. Note that the 250 years which separated these two examples have given the earlier chair a patination or deep glow (one can see it on the front stretchers) whereas the grain on the new example, clearly apparent in this photograph, has not had time to become patinated and therefore looks new.

Mid-17th century	With spiral uprights, back and seat in leather. £180 — £250.
	More for each chair if in sets of 4 or more.
	Yorkshire/Derbyshire type chairs each. £100 — £150.
	Simple oak with seats. £70 — £110 each.
Richly carved high backed	With arms. £80 — £100.
	A very well decorated one could be +£40.
	Without arms not so well carved. £60 — £90.
	If a bit shaky deduct £10 — £30.
Cabriole Legs	Fine early example with shepherd's crook arms, veneered splat with carved decoration. £1,000 — £2,000.

Early Queen Anne type (single). £120 – £180.

Early Queen Anne type (a pair). £350 – £600.

Small panels of marquetry, good colour and period needlework, push up the price to the top of the bracket.

Country made example. £70 – £120.

George I walnut of good quality style. £120 – £180. A pair £400 – £800.

A good cabriole leg Chippendale example with carved decoration and arms. £300 – £600.

Chippendale examples

        high quality. £300 – £500.

        reasonably plain. £100 – £200.

        crude without being too attractive. £30 – £80.

        Victorian reproduction for which quality varies widely. £40.

Hepplewhite

        high quality. £130 – £180.

        average shield back. £90 – £130.

        crude country. £20 – £30.

Looking very similar to the original, this Chippendale elbow chair is 1900-1920 the give-away from the photograph is the way the foot is turned out very markedly. On inspection the wood would look new especially on the unpolished wood revealed when the drop-in seat was removed.

Sheraton

fine example with arms. £300 — £450.
average. £40 — £70.
crude country. £20 — £50.
Sets of six, add between 50% to 100% for a single, except for really exceptional or very cheap which can be more. Country chairs, price affected by the wood. Walnut, laburnum and especially yew have their particular enthusiasts.

Regency Chairs
Will IV
Victorian

Sabre legs. £70 — £90
Turned legs. £40 — £70.
Turned. £20 — £40.
Balloon backs. Good examples c.1850. £30 — £40.
Flat sides to uprights, heavy and late corruptions. £10 — £20.

Museums
Nearly every museum in Britain has a number of pieces of antique furniture.

Reading List

Andrews, John. The Price Guide to Antique Furniture. Woodbridge, 1969. The Price Guide to Victorian Furniture. Woodbridge, 1972.

Aslin, Elizabeth. 19th Century English Furniture. London, 1962.

Edwards, Ralph. The Shorter Dictionary of English Furniture. London, 1964.

Fastnedge, Ralph. Sheraton Furniture. London, 1962.

Jarvis, Simon. Victorian Furniture. London.

Jourdains, Margaret revised by Fastnedge, R. Regency Furniture. London, 1965.

MacQuoid, Percy. A History of English Furniture. (4 volumes) New York, 1972.

Rogers, John C. English Furniture. London, 1967.

Symonds, R.W. & Whineray, B.B. Victorian Furniture. London, 1962.

DOLLS

Small human figures intended as children's playthings have been recorded over the past 4,000 years. In many cases these figures also have some quasi-religious significance. From the collector's viewpoint, however, the field is restricted to the period from about 1750 to the present day. Earlier dolls are of the greatest rarity and fine examples in contemporary costume would now be priced in thousands rather than hundreds of pounds. The only early dolls which the collector is likely to encounter are rather crudely fashioned 'babies' (carved wood, composition or stuffed rag) and crèche dolls, which were not intended as playthings but were religious figures produced in the Catholic countries to decorate tableaux connected with the Nativity, the Passion and other events in the Christian calendar. Date-lines are relatively insignificant, since any of the earlier types have continued to be produced to the present day, or enjoyed a very wide time span. Values depend primarily on type and quality, though when other factors are equal age is also an important criterion.

Left: 'Penny Dutch or Deutch' doll, showing crude construction. This is the type dressed by Queen Victoria. Earlier ones had top knots and painted side curls. Right: A 'pumpkin' head, of 1840.

166

Pegwooden or Dutch Dolls

Early examples (pre-1750) are rare, since they were the first type of doll intended for actual child's play and very few would have withstood rough usage. 18th century pegwooden dolls are comparatively crude and, as their name suggests, were usually carved from a single large wooden peg, with rudimentary features painted on the rounded end. In the earlier variety limbs are vestigial or entirely non-existent. The value of early wooden dolls (up to about 1820) is problematical, and would depend to a large extent on the clothing and accessories. Crudely carved Dutch dolls of this period may be worth as little as £25. On the other hand, finely turned and carved examples with jointed limbs and good quality contemporary clothing are now in the range £200 – £400.

The majority of pegwooden dolls with articulated limbs date from 1830 and were made extensively in Germany and the Netherlands. These remained very popular at the lower end of the market until the end of the 19th century, and have been revived fitfully in more recent years. £20 – £50.

Wax Dolls

The earliest wax dolls date from the late 18th century and were an English speciality. The earliest are known as Pumpkin Heads, with the hair, head and bust moulded in one, with pupil-less brown glass eyes. £50 – £120.

From about 1820 more realistic wax dolls were produced by pouring up to ten layers of wax over painted papier mâché to produce a soft pale complexion. These dolls are known as Slitheads, on account of the slits in the head by which a wig was held in place. Holes were often made for the eyes, which could be moved by manipulating a string or wire through the body. The bodies were more realistic, and were made of stuffed cotton or linen, or more rarely kid. Examples of Slithead dolls in superb condition are very rare, since the wax has a tendency to crack and discolour badly. Prices for average dolls of this kind are the same as for Pumpkins. Really superb examples, up to £400.

Poured wax dolls date from about 1860 and had solid wax heads, arms and legs and were realistically modelled. The important feature of these dolls is their hair, often inserted into the wax scalp singly or in groups, using a hot needle. The best English wax dolls were made between 1860 and 1900 by the Pierottis, Montanaris and Charles Marsh. Wax dolls which can definitely be identified as manufactured by these firms (especially if still with the original box) are highly prized. £300 – £500.

Many wax dolls, however, are unmarked, and their value will depend on both quality of moulding and fineness of the clothing. £150 – £300.

The earliest fashion dolls, exported by the French couturiers; all over Europe and America, often had wax heads. These dolls portray adults, rather than children, and their clothing is generally much more sophisticated and complete to the minutest detail, including fashionable coiffure and matching accessories. £250 – £400.

At the other extreme are the mid-Victorian wax baby dolls, with poured wax heads, seldom equipped with hair. They are usually dressed in baby linen and their value depends largely on the quality of the hand-sewn clothing, usually made by their youthful owners and their fond mamas. £80 – £150.

Portrait dolls in wax were an extension of the traditional craft of two-dimensional relief portraits in wax. They reproduced the features of Queen Victoria, the Empress Eugenie, the Princess Royal, etc. and were exquisitely clothed to match. They are very rare. £450 – £600.

Papier Mâché Dolls

During the period of the early 19th century when papier mâché was fashionable for articles of furniture, it was also applied to dolls, either as a basis for the layered wax Slitheads or used on its own. Papier mâché dolls, often with bodies and limbs of the same material, were made between about 1820 and 1850. £120 – £200.

Similar, but greatly inferior, dolls were made of papier mâché or composition in the late 19th century and early 20th century in an attempt to undercut the prices of the china dolls then fashionable (see below). These later papier mâché dolls were cheap and mass-produced and are unlikely to deceive the collector. Their value depends entirely on clothing and accessories. £5 – £30.

Paper Dolls

Two-dimensional paper or card cut-out dolls date from the 1820s and have continued to appear down to the present day. The more elaborate versions were fitted with a small wooden stand. On to the card body could be slipped or slotted various costumes and accessories. The most expensive of these paper dolls are the early examples, from 1825 to 1850. Because of the fragile nature of the material dolls of this period are very rare and their value depends on such factors as the number of interchangeable outfits provided, whether the figure is modelled on a contemporary celebrity, and whether it is intact with the original box. £40 – £100.

Later paper dolls (1850-1950) are much more plentiful, though the same criteria of age, number of outfits and historical associations with famous people apply. £2 – £25.

French doll with porcelain head, the head marked Depose Tete Jumeau, 21ins. high.

French doll with bisque head 18ins. high.

Glazed China Dolls

Dolls of this type appeared about 1840 and were fashionable for two decades. As they were often produced as a sideline of the famous porcelain factories of Europe, they were often exquisitely modelled. All features and hair were modelled on the porcelain and painted by hand before firing. The hairstyles found on china dolls provide fashion historians with an accurate picture of the coiffures between 1840 and 1860. Limbs were also made of porcelain on a stuffed cloth or kid body. Apart from hairstyles they can be accurately dated by certain features. Thus the earlier examples have sloping shoulders, a faint red line over the eyelids and painted slippers, while the later types have button boots. They were expensive at the time of manufacture and were dressed accordingly. China heads were fitted to the earliest walking dolls, operated by clockwork. Prices for non-automated china dolls are in the region of £150 − £300; clockwork dolls £200 − £450.

Parian Ware Dolls

Dolls with heads made of Parian ware appeared about 1850 and were produced up to about 1890. They were heavy and white, with a matt, unglazed surface, except for the eyes, mouth and hair, which were painted and glazed. Bodies were made of wood, papier mâché or stuffed cloth, with limbs in Parian ware. A rarer variant has inset glass eyes. Prices for Parian ware dolls are from £60 to £100 for those with painted eyes; £80 – £150 for glass eyes.

Bisque Dolls

Matt-surfaced porcelain at the biscuit stage (when the paste is first fired and left unglazed) was used for dolls' heads from about 1860 till the First World War. The delicate modelling and colouring of these heads represent the acme of the dollmaker's art and this group includes some of the most expensive dolls in the collecting field. Bisque dolls were first made in France and later in Germany. To a much lesser extent they were also made in Britain and the United States, but these are of lower quality. Early bisque dolls had the heads and shoulders in a single piece, with closed mouths and often with pierced ears. The bodies of these early dolls were made of stuffed kid and their limbs were gussetted and jointed. Later dolls had swivel heads, separate shoulders and open mouths (often showing their teeth). Bodies were made of composition and had ball and socket joints and elastic stringing. Later dolls had moveable eyes. The earliest bisque dolls may have been produced as coutouriers' models and this is reinforced by the brilliance and variety of their costume and accessories. These dolls had slender, elegant faces. Those made by Huret of Paris always had double chins. Other makes to look for in this category are Rohmer, Martin and Jumeau, whose marks are to be found on the back of the head, neck, shoulder or body. £500 – £1,000.

From about 1875 onwards bisque dolls were made to look like babies or young children – a significant departure from the earlier fashion dolls. These dolls were known as 'bébés' and are recognisable by their chubby faces and large eyes. The bodies of bébés had hollow limbs with ball joints and elastic stringing, covered with papier mâché composition, often painted a lurid orange-pink. The best of the bébés were made by Decamps, Jumeau and Bru. Dolls by Bru were not marked thus until 1891, though earlier unmarked dolls may be identified by their stuffed kid bodies and bisque limbs. Dolls can also be recognised by certain facial characteristics. Jumeau bébés have large liquid eyes, set close together, whereas Bru dolls have them wide apart in a rather startled expression. Jumeau bébés after 1888 had expansive smiles and parted lips. Bru dolls are generally heavier than Jumeau dolls. Jumeau dolls are invariably marked in some way, the early ones (1844-78) with the initials E.J. Later dolls had more elaborate marks and can be dated accurately by references to the medals and diplomas awarded between 1878 and 1899. In that year Jumeau combined with other French dollmakers to form the Société Française de Fabrication de Bébés et Jouets. Dolls produced by this combine are marked S.F.B.J. and were made up to 1910. Dolls of this period, however, are inferior in quality to the earlier Jumeau dolls.

Bisque bébés of the period 1875-1900, £100 – £300.

S.F.B.J. dolls of 1900-1910, £50 – £150.

Left to right: A Simon and Halbig bisque head doll, 24ins. high, dressed in a full national costume; a Simon and Halbig bisque head doll, fully dressed.

The German dollmakers began emulating their French rivals with bisque dolls about 1870 and, although they never surpassed the best of the French bébés, they were competently made. As they were exported in vast quantities to Britain and America (and even to France itself), they are relatively plentiful. The names to look for are Armand Marseille, Heubach Brothers, Simon & Halbig and Kammer & Reinhardt. Heubach produced a large range of character dolls with widely differing facial expressions. Armand Marseille dolls had a very 'English' look about them, though later he diversified into Chinese and Negro dolls Bodies were usually made of Elastolin and other German papier mâché composition substances. German bisque dolls are in the price range £50 – £150.

Dolls by Heubach are rather more expensive. £80 – £200.

German bisque dolls with matching cases and trousseaux. £150 – £350.

Automata

An important class consists of dolls incorporating mechanisms for walking, talking, sleeping, crying or other bodily functions. Many of these were produced in the United States, beginning with the Autoperipatetikos (self-walking doll) of 1862 and culminating in the talking and singing dolls patented by Edison in the 1890s, which concealed a tiny phonograph and records in their bodies. The prices of automata vary considerably, from around £100 for an early sleeping or crying doll, to £400 − £600 for the Autoperipatetikos and even more for the Edison talking and singing dolls. These prices assume that the dolls are in perfect working order.

Autoperipatetikos, 1862.

20th Century Dolls

A much wider variety of materials has been used in the production of dolls since the early 1900s. In most cases these were designed to undercut the more expensive bisque or composition dolls and take the form of various substitutes, such as rubber or celluloid, which unfortunately have not stood the test of time. Examples in good condition are scarce, but do not attract the attention shown to the earlier dolls. In this group come the Kewpie and other American character dolls, the English 'Diddums' designed by Mabel Lucie Attwell and similar dolls current in the 1920s and 1930s. Other dolls to look for are those reproducing child film stars, such as Shirley Temple and Jackie Coogan. German dolls of the inter-war period were made with hollow metal hands, with moulded and painted hair. Bakelite, vulcanite and other early plastic substances were widely used in the 1930s. Value depends on the degree of interest attached to the doll, particularly those with literary or historical connections. Costume tends to be more mass-produced, but hand-made dress rates a premium. £5 − £30.

A fine 19th century French Automata doll, 20ins. tall.

Points to look for

Condition is of paramount importance, although missing hair can be replaced and chips and cracks repaired by experts. Wax dolls can be re-waxed, though it may be better to keep them in original, if shabby condition. The same applies to clothing and accessories. A faded but original dress is preferable to one newly made to reproduce the style of the period. Prices have been quoted for good average specimens with a single complete outfit. Dolls with an extensive wardrobe or trousseau, together with matching accessories, are invariably worth a great deal more.

Pitfalls

The enormous demand for antique dolls, especially the bisque dolls of the late 19th century, has stimulated a major industry in modern reproductions. In particular it appears that the original Jumeau moulds have got into the wrong hands. These modern 'reproductions' have been selling at £35 − £50 but are virtually worthless as an investment. An expert can detect the subtle differences in the bisque itself, but more obvious points to look for are the use of nylon hair, soft glove-kid bodies of a chalk whiteness, oddly proportioned bodies and machine-stitched clothes (even if the material itself is original). A certain amount of faking is inevitable, and to some extent is permissible. In this case genuine bisque heads have been detached from the original bodies (either worn out or limbless) and attached to bodies and limbs of more recent vintage. As the chief value of a doll lies in its head (and, indeed, heads themselves are eminently collectable) the attachment of old heads to new bodies is not as serious as it might seem, though obviously it will detract considerably from the value. Repairs and replacements often occurred at the time these dolls were current. Similarly clothing was often updated, from one generation to the next.

Museums

Bethnal Green Museum, London.
British Museum, London.
London Museum (Queen Victoria's Dolls), London.
Pollock's Toy Museum, London.
Victoria and Albert Museum, London.
City Museum and Art Gallery, Birmingham.
Art Gallery and Museum, Brighton.
The Grange, Rottingdean, Brighton.
Blaise Castle Folk Museum, Bristol.
Beamish Open Air Museum, Chester-le-Street.
Museum of Childhood, Edinburgh.
Royal Scottish Museum, Edinburgh.
City Museum, Hereford.
Cliffe Castle Museum, Keighley.
Museum and Art Gallery, Leicester.
Museum of Miniatures, Lyme Regis.
Central Museum and Art Gallery, Northampton.
Strangers' Hall, Norwich.
Salisbury and South Wiltshire Museum, Salisbury.
The Toy Museum, Rottingdean.
City Museum, Sheffield.

County Museum, Stafford.
City Museum and Art Gallery, Stoke-on-Trent.
Elizabethan House, Totnes.
Royal Tunbridge Museum and Art Gallery.
The Doll Museum, Warwick.
Windsor Castle, Windsor.
City Museum and Art Gallery, Worcester.
Snowshill Manor, Worcester.
Museum and Art Gallery, Worthing.
Castle Museum, York.
Musée des Arts Decoratifs, Paris.
Villa Sauber, Monaco (Galea collection of Dolls and Automata).
The Toy Museum, Nuremberg.
Historical Society Museum, New York.

Reading List

Bateman, Thelma. Delightful Dolls. Washington, 1966.
Boehn, Max von. Puppen. Berlin, 1929.
Bullard, Helen. The American Doll Artist. Boston, 1965.
Calmettes, Pierre. Les Joujoux. Paris, 1924.
Coleman, Elizabeth A. Dolls: Makers and Marks. Washington, 1963.
Coleman, Dorothy S., Elizabeth A. and Evelyn J. The Collector's Encyclopedia of Dolls. New York, 1968.
D'Allemagne, Henry Rene. Histoire des Jouets. Paris, 1903.
Early, Alice K. English Dolls, Effigies and Puppets. London, 1955.
Faurholt, Estrid and Jacobs, Flora G. Dolls and Dolls Houses, Tokyo, 1967.
Fraser, Lady Antonia. Dolls. London, 1963.
Gerken, Jo Elizabeth. Wonderful Dolls of Wax. Lincoln (Nebraska), 1964.
Hart, Luella. Directories of British, French and German Dolls. Oaklands (Calif.), 1964-5.
Hillier, Mary. Dolls and Dollmakers. London, 1968.
John, Janet P. The Fascinating Story of Dolls. New York, 1943. More About Dolls. New York, 1946. Still More About Dolls. New York, 1950.
Johnson, A. Dressing Dolls. London, 1969.
Noble, J. Dolls. London, 1968.
Singleton, Esther. Dolls. New York, 1927.
Yamada, Tokubei. Japanese Dolls. Tokyo, 1955.
White, G. Dolls of the World. London, 1962. European and American Dolls. London, 1966.

ENAMELLED BOXES

Small enamelled boxes were among the objects of vertu produced by jewellers and goldsmiths in France and throughout the rest of Europe in the 18th and 19th centuries. These elegant pieces, usually of enamelled gold, are now, however, rare and expensive. The present-day collector will have more scope in confining his attentions to the more modest enamelled boxes produced in England between 1750 and 1840. These boxes were made of thin sheet copper, coated all over with a special enamel paste which, when fired, fused to the metal and provided the basic surface for decoration. This consisted of painting with enamels, either entirely by hand, or over a transfer-printed outline. Rims of boxes and their lids were often covered by gilt copper strip or pinchbeck ornament punched and engraved by hand, though latterly this decoration was applied by machine. The presence of hand-tooling or machine die-stamping is a useful guide to date, the latter having come into use in the late 18th century. The production of enamel boxes was centred on a few towns in England. In the main, the factories operated for relatively short periods. Manufacture was carried on at Battersea in London, and in the Midlands, at Birmingham, and the South Staffordshire towns of Bilston and Wednesbury. The characteristics of boxes produced in these areas are noted overleaf.

Left to right: A Battersea enamel patch box on pink ground painted with flowers and a landscape panel; a Battersea enamel patch box on blue ground, the lid painted with 'Cries of London' scene entitled 'Fresh gathered peas'; a small Battersea enamel patch box on blue ground, the lid with verse dedication; a French enamel casket painted with figures in landscape.

176

Battersea

The finest boxes were produced at Battersea between 1753 and 1756, under the direction of Theodore Jannsen, Henry Delamain and John Brooks. The business failed when Jannsen's other business interests (linked to the South Sea Company) collapsed. The period of operation was very short and the number of genuine Battersea boxes must therefore have been relatively small. Battersea boxes can be identified mainly by their distinctive deep colours, great brilliance of flowing line and fine translucent colours. Characteristic colours are soft crimson, clear light blue and a warm dark reddish brown. Decoration was always over a transfer-printed design and the colouring is even and finely applied. Boxes are rectangular, oval or round, and were designed for snuff, bonbons, cachous, powder or patches. They vary in size from just over one inch to about three inches in length. The more desirable boxes have additional pictorial decoration on the sides, bottom and inside lid. £200 – £600. Battersea also made small portrait plaques, after the manner of portrait miniatures, taken from engravings and mounted in a gilt frame. £200 – £500.

Bilston

The manufacture of enamelled boxes probably started in Bilston about 1750 and continued till the end of the 18th century. Bilston was a prolific producer and boxes from this centre can be dated by colours and styles. At its best Bilston comes close to Birmingham in fineness and brilliant colouring and credit for this must be given to the French enamellers who lived in that area. Whereas Battersea enamels were

A good Bilston enamel snuff box.

177

occasionally inspired by the decoration on Meissen porcelain, those of Bilston were influenced by Sèvres, and this accounts for their more elaborate painting and the use of the popular Sèvres pink known as 'rose Pompadour'. The predominant colour of the backgrounds of Bilston enamels is a very rough guide to date: dark blue (early 1750s), pea-green (1757-60), turquoise and claret (1760-70) and silver, yellow and golden red (1770-80). Many of the designs used by Bilston were derived from Robert Sayer's treatise *The Ladies Amusement or Whole Art of Japanning Made Easy,* which included engravings of flowers, parrots and other birds, currants and overturned baskets of fruit. Other subjects, also derived from publications by Sayers, include

A very fine Bilston enamel étui.

Hancock's 'Tea Party', the 'Milkmaids' and the 'Fortune Telling Woman'. Landscapes, insects, nautical scenery and ships were also used. Other boxes, excluding Bilston, were decorated with calendars or almanacs, inscribed in French or English in black, blue, red, purple or gold on a coloured ground.

Bilston enamelled boxes with all-over motifs of the period 1750-80 rate £250 — £800.

Plus factors are snuff-boxes with tiny spoons set in their lids.

Bilston also produced étuis (£150 — £500) and boxes in fancy shapes including swans, bullfinches, and the heads of dogs, Turks and Negroes. £250 — £800.

Later Bilston boxes were mass-produced using mechanical processes and intended as cheap holiday souvenirs. They are usually oval, lacking base rims and often badly hinged. Colouring is blue, pink, turquoise and yellow with a printed border and lettering in black. The majority have such inscriptions as 'A Trifle from . . . ' followed by the name of a town; others have sentimental mottoes 'To My Sweetheart', 'Eternally Thine' or similar. The 'trifle' boxes were also widely produced in Wednesbury and rate £40 — £100. The 'sentimental' boxes are less in demand and are worth £20 — £60.

Wednesbury

Production of boxes began in 1776 when Samuel Yardley established a factory. Previously Wednesbury had provided painters and mount-makers for Bilston, so it is often difficult to distinguish between Wednesbury and Bilston, but generally the colours were harsher and more thickly applied. The bulk of the 'trifle' and 'sentimental' boxes probably came from Wednesbury, which continued to manufacture boxes as late as 1840. Wednesbury boxes have a characteristically hard, glassy finish. The earlier boxes have pastoral scenes in the manner of Watteau and Boucher. £100 – £400.

The later 'trifle' and 'sentimental' boxes rate much the same as Bilston boxes.

Birmingham

Production of enamelled boxes and also best quality painted boxes was in operation by 1750 at least, since Robert Hancock is recorded as having been engaged in making transfer-printing plates by that date. The Birmingham manufacturers acquired the plates formerly used at Battersea and continued to print from them in the 1760s. Birmingham transfer-printed boxes can be distinguished from Battersea boxes by the signs of wear in the printing, giving an overall lighter impression. Early Birmingham boxes have the same design characteristics as the South Staffordshire boxes, with a penchant for French romantic landscapes and groups. Boxes with pictorial elements on the lid and sides only rate £150 – £500. Those with additional pictures inside the lid and on the base rate £400 – £800.

Points to look for

A curious novelty of the late 18th century was the box with an inner lid. While the outer lid might have a perfectly innocuous picture, the inner lid depicted a frankly erotic subject. One theory is that young men might offer well-bred young ladies a scented cachou and then suddenly flick open the top lid to give them unseemly thoughts! Erotic enamels are relatively plentiful and add about 20% to the value of a box. The majority of boxes will be found to have damage to some extent, where the enamelling has cracked or even flaked off. Even the most superb boxes will be found to have minute hairline cracks. Since it is impossible to repair enamel effectively the more serious damage obviously detracts from the value and may reduce it by two thirds or more.

Pitfalls

Although English manufacture of enamelled boxes ceased by 1840, similar boxes continued to be made on the Continent. These boxes, of French or German origin, are generally inferior in the quality of enamel and colours. A useful guide to identification is the hinge on the lid. If the central part projects, it is usually of Continental manufacture. All English boxes had smooth cylindrical hinges with no projections.

Samson forgeries of Battersea and Bilston enamels were produced from about 1860 onwards and the earlier examples are very close to the originals. At first Samson added an S or entwined S monogram, always painted, never transfer-printed, to identify his work, but latterly dispensed with this to improve sales. It is very difficult to unmask these

A good Birmingham enamel snuff box.

Samson forgeries, though colouring and the quality of tooling on the gilt-metal mounts are guides to the expert. Subtle anachronisms in the designs may indicate a post-1860 Samson forgery masquerading as a pre-1780 Bilston original. It should be noted, however, that early Samson enamelled boxes are collectable in their own right and are now in the price range from £50 to £100. More recent enamelled boxes have the pictorial motifs entirely transfer-printed and these should not deceive anyone since the surface is dead flat and screening dots should be obvious under a glass. These boxes are of very little value.

Museums
British Museum, London.
Victoria and Albert Museum, London.
Waddesdon Manor, Aylesbury.
Museum and Art Gallery, Bilston.
City Museum and Art Gallery, Bristol.
Royal Scottish Museum, Edinburgh.
Central Museum and Art Gallery, Northampton.
Salisbury and South Wiltshire Museum, Salisbury.
City Museum, Sheffield.
Windsor Castle, Windsor.
Municipal Art Gallery and Museum, Wolverhampton.

Reading List
Hughes, C. Bernard and Therle. English Painted Enamels. London, 1951.
Ilford, Lord. Staffordshire Coloured Enamels. London, 1965.
Mew, E. Battersea Enamels. London, 1926.
Rackham B. Catalogue of the Schreiber Collection. Victoria and Albert Museum, 1924.
Ricketts H. Objects of Vertu. London, 1971.
Watney B. and Charleston R. Transaction of the English Ceramic Circle. Vol. VI, Part II. London, 1966.
Watney B. English Enamels in the 18th Century. Antiques International. London, 1966.

FANS

Dismounted fan leaf, Diana and her huntresses, c.1720.

Fans exist in two major types, rigid and folding. Rigid fans, with a single large leaf attached to a pole handle vary enormously in size and age, having been produced in Assyria and Egypt at least 2,000 years B.C. This style of fan was favoured in Oriental countries, and many distinctive types may be found from Pakistan and Persia to China and south-east Asia. Rigid or screen fans are difficult to date since styles were retained unchanged for hundreds of years. There was a vogue for rigid fans in the second half of the 19th century, following the introduction of Japanese ideas on interior decoration. Small Japanese rigid fans were often affixed to screens and drapes for decorative effect.

From the collector's viewpoint, however, it is the second category — folding fans — which command most attention. The folding fan originated in China under the Ming dynasty and was brought to Europe by the Portuguese early in the 16th century. Fans spread rapidly to other western European countries and became an indispensable fashion accessory until the First World War. Fans can be dated stylistically, according to the decoration on the leaves and the ornamental treatment of sticks and guards. Different materials have been used at various times and these are also a useful guide to dating, although certain materials and techniques remained in use for centuries. France was the chief centre of fan-making, although indigenous styles were developed in other countries. A number of distinctive types of fan were produced at various times for specific purposes and these special types are discussed separately.

182

A fan printed with a dying hero, probably Genoese, c.1720.

Date-lines

1550-1660   Tudor and Stuart fans made of vellum, cut and pierced to simulate lace. Very expensive to produce and now extremely rare. Should they appear on the market they might well not be very attractive and as a result could well fetch much less than their age and scarcity might suggest. £300 – £800.

1660-1685   Earliest painted fans. Sticks decorated and pierced. Arc of fan up to 160°. 14-18 shouldered sticks, with the mount (fan-leaf) covering about two-thirds of the sticks. £350 – £600. Again only attractive ones would make these prices, others £40 +.

1685-1750   Number of shouldered sticks increased to 24 or 26 (up to about 1730) and then decreasing again to 18-21. Sticks becoming longer after 1730, leaving less space for the mount. Again attractiveness very important. £35 – £250.

German fan printed with the Rape of the Sabine women, c.1730.

A fine neo-classical fan in the style of Zucci, Italian late 18th century.

1750-1800	Arc of fan increased to 180° or more. Shoulders gradually disappear; ornament complete on each stick. By 1770, however, ornament spreads across the sticks, and a wide range of techniques employed – carving, painting, staining, lacquering, etc. Design across two, three or four sticks at first, eventually extending across entire range.
1715-1800	Brisé fans, completely consisting of sticks, tapered towards the foot, and made of thin flexible ivory, tortoiseshell, wood or horn, delicately fretted to simulate lace. Sticks joined at the top by short lengths of ribbon. Very attractive ones might fetch more. £10 – £80.
1740-1800	Brisé fans decorated with a type of clear lacquer known as *vernis Martin*. Vignettes of pastoral or classical scenes surrounded by flowers. Lacquer usually applied to unpierced ivory sticks. £200 – £450.
1775-1800	Minuet fan, similar to the brisé fan, but rather larger, with sticks of carved and fretted bone or ivory, displaying a large central vignette when unfolded; vignettes after Poggi, Bartolozzi, Cipriani and Boucher. £100 – £400. £30 – £80 if vignette is a print.
1800-1840	Brisé fans with sticks of sandalwood or cedarwood. Quality of carving and fretting not as intricate as on earlier fans. Wide variety of painted decoration in neo-classical style. Print £10 – £30. Painted £50 – £100.
1700-1800	Folding fans with mounts of silk or hand-made paper. Sometimes small silk vignettes were printed on silk and

applied to the silk mount, painted over by hand. Paper mounts decorated with gouache. Often elaborately decorated with figures and straw-work etc. Pastoral scenes predominate, though from 1760 scenes by Ravenet, Watteau and Boucher are also popular. Fans with general scenery and landscapes are worth from £30 to £120. Those with topical scenes, or depicting ballooning (popular in the 1780s) are worth more. £100 – £200.

1780-1840   The main period for disposable paper fans, with paper leaves reproducing a variety of subjects and prints, though there are printed fans from 1700 onwards, pastoral £40 – £60, early 18th century allegorical fans £80 – £150. In this period fan-leaves became a popular propaganda medium: politicans and even royalty were lampooned, victories celebrated, plays and popular songs publicised. These topical event fan-leaves were rather ephemeral and though cheap at the time are now rare. 1780-1800, £50 – £100. Early 19th century, £20 – £60.

1820-1900   Silk fan-leaves, decorated with sequins, embroidery, beads. £10 – £30.

1840-1910   Chinese (or chinoiserie) feather fans, with painted feathers, depicting birds. £8 – £20.

1860-1914   Mandarin fan, imported from China. Paper fan-leaves decorated with Chinese scenes. Faces of human figures consist of tiny pieces of ivory, and clothes of applied silks. £15 – £25, if very fine, sometimes more. Victorian painted fans, £10 – £80+; lithographic, £5 – £50.

One of a pair of Swiss fans, c.1780.

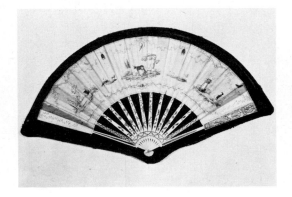

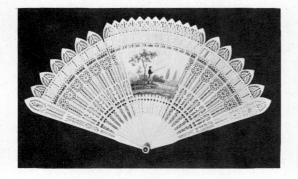

Rare double-image brisé fan (it reverses to produce four vignettes in all), 1820.

Points to look for

Unusual decorative features on the sticks and the pinion holding them together are worth a premium. The use of piqué or other forms of inlay is a plus factor. Fans with personal associations with historic personalities can be worth very much more than their style and quality might generally warrant, but much depends on their provenance. Special cases were provided for fans when not in use. The earliest cases were lined with velvet and covered with dark leather. Some 18th century fans have original papier mâché boxes with shop labels. After 1720 boxes had red or green covers with silver mounts or gilt patterns. Silver mounts were sometimes hallmarked up to 1790, when they were exempted. Fans with their original cases are worth a premium. Later cases often have the manufacturer's name and trademark in gilt lettering on a white satin lining.

A mid-18th century fan.

Pitfalls

Condition is of paramount importance and fans which have been damaged or carelessly repaired can be heavily discounted. This applies particularly to fans with mounts of silk or gauze. A rough and ready method of repair, when sticks were damaged, was to glue the broken one to its neighbour, but this spoils the symmetry of the picture when the fan is extended. Fan-leaves may often be found without their matching sticks, and even in this condition they are still quite collectable, although their value will be reduced by 60-80%. Rather more problematical are old sticks with more recent mounts. This may have been done quite legitimately, as fashions changed, but it may be suspect. More likely to have been faked are early mounts on sticks of a much later date. A metal loop was attached to the pinion from about 1816 onwards, for threading with ribbon. The presence of this feature on a fan whose mount is 18th century, would immediately be suspect.

Museums

London Museum, London.
British Museum, London.
Victoria and Albert Museum, London.
Waddesdon Manor, Aylesbury.
Royal Scottish Museum, Edinburgh.
City Museum, Hereford.
Temple Newsam House, Leeds.
Central Museum and Art Gallery, Northampton.
Museum and Art Gallery, Reading.
Blithefield, Rugeley, Staffordshire.
Salisbury and South Wiltshire Museum, Salisbury.
City Museum and Art Gallery, Stoke-on-Trent.
Elizabethan House, Totnes.
Royal Tunbridge Wells Museum and Art Gallery.
City Museum and Art Gallery, Worcester.

Reading List

Armstrong, Nancy. A Collector's History of Fans, London, 1974.
Fan Guild, Fan Leaves, Boston, 1961.
McIvor, Percival. The Fan Book. London, 1920.
Rhead, Wooliscroft. The History of the Fan, London, 1910.
Schreiber, Lady Charlotte. Fans and Fan Leaves — English. London, 1888.
Fans and Fan Leaves — Foreign. London, 1890.

FIRESIDE OBJECTS

Under this heading are grouped everything associated with fireplaces and their ancillary equipment, except fire-screens (q.v.). Fireplaces themselves became more decorative in the 18th century and the majority of collectable examples date from this period. Even the components of the fireplace may be collected individually. Decorative overmantels in carved and painted wood date from the Middle Ages and consequently vary considerably in value, depending on age, quality, detail of carving and condition. Mantelpieces consisting of a narrow wooden ledge supported by twin columns became fashionable in the early 18th century and likewise vary enormously in quality and price. Adam fireplaces and mantelpieces have long been popular with collectors and examples which could definitely be attributed to the Adam Brothers would now fetch four figures. Numerous mantelpieces in the Adam style exist and vary in price from £50 to £250, depending on condition, type of wood (pine is the commonest) and quality. Decorative features such as gilded carving and ceramic inlaid panels (especially Wedgwood) are important plus factors.

In the 19th century more elaborate mantelpieces came into fashion and the romantic revival brought carved oak back into vogue. Ornamental surrounds, with carved oak tops and supports in the form of carved figures would now be in the price range £150 − £400. Tiled fireplaces were an expression of the late 19th century Aesthetic Movement, and as individual tiles (q.v.) have distinct values it follows that complete sets mounted in the surrounds of fireplaces command a heavy premium. Good examples of late 19th century tiled fireplaces, with majolica tiling begin at about £200. Decorative tiling in Mason's ironstone rates £400 − £500, while run-of-the-mill Art Nouveau tiling on fireplaces ranges between £120 and £400. Fireplaces with Prattware (q.v.) tiling or sets of tiles by De Morgan and other artists of the Arts and Crafts period are now in the range from £450 to £1,000+.

Firebacks, otherwise known as fireplates, iron chimneys or reredos, consisted of cast iron plates protecting the wall behind the fireplace and radiating heat into the room. They were produced in Europe from the 15th century. Examples up to about 1690 are wide and low, but later types (1690-1750) are tall and narrow. Separate firebacks disappeared after 1750 when they became an integral part of the grate. The commoner firebacks had stylised floral or animal motifs and examples are worth £40 to £100 depending on age, quality and decorative appeal. Firebacks of a more personal nature, bearing initials and dates, are worth very much more, while those decorated with family coats of arms range from £200 to £500, depending on the family and historic associations.

Grates came into use in the early 18th century, when coal supplanted wood as household fuel. Stylistically the larger grates belong to the earlier period; by 1800 grates were very much smaller and tend also to be taller. There is relatively little market for old grates at present and even quite decorative wrought iron examples can often be picked up for little more than their scrap value.

Andirons and **Firedogs** date from Roman times, though the majority of collectable examples date from the 16th century. In the large medieval fireplace fire-irons were used in sets of six, comprising pairs of andirons at the outer extremities, firedogs and low creepers in the centre. The creepers, usually of scrolled ironwork, supported the main weight of the burning logs and embers, whereas the firedogs and andirons were similar in shape but in ascending size. They consisted of an upright bar at the front, often supported by tripod feet, with a long horizontal bar running back into the fireplace. The horizontal bars, taking the weight of the ends of the logs, were purely functional, but the frontal upright bars were frequently ornamented. The feet were sometimes cast in the form of animal or human feet and the most elaborate firedogs were actually cast in the shape of reclining hounds. Most 17th and 18th century examples have decorative columns surmounted by cast bronze or brass finials, often in the form of an animal or human head. After the adoption of grates in the 18th century andirons and firedogs became almost entirely decorative and to this period belongs the majority of the cast bronze figures. The most desirable of the decorative andirons are those with ormolu gilding. Cast bronze firedogs of the 16th century may be worth up to £1,500 the pair, since there is at present a great demand for them in Europe. Similarly fine ormolu firedogs of the mid-18th century may fetch from £500 to £1,500. At the other extreme, however, relatively plain wrought iron firedogs of the 17th century range from £30 to £70, though more elaborate examples are correspondingly dearer. There was a revival in andirons in the late 19th century and they may be found with curving feet and horizontal bar, and decorative panels in pewter, brass or copper. These firedogs range from £40 to £150, though fine Art Nouveau examples may be considerably more.

Fire Guards were first used in the mid-17th century and have continued to the present day. The earliest examples had a wire mesh enclosed by an all-round wrought iron frame slightly raised on small feet. Late 17th and early 18th century guards had decorative feet and often had ornamental finials in the upper corners. Polished brass

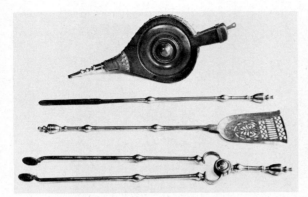

Fine lathe-turned fireside bellows with turned brass nozzle, brass nailed leather, c.1750, 20ins. long. Set of three George II fire irons comprising of heavy steel poker, 'fish tail' pierced shovel and hinged tongs, c.1750, 31ins. long.

ornament replaced the wrought iron top-rail in the 18th century and the more collectable (and more expensive) examples belong to this group. There is a wide variety of decoration found on the brass-railed fire guards of the 19th century. Late 19th century types had beaten copper panels, often with Art Nouveau motifs, and these are now much sought after. There is no hard and fast market for fire guards at present and prices seem to range from £10 to £20 for the plainer all wrought iron types, to £35 – £50 for the more decorative 18th century and Art Nouveau examples.

Fire irons came into use in the 18th century when coal superseded wood. The earliest sets consist of a shovel, poker and pair of tongs in iron or steel. The comparatively large fires of the time meant that the handles on these irons had to be much longer than their 19th century counterparts. As a rule, therefore, the longer the handle the earlier the set. The pans of shovels were frequently pierced and fretted in decorative patterns and the handles were surmounted with ornamental knops. Plus factors are handles of copper or brass and the most desirable types have gilt-bronze ornament on handles and swivel joints. Stylistically the earlier irons had straight shanks, but twisted or spiral shanks became fashionable about 1790. Shorter-handled irons continued till about 1850 when iron and steel were replaced by brass. At this point matching hearth brushes were incorporated in sets. With the advent of shorter fire irons holders and stands came into fashion and were decorated to match. Mid-Victorian brass companion sets vary from £8 to £30; 18th century iron or steel sets range from £20 to £50; and the more decorative gilt-bronze sets of the 18th century may be worth up to £150 if the decoration is unusual.

Coal scuttles came into use in the early 18th century but examples which can be dated prior to about 1840 are quite rare. The early scuttles resembled large scoops mounted on a raised circular base and

Left: Superb brass helmet-shaped coal scuttle with riveted swing handle. Repoussé scroll flower decoration with pineapple on the front. The two handles have lathe-turned lignum vitae hand grips, c.1830.
Right: Late Victorian copper coal scuttle with riveted swing handle.

were made of copper, often banded with brass. Though decidedly scarce the demand for them is small and examples have sold recently for £28 – £45. The helmet scuttle came into use in the early 19th century and is easily recognised by its large, round body and broad lip resembling an upturned helmet, the swing handle approximating to the chin-strap. Bases gradually became broader and lower as the century wore on. These scuttles were made of copper at first, but by 1860 brass was more common and in the late 19th century zinc scuttles came into fashion. Prices for helmet scuttles range from £20 – £30 for early, high-based copper scuttles, £15 – £25 for later low-based copper scuttles, £10 – £20 for Victorian brass scuttles (depending on amount and quality of decoration) and £5 – £8 for late 19th century zinc scuttles. **Coal vases** were smaller and taller than scuttles, usually highly decorative and made of japanned metal in a wide variety of styles (Baroque, Italianate, Gothic). Single vases range from £25 to £40 but matched pairs would fetch £60 – £100. **Coal boxes** were also produced in pairs and stood on either side of the fireplace. They may be found in many different styles, ranging from elegant, drop-front cabinets (popular in the late 19th and early 20th centuries) to boxes with lift-up tops which also doubled as fireside seats and were sometimes incorporated in the fender. These boxes usually have a detachable inner metal container for the coal, firewood, etc. Single coal boxes are worth from £5 to £15, depending on quality and such decorative features as

191

Fireside footmen and trivets to hold kettles or saucepans. Top: Oblong footman with hand-wrought cabriole front legs and decorative pierced cast iron top, unusual in having a pull out sliding barbecue grill underneath, c.1820, 17ins. wide. Bottom, left to right:

Blacksmith wrought iron horseshoe-shaped trivet with three splayed legs and burnt turned wood handle, two hooks on front to enable it to hang from the firebars on a grate, 9ins. high, c.1780. Oblong, finely pierced brass kettle stand on four turned cast brass legs with Chinese Chippendale fret top, 9½ins. long, 7ins. high, c.1770. Circular hand-wrought steel fireside trivet with triangular wrought iron decorative scrolled stretchers, c.1710.

beaten copper or brass mounts, short cabriole legs or upholstery. Pairs should be priced at about three times the value of singles. Patent scuttles invented by a Mr. Purdon are known as **purdoniums** and consist of sloping boxes with short feet, carrying handle, hinged lid in front and a metal liner. Purdoniums may be found in an all-metal construction with japanned surfaces and painted decoration, or in various kinds of wood with brass mounts and handles. A slot at the rear held a small shovel, and purdoniums with matching shovel still intact rate a premium. Worth looking for are purdoniums with back-painted glass panels set in the lid. Prices of purdoniums range from £10, for the plainer varieties, to £50+ for really fine specimens with polished wood surfaces, brass mounts and inlaid glass panels. Less desirable coal scuttles are simple bucket shapes and upright hods, often found in japanned tinware of late 19th century manufacture (£5 – £10). Copper hods with brass banding and loop handles, however, are worth rather more (£15 – £20).

Trivets were introduced in the 17th century as small stands for cooking pots in front of the fire. They consist of a broad plate on three legs with a long handle (often wooden-mounted) so that they could be moved to and from the fire. The earliest examples were of wrought iron but by 1700 brass was more commonly used and by 1730 pierced decoration was beginning to appear on the trivet plate. Examples with frontal hooks which secured the trivet to the bars of the grate, date from about 1750. By 1800 the rear leg had changed into a diagonal support. Trivets continued to be manufactured up to the end of the 19th century, when the introduction of cookers and stoves rendered them superfluous. Nevertheless it is likely that many of the small brass trivets found today date back no further than the turn of the century. The value of trivets varies from about £6 − £10 for the more ornamental late 19th century brass types to £40 − £50 for examples pre-1750.

Bellows for coaxing a hesitant fire have been recorded since Roman times and are to be found in many primitive forms all over the world, but the more collectable varieties developed in medieval Europe and have continued to this day. In their simplest form these bellows consist of two flat boards, of rectangular, triangular, heart, pear or oval shape, connected round their edges by a wide band of leather to form an air chamber. The boards are hinged at the pointed end and terminate in a fine nozzle, while handles are mounted at the other end. Air enters the chamber through a hole in the lower board and is ejected with considerable velocity from the nozzle when the handles are brought together. The wood, leather and metal construction of bellows afforded considerable scope for decorative treatment. Points to look for are

A kitchen beech wood handled steel herb and parsley chopper with double-sided sliding prongs to scrape off remains, c.1850, 14½ins. long. A cook's spoon with turned cherry wood handle, pewter bowl with stem stamped with a cockerel and 'London', c.1820. Rare four-pronged hand-wrought steel steak fork with flat handle and punched suspension hole, c.1720, 28½ins. long. Hand-wrought

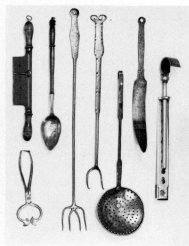

Queen Anne steel steak fork with ram's horn finial with punched and filed ornamentation, c.1700, 22½ins. long. Small George II brass cream skimmer, iron wire reinforced rim with copper riveted steel handle with suspension hook and hole, c.1740, 21ins. long. Late 17th century steel scone rake to pull cakes from an ingle-nook oven, 17½ins. long. Adjustable polished steel trammel or pot hook to hang a cauldron over an open down hearth fire from a chimney crane, 17ins. long adjustable to 26ins. long, c. 1780. Hand held steel sprung sugar breaker to cut up sugar loaves which were supplied by the grocer in the form of a cone, c.1790, 8ins. long.

Smoothing iron stands. Cast bronze cat face standing on four dumpy legs with pattern number cast into back, 27686, late Victorian, c.1880, 6ins. across. Typical cast bell metal, pierced top, flat iron stand on three legs, 9ins. long, c.1790. Cut sheet brass flat iron stand with pierced heart and diamond motif, the handle and feet are riveted to the top, 7¾ins. long, c.1820. Child's miniature cast brass flat iron stand with pierced scroll top and suspension hole, on three pyramid feet, 5¼ins. long, c.1840.

bellows with finely carved boards, decorative features on the brass nozzle, ornamental studs securing the leather to the boards and ornament on the handles. Early examples in working condition are rare and in many cases the leather will have been replaced by skins of much more recent vintage. Bellows may be worth from £10 to £80, depending on age, decorative features, size and quality of workmanship. More elegant forms, with ivory, tortoiseshell, brass or silver inlay, were fashionable in 18th century drawing rooms and would be worth considerably more, £100 – £300. Semi-mechanical types were developed in the 19th century and include the double bellows (giving a continuous blast) and the crank-operated centrifugal bellows, used mainly in Ireland where turf was burned instead of coal. These bellows are less decorative but because of their mechanical features they generally rate £40 to £50.

Toasters are an excellent example of a once useful object which is now prized for its decorative qualities. Long-handled forks with two or three prongs were in use from the 16th century till the late 19th century and many different types were evolved in that period. Typical toasters have turned wooden handles, bronze, brass or iron shafts, with brass, iron or steel prongs. Numerous patent devices appeared in the 18th century and included adjustable prongs, attached grease-pans (for toasting small game), tripods, stands and trivets. Early toasters (17th – mid-18th centuries) of a functional appearance are worth £15 – £30 each; decorative features, such as spiral shafts and prongs, add to the value. Mid-18th century patent toasters range from £20 to £50 depending on the type of device. Most of the highly decorative brass toasters are of 19th century manufacture and, though attractive in appearance, lack the antiquarian interest of the more functional types. Prices for brass toasters, with pierced heads and shafts, range from £5 to £15.

Museums
Geffrye Museum, London.
Wallace Collection, London.
Victoria and Albert Museum, London.
Museum and Art Gallery, Brighton.
Royal Scottish Museum, Edinburgh.
City Museum, Hereford.
Museum and Art Gallery, Leicester.
Central Museum and Art Gallery, Northampton.
County Museum, Stafford.
Museum of Country Life, Reading.

Stately homes are an excellent source of fireside material, but the following should be noted in particular:
Waddesdon Manor, Aylesbury; Hampton Court Palace; Anne of Cleves House, Lewes; Snowshill Manor, Broadway; Temple Newsam House, Leeds; Elizabethan House, Totnes; and Windsor Castle.

Reading List
Hughes, Therle. Cottage Antiques. London, 1967.
Kelly, Alison. English Fireplaces. London.
Lindsay, J. Seymour. Iron and Brass Implements of the English House. London.
Shuffrey, L.A. The English Fireplace. London.

FLATWARE

Generic term for sets of forks and spoons, derived from the fact that they were produced from flat strips of metal — as opposed to hollow ware (tankards, bowls and teapots) which were beaten up from sheets of metal into a hollow form. Spoons (q.v.) existed as separate items long before the introduction of forks in the early 17th century. The adoption of this Continental device soon led to the production of sets of forks and spoons *en suite,* with handles of a uniform design. Sets of flatware began to appear about 1660 and thenceforward can be dated by their shape, design and technical features. The first pattern for which complete services are known is the dog-nose. Flatware was produced in silver, less commonly in pewter, and in Sheffield plate (from c.1770) or electroplate (from 1840).

Date-lines

1660-1700　　Trefid pattern. Forks with two or three prongs. Knives have cannon handles with a tiny knop on the end.
Individual spoons in silver. £100 — £400.
Half sets of six, £1,200 — £2,000
Full sets of twelve, £5,000 — £7,000.
Individual forks and knives are much rarer than spoons. Double the value for lacy patterns on the backs of spoons.

1700-1710　　Dog-nose, wavy end or shield end. Forks still three-pronged but prongs now rounded, rather than flat, in cross-section. Rat-tail on the back of spoon bowls now loses its prominent rib and becomes simpler in design. Very elusive, but less expensive than trefid.
Individual spoons in silver, £30 — £150.
Cannon knives (individual) £20 — £25.
Half sets and full sets are virtually impossible to value due to scarcity.
Forks — individual, £20+; half dozen, £400 — £500.

1710-1730　　Hanoverian with rat-tail pattern on spoons only; end of stem now rounded and turned up at the end. Early examples have crests, initials etc. engraved on the backs of the stems; those after about 1760 have engraving on the fronts of the stems. Knife handles often shaped like pistol butts. Hanoverian forks still three-pronged and never found with rat-tails.

Spoons, pre-1730 with rat-tails, c.£20 each.

Pistol knives (plainer and heavier types are the more desirable) £15 − £20.

Table forks (individual) £25 − £30; dessert £30 − £35.

1730-1775   Hanoverian without rat-tail pattern on spoon. Rat-tail replaced by a single or double drop at the junction of the bowl and handle. Frontal rib less pronounced. Stems turned up at the end.

Single spoons, table, £10 − £20; dessert, c.£30.

Half sets of six spoons, table, c.£100; dessert, c.£200.

Full sets of twelve, table, c.£250; dessert, c.£500.

Single forks, table, c.£20; dessert, c.£30.

King's pattern flatware service with modern knives.

Half sets of six, table, c.£300; dessert, c.£450.

Full sets of twelve, table, c.£750; dessert, c.£1,000.

1760-1800   Old English pattern (with shoulders). Long, slim, tapering stems. Forks become four-pronged. This is the first pattern for which complete services become available (i.e. with all pieces made by the same maker in the same year). Full services are rare. The value of services largely depends on the degree to which the service is complete and original; the greater the number of additions of other dates or makers the lesser the value. Old English without shoulders followed.

Complete services of twelve tablespoons, table forks, dessert spoons, dessert forks, teaspoons and serving pieces. £1,200 – £2,000.

Half sets of six, £500 – £750.

1760-1780   Onslow pattern. Distinctive scroll end cast separately and soldered on with a sleeved joint. Fluted bowls are a plus factor (add 15%). This is a rare pattern, mostly found with serving pieces and is extensively faked.

Single spoons, c.£20.

1770-1780   Old English feather-edged pattern. Flatware with a narrow border of diagonal cuts. This style of decoration relates to Old English patterns of the period up to 1780. It may also be found on flatware of a much later date, but in such cases it is a copy.

Individual spoons, table, c.£15.

Half sets of six, table, c.£120.

Full sets of twelve, table, c.£250.

Individual knives, table, c.£5 – £10.

Full sets of twelve knives, c.£150 – £200.

1790-1810   Old English pattern with beaded edge followed by reeded edge or thread style of decoration.

Complete services of twelve, £1,000 – £1,700.

Half sets of six, £450 – £700.

1805-1850   Fiddle pattern, fiddle thread pattern and fiddle and shell. Stems and handles shaped like the body of a fiddle; thread motif engraved on the borders of the stem. Single-struck pattern (mainly Scottish) has the threaded border on one side only and is less desirable (deduct 15-20%).

Georgian services of twelve settings, £1,500 – £2,000.

Half sets of six, £450 – £700.

Victorian sets of twelve, £900 – £1,200.

Victorian sets of six, £350 – £500.

1815-1830   Fiddle, thread and shell pattern. As above, but with the addition of a shell motif on the ends of the handles. Complete sets of twelve, £1,600 – £2,300. Half sets of six, £500 – £800.

1815-1840   Hour-glass and king's pattern. Similar to the fiddle pattern, but with a more pronounced waist, accentuated by scrollwork. The 'hour-glass' derives from the pattern design half-way down the handle. Shell motif concave. Complete sets of twelve, £1,500 – £1,900. Half sets of six, £450 – £700.

1840-1870   Queen's pattern. As above, but with the fluting on the shell motif convex (i.e. raised from the surface). Queen's pattern flatware is always rather heavier than king's

Old English thread service with modern knives (as is quite acceptable).

pattern. Tendency in queen's pattern towards more florid ornamentation of handles, bowls and sides of forks.
Complete sets of twelve, £1,200 – £1,800.
Half sets of six, £500 – £800.

1850-1914　Later silver flatware tended to repeat or modify existing patterns. The earlier the date of the hallmarks the more desirable the service. Decorative features are important factors. After the middle of the 19th century specialised services began to appear. Of these the following are the most important:
Fish services: sets of twelve knives and forks, plus fish servers, with silver or mother-of-pearl handles, £150 – £300.
Half sets, £50 – £120.
Ivory handles, if nicely carved, £120 – £200.
Half sets of six, £50 – £80.
Dessert services (first produced in the 18th century); usually gilt to resist the acidity in fruit. These very elaborate services seem to have been designed as wedding presents with little thought of practical usage. They are usually found in their original plush-lined cases. Plus factors are the inclusion of the more esoteric items, such as grape-scissors, ice-cream servers and sugar-scoops.
Complete sets in cases, £600 – £1,500.

1760-1800　Early Sheffield plate. Bowls struck from sheet metal; stems of drawn wire beaten to the desired shape and soldered to the bowl. Backs and fronts of forks stamped separately, filled with lead solder and joined together. Faint seam lines down sides. Prongs tipped with silver.
Individual spoons (depending on size), £5 – £20.
Forks, £5 – £12.

1800-1840　Later Sheffield plate. Bowls struck from dies soldered to stems die-struck from thick plated metal sheet; edges hammered to a fine bevel to conceal the exposed copper. Forks made with steel prongs which were then close-plated.
Individual spoons (depending on size), £3 – £10.
Forks, £3 – £7.

1840-1860　Early electroplate, by Dixon or Elkington is highly desirable, but there is little market for later services, or those by lesser manufacturers.

Fiddle thread pattern flatware service.

Complete electroplate services by Elkington, £150 — £350.
Services by Dixon, £120 — £250.

Points to look for

Decorative features such as scrollwork and lacy pattern on early types of flatware are rare and worth a hefty premium. Full hallmarking on flatware up to 1790 is very desirable. On early pieces marks should be widely spaced along the stem. Full hallmarking on early knife handles is rare. Much research remains to be done on the marks of the 'small-workers' (sub-contractors) who produced the handles for knives, sold by the cutlers who made the blades.

Provincial variations exist and are worth looking for. Distinctive modifications of standard patterns were produced in Scotland and Ireland and have generally been rather neglected till now. It is not advisable to mix English, Scottish and Irish pieces in making up a service of a particular period or pattern.

Pitfalls

The paramount problems concern additions to existing pieces or conversions. Since the presence of monograms and crests on the stems of early flatware enhances their value, it follows that these embellishments may have been added at a much later date. The vexed question is whether these subsequent additions were made in good faith after the original period of manufacture, but still well within the antique period, or whether they are recent additions to enhance the value to collectors. Care and not a little research may be necessary.

Conversions are a much more serious problem. Three-pronged forks are relatively rare and are probably the most faked object in English antique silver. The usual method of conversion is the removal of the bowl from a Hanoverian spoon and the substitution of prongs, but this can easily be detected by soldering joints at the base of the stem (absent in the genuine article). More insidious is the beating-up and re-cutting of the metal from the bowl of a spoon, into the prongs of a fork. In this method the tell-tale soldering joints are absent. However, the proportions of prongs to stem are invariably wrong. Cast copies of forks taken from an original can easily be detected as they lack the tensile qualities found in genuine, hand-forged forks. In a set of cast fakes the hallmarks will appear in identical positions, whereas in genuine forks these hand-struck marks would naturally vary from one to the other.

Similarly fiddle pattern flatware can be converted to the more desirable Old English pattern by filing away the shoulders at the base of the stem and trimming down the wide top. Old English flatware with hallmarks after 1800 should be regarded with caution, and examined carefully for file marks.

Museums

British Museum, London.
Fenton House, London.
Victoria and Albert Museum, London.
City Museum and Art Gallery, Birmingham.
Museum and Art Gallery, Brighton.
Museum and Art Gallery, Bootle.
Royal Scottish Museum, Edinburgh.

National Museum of Antiquities, Edinburgh.
Museum and Art Gallery, Glasgow.
City Museum, Hereford.
Temple Newsam House, Leeds.
Museum and Art Gallery, Leicester.
Wernher Collection, Luton Hoo.
Stapleford Park, Melton Mowbray.
Central Museum and Art Gallery, Northampton.
Salisbury and South Wiltshire Museum, Salisbury.
City Museum, Sheffield.
City Museum and Art Gallery, Stoke-on-Trent.

Reading List
Bailey, C.T.P. Knives and Forks. London.
Bury, Shirley. Victorian Electroplate. London, 1971.
Harris, Ian. The Price Guide to Antique Silver. Woodbridge, 1969.
Hayward, John F. English Cutlery. London, 1956.
Singleton, Raymond H. A Chronology of Cutlery. Sheffield, 1966.
Snodin, M. English Silver Spoons. London.

See also *Apostle Spoons, Caddy Spoons, Knives, Spoons, Tongs.*

FRENCH ART GLASS

This category includes all decorative glassware produced in France between about 1870 and the beginning of the Second World War. The principal names in this period are Emile Gallé, Maurice Marinot, Daum Frères, René Lalique, Eugène Rousseau, Ernest Léveillé and François Décorchemont. It became common practice at this time to sign all art glass and so identification is considerably facilitated.

Emile Gallé
1870s

was probably the single most important influence on French glass production from the 1870s up till his death in 1904. Certain categories of production can be defined. Gallé's first experiments were with enamelling on clear glass. His early period, the '70s and '80s, is often referred to as his transparent period, though, in fact, the Gallé factory continued to produce enamelled wares at least up to the time of Gallé's death.

Early enamelled pieces, often with Islamic or medieval decoration, including services of decanter and glasses. £100 – £500.

Later more commercial vases, frequently enamelled with insects and often on a pale amber tinted glass body. £100 – £250.

A pâte de verre vase by Gabriel Argy-Rousseau.

A Lalique vase decorated with a raised design of small scaly fish, 9ins. high, signed R. Lalique, France.

A pâte de verre bowl by Décorchemont.

Left: A good Lalique figure, made for the Paris Exhibition of 1925.

Small vases of commercial manufacture and with little decoration. £50 – £150.

Clair de Lune glass as a basis for enamelling gives an added value. This glass is characterised by an opalescent milky colouring that turns to a rich amber with the light shining through it.

1889   At the Paris Exhibition of this year Gallé introduced his Cameo glass; this was glass built up with layers of colour and cameo-cut to leave the design in relief in one or more colours against a contrasting ground. There are various types of Cameo glass and it is hard to define distinct categories. The most ordinary pieces, which form the bulk of the production from the Gallé factory both during the '90s and long after Gallé's death, were made by acid etching and are characterised by rather uninspired forms and colours and generally by their frosty surface. The finest pieces are carved entirely by hand in rich quality glass, often having the appearance of semi-precious stone and often with a free-form body.

Ordinary factory pieces, depending on size and visual appeal. £50 – £500.

Factory pieces with some degree of hand work. £125 – £800.

Fine carved pieces by Gallé himself or one of his close collaborators. £500 – £3,000.

1897   In this year Gallé introduced his *marqueterie-sur-verre* technique. This involved pressing pieces of coloured glass into the body of a vase while it was hot from the furnace. A complex piece would involve constant re-heatings and the operation was clearly a difficult one with a high risk of breakage. These vases were made in very limited editions, though no two are ever identical. Price would depend on the amount of work in a piece and its artistic success. £750 – £7,500.

late '90s –
1904

In this period, the most important of Gallé's creative career, he made a number of important vases using applied glass. The technique was similar to marqueterie but the decoration was built up in relief rather than rolled in level with the surface. Major pieces of applied work have sold at auction in Paris for over £10,000.

Verrerie Parlante. Gallé was a very literary artist, deeply involved in the work of his contemporary symbolist poets. Often he would conceive vases around a theme drawn from a line of verse, matching the decoration to the mood of the poetry. He would then engrave the line on the body of the vase. Also, on occasion he would inscribe a dedication to a friend on certain special pieces. All such engraved work is described as 'Verrerie Parlante' and the presence of such inscriptions always increases the value of a piece.

Mould-Blown Vases. These were made in the later period, after about 1895. Molten glass was blown into a pattern mould with high relief to the decoration. The most unusual of the mould-blown series was Gallé's elephant design. Upwards of £400.

Points to look for

Gallé glass was invariably signed. The most usual signature to be found on factory-produced pieces was a cameo signature in simulated handscript rising from left to right. Often pieces bear a star before the signature – this is an indication that the piece was made after Gallé's death in 1904. This is not to say, however, that the lack of a star is a guarantee that a piece was made before 1904. Unusual signatures include the engraved word *etude,* indicating that the piece is an incompleted or not entirely satisfactory experiment, the engraved word *fecit,* sometimes abbreviated, indicating that a piece was made by Gallé himself, or dates, which usually are an indication that the piece featured in a major exhibition in that year. Virtually all good carved pieces, marqueterie or applied pieces are signed Gallé in fine engraved script, often in elaborate spaghetti-like lettering. The inscriptions

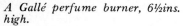

A Gallé perfume burner, 6½ins. high.　　　*A simple Maurice Marinot vase.*

'Modèle et Décor Déposés' or 'Cristallerie d'Emile Gallé à Nancy' are not unusual and it would be a mistake to read importance into them.

Other techniques used on occasion by Gallé included inclusions in the glass body of metallic foil and the application of carved or faceted glass cabochons. Occasionally Gallé had fine pieces mounted in silver by Paris *orfèvres*.

Daum Frères

The brothers Auguste (1853-1909) and Antonin (1864-1930) both joined their father's glass-making firm and in 1891 set up an independent glass-decorating workshop. They were greatly inspired by Emile Gallé and most of their work imitates techniques introduced by him.

Enamelled Wares. The Daum brothers produced a high porportion of enamelled ware including many vases and other pieces with snow scenes or forest views on mottled orange grounds, also many pieces with enamelled and gilt decoration on an etched ground. Prices in this category are generally not high. £50 – £100.

Cameo Glass. As with the Gallé factory the vast majority of glass produced was cameo, either acid-etched or more rarely wheel-carved. Daum's wheel carving tended to be broader than Gallé's, with larger facets, often looking like hand-hammering on silver. Price varies with quality. £50 – £750.

Later Cameo Glass. In the Art Deco period the Daum workshops turned their hand to heavy, one-colour, deep etched vases of geometric design. At their best these approach the work of Marinot in feeling. £50 – £500.

Pâte de Verre. The Daum workshops were probably the first to introduce pâte de verre on a commercial basis. These early examples usually bear the name Daum together with the name of the designer Amalric Walter. £150 – £500.

Other manufacturers

Glass, mostly in the manner of Gallé, was also produced by Muller Frères, Delatte, Arsall, Michel and Christian & Sohn of Meisenthal. Prices compare with those for more commercial Gallé pieces. Joseph Brocard made good enamelled glass contemporary with Gallé, Eugène Rousseau made cameo pieces even before Gallé, and their work, like that of another pioneer, Ernest Léveillé, is rare and much sought after.

Pâte de verre

A distinctive substance produced by the fusion at high temperature of glass paste with metallic oxides. It has a characteristic opaque quality and a matt, slightly frosty surface. The first to re-introduce the process was Henri Cros in the late 19th century. His work is very rare and shows the crudeness of an experimenter. His themes were classical. *Pâte de verre* rose to a peak of popularity in the '20s in the creations of Gabriel Argy-Rousseau and François Emile Décorchemont, and prices for the finest examples of their work have reached the £2,000 – £3,000 level. Early *pâte de verre* pieces by Albert Dammouse and Décorchemont are characterised by a totally opaque *matière,* an eggshell thinness and a wistful Art Nouveau decoration of trailing plants, usually in pastel colours. These pieces are very rare and none has appeared on the market in this country for several years.

Gabriel Argy-Rousseau was the great commercialiser of the process, producing ranges of vases, dishes, lamps and ornaments in many styles, from elaborate floral to strongly geometric. He experimented with the *matière* to achieve a fine, translucent body known as *pâte de cristal.* £50 – £2,500.

François Emile Decorchemont. His heavy, rich coloured Art Deco vases are the most sought after. All pieces bear an engraved date code on the underside and an impressed horseshoe shape signature. £400 – £3,000.

Amalric Walter. This artist started with the Daum brothers and then set up on his own. His best pieces are his vases and dishes, usually in shades of yellow and green modelled in full relief with lizards, frogs, chameleons or other creatures. £150 – £500.

René Lalique

Lalique started his career as a jeweller. He became possibly the finest jeweller of the Art Nouveau period and his speciality was the use of all kinds of enamelling. It was his interest in this vitreous substance that made him turn his attention to glass. Eventually his work as a jeweller was abandoned and he became the most important producer of commercial art glass in the period between the two world wars.

Cire Perdue Pieces. Lalique's first glass creations were made by the *cire perdue* process from wax models. They are characterised by a rough finish with evident signs of hand-modelling. Each piece was unique and these early experiments, dating from about 1910-15, are the most sought after of his glass creations. £1,000 upwards.

In the very early '20s Lalique opened a factory for the large-scale manufacture of glassware. His first commission had been for scent bottles for Coty, and Lalique continued to design highly inventive bottles which are keenly collected (and, in certain cases, still in production today). These sell for prices upwards of £30.

Opalescent Glass. Lalique created a type of glass that had a blue tint and became milky and opalescent if thickly moulded. This was used for every manner of domestic glassware in the '20s and '30s — vases, dishes, ashtrays, lampshades, decorative figures, etc. Prices depend on size, quality of design and rarity and range from about £20 — £30 for the most ordinary pieces to £300 — £400 for exceptional pieces.

Coloured Glass. Many of Lalique's designs were made in the usual opalescent or grey glass and also in rich coloured glass. This latter type is rarer and more desirable. The most usual colours are deep amber, burgundy red, blue, green and black. One also finds regular grey glass pieces enlivened with blue staining in the low relief.

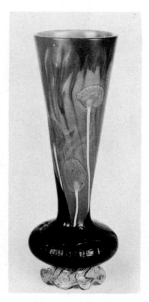

Left: An attractive Lalique glass pendant.

Right: A rare marqueterie - sur - verre vase by Emile Gallé.

Car Mascots. Lalique designed à splendid range of car mascots that have, in themselves, become very popular, with prices of over £500 for mint examples of the best designs.

Signatures. Virtually every piece of Lalique bears a factory mark, either an engraved or moulded signature in block letters or an engraved simulated handscript signature. It is a common mistake to assume that the presence of the handscript signature is an indication of superior quality. This is not so. All pieces that have a signature including the initial R. can be dated to the pre-World War II period, though not all pieces signed simply Lalique were necessarily made after the war.

Maurice Marinot

If Lalique has been mentioned in some detail at the expense of Maurice Marinot, this should not be taken as a reflection of their relative merits. Marinot was the more important artist in glass, but as his output was restricted to about 2,000 pieces in his working career it will suffice to say that prices of his glass are upwards of £1,500.

Museums

Bethnal Green Museum, London.
Victoria and Albert Museum, London.
Musée de l'École de Nancy, Nancy.
Musée des Arts Decoratifs, Paris.
Musée d'Arts et Métiers, Paris.
Corning Museum of Glass, New York.
Metropolitan Museum of Art, New York.
Hessisches Landesmuseum, Darmstadt.
Badisches Landesmuseum, Karlsruhe.
Staatliche Kunstsammlungen, Kassel.

Reading List

Bawelet, J. La Verrerie au France. Paris (undated).
Blount, B. and H. French Cameo Glass. Iowa, 1968.
Dermant, Janine Bloch. L'Art du Verre en France 1860-1914. Lausanne 1974.
Grover, Ray and Lee. Carved and Decorated European Art Glass. Rutland, Vt., 1970.
Hudig, F.W. Das Glas. Vienna, 1925.
Janneau, G. Modern Glass. New York, 1931.
Polak, Ada. Modern Glass. London, 1962.
Revi, Albert C. Nineteenth Century Glass. New York, 1959.
Rosenthal, L. La Verrerie Française depuis Cinquante Ans. Paris, 1927.

GAS-MASKS

Respirators giving protection to the eyes, nose and lungs against smoke and toxic fumes were developed from about 1860 for use in mines and factories. The main collecting interest, however, lies in gas-masks developed for military or civilian defence purposes. Interest in industrial respirators is mainly academic, although military masks were often modifications of industrial types. This aspect of militaria had its origins in the First World War, the earliest gas attacks dating from 1914 (French tear-gas raids) and April 1915 (German use of chlorine at Ypres). The earliest pad respirators were very primitive, but more sophisticated masks were developed as the technology of gas warfare advanced.

Date-lines

1916-1918   Period of primitive types and greatest variety, as gas-masks were rendered obsolete by developments in war gases. As many as eight types used by the British alone, from the Veil Respirator to the Small Box Respirator, Large Box or 'Tower' Respirator of 1918.

Left: Mark III 1924-30. Right: Mark V 1937-45. Crown Copyright.

Left: Civilian duty 1938-45. Right: Small child's respirator (Mickey Mouse). Crown Copyright.

	The French had similar complexity of types, but the Germans had two main types, of rubberised fabric (1916) or oiled leather (1917-18), the latter found with or without inner eye-guards.
1918-1938	Period of consolidation and improvements in existing designs. Thus British Mark III (1924), Mark IV (1931) and Mark V (1937) retained the basic features of the SBR (box filter and corrugated hose), but improved the face-piece and outlet valve. Box respirators (with hose and large canister) developed by United States, France, Russia, Poland, Belgium, Japan and Italy and these were still in use at the beginning of the Second World War. Germany alone scrapped the box respirator (1924-1931), and examples are consequently rare.
1936-1940	Development of special respirators for civilians or civil defence, including specialised masks for asthmatics, invalids, babies, young children. Civilian gas-masks developed primarily in Britain, Germany, U.S.A., Italy and Japan.
1940-1945	Light respirators, with filter screwed directly to the face-piece, pioneered by Germany in the First World War, adopted by most European countries and Japan. Filter attached centrally, opposite mouth or chin. British light respirator (1943) first to have filter attached at

212

side; subsequently adopted by U.S.A. and by several European countries in the post-war period.

Price Range

Main interest centres on the gas-masks of the two world wars. Those current in the inter-war period (e.g. the British Mark III and the German M-1924) are rare, but in little demand.

British Mark IV, Mark V (with hose and canister), £2 – £5.

British Light Respirator, Marks I, II or III, £1 – £3.

Civilian Duty Respirator, Civilian No. 4 Mark III, £2 – £4.50.

Small Child's Respirator (Mickey Mouse), £3 – £5.

Civilian No. 1, £1 – £2.50.

German M-31, S-35 military gas-masks with rubberised canvas, £6 – £12.

German G-42 (synthetic rubber face-piece), £5 – £8.

German civilian Volksgasmaske VM-37 (whole-head), £6 – £10.

German civilian VM-40 (with head-harness), £4 – £6.

French military types: M-2, A.R.S. or Fernez, £5 – £8.50.

Belgian, Dutch, Swiss, Danish, Swedish, Italian military, £6 – £10.

Left: Phenate hexamine (PH) helmet. Right: Phenate (P) helmet. Crown Copyright.

Italian civilian, £4 — £6.
Japanese civilian or military, £12 — £18.
American M-1, M-2, M-3 military, £8 — £12.
American M-9 (lightweight field protective mask), £3 — £6.
American naval diaphragm masks ND-1, 2, 3 or 4, £10 — £20.
ND-5 or M-17 (military or naval masks), £8 — £12.
American World War II civilian gas-mask, £3 — £5.
Russian, Polish or Czech gas-masks, £10 — £20.
World War I, German oiled leather face-piece, £15 — £25.
Ditto, rubberised canvas, 1916, £25 — £40.
British Helmet respirators P, PH, PHG types, £20 — £30.

Points to look for

Masks should be complete and filter canisters, outlet valves and harness should be intact. They are usually worth more (add 25-50%) when complete with original carrying cases and accessories (anti-dim compound, eye-shields, gas ointment, record cards, etc.). Perished or distorted face-pieces, broken or missing lenses, rusted filters: deduct 25-50%.

Pitfalls

Like other forms of militaria, gas-masks were usually clearly dated on all components. The only serious problem is the cannibalisation of parts from different respirators (i.e. face-pieces and filters of different masks brought together to produce a marketable specimen). This is particularly true of European examples which have a standard screw thread.

Museums

Imperial War Museum, London.
Science Museum, London.
Beamish Museum, Chester-le-Street.
Castle Museum, York.

Reading List — see *Militaria.*

GOSS CHINA

Term used rather loosely to denote any form of miniature white porcelain bearing an armorial crest, though strictly speaking it should apply only to those items bearing the marks of the Goss pottery. William Henry Goss founded the Falcon Pottery at Stoke-on-Trent in the late 1850s and for a quarter of a century produced the usual range of porcelain table wares and parian figures. In the early 1880s, however, the founder's son, Adolphus William Henry Goss, became a director and it was he, a heraldry enthusiast, who pioneered the miniature crested souvenirs. During 1887 Adolphus Goss obtained permission from the boroughs and cities of the United Kingdom to reproduce their coats of arms on pieces of miniature porcelain and the first of these souvenirs went into production the following year. A wide range of items was produced, covering almost every conceivable ceramic shape and style, and going back in time to the Greeks and Romans, cashing in on the popularity of archaeological excavations which were then topical. The objects were produced in plain white porcelain, decorated only by the armorial bearings of the British towns and cities. From the outset Goss only retailed these objects in the town whose crest was depicted, and immediately these souvenirs became immensely popular with the public who wanted a cheap memento of their visit. Goss china can be sub-divided according to period, type of object, decorative quality and markings.

Date-lines

1888-1914   'First Period' Goss. Objects marked on the base with W.H. GOSS and the falcon emblem of Goss Falcon

Three Goss cottages. Left to right: A Manx cottage, Shakespeare's House and Robert Burn's Cottage.

Bridlington quart measure. A pleasing little model, which is embossed 'E.R. 1601' on the side not shown in the photograph. Height 2ins.

Maltese vase 'A Canard', height 1¾ins.

	Pottery. Fine modelling, restrained enamelled colouring in armorial crests. Prices range from £2 to £20, depending on shape and the individual crest; rare pieces exist that would bring the price up to £200 and in one exceptional case to £500.
1914-1920	Miniature porcelain versions of guns, tanks, ships, aircraft, shells and other objects associated with the First World War. Prices range from £4 to £30, depending on the type of object reproduced (tanks are relatively common, while ships and despatch-riders are scarce). Most of these war souvenirs are crested as before; but examples which are additionally inscribed to commemorate a specific battle or event are worth much more.
1931-1934	'Second Period Goss'. Marked 'W.H. GOSS ENGLAND' up to 1936 when the firm was taken over by Cauldon Potteries; wider range of objects reproduced, included ancient pottery and folk objects, (shoes, clogs, etc.) of other countries. £2 – £5.
1936-1940	Original moulds were still used, although the quality of potting is poorer and the enamelled colours washed out by comparison with the earlier periods. £2 – £5.

216

Rival Firms

The spectacular success of the Goss company inspired others to emulate its wares. Firms which produced miniature souvenir china of the crested variety in the late 19th and early 20th century include Arcadian, Civic, Crescent, Florentine, Carlton, Grafton, Queens, Regency, Shelley and Swan and their wares are invariably marked fully on the base. In general these makes were inferior to Goss in quality of porcelain, moulding and decoration. The latter was often transfer-printed and lacks the distinctive raised surface of the Goss enamelled crests. Where crests were enamelled, the painting is usually coarse and the register inaccurate. Formerly little or no interest was shown in the Goss imitators, but with the rapid growth of interest in miniature china prices are beginning to rise. Prices for these makes are roughly half those for comparable Goss pieces of the middle period. Commemorative wares, with views of exhibitions all over the world, ranging from Chicago, 1893, to Auckland, 1913, are in the price range £2 – £5.

Points to look for

Goss produced a number of commemorative items for such events as the Golden and Diamond Jubilees of 1887-1897, the Silver Wedding of the Prince of Wales (1888), the Coronations of 1902 and 1911 and the death of Edward VII in 1910. These royal event souvenirs took the form of cups, saucers, mugs and beakers, with pictorial designs taking the place of the familiar crests. Early Goss miniatures bore a serial number, corresponding to the registered design numbers listed at the Patent Office. These numbers enable early pieces to be dated fairly accurately. This practice ceased in 1914 when the word 'Copyright' was substituted.

Museums

Art Gallery and Museum, Brighton.
Museum and Art Gallery, Derby.
Salisbury and South Wiltshire Museum, Salisbury.
City Museum and Art Gallery, Stoke-on-Trent.
Royal Tunbridge Wells Museum and Art Gallery.

Reading List

Galpin, John. Goss China. Portsmouth, 1972.
Vaughan, George. Goss for Collectors. Haslemere, 1974. The Goss Record. Haslemere, 1975. Goss and Crested China (monthly magazine).
Ward, Roland. The Price Guide to the Models of W.H. Goss. Woodbridge, 1975.

GRAMOPHONES

Instruments for reproducing sound, by transmitting the mechanical vibrations of a stylus in contact with a sinuous groove in a moving record. The term gramophone is now regarded as synonymous with the term phonograph and these words denote usage in Europe and America respectively. It is important to note, however, that prior to 1900 the terms were used side by side and then denoted two quite different types of machine. The principle of sound vibrations being picked up by a thin membrane was known to scientists early in the 19th century and was eventually utilised in the telephone, the microphone and the gramophone. In 1857 Leon Scott invented the Phonautograph which reproduced visually the pattern of sound waves, using a lever attached to the membrane and its free end moving against a rotating cylinder coated with soot. From visual to audible recording was a problem surmounted by Thomas Edison in 1876, whose phonograph recorded sounds by the membrane and lever method on to a tinfoil cylinder. The recording instrument could also be used to play back the sounds through the membrane, but the quality was poor and weak. In January 1877 Edison patented his invention, and all practical recording instruments and 'talking machines' date from that year.

Date-lines

1877-1888   Period of the earliest Edison phonographs. In the very earliest models the membrane is of parchment or gold-beater's skin, but by the end of the decade a thin glass plate had been substituted. Various improvements were made in the marker arm or stylus (originally steel and later sapphire). Indented tinfoil cylinders are exceedingly rare, as they were rapidly superseded by a brittle waxy material. Another important feature of the earliest models was the hand-cranked cylinder arm. £1,000 – £1,500.

1888 – 1900   'New Duplex' or 'Concert' phonographs by Edison. Main improvement was the use of a small electric motor to rotate the cylinder at an even speed. A plus factor in the older models is the fine screw adjustment of the stylus which had to be in the dead centre of the groove. £500 – £1,000.

1900-1910   Powerful triple-spring motor, wound up by hand, replaced the earlier electric motor. Circumference of wax cylinders increased from $6\frac{7}{8}$ to 15 inches. Amplifier horns mounted directly over the pick-up head. £250 – £500.

Other models of phonograph by Bell, Columbia, Tainter, Fleeming Jenkin, and Ewing, with modifications of the Edison system, using cylindrical records. Simple phonographs, taking records of either circumference. £300 – £600.

Compound phonographs (Columbia), with interchangeable rotating arm, capable of playing either $6\frac{7}{8}$ or 15 inch cylinders. £800 – £1,200.

Edison Home Phonograph, Model A, No. H124524 in green oak case (approx. 74 cylinders in carrying case), 1ft. 6ins. long, American, c.1901-04, with later additions.

1887-1897	Earliest gramophones, patented by Emile Berliner and using circular disc records. The earliest discs of vulcanised rubber with a galvano-plastic coating. Under-cutting of the grooves by the acid produced inaccurate results, but this problem was overcome by 1895 when shellac was adopted. Earliest Berliner gramophones had a metal diaphragm sound-box and hand-drive. £1,000 – £1,500.
1896-1900	Later Berliner gramophones had mechanical governing to regulate the speed of the hand-operated drive. £750 – £1,000.
1900-1905	Gramophones provided with clockwork motors. Celluloid diaphragms replaced metal, but were, in turn, superseded by mica diaphragms in 1902. These early gramophones were distinguished by relatively small, light horns attached directly to the sound-box above the pick-up stylus. £200 – £600.
1905-1910	Gramophones with very much larger horns connected by

A rare early Berliner gramophone c.1890.

a length of straight tubing, known as the tone arm, to the sound-box. The larger horn improved the volume and quality of sound, but was too heavy to be supported directly above the record. £150 – £400.

1910-1925   Tone arms designed as a tapering continuation of the horn, thus eliminating distortion. During this period there were many improvements in the construction of the cabinet and the horn. Value depends on the aesthetic qualities of these components, and the size of the instrument, the larger table models being more desirable. £30 – £300.

1920-1940   Horns inverted and placed within the body of the cabinet. The horn was regarded with disfavour by the public, hence this more compact arrangement. From the collector's viewpoint, however, these 'hornless' gramophones are very much less desirable. £10 – £25.

1925-1940   Earliest electric gramophones, substituting electric amplifiers for the horn.

1935   Earliest automatic changers introduced. Advent of the radiogramophone or radiogram, combining a wireless set with an electric gramophone. Very little interest has so far been shown in gramophones and radiograms from this date onward, apart from examples whose cabinets have a pronounced Art Deco appearance. Many of these pre-war models are still available in the price range £5 – £15.

Points to look for

The technical improvements in the horn gramophones and phonographs at the turn of the century, previously mentioned, superseded each other so rapidly that it is relatively easy to date these instruments. The majority will also carry a plate giving patent numbers and dates on which they were granted, and this also is a useful guide to the date. At present the chief interest lies in the early machines produced by the leading American and British companies. An area which is still re-

An early gramophone with horn.

latively unexplored concerns the early gramophones of European origin. France, Germany and Italy in particular produced many fine machines in the period 1900-1925 and these are currently undervalued.

Pitfalls

Very few as yet, since the collecting of gramophones is still in its infancy. The main point to watch out for is the alteration, modification or downright cannibalisation of instruments (e.g. the cabinet of one model forcibly married to the horn from another).

Museums

The Science Museum, London.
Beamish Museum, Chester-le-Street.
Royal Scottish Museum, Edinburgh.

Reading List

No books aimed at the collector have yet been produced.

HATPINS

Pins between six and ten inches in length (a few even up to twelve inches long), with ornamental heads, were fashionable from about 1880 till the end of the First World War, a period in which ladies' hats attained the ultimate in size and ungainliness and required several pins to anchor them firmly to the wearer's coiffure. The best and most interesting pins belong to this period, although less ornate examples have continued to be made down to the present day. The pins themselves vary

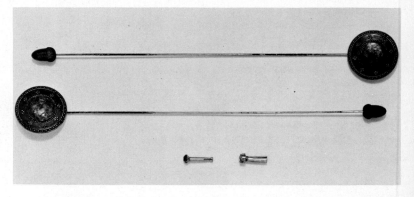

A pair of 1½in. diameter pressed silver headed hatpins. Central ¾in. diameter area is enamelled blue and green. Heads are hinged. Points are 'bayonet pointed' and marked 'PAT. 1679'.

considerably, from the simple steel shaft with a straight pointed end, to those with a flattened bayonet end, those with a spiral shaft, and those with a swivel joint attached to the head. Other refinements patented in the 1890s and early 20th century include various kinds of protectors, which were affixed to the point to protect the wearer. Hatpins were made all over Europe and also in America and the variety of decorative or novelty heads is infinite. A large group consists of pins with button heads and the decoration on these follows the same pattern as buttons (q.v.) of the corresponding period. Others have jewelled heads, using precious or semi-precious stones, pearls, glass paste, carved shell cameos, enamelling, amber, ivory, tortoiseshell and many other materials, usually set in silver and occasionally even in gold.

Price range

Prices of hatpins depend largely on materials and decorative treatment. Patent refinements, such as bayonet points, swivel heads,

A very fine pair of "thistle" headed silver hatpins in red box lined with royal blue velvet. The "thistles" are made of glass and one is amber coloured whilst the other is amethyst coloured. Hallmarked P & T, Birmingham 1911. 10ins. long pins.

screw-on protectors or spiral shafts, only marginally enhance the value of a hatpin.

Simple pins, with small plain glass, wooden or non-precious metal heads. 50p – £1.50.

More ornate pins in the same materials. £2 – £4.

Simple designs in silver, usually of the button variety. £2 – £6.

Ornate hallmarked silver hatpins, or novelty designs. £3 – £12.

Novelty pins incorporating a tiny peep-scope with scenic views. £10 – £20.

Jewelled hatpins in non-precious metals and stones. £3 – £5.

Jewelled hatpins in silver and semi-precious stones, pearls, etc. £7 – £40.

Pins with porcelain heads (including Satsuma porcelain). £3 – £10

Pins with metal regimental and private household livery buttons. £1 – £5.

More elaborate jewelled pins can cost from £50 to £200 each. A gold hatpin with pliqué-à-jour decoration by Lalique made £145 at Sotheby's in 1971 and would probably fetch substantially more today.

Pairs of jewelled or fancy hatpins rate 2-2½ times the price of singles. Sets of hatpins, especially those in their original cases or mounted on original cards, are worth a handsome premium. In addition there are sets of hatpins, with small belt buckles, garter clips, cravat and veil pins, all with uniform decoration, and these now rate a minimum of £10 a set for relatively simple designs.

Hatpin Stands

Associated with hatpins are the stands designed to accommodate them, and the majority of these were produced at the turn of the century. The most expensive of these were made of silver and consisted of an upright on a circular base, with a number of rings radiating from the top. Similar, though less expensive, models were made of silver-plated metal, brass, bronze or wood. Prices for these metal stands range from £5 to £25. More plentiful are the stands made of pottery or porcelain, and of these there are many varieties. Some are tall and balustroid, with a flattened top perforated like a pepperpot, so that the pins could be inserted and held upright. A simpler type had a tapering conical shape, with a large central hole at the top and smaller

Hatpin stands: a. China stand with pink glaze and flower; b. China stand with ornate flower design 5½ins. high; c. Cane-handled brass stand, 8½ins. high; d. Silver based stand, 4¾ins. high, hallmarked A & J.Z. Birmingham 1905; e. Silver based stand with blue cushion and amethyst coloured glass thistle, hallmarked A & LLᵒ Birmingham 1907; f. China stand with Bournemouth coat of arms, 5ins. high.

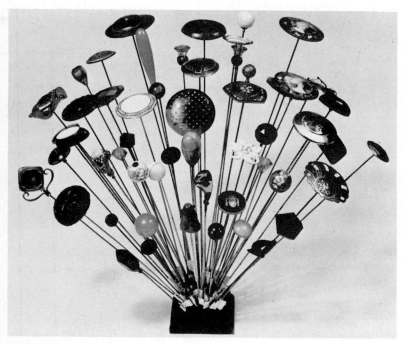

A selection of hatpins in a pincushion type display stand. The hatpin lengths vary up to 12ins. for the longest stems.

perforations round the circumference. This was a speciality of Goss (q.v.) and these may be found with different civic coats of arms in enamelled colours on their sides, and the words HAT PINS in gilt lettering near the top. Porcelain stands are worth from £1 to £7. An early 20th century patent stand has a cane handle top on a slender metal shank, with a perforated metal disc attached half way up its length. The shank terminates in a circular metal base with a narrow raised rim to hold the points of the pins in place. Such patent hatpin stands would be in the price range £4 – £10.

The commonest type of hatpin stand consisted of a large pin-cushion and these are found in a variety of shapes, with velvet or satin covers, occasionally decorated with beadwork. Prices vary from £2 to £6.

Museums

The Costume Museum, Bath.
The Costume Museum, Castle Howard, Yorkshire.
City Museum and Art Gallery, Birmingham.
Museum and Art Gallery, Leicester.
Castle Museum, York.

HELMETS & HEADGEAR

Top, left to right: French 1830 pattern Dragoon helmet; French 1845 pattern Dragoon helmet; 1873 pattern 6th Dragoon Guards; two mitre caps of the Prussian Guards. Bottom, left to right: 1873 pattern officer's helmet 1st Royal Dragoons; 1901 pattern officer's helmet 1st Royal Dragoons; 1901 pattern officer's helmet 7th Princess Royal's Dragoon Guards; 1847 pattern officer's helmet of the North Somerset Yeomanry; 1847 pattern officer's helmet of the 6th Dragoon Guards.

This is an enormous subject which can be broken down into such major categories as armour (morions, cabassets, bassinets and visored close-helmets of the 16th and 17th centuries), decorative regimental headgear (roughly from 1800 to 1914) and steel helmets of the two World Wars. Broadly speaking, these three major categories parallel developments in warfare. The armoured helmets of the late medieval period afforded protection against arrows, sword or pike thrusts and some measure of protection against the primitive firearms of the period. Helmets as a form of armour went out of fashion as firearms improved; as they ceased to give protection against bullets, there was little point in wearing such cumbersome headgear. There was a revival of helmets for decorative purposes at the beginning of the 19th century and this coincided with the growth of national armies and the development of the regimental system with its own strict codes of heraldry and insignia. The pageantry of these helmets died out with the First World War, but trench warfare gave new life to the helmet as a form of personal protection. Significantly the earliest British and French helmets were modelled on the sallets and bassinets of the late Middle Ages. Since then steel helmets have formed part of the standard equipment in every military force and in more recent years have been extended to ancillary forces, police, militia, fire services, etc., engaged on military or para-military service.

Date-lines

16th-17th centuries	Most elaborate type was the armet or closed helmet, associated with knights in armour, for both war and tournament. it was a close-fitting iron or steel shell with a movable visor and complete plating over the chin, ears and neck. It was joined to the rest of the armour by a gorget (q.v.). Armets vary considerably in complexity and decoration. £350 – £800.
1350-1475	Salade or sallet, an iron helmet with a shallow crown and a long brim or neck-guard, popular during the Hundred Years' War. Much plainer and simpler in construction than the armet but rare in good condition. £120 – £200.
1550-1650	Burgonet, a modified form of the armet, with a projecting brim shielding the eyes and a pronounced crest or comb. £450 – £750.
1520-1600	Morion, a much lighter helmet than the burgonet, much favoured by infantry. The typical shape has a high-domed crown surmounted by a comb, and a pointed brim fore and aft. £120 – £200.
1550-1600	Morion cabasset, a high-pointed helmet without the distinctive comb of the morion, but with a more or less curved and pointed brim. £90 – £120.
1600-1650	Cabasset, a simplified form of the morion cabasset with a high pointed crown but a much smaller brim. £75 – £120.
1600-1670	Spider burgonet, lobster-tail burgonet, modified forms of the burgonet with projecting neck-guards and metal bars protecting eyes, nose and chin. Much favoured by the Cromwellian forces. £150 – £200.

A close helmet probably by Anton Peffenhauser, c.1750/80.   *English lobster-tail helmet, c.1650.*

1640-1670   Pikeman's pot or iron hat, similar to the cabasset but with a lower, more rounded crown, sometimes fitted with an iron liner. £60 – £90.

Armoured headgear for use in warfare went out of fashion by about 1670, though decorative armets and morions survived for ceremonial purposes much later (cf. the Swiss Guard which wears decorative morions to this day). Various forms of hat, modified or based on contemporary civilian fashions, were worn by officers for much of the late 17th and 18th centuries. Leather or felt caps and hats were devised for ordinary soldiers, but it was not until the Napoleonic period (c.1800) that helmets came back into vogue. The most decorative helmets of the early 19th century were worn by cavalry and were made of burnished steel, brass or copper, often embellished with silver ornament. High-crowned cavalry helmets modelled on fanciful shapes associated with ancient Greece and Rome are in the price range from £300 to £600. Other types of 19th century helmet are listed below.

Tschapka or lance cap, based on the headgear worn by Polish cavalry and German Uhlans but eventually adopted by lancers in other European armies. Distinguished by a tall rectangular crest with a flat top. Other ranks' lance caps are from £80 to £120. Officers' tschapkas with helmet plates (insignia) in silver and gold are £400 – £800.

Pickelhaube or spiked helmet, adopted by Prussia in 1846, broke with the neo-classical traditions of the French-style cavalry helmets of the Napoleonic and subsequent periods. These helmets may be found with an all-metal construction, though this was later modified and sometimes incorporated a leather crown. Spiked helmets were worn by infantry, while artillerymen had helmets whose spike terminated in a ball. This type was eventually adopted by all German states prior to the establishment of the Empire in 1871, and spread to other armies, notably the British. German helmets were comparatively low and rounded, while British helmets were high and more pointed. German helmets have square or rounded visors, while British have pointed visors. £80 – £150 for all-metal helmets; spiked helmets of blue cloth construction were adopted in the British army in 1881 and continued to 1914, coinciding with the re-organisation of regiments by counties and offering a wide field to the collector of regimental insignia. £50 – £80. German pickelhaube of 1914-15 with *ersatz* cloth construction, were captured in vast quantities and kept as souvenirs. £10 – £20.

Albert helmets, introduced in 1861, with a horsehair plume replacing the classical crest of earlier types. Generally of all-metal construction, with high pointed crown and pointed visor. Earlier versions have the Royal coat of arms, while many later types have regimental helmet plates. This type of helmet went out of fashion for cavalry and yeomanry units at the end of the 19th century, though subsequently retained for dragoon guards and in service with the Household Brigade to this day. Present-day Household Cavalry helmets cost £200 to make, so prices of antique types are modest by comparison. Other ranks' helmets, £120 – £180; officers' helmets, £250 – £350.

The **busby** was a fur head-dress with cloth lining, plume-holder and plume, worn by hussars, some yeomanry units, Royal Horse Artillery and was the full-dress ceremonial headgear of the Royal Air Force up to 1939. £70 – £150.

The **bearskin,** now worn by Guards regiments, was formerly worn by officers in volunteer battalions. Good 19th century examples are still reasonably priced at £60 – £80.

The **shako** was a light infantry head-dress much favoured in the second half of the 19th century, with a circular flat top and a short square peak. £40 – £70.

The **pillbox** was similar to the shako, but without a peak and held in place by a chin-strap. Much favoured in more recent years as the head-dress of the Boys' Brigade, pre-war boy messengers of the Post Office and by hotel page-boys and bell-hops. Military pillboxes with identifiable insignia, £10 – £25; non-military types are of little interest.

Other military headgear of the late 19th century includes the glengarry (not confined to Scottish regiments, as it is today), the forage or side cap (remaining in use till superseded by the beret in World War II) and the short-lived Broderick cap, introduced at the turn of the century and based on the peakless flat-topped cap worn by other ranks of the German army. These caps should be complete with badges. £3 — £5.

Non-military helmets worn by police, gendarmerie and firemen. Good 19th century all-metal types, with helmet plates and crests, £35 — £80. Though less highly prized than their military counterparts, police and fire service head-dress have a steady following.

Steel helmets

The re-introduction of armoured head protection was brought about by the use of shrapnel and fragmentation grenades during World War I. The first steel helmets were adopted by the French in early 1915 and weighed 22 ounces. The extension of trench warfare meant that the head was much more vulnerable than the rest of the body, and armoured headgear was soon adopted by belligerents on both sides. The British helmet, modelled on the medieval sallet, was introduced in October 1915. In the German armies, steel helmets were issued to Stosstruppen (storm troops) in January 1916 and replaced the pickelhaube in other front line units later that year. French-pattern helmets had a comb and badge plate, German helmets had regimental insignia on decals at the sides, while British helmets were generally unmarked. French-style helmets were also worn by Belgian, Serbian, Rumanian and Italian forces and may be found with their respective insignia. British helmets were issued to Portuguese and American troops. First World War pattern helmets are in the price range from £10 to £20.

Distinctive national styles of steel helmet were evolved by many countries in the inter-war period, notably in Italy, Czechoslovakia, Spain, Japan and the Netherlands. Elsewhere, French, British or German patterns were used, or were manufactured under licence. Thus German-style helmets were used in the Baltic states, Finland and Eire, while British helmets were used in the United States prior to 1942 when the standard G.I. helmet with detachable liner was adopted. Russian troops used a spiked helmet based on the pickelhaube during the Russo-Finnish campaigns, but adopted a more streamlined form in 1942 and this has served as the basis for the many patterns developed by the Warsaw Pact countries since the war.

The German helmets of World War II were lighter and more streamlined than their 1916-18 counterparts, though World War I helmets may be found with Nazi decals and were issued to reserve formations, Volkssturm, etc. in the early part of the war. The greatest interest in World War II helmets centres on the German types, of which there were many variants and sub-types worn by the Wehrmacht (Army), Kriegsmarine (Navy), Luftwaffe (Air Force), Waffen-SS and SA units, and Reichsluftschutz (Civil Defence). Conversely helmets of

Officer's helmet of the Glasgow Yeomanry, c.1860.

A rare 1817 pattern officer's Roman style helmet of the Life Guards.

Czech, Polish, Austrian or Russian origin may be found with Nazi markings, reflecting the absorption of the military forces of occupied countries into the armies of the Third Reich. German helmets are in the price range £10 – £25.

Other steel helmets of the Second World War period: British, £1.50 – £3; Russian, £7 – £15; French, £4 – £8; Italian, £4 – £10; Japanese, £5 – £12: American, £6 – £15.

Specialist helmets (marines, naval gunners, tank crews, paratroops): add 50%.

Points to look for

Helmets should be complete and in good condition, complete with liners and chin-straps. Plus factors are original decals in good condition, especially on German, Waffen SS and Japanese naval helmets.

Pitfalls

German helmets in fibre glass are very common and have been produced in recent years as film props, but even they now change hands at £2.50 – £4 each. Beware of re-painted German helmets with faked decals, especially of SS, SA and other Nazi units which have regrettably acquired a glamour rating.

Museums – see under *Militaria*.

Reading List – see under *Militaria*.

HORSE BRASSES
AND
HARNESS

Brasses, partly for adornment and partly to ward off the evil eye, have been recorded from earliest times. Amulets of polished stones, iron, pewter and finally latten were popular in the Middle Ages and from this ancient custom was derived the practice of decorating horse harness with brasses. The earliest brasses were cut, chiselled, chased and hammered by hand from sheet latten and should show the marks of the hammer, especially on the reverse (or unpolished side). The earliest brasses which the collector is likely to encounter, however, date from the mid-19th century. Brasses are produced down to the present day, though the bulk of the modern examples (from about 1920 onwards) will never have been anywhere near a horse. The vogue for horse brasses as suitable decoration for cottage interiors developed in the 1930s and gathered momentum in the post-war years. As a result this medium is more beset with fakes, forgeries and reproductions than any other field of collectables.

An early brass depicting a war horse, made of hammered latten.

Four martingales. The left one, known as a flat brass martingle, is rather unusual, carefully balanced, beautifully backed with leather and has seen a lot of hard work in its time. The five brass martingale is genuine, but not exciting; these were thought to carry too many brasses. The third is a very interesting old martingale with four beautiful quality brasses mounted on thin scalloped leather.

Date-lines

16th century -1830

Brasses hammered by hand. Relatively heavy and tend to be two-dimensional in appearance. Stylised motifs are fairly simple, with infinite variations on traditional themes such as the sun, crescent moon, stars, concentric circles, hearts, clubs, diamonds and spades (playing-card symbols were especially favoured by gypsies). Other patterns were heraldic and included the floral emblems of the United Kingdom and animal figures taken from the crests of noble families in different districts.

Early brasses of this period and type are scarce. £10 – £40.

1830-1870

Cast brasses were fashionable. Still heavy, but with a more three-dimensional quality and can be identified by the cast marks on the reverse (though these and 'flashings' were often filed off). Casting techniques permitted a much wider variety of subjects and there was a craze for topical or commemorative brasses which continued to the end of the 19th century. Cast brasses with traditional motifs, heraldic designs and general decorative subjects. £5 – £12.

Cast brasses with commemorative inscriptions relating to the Golden or Diamond Jubilees of Queen Victoria, with or without her portrait. £12 – £25.

Cast brasses bearing other portraits (Disraeli, Lord Beaconsfield, Lord Randolph Churchill, Gladstone, the jockey Fred Archer, Joseph Chamberlain, etc.). £12 – £30 if old.

Commemorative brasses (County Shows, local events, R.S.P.C.A. and saddlers' advertising brasses). £7 – £25.

1870-1914

Brasses mass-produced by die-stamping from brass sheet. These later brasses were much lighter than the cast variety and more 'clean-cut' than the earlier hammered variety. Traditional motifs. £5 – £10.

Portrait brasses and commemorative brasses proliferated and seem to have been produced for every event and personality, both local and national. Brasses commemorating Derby winners were popular, as were the patriotic brasses at the time of the Boer War (1899-1902) and the Entente Cordiale of the Edwardian era. £8 – £20, depending on the importance of the subject.

19th century horse brasses all mounted on leather martihgale straps. They were mainly used by carters to decorate the horse when at agricultural shows or when taking wheat or barley to the miller or brewer.

Points to look for

Brasses incorporating a pottery or porcelain plaque are worth a good premium, though they date from the late 19th century only. Late 19th century brasses with enamel decoration are also worth looking for, and as many of these were of a commemorative nature, from the Diamond Jubilee of 1897 to the Treaty of Versailles in 1919, they are generally expensive, (£8 – £30). 19th century brasses designed as merit badges, awarded by the R.S.P.C.A. at horse shows, are usually worth a good premium, depending on the date and inscription.

Pitfalls

The current vogue for horse brasses as a form of interior decoration has stimulated an industry in reproductions, and this has risen to such a pitch that it has become difficult for the beginner to tell a genuine brass from a fake. Modern brasses usually follow the technique of 19th century brasses and are cheaply cast with two soft blodges of brass at the back. They tend to contain less brass than cast or hammered brasses of the earlier periods. The borderline between genuine brasses of the period 1870-1914 and modern reproductions is rather more subtle, but distinguishing features are signs of wear and degree of patina. Unfortunately wear, which on genuine brasses tends to appear at the lower edge of brasses, where they jingled against the harness as the horse moved, has been simulated on modern fakes by buffing, and patina has been reproduced artificially by pickling in acids. An added complication is the fact that many of the modern fakes have been cast and are dangerously like the early brasses in weight and thickness. It is very difficult to simulate both wear and patina accurately and these factors taken in conjunction should be considered very carefully.

Although brasses are often bought and sold singly they are worth much more as groups affixed to the original harness, including martingales, leading-reins, hame plates screwed into the bridle, face-pieces, loin-straps and the swinging part of the flyer. The number of brasses affixed to these pieces of harness varies. Thus four brasses were normal on a martingale for cart harness, but only three were used for plough harness; but sets of five, six or even more are occasionally found, though rare if genuine. Loin straps, on the other hand, usually have only one or two brasses. On martingales brasses were often mounted in matched sets, itself often a guide to genuineness. Genuine harness should show signs of wear in the right places: e.g. grooves on buckles where straps rub constantly, or rounded edges on leather. A common mistake with fakes is to use lightweight straps which would have been far too short in practice. Further problems include the replacement and substitution of brasses of later date on original harness, and this may have been done quite legitimately.

Other Harness Collectables
Though most attention has been focussed on brasses and martingales, other items are also worth noting. They include hame plates of nickel or brass, with a long rectangular base surmounted by a decorative feature, such as three horses, pair of horses and crown, often with a patriotic inscription and occasionally with dates. £20 – £50.

Bell flyers and plumes, attached to the poll strap terret and backty in plough harness or bridle, afford considerable variety. The more usual form is a circular mount with a brass attached to a swivel at the top and surmounted by an emblem (rose, crown, thistle, etc.). £5 – £20. Examples with compound or multiple swivels incorporating three or four small brasses are worth much more. £15 – £30.

The most elaborate examples incorporate bells and plumes and occasionally small brasses. Bell flyers were reserved for use in narrow lanes to warn other carters or for special occasions and are comparatively scarce. £10 – £40.

Museums
London Museum, London.
Victoria and Albert Museum, London.
Beamish Museum, Chester le Street.
Blaise Castle Folk Museum, Bristol.
National Army Museum, Camberley.
City Museum, Hereford.
Transport Museum, Hull.
Central Museum and Art Gallery, Northampton.
Pitt Rivers Museum, Oxford.
City Museum, Sheffield.
Somerset County Museum, Taunton.
Castle Museum, York.

Reading List
Hartfield, G. Horse Brasses. London, 1965.
Hughes, G. Bernard. Horse Brasses and Other Small Items for the Collector. London, 1962.
Richards, H.S. All About Horse Brasses. London, 1944.

INRO

Left: A very good example of the work of Shibata Zeshin, painter and lacquerer of the late 19th century.

Right: A rare sheath inro in gold and black lacquer by Shiomi Masarari.

Japanese for 'seal case', denoting small boxes or nests of boxes which were suspended from the *obi* (girdle) by a cord which was secured by the netsuke (q.v.) and used as a container for small objects, such as chops (seals), aromatic spices, medicines, tobacco and cosmetics. Twin cords passed through the sides of the boxes and were tied in a knot at the foot. A decorated bead *(ojime),* through which the cords slid, held the nest of boxes tightly closed at the top. Inro may be found with two to five compartments. The usual shape is a flattened oval in section with a rectangular form, slightly rounded at the corners. Other shapes include complete ovals, vases, cones and natural forms, the last-named being exceedingly rare. An inro in the shape of a mountain, with inlaid decoration of scenery and animals, fetched 2,400 guineas at auction in 1974. Inro originated in the late 15th century as small containers of simple form, but the characteristic shape and construction was well established in the early 16th century and continued with little variation until the late 19th century when the westernisation of dress (and the introduction of pockets) diminished the need for inro.

The majority of inro were made of wood covered in lacquer and are thus regarded as one of the principal media of the art of lacquer. Other materials, however, were occasionally used. Carved wood or ivory inro were produced by the craftsmen who made netsuke, and occasional examples will be found in bamboo or even types of fungi. Iron and other metal inro were made by the craftsmen who specialised in tsuba (q.v.) and other sword furniture, and these inro were patinated, inlaid and enamelled in the same manner as sword guards. A few inro were made of porcelain or pottery with deep glazes.

Date-lines

Late 16th-18th centuries .	Period of the finest lacquer inro. Shapes tend to be rounder and boxes smaller. Rather finicky detail characterises the decoration in 17th century inro.
Late 17th-early 18th centuries.	Inro often signed by masters and members of the various Schools.
Mid-18th-mid-19th centuries.	Inro becoming increasingly elaborate. The largest inro belong to this period and are relatively rare. Popularly known as wrestlers' inro, since they were much favoured by the rather flamboyant wrestling 'stars'.

Four attractive 19th century inro.

Late 18th-19th centuries. Main period of inro in carved wood, ivory, metal and pottery though lacquer predominant throughout.

Points to look for

Quality and variety of the lacquer are of paramount importance. Techniques such as flat lacquer, raised lacquer, carved or incised lacquer, addition of gold or silver dust, and inlays of base metals (pewter, copper, brass, bronze, iron) or precious metals (gold, silver), ivory, shell, mother-of-pearl, hardstones, porcelain and pottery indicate the variety which may be found. The more expensive inro are those which combine the greatest range of decorative techniques with mastery of detail and interesting or unusual motifs. Because they were produced to the order of nobles and court dignitaries, many inro were not signed by the maker out of deference to his patron. The presence of a signature by one of the outstanding masters of lacquer decoration would undoubtedly enhance its value; yet the record prices for inro in recent years have been paid for boxes which are unsigned, though attributed to the great masters on grounds of style, technique and decorative form. Inro which are positively attributed to such artists as Korin, Ritsuo and Tachibana Gyokuzan command very high prices (£1,000 – £2,500). These artists had extensive followings and their techniques were revived from time to time. Thus inro 'in the style of Korin' may range from £250 to £600. With such an enormous range of grounds and decorative treatments it is possible to identify inro and assign them to particular schools, if not specific artists. This is a very complex subject and the identification of schools, masters and styles is well documented (see **Reading List**).

The range of subjects depicted is also wide, and to a lesser extent this governs the desirability and value of inro: historical scenes and battles, poets and scholars of the Yoshiwara, gods and goddesses in dignified, humorous, grotesque or risqué situations; scenes from everyday life, both real, fanciful and whimsical; flowers, fishes, birds and animals

An inro in the manner of Ritsuo.

240

both real and mythological; abstract motifs and innumerable allusions from the **Ju** character to the **daikon** (in descending order of popularity). It must be stressed, however, that quality and craftsmanship are much more important than subject, and that the fashion for various subjects has fluctuated in the past. The minimum price for a three-case, late 19th century inro now seems to be about £150. Inro complete with matching ojime and netsuke are worth a premium.

Museums
See list under **Tsuba** and **Netsuke** and add:
Victoria and Albert Museum, London.
Walters Art Gallery, Baltimore.

Reading List
Boyer, M. Japanese lacquers in the Walters Art Gallery. Baltimore, Md., 1970.
Casal, U.A. Japanese Art Lacquers. Tokio, 1961.
Herberts, K. Oriental Lacquer Art and Technique. London, 1962.
Jahss, Melvin and Betty. Inro and other miniature forms of Japanese Lacquer Art. Tokio and London, 1970.
Joly, H.L. The Seymour-Trower Collection. London, 1913.
        The W.L. Behrens Collection.   London, 1913-14.
        Legend in Japanese Art.   London, 1908.
Joly, H.L. and Tomita, E. Japanese Art and Handicraft. London, 1916
Speiser, Prof. W. Lackkunst in Ostasien. Baden-Baden, 1965.
Stern, H.P. The Magnificent Three: Lacquer, Netsuke and Tsuba. New York, 1972.
Strange, E.F. Catalogue of Japanese Lacquer in the Victoria and Albert Museum. London, 1924.
Wrangham, E.A. Catalogue of Exhibition of Japanese Inro at the Ashmolean Museum. Oxford, 1972.
        Japanese Inro from the Collection of E.A. Wrangham. London, 1974.

JELLY MOULDS

The earliest record of jelly being served is at a feast of the Archbishop of York in 1466 although the practice of serving jellies and custards as a dessert was very unusual before the early 18th century. Individual silver moulds have been found with 17th century hallmarks, accompanied by silver saucers on to which the jellies were turned out — these may be mistaken for tea bowls and saucers. By 1750 the idea of forming them into unusual shapes had begun to develop and special moulds were produced from then onwards.

Moulds have been made in earthenware, stoneware and other types of pottery; in copper, Britannia metal, enamelled metal, tinware and glass. Age is not as important as the material and the type of mould though certain moulds can be dated stylistically.

Date-lines

1750-1770   Moulds of white salt-glazed stoneware in fairly simple shapes — stars, cogwheels, hemispheres, flat-topped ovals, etc. These early moulds were very small (often no more than an inch deep) and were intended for individual portions. £20 — £30.

1770-1830   Much larger moulds, designed for multiple servings. Still in salt-glazed stoneware, but the larger format permitted a much wider range of shapes. £15 — £30. Small moulds with very detailed decoration £3 — £10.

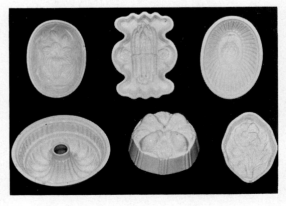

A group of 19th century white pottery jelly moulds. The lily (top left) is impressed Booths and the pineapple (top right) Wedgwood.

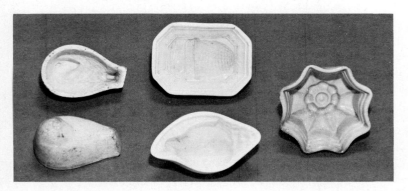

A group of miniature moulds; a pair of early 19th century partridges for savoury jellies; a late 18th century creamware beehive probably for honeycomb mould; a 19th century shell and an individual star-patterned mould.

1780-1820	Wedgwood Queensware moulds made in two parts, in the form of obelisks, pillars and wedges. Decorated and fluted interior piece was inserted into the liquid jelly When set the jelly was turned over, the outer mould removed, and the interior wedge used to enhance the decorative appearance of the jelly. The smaller moulds are most desirable. £100 — £150.
1785-1830	Moulds in pearlware, Leeds creamware and Liverpool pottery imitating Wedgwood, often with blue and white transfer-printed decoration on the insert. £25 — £50.
1830-onwards	Copper moulds, the interiors tinned to prevent verdigris poisoning. An infinite variety of shapes and sizes. Occasionally marked with maker's name or trademark, lozenge registration mark, etc. £10 — £25. Miniatures £3 — £4.
1830-1880	Britannia metal moulds, shapes similar to those in copper. Prices range from £5 to £30, those bearing the name of James Dixon of Sheffield being especially prized.
1835-1900	Stoneware moulds in many shapes (fruits, animals, birds, stars, geometric forms). Most potteries included them in their repertoire, though the specialists included Wedgwood, Copeland, Davenport, Booth and Minton. £2 — £10.
1850-1900	Bristol ware (a form of stoneware with a distinctively smooth glaze) or flint earthenware. £3 — £12.
1900-1940	Brown salt-glazed stoneware, often of European origin;

Left: Grimwade's 'shell' pattern mould, early 20th century. Right: Castellated mould in a fine but robust pottery by Shelley, probably 1930s.

	many different shapes and smooth interior glaze. £2 – £6.
1900-1935	Enamelled metal moulds; plain surfaces but wide range of shapes. £1 – £4.
1920-1940	Pottery moulds by Grimwade or Shelley. £1 – £5.
1935-1950	Glass moulds in traditional shapes, or animals in pressed or moulded glass of various tints. 50p – £3.

Points to look for

White salt-glazed stoneware and cream ware are always highly priced in comparison with later ware, and may be collected as a subject in their own right. Unusual shapes, especially realistic or detailed animals and birds, or a maker's mark will influence the price. Matching sets of moulds in graduated sizes or shapes are becoming scarce as many have been broken up and disposed of individually.

Whereas miniatures in creamware and pottery in general cost more than their larger counterparts, in copper the reverse applies. Because copper is bought as a decorative item as well as a collector's piece, the

Left to right: Back row, brown salt-glazed stoneware mould with shiny glaze inside, and two other 20th century moulds partly glazed in brown. Front, a glass hare and a tortoise, probably dating from the 1940s or 50s.

Copper jelly moulds of types to be found in retailers' catalogues of the late 19th century and often made earlier.

late 19th century moulds with intricate geometric designs, reflecting the light, tend to be as highly priced as earlier examples.

A few copper or ceramic moulds are still being produced, but in general plastics and aluminium have superseded traditional materials and lack their aesthetic appeal.

Museums

No museum collection specialising in this subject, though most include a few pottery or copper examples in their ceramic or metalwork sections. Rather more attention to the subject is given in the following museums:

Wedgwood Museum, Barlaston.
Beamish Open-Air Museum, Chester-le-Street.
English Museum of Country Life, Reading.

JETONS

French jetons. Left: late 14th or 15th century jeton of the French province of Dauphiné. Dolphin embowed, imitating coin types. Right: large jeton with a 14th century King on throne.

Coin-shaped discs, otherwise known as reckoning or casting counters; they gradually replaced coins on the counting or chequer board (thus Exchequer) which had been used for accountancy in England from some time in the 12th century.

During the 13th century the first jetons (so named in the sense of 'to push' as they were moved across the board to facilitate calculation in Roman numerals) were produced for the royal house in France. The use of these specially manufactured pieces spread to the French nobility, and by the end of the century the first English jetons appeared. Those used in official circles were modelled on the English sterling penny – in fact some were produced from the same punches as the coins but omitting the legend. There was also a variety of less easily identifiable types, including the larger module Wardrobe counters by the time of Edward III and Richard II. The metal most frequently used was latten (60 parts copper, 30 zinc, and 10 lead). Their value today is dependent, as with coins, on condition and rarity (£4 – £20 for English types).

Gold and silver coins were sometimes distributed as largesse, or made for the nobility's counting boards, and these could fetch up to £40 today.

The English series died out at the end of the 14th century and jetons produced by Tournai's copper industry were imported. Cruder and

Some 14th century English jeton obverses. A bishop's mitre (1) replaces the usual crown (5). (2) The Plantaganet badge of the Star and Crescent. (3) A fleur de lys between two birds, with typical Edward II border of pellets (4) Shield bearing the three lions of England. (6) Larger jeton of Richard II: bust of the Emperor Postumus. The legend in Lombardic lettering reads LE SOVDAM DE BABILONE.

French jetons of Louis XIV — child bust used from 1651 to 1654 and the periwigged portrait by Thomas Bernard in 1713 and 1715. In the centre is a reverse of 1678 showing the Sun King above a pile of weapons.

usually larger than the handsome French pieces on which they were modelled, the common varieties can still be bought for less than £1, while the earliest French rarities may cost nearly as much as the English. But there are also common French types for which not much should be paid.

A century later Nuremberg had become the centre of the jeton industry. The earliest types had jumbled legends, but later manufacturers names were compulsory. Of these the most prolific was Hans Krauwinckel who produced series of historical, mythological and biblical jetons with the collector in mind. Today one can pay £1.50 — £7 for better specimens in this series, but the extremely common stock-type should be purchased still for pence. The German families of Krauwinckel, Schultes and Laufer are complicated and many new names appeared later. The field demands extensive study. The Nuremberg stock jeton often features the city's Reichsapfel and is wafer-thin.

Meanwhile, in the Netherlands, some beautiful copper jetons were produced, chronicling the struggle against Spain. These can fetch from £3 — £15 today in top condition. This propaganda use was adopted in France by Louis XIV who established the *Academie des Inscriptions* to produce a series recording the triumphs and glories of his reign. These

German jetons. Bust of Mercury by Hans Krauwinckel, and a jeton by Wolf Laufer. Both these have the Nuremberg orb or Reichsapfel on the reverse.

were for use in Government offices, some in silver (£15 — £25 today perhaps) but the majority in latten or copper should not be more than £1.50 — £5. Many smaller variants of this series are to be found, often recognisable by the use of Rechen Pfennig or just R.(P.). These are very common and should be cheap, though those depicting our own monarchs are in great demand and likely to cost more.

But manual arithmetic was dying out and the French Revolution hastened the demise of the jeton. Thereafter Nuremberg adapted the industry to gaming. Although some of the pieces bear the word 'Jeton' or 'Spielmarke', they should not be confused with the true jeton used for reckoning. Gaming counters, often imitating gold in their brassiness, continued to be produced in great quantities. The imitation 'spade' guineas with the legend THE GOOD OLD DAYS are a typical English example. Like the 17th century Dutch jetons, these gaming counters sometimes had a political motive, such as the Cumberland Jack imitating the contemporary gold sovereign, produced in 1837 when the unpopular Duke of Cumberland succeeded under Salic Law to the throne of Hanover. There is a growing amount of interest in gaming counters, largely stimulated by the handsome dollar-sized counters struck by the Franklin Mint to replace the traditional silver dollars used in American casinos, but there is no hard and fast market as yet. Gaming counters may be picked up for as little as 10 pence, but expect to pay £1 — £3 for 19th century examples of unusual designs, or produced in silver.

Sets of silver gaming counters, complete with counter box, are scarce and are worth £30 — £50.

Reading List

Barnard, F.P. The Casting Counter and the Counting Board. London, 1916.
Berry, George. Medieval English Jetons. Spink, London, 1974.
Angus, Ian. Coins and Money Tokens. London, 1973.
Pullan, J.M. History of the Abacus.

Points to look for

Knives were being made in Sheffield from the 14th century at least (with references in Chaucer's *Canterbury Tales)* and makers' marks are known from the 15th century. The majority of collectable knives date from the 17th century and present a bewildering array of makers' punch marks, usually near the hilt. Names to look for include James Dixon, Rodgers, W. Edward Barnes, T. Read. Silver handles are not always fully hallmarked prior to about 1790, but usually bear the maker's initials. The appearance of engraved coats of arms on the handles is a plus factor. In the 19th century many popular styles of flatware such as King's pattern, Queen's pattern and Albert pattern had knives produced to go with them.

Pitfalls

Avoid, where possible, knives of which the blades are damaged or badly worn, unless the handles are particularly fine or ornate. Beware of new blades fitted to old handles — although this was done quite legitimately in historic times and would then be quite acceptable. It is generally accepted that 18th and 19th century silver-handled eating knives may be rebladed. Electroplated knives should be avoided altogether if they require replating, since this is very expensive if done properly. Another problem concerns blades (possibly of swords) which were broken and then ground down to convert them into knife blades. Again, this is acceptable if near contemporary to the knife handle, but be on guard for modern fakes. Silver-handled knives were made of very thin silver sheet which has a tendency to crack. Examine such handles carefully for dents and cracks or badly soldered repairs. Care should be taken in washing such knives, not to melt the resinous filling of the handles by the application of heat.

Reading List

Abels, Richard. Classic Bowie Knives. New York, 1967.
Himsworth, J.B. The Story of Cutlery. London, 1953.
Paterson, H.L. American Knives. New York, 1958.

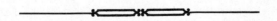

LACE

Top left: Reticella, Italian needlepoint. Late 16th century. Top right: Italian Cutwork, mid-16th century. Bottom: Genoese bobbin, early 17th century.

Various kinds of fine fabric distinguished by open work and created by plaiting numerous threads attached to individual bobbins (bobbin or pillow lace) or by working with a needle and a single thread (needlepoint lace). Both types of lace are known to have been produced in the Middle and Near East in pre-Christian times. The production of lace languished during the Dark Ages and was revived in medieval times. It attained its peak during the Italian Renaissance, when many of the styles in use to this day were formulated. Fine lace spread from Italy to France and Flanders in the 16th century and thence to England and Germany. The wearing of lace was in vogue from the 16th to the late-19th century, but hand-made lace gave way to machine-made lace from about 1840 onwards. Hand-made lace never quite died out, and has enjoyed a revival in recent years. Although avidly collected while it was fashionable, lace has been out of favour for many years and it is only within the past decade or so that serious collecting has been resuscitated. As a result, there is no hard and fast market for lace of various kinds though the following points may give some indication of current value. These comments are limited to the period for which examples of lace are available. Lace dating before the early 17th century is extremely rare, and virtually all of it now reposes in museum collections.

Date-lines

1600-1790 Zenith of European lace, with distinctive styles emanating from Italy (Point de Venise, Genoese and Milanese bobbin lace), the Low Countries (Brussels Point, Mechelin, Binche and Valenciennes, Point d'Angleterre). French lace attained its peak in the second half of the 17th century and continued till the outbreak of the Revolution. Distinctive styles include Point de France, Point d'Argentan and Point d'Alencon and Lille bobbin lace. In the late 18th century Chantilly became an important centre for the manufacture of Blonde lace, with a light mesh and floral sprays. English

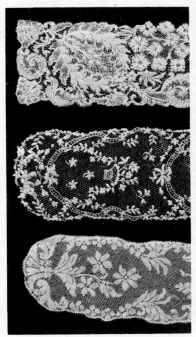

lace dates from the late 17th century (Honiton and Buckinghamshire), derived from Flemish laces. Drawn thread lace embroidered on fine muslin, was a German speciality (Dresden work), also known in Denmark as Tönder. Lace also made extensively in this period in Spain (Reticella) and Switzerland. Lace of this period is scarce and is now worth £15 – £25 per yard.

Small dress accessories (collars, cuffs, lappets) may cost from £25 – £60.

Larger items – christening shawls, aprons, babies' robes. £100 – £400.

18th century cap-lappets. Top to bottom: Point d'Angleterre, bobbin. Point d'Argentan, needlepoint. Valenciennes, bobbin.

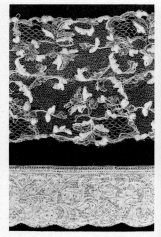

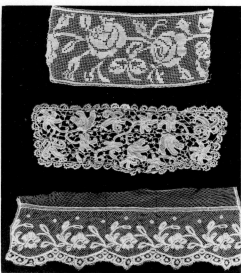

Above: Top. Buckingham-shire silk Blonde. Early 19th century (similar to 18th century). Bottom. Binche bobbin. Early 18th century.
Right: Top to bottom. Italian Filet. Darned net. Mid-19th century.
Irish crochet. Mid-19th century. Valenciennes bobbin. Mid-19th century.

1800-1900   Limp, semi-classical style, lacking the complicated frilled trimmings of the earlier period. Lace now softer and finer. Greater preference for bobbin lace (Flanders and English Midlands). Development of needlepoint and crochet lace in Ireland and the west of Scotland. Other forms include appliqué work and tambour (resembling darning). Embroidery on net also fashionable. Greater use of machine-made components, e.g. hand-worked motifs on machine-made net background. Individual sprigs joined with bridges made by needle or bobbin (guipures), a speciality of Brussels and Honiton. Mid-19th century lace generally more fussy and ostentatious. Fine flax thread gradually superseded by the much coarser cotton.

Prices for 19th century lace range from £1 to £10 a yard for trimmings, £15 – £40 for small dress accessories, and up to £50 for larger items.

Points to look for

The value of lace may vary considerably according to the precise style or locality of manufacture, together with unusual decorative

255

features. The subject is very complex and the reader is advised to consult books which illustrate the various styles in detail (see **Reading List**). The restoration, cleaning and maintenance of fine old lace is likewise a complicated subject, fully covered in the literature on the subject.

Pitfalls

The main problem confronting the collector is the distinction between hand-made and machine-made lace, the latter becoming increasingly common from 1820 onwards. The position is complicated by the fact that part of the fabric may have been machine-made while the more decorative patterns were worked by hand. However, even early machine-made lace (1820-1900) is attracting the attention of collectors, though there is no established market as yet. In this field decorative lace handkerchiefs of the 19th and early 20th centuries are worth looking for, especially if they have a souvenir or commemorative motif.

Museums

London Museum, London.
Victoria and Albert Museum, London.
Waddesdon Manor, Aylesbury.
City Museum and Art Gallery, Bristol.
Royal Scottish Museum, Edinburgh.
Museum and Art Gallery, Glasgow.
City Museum, Hereford.
Public Museum, Honiton.
Museum and Art Gallery, Leicester.
City Museum and Art Gallery, Nottingham.
Pitt River Museum, Oxford.
Salisbury and South Wiltshire Museum, Salisbury.
City Museum and Art Gallery, Stoke-on-Trent.
Elizabethan House, Totnes.
City Museum and Art Gallery, Worcester.
Art Gallery and Museum, High Wycombe.

Reading List

Caplin, J. The Lace Book. London, 1932.
Huetson, T.L. Lace and Bobbins A History and Collectors' Guide. Newton Abbot, 1973.
Jacksen, F.N. A History of Hand-made Lace. London, 1928.
Pollen, J.H. Seven Centuries of Old Lace. London, 1928.
Pond, Gabrielle. An Introduction to Lace. London, 1973.
Wardle, Patricia. Victorian Lace. London, 1968.

LACE BOBBINS

Bobbins used in the making of pillow lace, serving to identify each individual thread. The lace is made on pins placed on a pricked parchment pattern on a pillow. Between 20 and 500 different threads may be required to make a single piece of lace, and each of these will require its own distinctive bobbin. Pillow lace-making was introduced to England in the late 16th century by Huguenot refugees from France and the Low Countries.

Date-lines

16th century – 1800	Very early bobbins are of the greatest rarity. They were bulbous in shape with a long slender neck surmounted by a retaining knop. Mostly wood.
1800-1914	Bulbous shape replaced by a slim shaft, with a thinner neck and a double knop. Many different kinds of material used, in ascending order of scarcity — hardwoods, bone, pewter, brass, copper, ivory, glass. Enormous range of decoration (see *Types*). East Midlands bobbins had spangles attached to the lower end and these consisted of beads mainly, though carved shell cameos, coins, medalets and buttons have been recorded. Honiton bobbins are pointed at the lower end and have no spangles, since the Devon technique required the bobbin to be passed through the fabric.

Types

Leopard, Tiger, Butterfly: made of turned wood or bone inlaid with pewter, with spots, stripes and wing-shapes respectively.

Yak: a thick, heavy, turned wooden bobbin used for worsted lace — not to be confused with early bulbous varieties.

Baluster, Serrated: turned wooden or bone bobbins denoting styles of turned shank.

Old Maid: a thin, straight-sided bobbin with a plain turned shank.

Bitted: wood inlaid with contrasting wood or bone in various patterns.

Spliced: two different woods, or wood and bone, spliced together (often made from two broken bobbins).

Incised: bobbins with shanks decorated with grooves, dots and dashes, the incisions usually being coloured.

Wired: bobbins whose shanks are decorated with tightly bound brass or copper wire.

Wire and Bead: shanks decorated with tiny beads on wires set in grooves.

Trolley or Trailer: a fan bobbin with loose pewter rings or gingles. These bobbins are sometimes known as Henry VIII's wives, designated by the number of rings. Thus a one-ring bobbin is Catherine of Aragon and a six-ring bobbin is Catherine Parr. Complete sets of six are rare.

Mother-in-Babe: bobbin with a hollow shank containing a miniature bobbin.

Cow-in-Calf: bobbin in two sections which unscrew to reveal a miniature bobbin in the hollow interior.

Bird-cage: similar to Mother-in-Babe, but hollow compartment contains balls or beads.

Church Window: a hollow bobbin with narrow apertures, but not containing any miniature.

Mother-in-Twins, Mother-in-Triplets: similar to Mother-in-Babe, but containing two or three miniature bobbins.

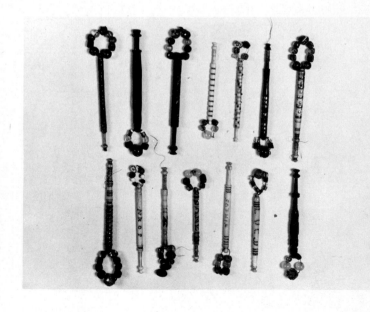

Selection of lace-maker's bobbins.

Price Range

Old Maids in turned wood	50p – £2
in metal (very rare)	£8 – £15
Decorative turned wooden bobbins (Leopard, Tiger, etc.)	£1 – £4
turned bone	£2 – £10
in metal, ivory or glass	£5 – £20
Bitted, Spliced, Wired, Wire and Bead bobbins	£3 – £15
Hollow bobbins (Mother-in-Babe, Bird-cage, Church Window)	£8 – £25
(Cow-in-Calf, Mother-in-Twins etc.)	£16 – £35
Trolley, Trailer, Henry VIII's Wives: single	£4 – £10
Sets of six	£30 – 75

Points to look for

Bobbins are greatly enhanced by the type and quality of the spangles. A traditional spangle consisted of nine beads – two small round clear glass beads, six square cut beads of clear or pink glass and a large central bead called a Venetian or Pompadour of glass with an enamel or coloured glass scroll round the middle. The incorporation of medalets (small medallions), coins, buttons of unusual design and carved cameo shells may double or treble the value of a bobbin.

Inscriptions on bobbins also add to the value, and these include Christian names (on wood, rare, £3 – bone £4 – £5), names of relatives such as My Dear Mother, Uncle George, Cousin Albert (add 70%), Christian and surnames (less popular). Spiral messages are usually 50% more valuable than straight ones. Any dated bobbin adds at least 100% to the value, and a bobbin inscribed with a name, date and name of the lace-making village would be worth about £30. Bobbins with two sets of names and dates, celebrating betrothal or marriage, or dates of birth and deaths are from £10 – £25, as are bobbins given as love tokens with expressions of affection, love knots etc. Slightly less valuable are bobbins with religious phrases, but ones with cryptograms would be slightly more. Bobbins inscribed with political or electioneering slogans are relatively scarce and their value depends on local associations. The most macabre bobbins of all are those bearing the names of convicted murderers and the date of their execution. It was apparently a custom for the relatives of murder victims to celebrate their execution by giving away lace bobbins inscribed with the murderer's name. No doubt a bobbin with thread wound round its neck resembled a man hanging from the gallows. These are rare and because of their high degree of human interest are quite valuable (£35 – £55).

It is important that the head of the bobbin is undamaged. No lace-maker will willingly work with a bobbin whose head is nicked or broken and such damage decreases the value of the more common varieties by 50% or more and the rarer types by at least 10%. Similarly, expanded pewter rotting away reduces value by half, and in wired and wire-beaded varieties a broken or loose wire is to be avoided.

Pitfalls

The revival in the craft of lace-making in recent years has resulted in the production of modern bobbins, but these are relatively plain and made of turned wood or even plastic substances. No doubt many of them will become collectable with the passage of time. The prevalent 19th century practice of repairing broken bobbins by splicing or dowelling parts from different bobbins means that hybrids are occasionally met with. As they served a genuine purpose, they should not be regarded as fakes, but are collectable in their own right. Wear and patination on shanks and knops are indications of age. Originally spangles were threaded with thin brass wire; re-threaded spangles are usually found with modern fuse wire. Lace bobbins are only now moving into the price range which would make them an attractive proposition to the faker or forger and this is not, as yet, a problem.

Museums

Luton Museum, Luton.
Aylesbury Museum.
London Museum, London.
Victoria and Albert Museum, London.
Art Gallery and Museum, Brighton.
Blaise Castle Folk Museum, Bristol.
Beamish Open Air Museum, Chester-le-Street.
Royal Scottish Museum, Edinburgh.
City Museum, Hereford.
Museum and Art Gallery, Leicester.
Central Museum and Art Gallery, Northampton.
Pitt Rivers Museum, Oxford.
Salisbury and South Wiltshire Museum, Salisbury.
City Museum, Sheffield.
City Museum and Art Gallery, Stoke-on-Trent.
Elizabethan House, Totnes.
Royal Tunbridge Wells Museum and Art Gallery.
Castle Museum, York.

Reading List

Huetson, T.L. Lace and Bobbins A History and Collectors' Guide. Newton Abbot 1973.

LOCOMOTIVE MODELS

Within a decade of the invention of the first practical steam locomotives model versions were being produced commercially as toys. These were the forerunners of a long line of model locomotives which continue to this day. Models may be divided into several categories (steam, clockwork or electrically operated) and fall into two broad divisions – commercially produced toys and accurate scale models. Different criteria of value apply in each case and they are discussed separately below.

Toy Locomotives

Clockwork models in tinplate date from about 1840, made in Germany, operating without rails, and generally in a circle, tied to a centre point. About 1870 American cast iron models and wagons began to be produced; these were made in two cast iron sections.

Small brass locomotives were also being marketed as toys by about 1840 and continued to be produced until they were superseded at the turn of the century by the first clockwork models. The earliest model engines had no tracks and were provided with serrated wheels to give them a better grip on the floor or carpet on which they ran. They were equipped with chubby pot boilers externally fired by methylated spirits. They were nicknamed Birmingham Dribblers because of their distressing propensity to leaking. They were almost invariably made from brass castings, with the lower part of the boiler only soldered to

American South Coast Pacific locomotive, c.1870, coal-fired and built to a scale of ¾in. to 1 foot.

the chassis; great care had to be taken in operating these engines to see that the boiler never ran dry, or else the heat would melt the solder and the boiler would disintegrate.

The earliest engines had four wheels (two small and two large), were driven by oscillating cylinders and had hand-rolled or soldered tubes with a seam up the side. These locomotives date between 1840 and 1850. £80 — £320.

After 1850 boiler tubes were drawn (machine-made and seamless). £60 — £500.

Early examples incorporating a tiny tender on two wheels — add £25 — £30.

By 1870 these engines were being mass-produced in the Birmingham area. Their value depends on the amount of brass taps and fittings, eye-appeal (some had flamboyant names like Ajax or Jupiter in a decorative panel or engraved on brass plates), and size (ranging from under 6 inches to about 18 inches). Other features which increase the value considerably include six main wheels instead of four, water tanks fitted on either side of the boiler, fixed cylinders instead of oscillating cylinders, proper valve gear (either slip eccentric valve gear or Stephenson's link motion). Prices for these engines, 1870-90, range from £50 — £80 for the smaller, simpler models, to £150 — £850. for the larger and more complex models.

1890-1910: More sophisticated models ('Iron Duke', 'Britannia', etc.) which were more realistic and modelled on contemporary locomotives. Size was tending to increase and models up to 24 inches long and 10 inches tall were being produced. After 1895 realism was heightened by the addition of litho transfers simulating the insignia of the railway companies. Also sold in construction kits, c.1900, so a greater variety of finish is found. £200 — £400.

Various firms in France and Germany (Radiguet, Ernst Planck, etc.) began mass-producing toy locomotives about 1890. These Continental versions largely avoided the brass castings of the earlier Birmingham Dribblers. German models have a brass plate inscribed 'D.R.G.N.', the emblem of the German Toy Federation. £40 — £1500.

After 1910 the model steam locomotive graduated into a more highly technical and sophisticated instrument (see below). Its place as a mass-produced toy was taken by the clockwork engines developed by Bassett-Lowke, Hornby, Lines Brothers and others. Clockwork locomotives originated about 1880 from Bing and Marklin of Germany; they were large, clumsy and cut from tinplate. The quality improved noticeably about 1900. The standardisation of the 0 gauge led to the widespread use of metal tracks and layouts. Price range for early clockwork models is £5 — £250 for the cruder varieties; £10 — £500 for

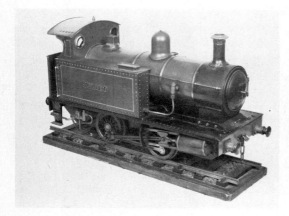

the more sophisticated types. Gauges 1 (1¾in.) and 2 (2in.) remained popular in the early 1900s (and still do today!) before the 0 gauge got under way, and complete layouts of these former gauges were sold.

From 1920 onwards there were enormous improvements in the manufacture of clockwork engines. Greater realism was imparted by the use of castings instead of die-stamped tinplate. The 00 gauge was first introduced in this country by a firm called "Trix" in the mid-'30s; Hornby (with "Doublo") and others followed after the Second World War. Price range of models 1920-40 much wider (£10 – £70), but the inclusion of rolling stock and accessories can increase the value even more.

Electric motors developed before the First World War, but not becoming common till 1920. Pre-1920 examples now rare (£40 – £80); later examples in the range £15 – £90.

Scale Models

Models which are accurately scaled down from real locomotives originated at the turn of the century, and were produced primarily for use in miniature railways which became a popular feature in large private gardens and of holiday resorts about that time. At the same time, however, even smaller scale models were being produced by Bassett Lowke, Henry Greenly and other model engineering companies as the hobby of railway modelling developed. The smaller models have always had an appeal to enthusiasts of complete railway layouts, as opposed to working steam models. The earliest scale models were powered by spirit boilers like the earlier toy locomotives, but by 1910 models were being produced which were coal fired. Running efficiency was sacrificed to accuracy of scale, but during the 1920s this trend was reversed and the size of boiler, grate and working parts gradually became exaggerated in relation to the over-all scale and so produced more satisfactory results. This was apparent in designs by L.B.S.C. (pen name), mainly before and just after the Second World War. Steam-working scale models range in size from about 24 inches to 6 feet and their price range is from £150 to £2,000, though exceptionally fine models have fetched prices up to £8,000. Accuracy and detail, quality of work and rarity of a particular model, are more important criteria than size or working condition in increasing value, though these factors are also important.

Scale models for display only and not intended as working models have also been produced since about 1890. They were intended originally as prototypes and display models in the offices of the railway companies, but latterly they have been produced for museum display. Display models are much rarer than working models and come on the market much less often. They are generally in the price range from £500 to £2,000.

Points to look for

The names found on 19th century models are those of the retailer rather than the manufacturer or individual model engineer, so they are not always relevant to the quality and hence the value of the model. Nevertheless names to watch for include Newton or Steven's Model Dockyard (mainly because they were among the earliest). Other names include Whitney, Clyde Model Dockyard, British Modelling and Electrical Co., Leeds Model Co., Lucas & Davis and H. Wiles. Continental names include Radiguet, Ernst Planck, Bing and Marklin. In the early toy locomotives plus factors are the number of funnels, taps, blow-off cocks, whistles and other extravagances, but care should be taken to see that these are original and not additions of a much more recent date. With the later scale models accuracy is all-important, down to the finish and paintwork of the original railway company.

Pitfalls

In working models the condition of the boiler is of paramount importance. Beware of rusted steel boilers, brass boilers with faulty seams, poorly made or soft-soldered copper boilers, missing parts and indifferent workmanship. It is advisable to obtain a boiler test certificate, or steam test, before steaming up. Old-style 'dribblers' have been revived in recent years (£40 – £80) but their brasswork is too bright and lacks the patina and wear found on genuine 19th century examples.

Other Models

In addition to models of railway engines, interest in other forms of steam locomotion have developed since 1900. Working scale models of tramways, traction engines and steam rollers follow the same general criteria as railway engines and are in the price range £150 — £10,750.

Museums

Museum of British Transport, London.
Science Museum, London.
Pendon Museum, Abingdon.
Tramways Museum, Crich, Derbyshire.
Bressingham Hall, Diss, Norfolk.
Museum of Science and Industry, Birmingham.
City Museum and Art Gallery, Bristol.
Beamish Museum, Chester-le-Street.
Museum and Art Gallery, Derby.
Museum of Childhood, Edinburgh.
Royal Scottish Museum, Edinburgh.
Museum and Art Gallery, Glasgow.
Museum of Transport, Glasgow.
Museum and Art Gallery, Leicester.
Museum of Transport and Technology, Leicester.
Science and Engineering Museum, Newcastle-upon-Tyne.
Norwich Museum, Norwich.
Locomotive Museum, Penrhyn Castle.
Salisbury and South Wiltshire Museum, Salisbury.
City Museum, Sheffield.
Staffordshire County Museum, Shugborough Hall, Stafford.
City Museum and Art Gallery, Stoke-on-Trent.
Industrial Museum, Swansea.
Swindon Museum.
Towyn Wharf Museum, Towyn.
Railway Museum, York.

Reading List

Flick, Pauline. Toys and Toy Museums. Shire Publications, Tring.

MAUCHLINE WARE

Name given to a distinctive type of wooden souvenir ware. Boxes and other small articles of sycamore wood were varnished and decorated with a transfer print, usually of scenery or some prominent landmark. The distinctive Mauchline ware takes its name from the Ayrshire town where the firm of A. and A. Smith were active from about 1820 till the Second World War. The Smiths originally quarried stone for razor strops and their earliest woodware consisted of the mounts and cases for razor hones. They soon extended their boxmaking business to include wooden snuff boxes (q.v.), a speciality of Laurencekirk, Alyth and other towns in eastern Scotland since the late 18th century. The Smiths opened a warehouse and showroom in Birmingham in 1829 and subsequently established a branch factory in that city. By the end of the 19th century the Smiths did for treen what Goss was doing for miniature porcelain. A wide range of articles, from snuff and stamp boxes to napkin rings, needle cases and string-holders, was decorated with tiny transfer prints of scenery from every part of the British Isles, and also overseas countries (such as the United States, India and Australia) which had close ties with Britain.

Group of Mauchline tartan ware; stamp boxes, rouge pot and needle case. Stamp boxes with varnished Penny Red stamp are worth 50% more than plain boxes.

The manufacture of souvenir treen reached its peak in the 1860s, when the Smiths were employing over 400 people and had absorbed their competitors. Thereafter the business declined steadily. A serious blow was the amalgamation of the Scottish thread manufacturers to form a single combine. Previously the various companies had vied with each other in selling cottons and silks in attractive Mauchline boxes. Various attempts were made to revive sales, by introducing such novelties as tartan boxes, lacquer boxes and fern ware (dealt with separately below). A fire at the Ayrshire works in 1933 seriously affected output and the outbreak of war in 1939 was soon followed by the closure of the firm.

Left: Princess Louise tartan egg. Right: Stuart tartan egg.

Date-lines

1821-1850	Earliest boxes decorated by hand with pen and ink, evolved from the earlier east coast tradition of hand-painted boxes in a style thought to have been introduced from Russia. £20 – £50.
1820-1840	Boxes decorated with tartan painted directly on to the wood by hand. Early tartan ware produced by several firms including the Smiths. £10 – £20.
	Tartan boxes with hand-painted portraits of Bonnie Prince Charlie, Robert Burns, etc. £25 – £40.

<table>
<tbody>
<tr><td>1840-1880</td><td>Later tartan ware, using a semi-mechanised process involving painting on to paper which was then glued to the wood. Joins concealed by gilding. Earliest tartans unidentified, but by 1850 the name of the clan was shown in gilt lettering. Pill-boxes, rouge pots, stamp boxes. £4 – £10.
Larger articles (blotters, darners, parasol handles). £7 – £20.</td></tr>
<tr><td>1850-1900</td><td>Transfer-printed wares. A very few earlier examples are known which can be dated to 1832-7, but these are rare (snuff boxes, razor strops). £25 – £30.
Wide range of articles decorated with black transfer prints. Prices depend on subject and local appeal, innate interest (e.g. early railway scenes) and date, though most subjects are relatively timeless. The commonest objects in Mauchline ware are small boxes, needle cases and threadwinders, £4 – £8, rulers, paper-knives, darners, pin-cushions, £7 – £15, larger items – tea-caddies, reel boxes, spill-holders, eggs (always highly prized) etc., £10 – £20.</td></tr>
</tbody>
</table>

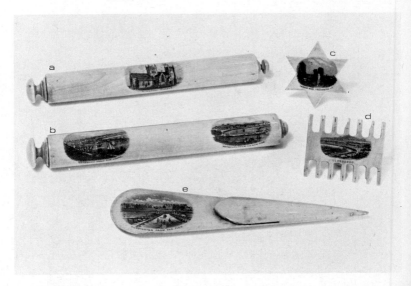

(a) Ruler (Wimborne Minster); (b) ruler (Weymouth from the North, and Weymouth from The New Pier); (c) star thread winder (Arched Rock, Freshwater, I.O.W.); (d) comb thread winder (Llandudno); (e) letter opener (Hunstanton from the Pier).

1900-1940	19th century scenes continued probably into the 1920s and are indistinguishable from the late-19th century items. A few more up-to-date subjects are known and these are highly prized. £10 – £25.
1870-1890	Imitation lacquer ware and Scoto-Russian niello ware – floral designs on a black or cream-lacquered ground. Mostly found on small boxes and miniature barrels but very rare and often in poor condition, as the gilding and lacquering were poor. £10 – £25.
1900-1930	Fern ware. Boxes, napkin rings, etc. decorated with ferns (gathered in the Isle of Arran), applied to wood and then varnished. £8 – £20.
	Later fern ware used paper with a simulated fern pattern and lacks the characteristically uneven surface left by real ferns. £2 – £5.

(a) Thimble case (Bournemouth Pier); (b) napkin ring (Malvern from the College Fields); (c) disc pin cushion (Old Mill on the Stock, Ambleside); (d) tubular pin cushion (Arched Rock, Freshwater); (e) seal box (Sandown Bay); (f) disc pin cushion (St. George's Church, Llandudno); (g) standing needle-case (Arched Rock, Freshwater).

1930-1940   Whitewood boxes sold undecorated for amateur artists to apply their own ornament. Value depends on the artistic skill lavished on them, but the majority are of no account.

Points to look for

Items with more than one picture are especially desirable. Pictures of landmarks in the United States, Canada, Australia or India are scarce and would at least double the value of an item. Apart from the types of object mentioned above, there are many other articles which can be grouped thematically — medical, cosmetic, domestic crafts, smoking accessories and writing materials — each of which has a following and this tends to boost prices. The most desirable items include money boxes in various novelty shapes, boxes with secret compartments or trick lids, tape measure holders and caskets, and miniature work boxes, especially if complete with such accessories as needle case, thimble, scissors and bobbins. Items with some commemorative aspect in their pictorial vignettes are worth a premium. These are often of a literary nature (e.g. Burns's centenaries in 1859 and 1896, Shakespeare's tercentenary, 1864).

Pitfalls

Because Mauchline ware was despised or neglected until relatively recently, there has been no incentive to fake or forge items. The only points of caution concern the distinction between hand-painted and transfer-printed wares, between tartan decoration applied direct to the wood and tartan-paper wares, and between genuine fern ware and the later fern-printed paper wares.

Museums

City Museum and Art Gallery, Birmingham.
The Manx Museum, Douglas, Isle of Man.
National Museum of Antiquities, Edinburgh.
Royal Scottish Museum, Edinburgh.
Art Gallery and Museum, Glasgow.
Burns Museum, Mauchline.

Reading List

Buist, John S. Mauchline Ware. Edinburgh, 1974.
Pinto, Edward H. Encyclopaedia and Social History of Treen and Other Wooden Bygones. London, 1969.
Pinto, Edward H. and Eva R. Tunbridge and Scottish Souvenir Woodware. London, 1970.

270

MEDALS & DECORATIONS

Awards primarily associated with naval or military service, though in more recent times also awarded to police and civilians. The interest of collectors is predominantly centred on awards to armed forces. Although medals can trace their ancestry back to the gold buttons of biblical times, in their present form they date from the mid-17th century. Earlier medals were quasi-commemorative and included the famous Armada Medal of 1588. A few medals in silver or gold were awarded to officers for distinguished service during the Civil War, but the first general issue of medals to all taking part in a particular action was in 1650 when Parliament conferred a medal on troops engaged in the Battle of Dunbar. This practice fell into abeyance during the 18th century, though there were several awards of a private or semi-official nature, and medals were also awarded by the Honourable East India Company to its troops.

The first general issue of medals to British forces took place in 1816 when a silver medal, fitted with an iron suspension ring, was awarded to all personnel taking part in the Battle of Waterloo. Belatedly an Army General Service Medal was instituted in 1847 and awarded to those taking part in the land campaigns of the French Revolutionary and Napoleonic Wars, 1793-1814, with about thirty campaign clasps denoting individual battles. Simultaneously a Naval General Service Medal was instituted, but differed in two major respects. Firstly it was awarded for naval service over a much longer period, spanning not only the Napoleonic period but more recent naval engagements in Greece and Syria; secondly it had a much larger number of clasps – some 231 covering battles and even individual boat actions. At one extreme the Naval G.S.M. with bar for Syria is relatively common; at the other the same medal with a bar for an obscure boat action of the Napoleonic period may only have been awarded to a handful of men, and there are several instances of bars which were never claimed at all. This extreme disparity has given rise to faking, transforming a common 'Syria' medal into a rare 'boat action' medal (see *Pitfalls*).

Subsequently silver medals were struck for many individual campaigns, and also a number of general service medals covering a certain area, with clasps awarded for minor expeditions and campaigns which were not sufficiently important to warrant a medal of their own. The major conflicts resulted in several medals. The second Boer War (1899-1902) had the Queen's and King's South Africa Medals, bearing the profiles of Queen Victoria and King Edward VII respectively, and the First World War resulted in the familiar medal group (nicknamed 'Pip, Squeak and Wilfred'), consisting of either the Mons Star or 1914-15 Medal, the British War Medal and the Victory Medal.

The campaigns of the inter-war period were covered by general service medals for the Navy, Army and Air Force and for service in India. The Second World War was covered by a number of bronze campaign stars, often combined with clasps, the Defence Medal and the War Medal (both in white metal). Subsequent campaigns have been covered by Army or Navy general service medals with bars for the appropriate campaign. A distinctive medal was awarded for Korea (1950-53), together with the U.N. medal.

Points to look for

The vast majority of British campaign and war medals, with the exception of those awarded during the Second World War, bear the number, rank, name and regiment or unit of the recipient, and herein lies the most important factor governing the value of the medal. This personal element largely transcends all other considerations. The authenticity of a named medal can be verified by reference to the medal rolls, preserved in the Public Record Office and most regimental museums. The relative rarity of a medal with a particular bar, or combination of bars, can be ascertained by reference to Gordon's *British Battles and Medals* (see *Reading List*) which gives the breakdown of awards in many actions where few medals or bars were awarded. Thus a medal may be worth £5 if awarded to a soldier serving in the principal regiment involved in a campaign; but £50 if awarded to a man serving in a unit from which only a handful of soldiers are known to have been seconded. Alternatively a medal awarded to a soldier whose regiment took part in the actual fighting of a battle will be worth much more than the same medal awarded to a man serving in a reserve unit which was not actually involved in the fighting.

Medals with clasps awarded for participation in subsequent engagements are invariably worth much more than the basic medal. The greater number of bars the more valuable the medal. For 19th century medals the value of a medal may be multiplied by the number of the bars (except the Boer War Queen's medal, in which case bars add 30-50% to the value). Rare bars, of course, may increase the value much more, out of all proportion. Thus the Naval G.S.M. with bar for Syria may be worth £20, but the same medal with a bar for a rare boat action may be worth £600. Again, relative value can only be determined by reference to all the circumstances of the award.

Combinations of medals, or medal groups, awarded to the same recipient, are worth much more than the aggregate value of the medals taken separately. Certain groups are fairly common, such as the First World War (£7 − £15) or the Boer War pair (£20 − £50, depending on number or combination of bars); but earlier groups escalate rapidly. The Indian Mutiny and Crimean medals as a pair would be worth £50 upwards (more if the Crimean Medal bore all four battle clasps). The inclusion of other medals (long service and good conduct, yeomanry, territorial or volunteer medals) also adds to the value of a group. Second World War medals were issued unnamed, but are often found as part of a group in which some of the other medals at least are named.

Condition and authenticity have a major bearing on valuations. The medal itself should be in first class condition, though one school of thought prefers a medal or group of medals obviously to have been worn, and with tatty ribbons cobbled by the wearer. They hold that the recipient treasured his medals and wore them frequently. The opposite school prefers medals in pristine state, with new ribbons, the old being easily replaced. These two points are naturally a matter of individual preference but, as always, do affect valuations.

Pitfalls

The chief problems are the faking of bars and the substitution of names on the medal rims. Examine the rivets closely for signs of file marks, soldering or any other form of tampering which might indicate that rare bars had been added to a medal to improve its value. Check the diameter of the medal with callipers. If the rim is at all uneven the medal may be suspect. A medal named to someone in a plentiful regiment, or to a non-combatant, may have had the original name erased by careful filing, and a new name, rank, number and regiment added. It is advisable to study one of the detailed handbooks concerning the naming of medals, as to the style of lettering and method of punching or engraving used (see *Reading List*).

Decorations

Awards for distinguished service are not usually rated as highly as gallantry awards. Exceptionally, breast stars and collar badges of orders involving the use of gold and precious stones have an aesthetic and intrinsic value which raises then above more mundane decorations. Unfortunately many bravery awards were issued unnamed and can often be authenticated only when they form part of a named medal group. Even when supported by the original citation or other supporting documentary evidence, care must be taken since it is not uncommon for recipients to purchase copies of their decorations. There is obviously a vast difference in the value of a genuine Victoria Cross (anything from £2,000 to £8,000) and an excellent copy (£2 − £5),

*A collection of military medals including the Victoria Cross, C.B., D.S.O.
and Crimean Campaign medals.*

1914-1918 medals. The Victory medal, D.F.C.,
General Service medal, Croix de Guerre Belgium,
Croix de Guerre France, 1914 Star, The Legion of
Honour, D.S.O., Order of Leopold.

even when the copy was purchased in good faith by the original
recipient.

The value of decorations, where their provenance can be
unquestionably established, will depend largely on the decoration itself,
whether awarded to an officer or an enlisted man, the circumstances of
the award, the campaign concerned and the personal details of the act
or acts of bravery. These factors are difficult to quantify, hence the
apparent discrepancies in the prices fetched by decorations in auction.

The addition of even relatively common decorations, such as the
Military Cross or the Military Medal to the First World War medal

group, invariably enhances its value very considerably (£25 – £40). The addition of bars for subsequent awards likewise rates a good premium.

Foreign Medals and Decorations
In most cases foreign campaign medals and decorations are not named to the recipient, and as records are either difficult to obtain or non-existent, it is seldom easy to verify these medal groups. Consequently interest in foreign medal groups is substantially less than British groups and their value is affected accordingly. Individual foreign medals and decorations can only be assessed on their innate merits and the relative scarcity of the medal. The most popular medals are also among the most plentiful – the medals and decorations of Nazi Germany. Excellent copies of the Iron Cross and Pour le Merite are plentiful, but there has been less incentive to forge the campaign medals of 1939-45 which range in value from £3 for a War Merit medal or a Russian campaign medal, to £20 for a Cross of Honour for the Spanish Campaign.

The value of other foreign medal groups depends largely on intrinsic value, aesthetic appeal, combination of unusual medals and decorations and association with some famous recipient. Such groups are best purchased with supporting documentation, preferably the original citations.

Museums – see **Militaria**

Reading List
Angus, Ian. Medals and Decorations. London, 1973.
Dorling, H.T. and Guille, F. Ribbons and Medals. London, 1974.
Gordan, L.L. British Battles and Medals. Aldershot, 1962.
Hieronymussen, Paul. Orders, Medals and Decorations. London, 1967.
Joslin, E.C. Standard Catalogue of British Orders, Decorations and Medals. London, 1972.
Mackay, James. Value in Coins and Medals. London, 1967.
Mericka, V. Orders and Decorations. London, 1967.
Neville, D.C. Medal Ribbons and Orders of Imperial Germany and Austria. London, 1974.
Poulsom, N.W. Catalogue of Campaign and Independence Medals. Newcastle (n.d.).
Purves, Alec A. Collecting Medals and Decorations. London, 1968.
Smyth, Sir John. The Story of the Victoria Cross. London, 1964.

MICROSCOPES

Optical instruments for viewing very small objects. Microscopes fall into two basic groups: (a) the simple microscope, consisting of a single lens, which may be made up of two or more elements in close proximity, and (b) the compound microscope, in which the magnified image formed by the primary (objective) lens is further magnified by an eye lens. The properties of simple microscopes (magnifying glasses) have been known for many centuries, and the magnifying power of a round flask of water was noted by Seneca more than eighteen hundred years ago. By the 17th century workers in glass could produce the small, deeply curved lenses needed for high magnification, and the development of simple and compound microscopes proceeded side by side. The credit for making the first powerful, simple microscopes (over 250 diameters magnification) goes to Antony Van Leeuwenhoek of Delft about 1660, but the inventor of the first compound microscope cannot be stated with any certainty. In 1665, Robert Hooke published *Micrographia*, and without prejudice to the claims of earlier pioneers, it was Hooke's work that set the compound microscope upon the road leading to the complex and precise instruments of today.

Date-lines

Pre-1700   Simple microscopes, mainly of brass, with fittings of wood and ivory. Compound microscopes, with cardboard tubes covered in leather or vellum, and turned hardwood mounts. Almost never found outside museums.

1700-1745   Simple microscopes include the screw barrel type, attributed to James Wilson, often in ivory, and the 'compass' microscope, in which one leg carried the lens in its mount, and the other leg takes the form of fine forceps, to carry the specimen. Compound microscopes are still of vellum-cardboard-wood construction, and were designed for the viewing of opaque specimens, until the appearance of the Culpeper design, about 1725. Culpeper, and Culpeper-type, microscopes have a circular base of turned wood, supporting the stage for the specimens on three turned legs, and above the stage, three further smaller turned legs carry the leather covered body tube. This design had a small concave mirror mounted on the base below the centre of the stage, to illuminate transparent specimens. Any sort of microscope of this period is very rare, and valuation must depend on careful and expert examination of each individual example.

1745-1800   About 1745 the first Cuff microscopes appeared. John Cuff produced a microscope constructed of brass in which the body tube and stage were overhung from a square brass column, allowing for easier handling of the specimen. These instruments are mounted on a square box-form base, fitted with a drawer for accessories. Examples signed by Cuff should make £800 – £1,400, depending on condition and completeness. Cuff-type microscopes by other makers, about 25% less. One effect of Cuff's work was that other makers turned to brass, and it is in this period that brass Culpeper-type microscopes are found. These usually have a square base, and a pyramidal case, reminiscent of a metronome. The tripod legs between the base and the stage are often in 'S' form. Other fine makers of this period are Adams, Martin, Dollond and Cary. Adams in particular produced some highly ornate work, and the period is characterised by fine workmanship, mechanical ingenuity, and optics often of high magnification, but poor image quality. Simple microscopes in this period vary little from the earlier period, but are not uncommon, and may often be picked up for a few pounds; they are a fruitful and little explored collectable.

1800-1900   This century saw the final flowering of English craftsmanship in brass, and immense advances in optical

Three 18th century microscropes, from left to right, by Cary, Culpeper and Geo. Adams.

Late 19th century English brass binoculars microscrope, 20ins. high

Andrew Ross, 1839.

design. The microscope evolved from being almost solely an instrument for the delectation of the dilettante, and became a serious scientific tool. Design became functional without, in the best examples, any loss of elegance. By about 1760, Dollond had produced large lenses for telescopes which were achromatic — lenses which did not break white light into colours, producing spectrum-fringed images — and as the 19th century

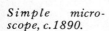
Simple microscope, c.1890.

progressed, it became possible to apply the same principles to the tiny lenses of microscope objectives. Selligue in France designed an achromatic microscope, which was made by Chevalier, while in England the full formulation of achromatism was arrived at by J.J. Lister, father of the famous surgeon. Lister's work was put into practice by Andrew Ross, the greatest of the English craftsman-opticians of the 19th century. Makers in this period are legion, and good ordinary compound microscopes may be expected to fetch from £50 – £200. However, fine examples of the work of Andrew Ross, Hugh Powell, and later in the century, Powell and Lealand, Thomas Ross (Andrew's son), Watson, Smith and Beck, and R. and J. Beck, can fetch considerably more, particularly when the microscope is cased as an outfit, with all its accessories.

Points to look for

Plus factors are fine decoration in 18th century microscopes, unusual technical features on 19th century examples. Names to watch for are Abrahams, Aronsberg, Beck, Lealand, Powell, Ross, Leitz and Zeiss. For Museums and Reading List – see *Scientific Instruments*.

Mid-19th century brass binocular microscope by Hugh Powell of London, 18½ins. high.

A brass microscope by W. Watson & Sons Ltd., London.

MILITARIA AND NAVALIA

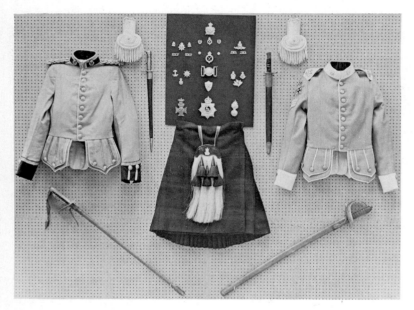

Items of militaria.

Generic terms for anything collectable associated with military or naval forces, but more specifically limited to items of equipment and miscellaneous pieces of uniform. The collecting of militaria falls into two main forms, either concentrating on the assemblage of every item connected with one particular army or period, with the aim of building up a complete set of uniforms and accoutrements for a typical soldier or sailor of a given period; or concentrating on a specific item of equipment and collecting every kind and variation of it regardless of period or country of origin.

Certain categories of militaria are more fashionable than others, or are more capable of study according to their subject, and these are dealt with separately in this book. On the other hand, most collectors of militaria prefer to limit their interests to the equipment associated with a single army or period. In the latter case, certain armies and periods are more popular than others. Operating on the principle that the vanquished are always more interesting, the fashion in militaria has so far concentrated largely on the relics of Nazi Germany, with the equipment and uniforms of the Confederate States of America a close second. The bulk of the more specialised literature (see **Reading List**) is devoted to these two periods. Trailing behind in popularity come the militaria associated with Imperial Germany (mainly 1914-18), Japan (mostly fashionable in the United States), Italy, Britain and the United States.

Availability of Material

Availability of material to a large extent governs not only the interest in, but also the demand for militaria. Thus it follows that the strongest interest in Britain, outside Nazi relics, should be in British militaria, since that is the material which should be most readily available through surplus stores. Curiously enough, this is not always necessarily true, on account of the thriving industry in the export of surplus military equipment. Thus many items of British equipment are more easily available in the United States. Former Nazi equipment is difficult to obtain in Germany itself, for fairly obvious reasons, but is available in some quantity in such countries as Belgium and Norway, whose military forces were re-equipped after the Second World War with captured German equipment. A fertile source of the more exotic forms of militaria, including badges and insignia, lies in countries to which the victors in various wars returned home with their trophies and souvenirs. This explains why interest in Nazi militaria is so strong in Britain, or Japanese equipment in the United States.

Scope of Militaria

The scope of militaria and navalia is almost endless. Most collectors, however, concentrate on completing the uniform and personal equipment of a single soldier or sailor and this, on average, comprises cap, steel helmet, tunic, breeches or trousers, boots, anklets or gaiters, greatcoat, packs, belts, straps and pouches, bandolier, gas-mask, water bottle and bayonet frog. These may be termed the bare essentials or external items. Taking it a stage further the collector will try to acquire the minor items, including regulation footwear and underwear, eating irons, mess tins, field dressings, identity discs and cleaning equipment. Under the heading of military ephemera come pay books and manuals, warrants, commissions, passes, invasion money and military payment vouchers. Cloth and metal badges of rank, regimental or formation insignia, medals and medal ribbons, brassards, armbands, cuff titles and hat bands, aiguillettes, lanyards and epaulettes, sashes and gorgets comprise the more decorative items of military apparel and all of them are collectable, either as a class by themselves or as part of a particular uniform.

Among the 'non-personal' items of militaria and navalia which are collected in association with the equipment of a particular formation, may be mentioned bayonets, firearms, grenades, trench-knives, trenching tools, trench periscopes, range-finders, field telephones, wireless equipment, compasses and binoculars.

Points to look for

Most items of militaria and navalia are clearly marked (often on each

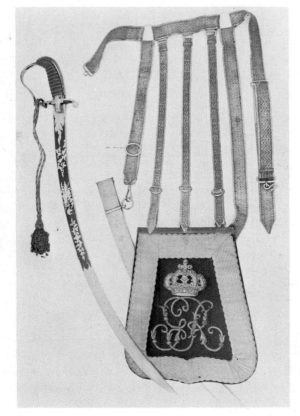

A full dress sabretache bearing large bullion Hanoverian crown and an officer's 1796 pattern cavalry sword.

component) with the names or initials of manufacturers, government emblems, serial numbers, mark numbers and dates. British and American equipment usually also bears a lot number, denoting the batch of production or issue, while German equipment bears the eagle, swastika and *Waffen Amt* (equipment office) number. Similar markings are to be found on the equipment of other armed forces, which enable the collector to identify and date material accurately. There are, of course, many apparent anomalies, such as 1918 pattern Imperial German helmets with Nazi *Waffen Amt* markings, French helmets with Italian markings (1918) or, Czechoslovak gas-masks with Nazi or French markings, but the collector will usually find that there is a very good historical reason, which merely adds to the interest (and value) of such items.

Pitfalls

Although militaria is a hobby of thirty years' standing it is still young enough to have avoided the attention of the faker or forger, except in certain clearly defined areas, where demand long ago outstripped supply. Most of the uniforms and many of the helmets relating to the Nazi period, now on the market are not original, but were produced at some time or other as film props. The helmets can be readily identified, since the majority of them are made of light fibre glass, unlike the steel of the originals, but the uniforms and caps are more difficult to detect. Similarly German medals have been reproduced. A close examination will reveal whether they have been struck (original) or cast (fake), the latter also being slightly smaller in overall dimensions. Many military badges and buttons have been re-struck from original dies, purely for sale to collectors, and are virtually impossible to detect, though genuine originals will usually have some signs of patina or wear.

Museums

Imperial War Museum, London.
National Army Museum, London.
National Maritime Museum, London.
Scottish United Services Museum, Edinburgh Castle.
The Castle Museum, York.
A full list of British regimental museums appear as an appendix to *Militaria* by Frederick Wilkinson.
For worldwide museums, consult *Directory of Museums of Arms and Military History* (1970) published in Copenhagen by the International Association of Arms and Military History.

Reading List

Barnes, R.M. History of Regiments and Uniforms of the British Army. London, 1957. Military Uniforms of Britain and the Empire. London, 1960.

Blakeslee, F. Army Uniforms of the World. Hartford, Conn., 1919. Uniforms of the World. New York, 1929.

Carman, W.Y. Indian Army Uniforms. London, 1968. British Military Uniforms from Contemporary Pictures. London, 1968.

Coggins, Jack. Arms and Equipment of the Civil War. New York, 1969.

Funken, Liliane and Fred. Arms and Uniforms. (5 volumes) London, 1973-75.

Harwell, R. Uniforms and Dress of the Army and Navy of the Confederate States. Philadelphia, 1960.

Hyatt, S. Uniforms and Insignia of the Third Reich. New York, 1962.

Irlam, D. Ranks and Uniforms of the German Army, Navy and Air Force. London, 1939.

Johnson, A.C. Chats on Old Military Curios. London, 1915.

Lachouque, W. and Brown, A.S. Anatomy of Glory. London, 1962.

Lawson, C.P. History of Uniforms of the British Army. (5 volumes) London, 1940-67.

Mollo, J. Uniforms of the Royal Navy. London, 1965.

Martin, P. European Military Uniforms. London, 1968. Military Costume. London, 1967.

Parkyn, M. Shoulder Belt Plates and Buttons. London, 1956.

Smitherman, P. Cavalry Uniforms of the British Army. London, 1962. Infantry Uniforms of the British Army. London, 1965. Uniforms of Royal Artillery. London, 1966. Uniforms of the Scottish Regiments. London, 1962. Uniforms of the Yeomanry Regiments. London, 1967.

Wilkinson, Frederick. Antique Arms and Armour. London, 1972. Battle Dress. London, 1970. Militaria. London, 1969.

See also *Aeronautica, Badges, Buttons, Gas-masks, Helmets and Headgear, Medals and Decorations, Model Soldiers, Weapons.*

MIRRORS

Silvered looking-glasses were imported from the Continent until the late 17th century and were extremely expensive. English mirrors date from 1665 when the Duke of Buckingham established a glassworks at Vauxhall, London. The earliest English mirrors are relatively small, owing to the problems of producing plate glass without surface distortion, though several plates could be joined together to make multiple mirrors for stately homes. Mirrors vary enormously in size, shape and purpose. Age itself is of little importance in assessing the value of a mirror, since the bulk of the value lies in the frame and not the glass itself. Consequently the various types of mirror and their decorative styles are discussed below according to purpose rather than date. Within each group, however, the variations are described in chronological order.

Girandoles or Wall Mirrors

The earliest type collectable is the cushion type which appeared about 1700. In its commonest form this plain rectangular or square mirror had a pine frame veneered with walnut. By 1710 these mirrors were being bevelled and often shaped with a rounded top. £200 – £450.

More elaborate mirrors of the late 17th century and early 18th century were decorated in the Dutch manner, with marquetry borders decorated with floral or foliate motifs. £800 – £2,500.

Verre églomisé with good blue borders, 1680-1710. The more elaborate examples of the Queen Anne period had a semicircular carved and gilded cresting. Value depends on the degree of intricacy of carving in the crested hood (though many mirrors of this type have lost their crest). £400 – £2,000.

During the 18th century frames became increasingly elaborate. Those with highly ornate carved wood frames, gilded and burnished, are now very expensive. £400 – £1,000+.

Frames made of pine with a polished walnut veneered surface, enriched with carved wood, gilded and burnished. Carved gilt strip inserted between the walnut and the glass for extra decorative effect. The larger and more decorative the better. £300 – £1,000.

Frames of gesso (plaster of Paris, carved and gilded) in low relief. £200 – £450.

Mahogany frames decorated with giltwood carving, popular from about 1730, and usually in extravagant rococo styles. Tops straight with rounded corners (less desirable). Tops decorated with broken pediments, or swan's neck pediments (more desirable). Elaborately crested tops, with C and S scrolls in the borders, foliage and animal motifs. Value depends on the quality of the carving and gilding. £450 – £1,500.

More formal, though delicately symmetrical, forms, reflecting the Neo-Classicism of the late 18th century. Comparatively plain mirrors with oval frames, embellished with classical motifs (Grecian urns, acanthus leaves, rams' heads, griffons, garlands and cupids). Generally the simpler motifs are in gilt or painted wood. £100 – £250.

Frames of plaster composition on wire, carved and gilded in Neo-Classical style. £250 – £800. Condition very important as re-gilding costs £100 – £200.

Mirrors produced during the Regency period fall into two broad styles. Circular mirrors with a convex surface were framed in giltwood with restrained decoration. £50 – £150.

Similar mirrors surmounted by an eagle often with balls in the concave moulding (a fashionable device at that time) are highly desirable because of their American appeal and rate £100 – £250.

The other main Regency type is rectangular with a decorative panel at the top, often in a combination of carved giltwood and composition material. Other forms of decoration include a brass lattice work grille or Wedgwood jasperware inset plaques. Mirrors of this type range in quality and decorative appeal. £60 – £200. But a good Wedgwood plaque mould increases the price above this level.

Similar mirrors with a glass painting in the top panel are very desirable. £100 – £250.

Victorian girandoles may be found in circular, oval or oblong forms, with giltwood or carved gilt and ebonised frames but normally plaster. Value depends on the quality, restraint in decoration, condition and size. It must not be too big. £50 – £250.

Early 19th century European girandoles with irregular shapes surrounded by lavishly carved giltwood frames were sometimes produced in pairs. Singles £250 – £400; pairs £600 – £1,000.

Late 19th century wall mirrors with wooden frames inset with repoussé copper, pewter and enamel decoration in the Art Nouveau manner. £50 – £120.

Toilet Mirrors or Dressing Mirrors

Small upright mirrors mounted by swivels between vertical supports with a drawer or bank of drawers underneath came into fashion at the beginning of the 18th century and sat on dressing-tables or tallboys. The style of these mirrors usually parallels that of girandoles of the corresponding period. The earliest type (1700-1740) had a bevelled mirror, sometimes with a gilt edge, with the drawer cabinet in deal

A George I period giltwood and gesso wall mirror.

George II giltwood wall mirror, 4ft. high.

veneered in walnut. Considerable variety exists in these miniature cabinets, from a single shallow drawer £150 − £200, or set of three £120 − £180, to miniature bureaux enclosing tiny drawers, £300 − £400.

Similar toilet mirrors with japanned woodwork are particularly desirable. Good original lacquerwork, £500 − £700; heavily restored, £300 − £450.

Mahogany mirrors were fashionable from 1740 to 1800. The base cabinet was normally of pine with a mahogany veneer. Mirrors usually upright rectangular with chamfered corners. Supports straight and tapering with turned finials. Good colour of hood important. £90 − £150.

Late 18th century examples were more elaborate, with the base cabinet on ogee bracket feet, and curved supports to accommodate the oval or circular mirror. Plain examples range from £80 to £130, but those with inlaid decoration, e.g. shells, are worth more. £100 − £250 depending on decoration and condition.

288

At the end of the 18th century fluted or reeded uprights were popular. Mirror frames and cabinet work were decorated with cross-banding. The front of the cabinet was often bowed slightly. £80 – £140.

Late Georgian and Regency toilet mirrors had plain rectangular mirror frames, and turned balustroid supports. Decorative effect was achieved by figured veneers, which govern the desirability and therefore value. £30 – £60.

Victorian examples were invariably made in mahogany, usually with rounded tops to the frames, various fancy styles of upright supports and seldom with a drawer in the matching stand. £15 – £40.

Cheval Glasses

These mirrors on swivel mounts between upright supports without the base cabinet of toilet mirrors. Cheval glasses may be quite small and mounted on bracket feet for display on top of a dressing-table or tallboy, or they may be quite large (up to 5 feet tall) and intended to stand on the floor. The majority of cheval glasses date from 1750 onwards. They are usually fairly plain, with slightly rounded corners at the top, plain straight corners or slightly chamfered corners. The supports are usually square tapering, with or without gilded finials. £80 – £150.

They returned to popularity in the 19th century. Like the 18th century cheval glasses emphasis was laid on function and decoration was kept to a minimum. Plain rectangular, slightly rounded or stepped tops to the mirror frames. There was a brief fashion for elaborate supports and paw feet, c.1850, but otherwise supports and feet were relatively plain. £50 – £100, depending on size.

Overmantel Mirrors

The majority of these mirrors now extant belong to the 19th century and vary considerably in hideousness. Formerly they were not considered collectable and were often broken up and cut into smaller pieces of mirror glass. Generally speaking the smaller the mirror the more desirable it becomes, though size tends to be less important where the quality of carving, gilding and plasterwork is superb. Smaller overmantels are in the price range £50 – £120; larger overmantels, £50 – £120.

Pier Glasses

The name is derived from the piers, or upright narrow wall spaces between two windows. Mirrors of this type tend to be tall and comparatively narrow and were intended to occupy the wall space above a matching pier table. The most elaborate pier glasses belong to the second half of the 18th century and were extravagantly carved and gilded with enormous pediments and often with a band of carving across the upper portion of the glass dividing it into two areas. Prices vary enormously due to quality of carving, from £400 to £1,200+.

Late 18th and early 19th century pier glasses in mahogany frames with scrolled crests and giltwood cartouches are more plentiful. £100 – £250.

Later pier glasses follow the style of girandoles, but because of their large size are generally less desirable. Mirrors over 3 feet high, deduct 30% from the price of corresponding girandoles.

Shop Mirrors

During the second half of the 19th century the fashion rose of having shop and pub mirrors decorated with floral motifs, fancy lettering and latterly with trade advertising. Genuine examples have an indefinable quality of age about them. Generally speaking, the colours are more muted and inevitably there will be signs of wear. The glass itself is usually darker and spotted in places with age. Genuine shop and pub mirrors have become very collectable in recent years and are in the price range from £20 to £70, depending on size, and decorative interest. Imitations have already flooded the London street markets and certain boutiques, and are now spreading into the provinces. They are cleanly silvered with bright colouring and crisp, intact decoration. While they have a certain charm, they are scarcely worth the fancy prices asked.

Points to look for

In most cases the gilding shows some sign of wear, and many 19th century examples show degrees of tarnishing as a result of the use of cheaper substitutes. Gilding in superb, bright condition is a very important plus factor. Frames can be regilded, but this is so expensive that it adds considerably to the cost, although enhancing the value of the mirror. When the original gilding is in passable condition, however, it is best left alone. Considerable controversy ranges over the vexed question of original glass. A mirror with its original silvering in a good state of preservation is the most desirable. In many cases, however, the silvering has flaked off or become badly spotted, almost to the point of giving no reflection. Unless the frame is of outstanding historic interest in its own right, it is advisable to have the glass re-silvered.

Pitfalls

While re-silvering of the original glass is permissible without a consequent drop in value, replacement of the glass will seriously affect the value. Old glass is usually very thin, whereas more recent replacements are $\frac{1}{8}$-¼ inch thick. Test by placing the edge of a twopenny

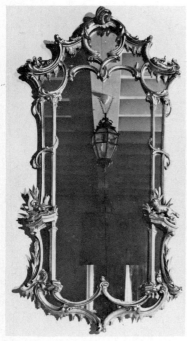

Above: A pair of oval-shaped mirrors with C-scrolls.

Left: 18th century wall mirror in Chinese style.

coin to the glass and measuring with the eye the reflection distance through the glass. This will give a rough idea of the thickness. The back of the glass is also useful in dating. If, when exposed, it shows a pink or maroon paint it indicates that either the glass or the silvering is after 1820. Mercury and tin-type silvering used prior to 1820 shows on the back of the glass as a dull silver or pewter colour.

Museums

British Museum, London.
Geffrye Museum, London.
Victoria and Albert Museum, London.
Wallace Collection, London.
Waddesdon Manor, Aylesbury.
Royal Pavilion, Brighton.
Royal Scottish Museum, Edinburgh.
Central Museum and Art Gallery, Northampton.
Pilkington Glass Museum, St. Helens.
City Museum and Art Gallery, Stoke-on-Trent.

Reading List

Roche, S. Mirrors. London, 1957.
Wills, Geoffrey. English Looking-Glasses. London, 1965.

MODEL SOLDIERS

Elastolin, German 1930s, composition figures of German leaders.

Miniature figures of soldiers made of a lead or tin alloy were a speciality of the Nuremberg toymakers from the 16th century. These two-dimensional *zinnsoldaten* attained the height of their popularity in the 18th and 19th centuries and were exported to other parts of Europe. These 'flats' may be found in the uniforms of every European army of the period and they range in size from little more than one inch to about 2½ inches. These early German soldiers are difficult to date, since little attention was paid to fine detail and the same designs were retained for very many years. The quality of design and the accuracy of detail began to improve from about 1830 onwards, and the size was standardised gradually after 1848 when Heinrichsen introduced the 30mm. Nuremberg scale. Nevertheless the earlier 54mm. scale continued to be very popular, and models of this size are made to this day.

Model soldiers became more three-dimensional about 1870 when French toymakers adopted the *rond bosse* method of casting figures. These 'solids' were made by the European toymakers up to the time of the First World War. The industry was revolutionised in 1893, however, when William Britain of England began using the hollow-cast process which used much less metal and thus enabled him to undercut his competitors. Though crude and naive by present-day standards, the Britain models were much more detailed than their contemporaries and rapidly captured the world market. Soldiers were modelled in the

292

Rare Britain's (c.1900) Royal Horse Artillery Gun Team, first version.

uniform and equipment of virtually every army from the period of the Spanish-American War and the Anglo-Boer War onwards, though the perennial favourites were models of British soldiers, especially in the uniforms of the Brigade of Guards and the Highland regiments. The production of model soldiers was severely curtailed during the Second World War and in the post-war years the increasing use of plastics led to the demise of the commercially produced lead soldier in 1966. The dramatic rise in the popularity of war-gaming, however, has led to a revival of interest in lead soldiers and the real collector's pieces of the present time are those made in traditional metals, cast, chased and painted by hand.

Date-lines

1775-1848   Earliest German 'flats' in varying sizes, but invariably very thin and mounted on a narrow base. Often unpainted, or painted in monochrome. Prices vary from a few pence upwards for single items, though sets range from £10 to £100.

1848-1900   Standard 'Nuremberg' 30mm. scale. Models still two-dimensional. Greater attention to detail and wider

Britain's King's Royal Rifle Corps, lead soldiers, early 20th century.

A John Hill & Co., 1937 Coronation coach and figures, including Yeomen of the Guard, Life Guards, etc.

use of colour. Figures made by such firms as Heinrichsen of Nuremberg and Heyde of Dresden, 50p – £5 each; £15 – £50 for sets.

1870-1914 French *rond bosse* soldiers; larger and more rounded than the German models. Great precision in detail and painting. £1 – £7 each; £20 – £50 sets.

1893-1914 Early Britain models. Hollow-cast figures on 54mm. scale (invariably with one moveable arm). Round bases stamped 'Made in England by Britain Ltd.' Mounted figures £2 – £15; foot soldiers £1 – £10.

1914-1940 Later Britain models with square bases. Markings vary, but often only the word BRITAIN appears. Mounted figures £1 – £10; foot soldiers 50p – £3.

Britain's model soldiers, c.1920.

Courtenay figures. Sir Walter Woodland, banner bearer to the Black Prince on prancing horse; and Sir Howel y Fwyall, on foot, with Wessex Dragon standard (No. 7).

1940-1966	Last period Britain soldiers — similar to the earlier ones but usually much lighter as the moulds wore out; greater range of figures reflecting the Second World War period. 50p — £2.

Other firms active in this period include Timpo and Johillco whose models are generally rated less highly than Britain's. 30p — £1.

Points to look for

The real collector's pieces are of too recent manufacture to qualify for detailed comment here, but it is worth noting the names in passing. The finest hand-made models are made by Charles Stadden, Russell Gamage, Hinton Hunt and individual craftsmen such as Courtenay, Ping, Greenwood and Ball. These models are remarkably detailed, often with fully articulated limbs, and naturally are expensive to buy initially: £7 — £15 for foot soldiers; £25 — £50 for mounted figures being not unusual prices. Of the commercial manufacturers, there is little market for their plastic figures. The lead figures of the period prior to 1966 are still fairly plentiful. Points to look for are soldiers in the uniforms of less popular regiments and the more esoteric armies (e.g. Montenegrin, 1914, or Abyssinian, 1936). Sets, complete with their original boxes are worth a good premium. Highly prized, for example, are the Pontoon, Medical and Balloon sets and gun crews dating before the First World War. These all fetch £40 or more.

Pitfalls

Inevitably many model soldiers were subjected to rough usage and casualties are high. Consequently examples in really fine condition are scarce. However, the usual criteria of repair and faking do not apply to model soldiers, since the 'cannibalisation' of broken figures is an accepted practice among modelling enthusiasts, as is the conversion of common figures into something rare and exotic, by moulding, hammering, chasing, filing and repainting. The value of the end product depends on the skill, artistry and labour expended on it.

Museums

Imperial War Museum, London.
National Army Museum, London.
London Museum, London.
Blaise Castle Folk Museum, Bristol.
Museum of Childhood, Edinburgh.
Museum and Art Gallery, Leicester.
Childhood Museum, Menai Bridge.
Elizabethan House, Totnes.
Royal Tunbridge Wells Museum and Art Gallery.
Blenheim Palace, Woodstock.

Reading List

Blum, Peter. Model Soldiers. London, 1971.
Featherstone, Donald. Handbook for Model Soldier Collectors. London, 1969.
Garratt, John G. Model Soldiers: A Collector's Guide. London, 1961.
Harris, Henry. How to Go Collecting Model Soldiers. London, 1969.
Harris, Henry. Model Soldiers. London, 1962.
Nicollier, J. Collecting Toy Soldiers. Rutland, Vt., 1967.
Richardson, L.W. Old British Model Soldiers, 1893-1918. London, 1970.

MONEY-BOXES

Small containers for coins are of the greatest antiquity, as coin hoards testify, but the earliest boxes designed specifically for savings date from the 17th century and were made of earthenware. The origins of the piggy-bank are wrapped in mystery, but certainly by the 1670s this shape was well established in western Europe, no doubt from the fact that the pig is a very economic animal to rear and provides an excellent return for the labour and foodstuffs expended. By a process of transference the term pig came to be applied to any small pottery receptacle for money, or even to pottery vessels which ante-date hot water bottles. Money-boxes of this type, not necessarily pig-shaped, were known as pirley or pinner pigs. More elaborate money-boxes, in metal, wood or ceramics, appeared in the 19th century and culminated in the mechanical bank, an American invention. Traditional pottery piggy-banks survive to this day, though the mechanical banks offer the greatest scope to the collector.

Date-lines

1670-1700   Pottery pigs; tin-glazed earthenware or delftware, often fish-shaped and sometimes combining both fish and pig in the same article. £75 — £150.

Two metal toy money-boxes.

1700-1800	Elliptical, oval or oblong pottery banks in earthenware, stoneware, creamware, slipware or pearlware. Various styles of decoration, but usually fairly coarse. £10 – £25. More elaborate boxes in the shape of pigs, dogs, fishes, fowls. £20 – £45.
1750-1840	Staffordshire pottery banks in the form of cottages or castles. £15 – £50.
1800-1880	Staffordshire banks in the form of pigs (fairly common), dogs' heads, cattle or sheep, human figures. £10 – £30.
1850-1920	Wide range of pottery pigs, many of Continental origin though very few marked. Price depends on size and quality of the decoration. £7 – £20.
1870-1900	American mechanical banks, majority produced by the Stevens Company. The commonest is the Sambo (from 1882 onwards), whose eyes roll as the coin drops into his mouth. Price depends on size and date. £7 – £25. Among the more elaborate types are the William Tell. £60 – £100. Tammany Hall bank (fat gentleman swallowing the coin). £70 – £150. 'Always did 'spise a Mule' (negro kicked by mule). £80 – £150. Trick Pony (1885 onwards), coin dropped into manger. £60 – £100. Lion and Monkeys (1883). £75 – £150. Uncle Sam (standing figure) (1886 onwards). £50 – £90. Indian Hunter and Bear. £60 – £100.
1880-1920	Numerous money-boxes produced in Europe in this period, using cast iron, pressed steel, tinplate and brass. Value depends on decorative qualities, souvenir or local inscription. Letter-boxes and clocks are the commonest; houses, monuments and other fancy shapes relatively scarce. £10 – £50.

Points to look for

Condition is the most important factor. Good colour in pottery examples is worth a premium. Boxes should be undamaged and mechanical banks should be in working order. The American mechanical banks can often be dated by their patent numbers.

Pitfalls

Certain types (especially the Sambo) have been revived in recent years, or have remained popular over a very long period. Beware of cheap French or German tinplate money-boxes made between 1920 and 1940, which are worth very little as yet, and should not be confused with the late 19th century originals. Since 1950 plastics have largely superseded both ceramics and metal in money boxes, so that *any* boxes in the pre-plastic era should be worth collecting as a long-term investment.

Museums
Bethnal Green Museum, London.
British Museum, London.
London Museum, London.
Pollock's Toy Museum, London.
Victoria and Albert Museum, London.
Art Gallery and Museum, Brighton.
Beamish Museum, Chester-le-Street.
Museum of Childhood, Edinburgh.
Royal Scottish Museum, Edinburgh.
Museum and Art Gallery, Leicester.
Museum of Childhood, Menai Bridge.
Central Museum and Art Gallery, Northampton.
Toy Museum, Rottingdean.
Blithfield Museum, Rugeley.
City Museum, Sheffield.
City Museum and Art Gallery, Stoke-on-Trent.
Castle Museum, York.

Mid-19th century iron money-box.

Reading List
Dunham, Leonard W. Money Boxes. London (undated).
Hughes, Therle. More Small Decorative Antiques. London, 1962.

MUSICAL BOXES

Mechanical contrivances for playing music, popular in the 19th century before the advent of the phonograph or gramophone. They developed out of the musical movements incorporated in 18th century watches and their manufacture was originally a sideline to watch-making. The musical box in its present form, however, did not develop until the early 19th century. The cylinder with pins arranged in such a manner as to strike notes against tuned steel teeth when rotated was invented in 1796 by the Swiss Antoine Favre. Cylinder musical boxes spread to other parts of Europe in the early 19th century, though Switzerland continued to be the main producer. Boxes vary considerably in complexity, from simple mechanisms playing a single tune, to complex boxes playing a wide variety of melodies, accompanied by bells and other special effects, playing up to three hours non-stop. The majority of cylinder musical boxes play between 4 and 12 tunes per cylinder and most were housed in rosewood boxes. Few boxes bear the name or date of manufacture, though those produced by Nicole Frères are invariably marked and rank among the more expensive boxes today. Although the cylinder musical box continues to be produced to this day, there was a vogue for disc musical boxes around the turn of the century and they constitute a quite separate category.

The late 19th century also witnessed the development of larger mechanical innovations. These mechanical music-makers range in size all the way up to fairground organs and may be classed as mechanical musical instruments rather than musical boxes in the strict sense.

Date-lines

1800-1830	The earliest boxes had tuned teeth cut singly and grouped in ones, twos, threes, fours or fives, and screwed to a long brass base plate. Sectional comb boxes are now very rare. £200 – £900.
1820-1840	Earliest single piece combs, with tuned teeth cut from a single comb. Cases of plain fruitwood. Controls at left side of case, often extending beyond the side. £200 – £900.
1840-1850	Flap added to enclose the controls, separate key compartment on right side. Decorative inlay beginning to appear on the case. £300 – £1,000.
1850-1860	Glass lids fitted to protect the movement and controls

from dust. Earliest lids simply plain glass piece set into a groove above the movement; later glass lids have a wooden frame; and by 1860 frames were hinged at the back. £250 − £1,000.

1860-1875   Key replaced by a ratchet lever; glass lid shortened so that movement could be wound without raising it; controls moved to right side. Cases now a little wider than before and usually more decorative. £150 − £350.

1875-1895   Cases becoming much larger in proportion to the movement. Mass-produced boxes now made for the general market, pioneered by E. Paillard of St. Croix. Good boxes still produced, £200 − £600, but most boxes of this period were machine-made and of relatively poor quality, £100 − £150.

1895-1914   Cases enlarged even further, until the movement occupied no more than 25% of the interior. Cheaper boxes decorated with transfer motifs. Movement often nickel-plated. Hey-day of the garish souvenir musical box. £100 − £250.

Points to look for

Musical boxes should be in good working, playable condition. Most mechanical parts of the movement should be capable of repair by a competent watchmaker, but damage to the cylinder or comb is much more serious. Watch for damaged, worn, bent or missing pins on the cylinder or broken teeth on the comb, factors which seriously detract from the value. Check that the dampers are intact (small pieces of metal below the tips of the teeth at the base end of the comb.) With the exception of Nicole Frères, names are comparatively unimportant and few makers marked their boxes in a readily identifiable way. However, the maker's initials or trademark may sometimes be found on the bedplate or comb and these marks are occasionally identified in books on the subject (see *Reading List*). Boxes with interchangeable cylinders were marketed from 1850 onwards and examples with sets of cylinders are worth a good premium, usually with sets of four or six cylinders.

Types to look for

The date-lines cover the evolution of cylinder musical boxes from 1800 to 1914 and prices are given for good average examples of single cylinder boxes in each case. There are a number of rare types, belonging mainly to the late 19th century which are prized for their technical features. These types are described individually below.

Overture: a box playing a selection of operatic overtures, but

A beautiful overture box by Nicole Frères, grande format, c. 1850-55, in superb condition and therefore top price range.

A late 19th century example in an inlaid walnut and rosewood box by Billon-Haller. Three 6 ins. interchangeable cylinders. Poor quality and musically brash short tunes but interesting for the stop/start mechanism which was a patent of Billon-Haller.

A Swiss overture musical box playing four airs by F. Lecoultre, c. 1830. In mahogany case, 13 ins. wide. All of this period are plain. The extra thickness of the cylinder is good, more than usual even for an overture.

distinguished by the much larger diameter of the cylinder and the fineness of the teeth on the comb, permitting a greater number of teeth per comb, and hence a wider variety of notes. The combination of large diameter and fine teeth produces music of a very high quality. Variations of the overture box are the part overture (playing a combination of overtures and other melodies). £500 − £2,000.

Mandoline: a box whose notes simulate the sustained tremolo sound of a mandoline. The cylinder is pinned in order to strike the teeth (arranged in groups) in rapid succession to produce the distinctive sound. £300 − £750.

Forte Piano: a box whose movement employs two combs, playing softly and loudly, each with bass and treble clefs. This movement results in greater tonal variation, with soft, loud or combined to produce very loud sound. £300 − £750.

Forte Piano-Mandoline: a rare combination of the mandoline and forte piano types, usually playing four melodies only. £400 − £1,200.

Harpe Eolienne: similar in appearance to the forte piano, with two combs. In this case, however, the smaller comb is employed contrapuntally, not for a softer effect. £250 − £650.

Sublime Harmonie: a box with a complex movement employing up to four combs playing in harmony, patented by Charles Paillard in 1874. Numerous variations have sub-titles such as Piccolo, Tremolo, Octavo and Quatuor. Originally intended for use in coin-operated mechanisms, they are capable of a greater volume than standard boxes. £250 − £750.

Organ Celeste: a box combining normal cylinder and comb movements with a set of organ or harmonium reeds which produce the main melody. £350 − £850.

Piéce à Oiseau: a very rare variant of the above in which reeds are used to produce bird notes, accompanied by the music on the combs. A small mechanical bird is mounted in front of the movement and visible through a glass window in the front of the case. £850 − £1,500.

Orchestra Box: an Organ Celeste box incorporating drums, castanets and bells. £550 − £1,500.

Revolver Box: an interchangeable cylinder box with the cylinders mounted on two wheels so that any cylinder can be brought into play by turning a wheel. Last one sold 1,500 gns.

Table Box: a large interchangeable cylinder box set on a table with drawers for spare cylinders. £500 − £2,000.

Disc Musical Boxes

This category is quite distinct from the cylinder boxes and flourished briefly in the period between 1885 and 1914. The origins of

A fine key-wind Forte Piano box by Nicole Frères, c. 1860. The glass lid is framed and hinged to the case and has the original time sheet.

A 19th century Swiss example in a burr walnut case with matching table in which there should be two other cylinders. Value points are the interchangeable cylinders, the table, double spring barrels and less important, the time indicator and zither.

the disc box are obscure, though it has been stated that Miguel Boom of Haiti invented the first of this type in 1882 and patented it in the United States. Three years later, however, Ellis Parr in England and Paul Lochmann in Leipzig independently invented disc boxes. Parr and Lochmann subsequently combined to market the Symphonion disc musical box, produced in Leipzig. Within five years two employees of the Symphonion factory had established their own company and began marketing the Polyphon. One of these men, Gustave Brachhausen, moved to the United States in 1892 and founded the Regina company. Most of the disc boxes in existence today were made by these three companies. They were rendered obsolete by the development of the gramophone. Disc boxes are found in two basic types, either upright or horizontal and they vary considerably in size, from small table models, usually with rectangular cases, to the large upright models. Many disc boxes are of the greatest rarity, though this in itself does not govern the price. The most important factor is the availability of discs suitable for playing on a machine. The ideal combination would be a box which was so expensive at the time of manufacture that very few were ever sold, but capable of playing discs produced by the same manufacture as for the more popular models. As with cylinder boxes, disc boxes are valued according to type, as follows:

Disc Box with Bells: bells and castanets enhance the movement (in cylinder boxes this is often the reverse and bells were substituted for part of the movement, to the detriment of the music). Unfortunately discs for boxes incorporating bells are very hard to find and this detracts somewhat from the value of these rare boxes. £250 – £600.

Automatic Disc Changers: an extremely rare type of machine which changes its disc from a rack in the base. Made by all three major companies – Polyphon, Regina and Symphonion in ascending order of rarity. £1,500 up for Polyphon and Regina; Symphonion automatic disc changers are known to have been made but only two have ever come on the market.

Multiple Disc Boxes: boxes capable of playing two or three discs simultaneously. A speciality of Symphonion, who marketed the two-disc table model and the three-disc 'Eroica' upright model. Sets of the special discs are unfortunately very rare, which detracts from the price which these undoubtedly rare machines ought to fetch. £800 – £2,000.

Disc Playing Clocks: clocks incorporating musical disc movements ranging from 4-inch to 24½-inch discs fitted to mantelpiece or hallway models respectively. Average sizes are 9-inch or 12-inch models standing 5-7½ feet high. These models play discs of the standard Polyphon, Regina or Symphonion types. £750 – £2,500 (for large 24½inch.)

Disc Orchestrions: very rare disc boxes produced between 1901 and 1914, producing sounds of piano, percussion and bells. This type was pioneered by Lochmann after he left the Symphonion company about 1900, but they were also made by Polyphon and Regina. A later version used a paper roll instead of metal discs to play the mechanisms. All disc orchestrions are extremely rare and are now in the range £1,000 – £2,500.

Sirion Double Tune Disc Box: a box produced by the Sirion company with a disc which played a tune and then, by altering the central spindle, a second set of projections was brought into play. This novel type was produced by only one company and very few examples are known. Very difficult to price, since they are of the greatest rarity, but the chance of finding discs for them militates against their popularity. £750 – £1,500.

Disc Machine Gramophone: a creditable, though ephemeral, attempt by

Regina to combat the threat from the phonograph or gramophone by combining features of both gramophone and disc musical box. Extremely rare in America and virtually unknown in Europe, though Polyphon are also believed to have made them. Impossible to price.

Rare Case Designs: unusual designs were used for the cabinets of many disc musical boxes, especially those intended for use in cafes and public houses. The best-known include the Gambrinus or King of Beer design by Symphonion, the Rococo by Symphonion (simulating the ornately carved wooden furniture of the Rococo period), the Desk by Regina with a cabinet in the form of a full-sized roll-top desk, and the drum table model, also by Regina, decorated with scenery. £500 – £1,500.

Points to look for

Coin-fed boxes are usually worth much more than hand-started ones. The general size of discs for table or horizontal boxes is up to 15½ inches; upright (coin-fed) boxes with larger discs are more highly regarded and sought after. Rare, unusual or particularly decorative cases are an important plus factor.

Mechanical Musical Instruments

The largest category, both physically and in variety, of mechanical musical box may be considered under the general heading of mechanical musical instruments. They are usually capable of a much greater variety of musical sound, by the employment of mechanisms involving pipes, bells, strings and reeds. In size they range from the serinette or miniature bird organ, popular from the 17th to the late 19th centuries, to the giant fairground organs (themselves ranging from 4 to 28 feet in length) with a mechanism capable of reproducing most of the sounds in an orchestra, after a fashion. Below are enumerated a few of the more representative types. Others are omitted because they are either virtually unique or because their great size precludes the possibility of most collectors finding the house-room for them.

Serinette: otherwise known as the bird organ, dating from about 1670, and originally designed for training song-birds. This instrument resembles a miniature barrel organ and is hand-operated, with a single bank of about a dozen pipes emitting a series of bird notes. Clockwork serinettes were produced in the 18th and 19th centuries, and were sometimes incorporated in bird-cage automata. £150 (for 19th century hand-operated serinettes) to £2,500 (for 18th century clockwork examples).

Chamber Barrel Organ: mechanical pipe organ, with hand-crank attached to the front. Popular from the 18th century onwards and made extensively in Europe until the early 20th century. Smaller and

Left: A George III mahogany barrel organ by George Astor of Cornhill, London. Beautiful instrument but these always need major rebuilding (at a high cost) when found in auctions.

Right: A table model Symphonion 'penny in the slot', fitted with two combs of 53 teeth and 40, $19\frac{1}{8}$ins. in a mahogany case.

more elegant version of the large church barrel organs of the same period (1740-1880) but providing a much wider repertoire. These organs often have interchangeable barrels, each playing up to ten melodies. £350 – £1,000.

Street Barrel Organ: a more robust version of the above, often mounted on some form of carriage for greater mobility. The smallest variety, however, was fitted with straps and could be carried by the 'organ grinder'. An intermediate type was mounted on a pole or rudimentary stand. £500 – £1,800.

Flute or Bell Clock: reed mechanisms fitted to clocks, ranging from French *petite armoire* clocks of the 18th century to large Black Forest longcase clocks of the late 19th century. Prices for flute clocks can be influenced by their horological interest and range from £600 to £2,000 (or more). Bell-playing musical clocks (as distinct from clocks incorporating musical chimes) are mainly of the bracket variety and were produced in the 18th and early 19th centuries. Here again, the value depends primarily on the fact that it is a clock and prices may therefore rise from £600 to £2,000.

Stringed Musical Clocks: musical clocks with a stringed movement were produced in the 18th and early 19th centuries, either as wall clocks, with strings on a frame, or longcase clocks. The most elaborate stand up to ten feet high and have chests of drawers *en suite* housing spare barrels. Stringed musical clocks are rare and are priced from £800 to £10,000.

Mechanical Pianos: a very wide field, ranging from the small street barrel piano, first cousin to the street barrel organ, to the large instruments mounted on a hand-cart. A less mobile form was the pub piano, with a coin-operated clockwork motor (sometimes known as a pennyano), the European barrel piano orchestrion, resembling a large wardrobe in size, disc-operated piano orchestrions or nickelodeons and Encore Banjos, Wurlitzer Harps, Violano Virtuoso, etc. These are all expensive, the latter about £4,000. Reproducing pianos, produced by the German company of Welte and Son, faithfully reproduced the actual playing of celebrated pianists, translating their style and fingering on to rolls of perforated paper which then operated the piano movement by pneumatic action. Mechanical pianos are still fairly plentiful and are relatively unpopular on account of their size. Prices range from £100 to £2,000.

Reed Organette, Player-Organ, Mechanical Harmonium: the reed equivalent of the mechanical stringed instruments listed above. The reed organette was developed in the late 18th century, with bellows supplying air, via perforated paper roll, paper or metal disc, to a bank of organ reeds. Much less popular than musical boxes, reed organettes have only recently begun to attract serious attention and prices are therefore relatively low (£60 − £200). The paper roll principle was expanded and extended to full-size organs and harmoniums, especially in Germany and the United States where the Aeolian Company specialised in mechanical organs operated in this fashion. Many of the original pedal-operated player-organs were later converted to automatic electric operation. Prices as for player-organs.

Points to look for

While good decorative features are worth a premium, it is much more important to consider mechanical qualities. Prices quoted are for examples in reasonable working order, but specimens of mechanical instruments, especially the larger and more complex varieties, with defective mechanisms may be worth a great deal less, the difference being the cost of making good the defects. In extreme cases this may entail the virtual rebuilding of the instrument, and this is only practicable if the initial cost of purchasing dilapidated specimens is negligible.

Museums
London Museum, London.
British Piano Museum, London.
Waddesdon Manor, Aylesbury.
City Museum and Art Gallery, Birmingham.
Art Gallery and Museum, Brighton.
Elizabethan House, Totnes.
Royal Scottish Museum, Edinburgh,
Art Gallery and Museum, Glasgow.
City Museum, Hereford.
Museum and Art Gallery, Leicester.
Central Museum and Art Gallery, Northampton.
City Museum, Sheffield.
Blithfield, Rugeley, Staffordshire.
West Cornwall Museum of Mechanical Music.
Windsor Castle, Windsor.

Reading List
Clarke, J.E.T. Musical Boxes: A History and Appreciation. London, 1961.
Mosoriak, Roy. The Curious History of Musical Boxes.
Ord-Hume, Arthur W.J. Collecting Musical Boxes. London, 1967.
Tallis, David. Musical Boxes. London, 1971.
Webb, Graham. The Cylinder Musical Box Handbook. London, 1968.
Webb, Graham. The Disc Musical Box Handbook. London, 1971.

MUSIC COVERS

Although the earliest recorded pictorial music title was engraved by William Hole as early as 1611, the covers of sheet music remained relatively plain until the beginning of the 19th century, when the process of lithography was invented by Alois Senefelder. Hitherto music was engraved from copper plates and the ornament on the cover was confined to elaborate lettering. The rise of the more pictorial music covers coincided with the growing popularity of home entertainment in most classes of society, and for that reason it tended to drop to the lowest common denominator, the respectable working class to whom the possession of a piano in the front parlour was a very important status symbol. The heyday of the pictorial music cover was the period from 1840 to 1900, when covers became more colourful following the advent of chromolithography and countless thousands of titles were produced with the ballads which attained temporary eminence through the medium of the music hall. Although the most collectable music covers belong to the Victorian period, later titles should not be ignored. Those of the First World War, with their strongly patriotic sentiment, and those of the inter-war period with their Art Deco lettering and *moderne* symbolism, are now rapidly rising in favour.

Date-lines

Pre-1800	The 18th century covers are prosaic in appearance; any decorative effect achieved was entirely through the medium of contrasting styles of lettering. £1 – £2.
	Relatively few examples of this period incorporate a small pictorial vignette on the cover. £2 – £3.
1800-1820	Increasing use of pictures. Small engraved vignettes. £1 – £2.
	Larger engraved pictures, occupying the top half of the cover. £2 – £3.
1800-1818	Lithographed covers with lettering and no pictures. £1 – £2.
1818-1840	Lithographed pictures in black and white, occupying the centre of the cover. £2 – £5.
	As above, but hand-coloured. £5 – £10.
1840-1880	Chromolithographed covers. Value depends on artist, subject matter and rarity. Average prices for covers with scenic pictures. £1 – £3.

'Olga', cover by John Brandard, c.1845. Covers such as this, which are exquisitely coloured, are widely collected and demonstrate the capabilities of the new medium of chromolithography, introduced c.1840.

Those depicting figures in contemporary situations. £3 — £8.

Covers for ballet music (usually of a higher quality). £7 — £15.

Patriotic covers, alluding to the Crimean War, American Civil War and other campaigns, depicting battle scenes, £4 — £10. Unless of particular military interest, then more.

Covers bearing the imprint of Concanen or Brandard, £5 — £15. A very few rare titles, dependent on the age of the paper or colour, £25 — £40.

1880-1914 Last period of chromolithographs, usually of a much poorer, blurred quality. Colouring tends to be more garish. £2 — £4.

Boer War patriotic music covers, often portraying popular heroes. £5 — £10.

1890-1914 Covers illustrated with letterpress, line drawings or half-tone blocks; restricted use of colour, or merely in black and one other colour. £1 — £3.

311

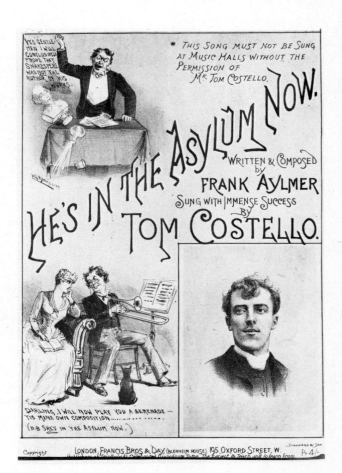

'He's in the Asylum Now', cover by H.G. Banks. Banks belonged to the generation succeeding that of Concanen and worked with him for a time. His vignettes have the vigour of Concanen, but the covers themselves are devalued by the typography.

1914-1920   First World War patriotic song sheets and music covers. £1 – £4.

1920-1940   Covers printed by two- or three-colour lithography, photogravure or letterpress. Value depends on the subject (including the artist who popularised the song) and the artistic quality of the design. £1 – £3.

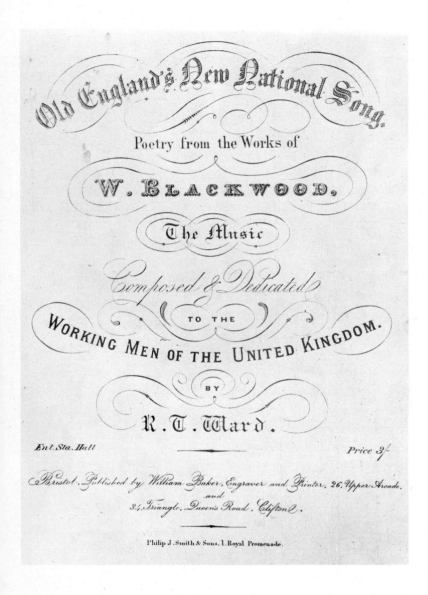

'Old England's New National Song', with a pre-1850 typographical cover. The wide variety of type faces are neatly combined and this type of cover has increased in popularity with collectors.

CALL HIM BACK,
BEFORE TOO LATE,

Then call him back before too late.
In Anger dont dismiss him.
And when your arms are round his neck,
What can you do but kiss him.

WRITTEN BY
CHAS. LINDA.
COMPOSED BY
CARLO MINASI.
SUNG WITH IMMENSE SUCCESS BY
MISS LOUIE SHERRINGTON.
London, HOPWOOD & CREW, 42, New Bond S.t

'Call him back', cover by Henry Maguire the younger.

Points to look for

The best music covers were those produced by John Brandard (1812-1863) and Alfred Concanen (1835-1886). Brandard's speciality was the stage, whereas Concanen concentrated on the music halls and gin palaces. Early titles by these artists are the most desirable of all music covers. Brandard's earliest titles bear the initials J.B. and include some excellent three-quarter length portraits of contemporary celebrities. Early prints by Concanen bear the imprint Concanen & Lee; subsequently imprints were Concanen, Lee and Siebe, and then Concanen, Siebe & Co. Later Concanen prints bear the imprint of Stannard & Dixon, which also changed subsequently to Stannard & Co., Stannard & Son and eventually W.T. Stannard. Concanen covers from 1880 onwards have a coded datemark after the signature, using letters to denote the year (A = 1, H = 8, etc). Also covers depicting animals.

Lower down the scale comes Thomas Packer, best known for his scenic series such as Cathedral Gems, Riverside Reveries and Operatic

'Complaints', cover by Alfred Concanen (fl.1858-1886). Single figures by Concanen are not so sought after as his genre scenes.

Gems. Much of Packer's work was also printed by Stannard & Dixon. The covers by Robert Hamerton (1809-1905) are almost as sensitive as those by Brandard, but the colouring is more subdued. Other names to look for include S. Rosenthal, Frank Trevisany, William Michael Watson, Alfred Bryan, Augustus Butler, Richard Childs, Alexandre Laby, G.E. Madeley and Henry Maguire.

Prices quoted are for covers with their music intact and, most important of all, in good condition. Other covers minus the contents, or fronts (often framed for their pictorial attraction) should be heavily discounted.

For example, at auction, for covers only, prices tend to be much lower for bundles of 20-50 covers:—

Pre-1800, £5 — £10.
1800-1818, £2 — £5.
1800-1820, £10 — £20.
1818-1840. Black and white, £2 — £5.
1818-1840. Coloured, £8 — £15.
Concanen and Brandard, about £5 each.
1880-1914, £2 — £6.

This seems to be one of the collecting subjects which has 'gone off the boil' at the moment but it may well revive.

Pitfalls

Beware of cheap and nasty music covers of the late Victorian period drawn by an eminent vulgarian named Sydney Kent. The designs are badly drawn, garishly coloured and poorly executed. Inevitably even these travesties of the art are now attracting attention by virtue of their age and curiosity alone, but do not pay fancy prices for them.

A major problem centres on those titles which, on account of their popularity, became 'standards' of the period and were reprinted over a very long time. Early editions of such works as *The Bridge* by Longfellow (a long-time favourite) are worth buying, but late 19th century re-issues are of little value. Editions can usually be dated fairly accurately by the style of the printer's and publisher's imprints and the music itself often bears a date or a reference to the edition.

Museums

The Music Room at the British Library (formerly Department of Printed Books, British Museum) contains a vast number of music covers, deposited under the Copyright Act since 1842, and invariably stamped by the Museum with the date of acquisition. These date-marks can only be regarded as an approximate guide, since publishers often sent their titles to the Music Room years in arrears.

Reading List

Imeson, W.E. Illustrated Music Titles. London, 1912.
King, A. Hyatt. English Pictorial Music Title Pages, 1820-1885. London, 1950.
Pearsall, Ronald. Victorian Sheet Music Covers. Newton Abbot, 1972.
Spellman, Doreen and Sidney. Victorian Music Covers. London, 1969.

MUSICAL INSTRUMENTS

This is an enormous field and within the scope of this book it is possible only to give brief outlines concerning the principal categories of collectable instruments. They are discussed below in sequence of stringed, wind, percussion and keyboard instruments.

Stringed Instruments

Among the oldest and most widespread of musical instruments are those whose notes are produced by strumming or plucking strings, the sound then being amplified by a soundboard. Various forms of harp or lyre have been recorded in use since the first millenium B.C. From the collector's viewpoint, however, stringed instruments date from the 16th century. Authentic lutes of the Elizabethan period are among the most highly desirable of all instruments, on account of the artistry and craftsmanship lavished on their cases, but they are extremely rare and any examples coming on the market now would fetch from £1,000 upwards. During the second half of the 16th century various other instruments were derived from the lute and these turn up at auction in the £1,000+ range. Little is known about such early instruments as the strump and the poliphant. A related instrument, the orpharion, is known. The lute (as opposed to the English guitar) superseded the cittern by nearly a hundred years. The cittern especially underwent numerous modifications, transforming it from the bulbous-backed lute to the flat-backed English guitar, which should not be confused with the classical guitar. Early guitars of the period 1720-60 are in the price range from £80 to £200, depending on the quality and form of decoration.

More elaborate guitars were evolved in France and Spain in the early 18th century and attained their peak in the 1780s. Two of the greatest guitar makers of the early 19th century were French and English, namely Lacote and Panormo, and the guitar enjoyed a tremendous vogue in Spain and Italy, and also in the Latin American countries. Spanish guitars were often ornately finished and inlaid with mother-of-pearl and ivory. Elaborate fretting on the sound hole and the bridge enhances the value of these instruments. Early 18th century guitars differed from their later descendants in the number of strings, having ten instead of six, (these were tuned in pairs, technically five double courses of strings) and in the more elegant outline with gently curving sides. After about 1750 the 'New Spanish Guitar' became less

317

ornate, the six-string arrangement became standard and the sides of the sound box were widened considerably. In place of the overall decoration ornament was confined to purfling (an inlaid border round the back and belly), and simple circular motifs of ivory and ebony round the sound hole. Since the guitar was considered a ladies' drawing-room instrument, styling continued to be elegant and refined and examples from 1800 to 1850 are still relatively plentiful. Names to look for (their labels can be seen through the sound hole) include Louis Panormo of London (the rest of whose family were primarily violin makers) and Stauffer of Venice.

After 1850 guitars became more practical and much less decorative, reflecting the move from the drawing-room to the great outdoors. The instrument was relatively unfashionable in the late 19th century, but returned to favour in the 1920s. Instruments after that date are common, but often have unusual technical features which enhance their value.

The small, elegant, French, Italian and Spanish guitars of the 18th century are in the price range £700 to £3,000, depending on decorative features. The less decorative, more robust models from 1750 to 1850 are in the price range from £100 to £400. Early 19th century English guitars by the Panormo family, for example, are in the range £50 to £100. Plain Italian, French or Spanish guitars from 1840 onwards range from £30 to £90.

During the second half of the 18th century the mandoline group of instruments was very popular and almost ousted the guitar from favour in Italy and England, the other great centre of mandoline playing being Vienna. Another descendant of the lute, the mandoline had a bulbous sound box. Similar types of instrument include the mandora (the generic name for the small soprano lute from which the mandoline is derived), the chitarra battente (a wire strung guitar only distantly related to the mandoline which it preceded) and the chitarrone (related to the lute, its other name being the arch lute). Most of these instruments are relatively plain and are in the price range £100 — £300, although fine examples can be very expensive, a chitarra battente recently realising £10,000. The mandoline continued to be very popular in the Mediterranean countries and Britain throughout the 19th century and examples from Naples or Milan range from £25 to £80.

The late 18th century was a period of much experiment and hybridisation of instruments. The features of several distinct instruments were often combined in various forms to produce hybrids which were supposedly more easy to play. To the period from 1780 to 1830 belong such curiosities as the harp-lute and the harp-lyre. Many of these hybrids were made by Edward Light and they were elegantly decorated in the Regency manner. These small harp-like instruments are in the price range £45 – £120.

Harps themselves had a very long history as orchestral instruments, but they became fashionable in the drawing-room in the late 18th century and remained popular for much of the 19th century. Since then they have been revived from time to time. Double-action English harps, with Grecian or Gothic styling, were fashionable in the 19th century and are in the price range £250 to £500. The much smaller Irish harp or clarsach also enjoyed a revival in this period, the principal manufacturer being Joseph Egan of Dublin. These Irish harps were elegantly decorated with gilt gesso ornament and, though about half the size of the English double-action harps, are in the same price range. Considering that new harps, mainly of French or Italian origin, cost twice as much, antique harps are by no means appreciated at their true value as yet.

A Gothic concert harp by Erard of Paris, in the style of Louis XVI.

Dital harp by Edward Light.

At the other extreme comes the banjo, an instrument which had its origins on the slave plantations of America in the late 18th century. Unlike other European stringed instruments it had a sound box of parchment stretched over a circular wooden hoop. It usually has four or five strings and attained the height of its popularity and technical excellence during the first half of the 19th century. The finest banjos of this period have uncovered wooden rims, no frets and lavish ornament with inlays of mother-of-pearl, ivory or ebony. The vellum was kept taut by means of brass tensioners arranged round the rim. The greater the number of these 'tackheads' (as they were popularly known) the more valuable the instrument. Examples range in price from about £40 for a banjo with six tensioners to £100 or more for one with up to 40 tensioners (though there are some early banjos with relatively few tensioners which are more valuable than later ones). Few banjos are marked with a maker's name, though the most desirable are those made by Da Silva, whose instruments are distinguished by the intricacy and beauty of their inlaid patterns. A fine Da Silva banjo may cost up to £200, whereas a plain, 'common-or-garden' banjo of the late 19th century may be as little as £10 – £15.

The violin developed in Europe in the 16th century, probably evolving out of the earlier vihuela da arco or bowed guitar, though its origins are obscure. The earliest violins had three gut strings, though by the late 16th century the four-string arrangement had been adopted. The finest violins were made in northern Italy, especially Brescia and Cremona, and the best were produced by several families (Amati, Guarneri and Stradivari) whose instruments are the most highly prized to this day. The violin is deceptively simple in appearance, but the quality of tone depends on a number of subtle, yet highly complex factors, including the type and quality of wood, the seasoning, the varnishes and the craftsmanship – all factors which tend to defy definition. The most expensive of the Italian violins are those dating from 1600 to 1800, by the better known Italian makers and are in excess of £5,000. The highest auction price for a Stradivari is £84,000. At the other extreme are late 19th and early 20th century instruments, manufactured in many parts of Europe and America, which can still be picked up for £5 – £10. It is impossible here to go into the complex factors which govern the value of a violin. Moreover, the large number of instruments which have forged labels pasted inside the sound box and purport to be the work of Amati or Stradivari, make this an exceedingly difficult field for the collector, who would always be well advised to consult an expert before contemplating a purchase, even of a relatively inexpensive instrument.

The violin family also includes the larger viola, violoncello and double-bass, to which the same cautionary remarks must apply. The viol was popular in England in the 17th and 18th centuries but was gradually superseded by the violin. Broadly these instruments resemble an elongated violin with six strings, are very rare and range in value from about £2,000+ (top limit perhaps £5,000), depending on condition, make and quality of decoration. The best English instruments were made by Henry Jaye and Barak Norman.

A violin by Giacomo Zanoli, Verona, bearing a label 1740 — length of back 14ins.

A violin by Hendrick Jacobs, Amsterdam 1693, length of back $14\frac{1}{16}$ins.

Wind Instruments

The most universal of the wind instruments is the flute, found in diverse forms all over the world and known to have been used in Egypt in the pre-Christian era. In its modern form, however, the flute dates from the 17th century when the French bagpipe-maker, Jean Hotteterre, invented the one-keyed flute, consisting of straight tubes of boxwood with seven holes, one covered by the key, and three joints. These early flutes are rare and would now be worth from £1,000+ (top limit perhaps £10,000). By 1760 an extra joint was added and ivory rings reinforced the joints. The number of holes was also increased, so that the head joint had a single hole, the two middle joints had three each, and the bottom joint had a single hole which was kept closed by a brass or silver key. Later developments, which help to date flutes, were further metal keys added in the late 18th century to facilitate the playing of semi-tones. These keys increased in number and complexity between 1770 and 1840, until the standard eight-keyed flute was in use. Early one-keyed boxwood flutes range from £60 to £200; later multi-keyed flutes in the same material range from £30 to £120. Rare examples are known with up to eleven keys and these are also very desirable (£100 – £150).

Early in the 19th century boxwood was gradually replaced by other materials, such as ebony or crocus-wood and these are generally less expensive than the boxwood variety (£25 – £90).

The structure of the flute was revolutionised in 1831-32 by the Munich flute-maker, Theobald Boehm, who used the 'axle and ring' system of metal keys. Early Boehm flutes are rare, and technically of immense interest since they underwent several major changes in fifteen years. By 1847, however, Boehm had perfected the modern orchestral flute. The 1847 flute had a different arrangement of keys and padded metal plates in place of the rings. Manufacturers found that boxwood was no longer satisfactory and switched to rosewood and African blackwoods which were less prone to distortion. There was considerable resistance to the new system of fingering introduced by Boehm and many English manufacturers devised improvements on the existing 'simple system' flutes.

Names to watch for are Nicholson, Siccama Clinton, Pratten, Rockstro and 'Carte and Boehm Combined'. The simple-system, eight-keyed flute remained popular throughout the rest of the 19th century, the later models being shorter than the earlier ones to suit the higher pitch which was fashionable between 1860 and 1900. These

Seven-keyed flute by Monzani & Co., 28 Regent Street, Piccadilly, London. Ebony, with silver bands and keys, hallmarked 1821.

One-keyed flute by T. Prowse, Hanway Street, London. Boxwood and ivory, with brass key. c.1815.

Four-keyed flute by Potter, Johnson's Court, Fleet Street, London. Boxwood and ivory, with silver keys, c.1810.

Ivory, gold-mounted concert flute by Thomas Stanesby Junior, London, c.1740.

instruments are in the price range from £5 to £100 depending on quality and the materials used, the more expensive items being lavishly decorated with ivory and silver. These English simple-system flutes should not be confused with similar, low-priced German flutes produced in vast quantities especially between 1900 and 1914. They seldom bear any maker's name, and the metalwork is in German silver or some other base white metal. They are often high-pitched for military band work and have very little value.

In addition to the various kinds of flute there are its relatives, the double or triple flageolets. These smaller instruments were very popular in the Regency period and were produced in England, mainly by Bainbridge and Halstrick. These instruments would now be worth from £100 to £250 for double flageolets and £500 – £1,000 for triple flageolets. Single flageolets are also common. £60 – £100.

Brass instruments are an enormous subject in themselves, and often have the additional interest of a military connection, hence their value to collectors of militaria. Early regimental trumpets, horns and bugles (up to about 1800) are now rare and could well be in the price range from £250 to £750, depending on decoration or other markings establishing their provenance and date. Later military bugles are more plentiful, but those with regimental insignia can be worth up to £200 (especially if the ornament is in silver). Even bugles of the Third Reich are currently worth £70 – £120. Plain brass or silver-plated bugles without keys are worth from £5 to £20.

Kent bugles, incorporating one or more keys, were invented about 1810 and named after the then Commander in Chief of the British Army, the Duke of Kent. Otherwise known as a keyed bugle, this instrument was immensely popular in the early 19th century. The, earlier the bugle, the fewer the keys. By 1840 as many as seven or eight keys were incorporated. These instruments were made of copper with brass keys and fittings and usually have the maker's name inscribed on the bell. Names to look for include Rudall Carte, Clementi, Kohler, Mickleburgh, Potter, Mayers & Harrison, Reynolds, Keat (all English) and Alexandre and Courtois (both French). The interest of keyed bugles lies in the fact that they come in an infinite variety of styles. At one extreme they are quite plain and devoid of ornament; at the other they are highly elaborate with keys shaped like miniature scallop shells. Relatively plain Kent bugles are in the price range £50 – £100; the more decorative examples may go as high as £150.

Kent bugles were superseded about 1850 by the cornet, a similar-looking instrument with keys operating on a vertical plunger system. Late 19th century cornets are relatively plentiful in a wide range of sizes and technical quality and are worth from £10 to £40.

A larger version of the Kent bugle, developed about 1820, was the ophicleide which remained popular until the end of the century. During its fairly long life the ophicleide grew in number of keys. The most desirable are those with fewer than eight keys (belonging to the period 1820-40). By the middle of the century, however, up to twelve keys was commonplace and that maximum remained standard till 1900. Like the Kent bugle the ophicleide was made of copper with brass keys and mounting. Earlier ophicleides are rare and are worth from £80 to £150; later examples, with more keys, are more plentiful and range from £60 to £100, depending on decorative features and condition. The ophicleide was superseded at the turn of the century by the tuba.

Other instruments which are worth considering are the piccolo and the clarinet, both developed in the late 18th century and undergoing a number of important technical changes in the 19th century. Boxwood was superseded by ebony and the development of keys paralleled the progress of the flute. Prices for these instruments range from about £25 for late 19th century piccolos to £60 for those about 1800, and from £50 to £120 for clarinets of the corresponding periods.

Keyboard Instruments

Early keyboard instruments include the virginals, whose keys activated a plucking system and produced the characteristic tinkling sound, and the harpsichord. The spinet retained its popularity till the late 18th century as a boudoir instrument and many elegant examples have survived with walnut or mahogany cases, occasionally elaborately inlaid with ivory, brass or mother-of-pearl. The spinet had no pedals and there was no method of varying the tone and volume of sound. Because of the very long period in which they were current, the prices of spinets vary enormously, from under £800 to £4,000, depending on age, maker and decorative features. As a rule the maker's name, and often the date, appear on an inlaid panel above the keyboard.

The larger and much more powerful instrument of the 16th-18th centuries was the harpsichord. These instruments were expensive to produce and required a large room to house them adequately. Consequently they were the prerogative of the wealthier classes and were usually decorated accordingly. The lid was frequently painted with flowers, scenery, classical or allegorical compositions and the use of gilding and lacquering boosted the initial outlay and enhanced the subsequent value. For these reasons, most harpsichords of the 18th century are very expensive and are in the price range from £5,000 to £10,000. It is interesting to note that with the revival of interest in the harpsichord as a contemporary instrument, modern harpsichords can cost from £2,000 to £5,000, and have minimal antiquarian value as yet!

It is important to emphasise that there is a greater disparity in the price of keyboard instruments than with other musical instruments – or almost any other form of collectable antique. Consequently, while four-figure prices for harpsichords are more often than not the case, relatively plain examples in reasonable condition have been known to change hands for £350 to £600 in recent years.

The same remark can be applied to other keyboard instruments, introduced in the second half of the 18th century and developed throughout the 19th century. The first grand pianos appeared in the mid-18th century, adapting the clavichord with its hammer action and adding pedals which controlled dampers and helped produce the soft (piano) and loud (forte) range of volume. Although the first practical grand piano was invented by the Italian Cristofori in 1709, it was in Germany that it attained its peak of technical perfection. Names such as Bechstein, Bluthner, Bosendorfer, Steinweg and Goss and Kallmann are household words to this day. The size and technical features of grand pianos vary greatly, and this is reflected in the price which may range from a mere £50 to £5,000. Generally the more expensive are the full-sized concert grands by the more renowned manufacturers, very early examples (1760-1800) by German or Italian emigré craftsmen working in London (Zumpe, Pohlmann, Beck, Backers, Geib, Buntebart, Clementi), with the early grand pianos of indigenous English craftsmen (Broadwood, Kirkman, Collard and Challen) in the middle price range from £500 to £2,000. Other factors which have to be considered are the size (concert, semi-grand, boudoir grand – in descending order of value) and decorative features. Most pianos were

A tulipwood salon piano by J. Broadwood & Sons, c.1860.   *A fine single manual harpsichord by Jacob Kirckman, 1766.*

An elaborate painted concert grand piano by Erard.

produced in mahogany or walnut, but such features as marquetry and boulle work enhance the value considerably. An imponderable factor is association with a famous composer or pianist, and, where the provenance of such association can be authenticated, the value can be greatly boosted.

A much cheaper version of the grand was the square piano, introduced to England by Zumpe about 1742 and subsequently made in London by the great Anglo-German manufacturers already mentioned. The earliest square pianos (1750-1800) were small, with a compass of five octaves or less, constructed entirely of wood with small leather hammers. They rested on a trestle table with four or six legs. From about 1800 the legs were screwed directly into the base of the instrument. Various improvements were made in the late 18th century, including levers for raising the bass and treble dampers for producing a pizzicato effect. These refinements were short-lived and had been abandoned by 1800 when the first pedals were introduced. Pedals giving soft and loud effects on the same lines as the grand piano were introduced about 1820. Thereafter square pianos gradually increased in size, until they were every bit as large as the grands they were intended to replace and were usually a great deal uglier. From about 1850, however, the square piano was superseded by the upright, though it survived till the end of the century in northern Europe and in America. The prices of square pianos seem to have remained fairly static over the past five years. The smaller, more delicate and more beautifully decorated examples prior to 1820 are in the price range £100 – £500+, while the post-1820 examples are generally in the price range £40 – £80 (some piano prices are now moving up rapidly).

Although the upright piano was patented as early as 1800 by Dr. John Hawkins of Philadelphia, it did not supersede the square piano till about 1860. Uprights were, however, being made on both sides of the Atlantic during the first half of the 19th century and these are now highly desirable. The upright piano was probably the most 'architectural' piece of furniture ever devised, and it afforded considerable scope to designers and craftsmen who covered its surfaces with gilding, lacquer, balustroid and fluted pillars, cabriole legs, grotesques and animal masks, bracket candlesticks, fretwork panels backed with silk and other decorative extravagances. The earliest pianos were also lavishly decorated with marquetry and boulle work. Elegantly chased brass mounts and handles were another popular feature. Consequently the more decorative uprights of 1800-50 may be worth from £250 to £800, though it should be noted that there are many uprights of the second half of the 19th century of such unrelieved ugliness that until a decade ago they were fit only for firewood. Even now, when Victoriana has become fashionable, these musical monstrosities are still generally in the £15 – £50 price range. An important point concerning pianos is their condition, and such defects as a cracked or distorted sound-board, frame damage or worn hammers will seriously detract from the value. Restoration is now so expensive that it can easily cost four figures to put a piano into good working order – and this consideration may make the initial purchase price prohibitive.

Museums
British Piano Museum, London.
Fenton House, London.
Geffrye Museum, London.
Horniman Museum, London.
London Museum, London.
Royal College of Music, London.
Victoria and Albert Museum, London.
The Wallace Collection, London.
Waddesdon Manor, Aylesbury.
Art Gallery and Museum, Brighton.
Fitzwilliam Museum, Cambridge.
Royal Scottish Museum, Edinburgh.
St. Cecilia's Hall, Edinburgh.
City Museum, Hereford.
Museum and Art Gallery, Leicester.

City Museum, Liverpool.
Ashmolean Museum, Oxford.
Pitt Rivers Museum, Oxford.
Central Museum and Art Gallery, Northampton.
City Museum, Sheffield.
Blithfield, Rugeley.
City Museum and Art Gallery, Stoke-on-Trent.
City Museum and Art Gallery, Worcester.
Snowshill Manor, Worcester.
Windsor Castle, Windsor.
Boston Museum of Fine Arts, Boston, Mass.
Metropolitan Museum of Art, New York.
Smithsonian Institution, Washington.
Library of Congress, Washington.
Conservatoire Royal de Musique, Brussels.
Conservatoire de Musique, Paris.
Gemeente Museum, Hague.
Musikinstrumenten Museum, Berlin.
Germanisches National Museum, Nuremberg.
Kunsthistorisches Museum, Vienna.

Reading List
Baines, Anthony. Musical Instruments Through the Ages. Harmondsworth, 1961. European and American Musical Instruments. London, 1966.
Bragard, Roger. Musical Instruments in Art and History. London, 1968.
Gilpin, F.W. Old English Instruments of Music. London, 1965.
Harding, Rosamund. The Pianoforte. London, 1933.
Marcuse, Sybil. Musical Instruments: a Comprehensive Dictionary. London, 1966.
Russell, Raymond. The Harpsichord and the Clavichord. London, 1959. Catalogue of Keyboard Instruments in the Victoria and Albert Museum. London, 1968.
Sachs, C. The History of Musical Instruments. London, 1942.
Winternitz, Emanuel. Musical Instruments of the Western World. London, 1966.

NETSUKE

Small carved toggles (from the Japanese verb *tsuke,* to fasten) used to secure by means of a cord the inro (q.v.) and pouches attached to the sash of the kimono. Considerable ingenuity was displayed in carving these objects into an infinite variety of forms, human, animal and mythological. Certain limitations were dictated by the requirements of these toggles. Primarily netsuke had to be small, bereft of awkward projections which might catch and tear clothing, and compact in design; but most important of all it had to have apertures (cord-holes) through which the cord was passed. At one extreme, the cord holes in many wood netsuke are lined with ivory to prevent wear and are a highly distinctive feature; at the other extreme, however, are ivory netsuke in which the holes are cunningly disguised in the limbs of the figure. Small carvings without tell-tale cord holes are known as okimono and were intended as small ornaments.

Date-lines

Netsuke came into use in the 16th century, but at this early date they consisted merely of simple pieces of wood, bamboo, bone or ivory with a rudimentary attachment for the cord. As collector's pieces netsuke date from the mid-17th century and reflect the period of peace and prosperity that developed under the Tokugawa shoguns from 1620 onwards. Sculptors and carvers, hitherto employed in making religious figurines, now turned increasingly to netsuke. Netsuke of this period tend to be simple in line and subject, with little or no surface decoration and relying mainly on the patina of the ivory for effect. The earliest netsuke were *manju* (bun-shaped) but by the end of the century

 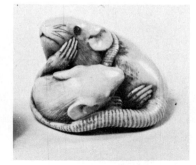

Left: Ivory model of tiger. Right: Ivory group of two rats. Both popular 18th century types.

animals, human figures and deities of the Buddhist and and Shinto religions were becoming more popular. Early netsuke are invariably unsigned.

By the middle of the 18th century schools for carvers were established at Edo (now Tokyo), Osaka, Kyoto, Nagoya, Gifu, Yamada, Wakayama, Ise and Echigo. Each school developed its own distinctive styles of carving and subject matter and tended to favour certain materials such as ivory (Kyoto, Osaka), cherry and box wood (Nagoya, Gifu), Korean pine (Wakayama). The subjects became much more

A very fine and popular 19th century netsuke by Tomotada.

varied, the emphasis moving from figures of the Sennin (immortals) to animals, both real and mythological. Historic figures were popular, but so also were figures from everyday life — actors, workmen, children — the masks and costume of the Noh drama and Kabuki theatre, household implements and plant life. The signs of the zodiac and the rich field of Japanese folklore were also immensely popular. The finest netsuke were produced in the late 18th-early 19th centuries. Thereafter forms became rather stereotyped or too elaborate for practical use.The rapid westernization of Japan after the Meiji Restoration of 1868 led to a decline in netsuke, though this has, perhaps, been overstated by most writers on the subject. The Tokyo School of Fine Arts, founded in 1878, did much to foster interest in traditional crafts. Miyazaki Joso (1855-1910), a pupil of Kojitsu of Tokyo, formed his own school and carried on the carving of fine netsuke in the traditional manner. Artists of the So School have continued to produce netsuke down to the present time and in recent years the art of netsuke carving has spread to other parts of Japan.

Points to Look for

The criteria governing the value of netsuke are quality, name of carver, novelty, material and period of manufacture in that order. Quality is almost impossible to define and accurate assessment comes only with a very long acquaintance with the subject. Mastery of the medium, detail in engraving and treatment of the subject are a guide, to

19th century fine netsuke by Kwaigyoko Masatsugu.

Attractive and popular type, early to mid-19th century.

which one should add compactness and restraint. Many of the later netsuke, especially of the So school lack the compactness essential in a good toggle and have been dubbed Okimono-style. As many of them are of a very high artistic quality, however, they still command fairly high prices, in the general range from £70 to £300; although some pieces fetch up to £5,000.

Many 18th and 19th century netsuke are signed by the carver, and the presence of a signature identifiable as that of one of the recognised masters, such as Masanao, Tomotada, Okatomo or Okatori, often enhances the value of the piece. Fine netsuke by the acknowledged masters would now be worth in excess of £5,000 (ten years ago the top price for signed netsuke would have been about £300). Signed netsuke by minor artists even of the Meiji era now range from £150 to £1,000. Simple netsuke of the 19th century, without signature, are in the £20 – £150 range.

Material is not as important a criterion as is popularly imagined. The fact that the best netsuke of the elite Osaka, Kyoto and Edo schools were carved in ivory may have created the impression that ivory netsuke are always preferable to wood, but it should be borne in mind that whereas many poor quality netsuke of the late 19th century were carved in ivory for the western export market and are still worth no more than £15 – £20, the wood netsuke of such masters as Suzuki Masakatsu and Miyake Masanao are now well over the £1,000 mark. Signed wood netsuke range from £150 to £600 and are often comparable in price with ivory netsuke of the same quality, period and school. Other materials used in netsuke include bamboo, narwhal tusk, rhinoceros horn or bone. The presence of inlays of amber, tortoiseshell, black horn (to impart realism to the eyes of the figures) or the use of lacquer or metal usually rate a handsome premium. Netsuke incorporating novelty or 'trick' forms also rate a premium; they include netsuke with a rattle (such as seeds in a lotus pod), a worm slipping in and out of rotten fruit, snake in a skull, mouse darting in and out of clothing, etc.

Pitfalls

The demand for netsuke for the western export market far exceeded the supply and encouraged a spate of late 19th and early 20th centuries fakes and forgeries. The fakes consist of genuine small carvings produced as ornaments which were converted to netsuke by boring cord holes through them. The absence of ivory lining in the cord holes of wood netsuke should put one on guard, though this is not an invariable feature. In genuine netsuke the apertures for the cords should be as unobtrusive as possible; in fakes the holes seldom look or feel right. Copies of traditional netsuke are frequently met with, but lack the fine detail, patina or indefinable qualities of genius which are the hallmark of the genuine article. The worst kind of copies are those made from ivory dust, compacted and moulded into shape; these items lack the characteristic cuts and engraving found in real ivory carving. The borderline between a modern 'interpretation' of an antique style, an early 20th century 'copy' and a late 19th century example following traditional lines but having degenerated into a stereotyped form is debatable and explains the somewhat erratic pricing of late netsuke.

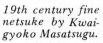

19th century fine netsuke by Kwai-gyoko Masatsugu.

Museums
British Museum, London.
Victoria and Albert Museum, London.
Fitzwilliam Museum, Cambridge.
Ashmolean Museum, Oxford.
Pitt-Rivers Museum, Oxford.
Royal Scottish Museum, Edinburgh.
City Museum and Art Gallery, Bristol.
Museum and Art Gallery, Leicester.
City Museum and Art Gallery, Stoke-on-Trent.
Brodick Castle, Isle of Arran.
Musée d'Ennery, Paris (Sundays only).
National Museum, Tokyo.
Museum of Fine Arts, Boston, Mass.
Freer Gallery of Art, Washington, D.C.

Reading List

Brockhaus, A. Netsuke. Leipzig, 1905.
Bushell, R. The Netsuke Handbook of Ueda Reikichi.   Tokyo, 1961.
    Collectors' Netsuke. Tokyo, 1971.
Davey, Neil K. Netsuke: A study based on the M.T. Hindson Collection. London, 1974.
Eskenazi, Giuseppe. Japanese Netsuke formerly in the collection of Dr. Robert C. Greene. London, 1973.
Jonas, F.M. Netsuke. Kobe, 1928; London, 1969.
Meinertzhagen, Frederick. The Art of the Netsuke Carver. London, 1956.
O'Brien, M.L. Netsuke: A Guide for Collectors. Rutland, Vt. and Tokyo, 1965.
Oakada, Y. Netsuke: A Miniature Art of Japan. Tokyo, 1951.
Reikichi, Ueda. A Study of Netsuke. Osaka, 1943.
Ryerson, Egerton. The Netsuke of Japan. London, 1958.

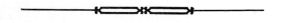

NUTMEG GRATERS

Cylindrical ⌐.1700. London. Length: 2½ins. The grater is marked on lid, grater and base of case with maker's mark only.

Pocket graters for powdering nutmeg were fashionable from about 1670 to 1840, the grated nutmeg being added to drinks or used as a condiment to make meat more appetising. It became the custom for gentlemen to carry small graters with them when dining out or drinking in public. The majority were made of silver, either wholly or partly, and several distinct forms evolved during the period when they were current.

Date-lines

1670-1730   Plain cylindrical form consisting of a cap, tubular grater and outer case. The grater itself may be found in iron or silver. The outer case was usually quite plain, but occasionally line engraving, or even pierced decoration, may be found. Usually from two to three inches in length. £80 – £150.

                          Early heart-shaped graters. Over £150 if 17th century.

1700-1750   Heart- or tear-shaped form, comprised of three parts: a lid and base which detach from the main part in the top of which is set the grater. The grater was usually of iron or other base metal and conceals a compartment in which a nutmeg could be stored. Decoration on this type is usually fairly simple, consisting of shallow line engraving. £100 – £150.

1730-1760	Acorn-shaped graters between 1¼ and 2½ ins. high. Composed of three parts, with the dome of the acorn unscrewing to reveal the grater which, in turn, conceals the nutmeg. £40 – £70.
1760-1780	A rare variant of the acorn-shaped grater has a corkscrew attached and measures 3-4 ins. in height. These combined graters and corkscrews were known as maces, and often thus shaped – a pun on the word mace meaning the outer layer of the nutmeg which was itself used as a spice. £100 – £150.

Acorn shape, c.1770. Maker: S. Massey, London. Length: 1½ins.

1750-1800	Egg-shaped form. Like the earlier graters, this type usually only bears a maker's mark prior to 1790, and full hallmarks after that date. Wide range of sizes, from ½ to 1½ ins. in length. Often decorated by chasing, bright-cutting and reeded banding. Three parts as before, usually unscrewing though some later examples merely pull apart. £35 – £80.
1760-1810	Barrel-shaped graters – probably the commonest shape of all, coinciding with the high point of the popularity of nutmeg graters. Generally 1-2 ins. tall and in three sections as before. Hallmarks and decoration as for egg-shapes. £35 – £60.

1770-1785. Oval pull-off graters, from 1 to 2½ins. in length. Lid and base pull off in same manner as the heart-shaped graters. Stylistically the decoration shows the influence of the Adam Brothers. £40 – £70.

Oval pull-off c.1780. Maker S. Massey, London. Length: 1¼ins. Height ¾in.

Hydrant shape. 1819. Silver hallmark, Birmingham. Maker: Samuel Pemberton.

1780-1810	Hydrant-shaped graters, similar in structure to the oval pull-off, but has a distinctive drum-shaped body and domed cap, like a fire-hydrant. Relatively plain, this type was favoured by the Birmingham makers, especially Samuel Pemberton whose mark is found on later specimens. £50 – £90 (plain). £100 – £150 (bright cut).
1780-1820	Box-shaped graters, from 1 to 2½ ins. in length. The majority have an oval section, though squares, rectangles, octagons, squares with cut or chamfered corners are also known. Lids either lift off or are hinged; bases are usually attached by means of an invisible hinge. Names to look for are Thomas Phipps and Edward Robinson. Wide variety of decorative treatment on sides and lids. £40 – £150.
1790-1815	Hinged cylinder graters, consisting of an oval cylinder with a side cut away to reveal the grater inside. Hinged base and lid, the latter clipping over the top of the grater to seal it. £50 – £80 (premium for examples inscribed 'Rub this and remember me').
1790-1820	Urn-shaped graters, usually 2½ to 3½ ins. high. A development of the cylindrical form, but shaped like a classical urn on a square plinth. When the lid is lifted the front falls away to reveal the grater inside. Often decorated in classical form. £100 – £150.

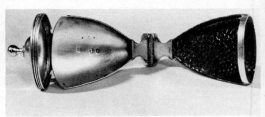

Urn shape. 1804. Maker: Phipps and Robinson, London. Height: 2½ins.

Rectangular. 1836. Maker: Charles Reily and George Storer, London. Length: 1¾ins. Height: 1⅛ins.

1800-1840   Plain rectangular graters, generally larger than the earlier types, with lid and base hinged to the body. A wide variety of decorative styles, including novelties such as shells, fruits, walnuts, etc. £40 – £70.

Points to look for

Graters should be in good working condition, solidly made, with hinges intact. Plus factors are names or initials of the better manufacturers, personal inscriptions alluding to betrothals, marriages, etc., and good decorative features. The above descriptions concern silver graters, but examples may also be found in Sheffield plate, brass, pewter, wood, bone or ivory (invariably incorporating steel graters). Graters in materials other than silver have attracted comparatively little interest so far and no hard and fast market for them yet exists. Prices range from £5 upwards for wooden graters in good condition.

Pitfalls

With all examples beware of replacement graters and, on early cylindrical examples, pull-off lids.

Museums
Victoria and Albert Museum, London.
Wallace Collection, London.
Royal Scottish Museum, Edinburgh.
City Museum, Hereford.
Museum and Art Gallery, Leicester.
Central Museum and Art Gallery, Northampton.
City Museum, Sheffield.
City Museum and Art Gallery, Worcester.

Reading List
Miles, Elizabeth B. The English Pocket Nutmeg-Grater. Cleveland, Ohio, 1966.

OIL LAMPS

Form of illumination used from the earliest times until the advent of electric light. Oil lighting has survived in many parts of the world to the present day and lamps are still being produced, though mainly for export. The revival of 19th century oil lamps for interior decoration in recent years has stimulated a demand for them, either in their original form, or converted for electric light. There are many different types of lamp, varying in technical complexity and decorative appearance and these factors, rather than age, govern the value of lamps.

Types

Early lamps were shallow saucer-like vessels, with a wick of moss or wool which floated in the oil, and gave a poor light with much smell. The Crusie, widely used in Scotland and Ireland, was a hand-made iron type and can be found from £6 for simple specimens to £20 for the double decker and lidded types. The Roman lamp with a covered top and spout-like aperture resembled a flattened teapot and was made in terra cotta and in bronze. Many fakes and replicas of these are still made and genuine lamps in either metal or terra cotta would cost several hundred pounds.

Hand lamps start off with small tinplate specimens with Gem or Star burners at £2 — £4 followed by a large variety with glass containers, mainly common flint with Gem, Star, Slip and Eureka burners; these in optic, moulded opal, decorated opal and moulded crystal, £4 — £14. Cut crystal, £12+. Brass hand lamps generally had Kosmos burners though Star, Slip and Duplex were all used. Production was constant for some 60 years and Kosmos specimens are best bought complete with chimney as the glassware can be elusive. Prices vary from £5 to £15 according to size and type. Many attractive night lights such as Pixie and Kelly were produced as well as the nursery rhyme and fairy tale patterns. £1 — £3.

Scottish iron two-valve crusie lamp.

Slip burner model.

Portable Lanterns are generally more utilitarian and less decorative than small hand lamps, and of a more robust construction since they were invariably used out of doors. They range in size from the small lanterns carried by policemen, nightwatchmen, railwaymen and bellmen (the early 19th century equivalent of postmen), to the large rectangular or cylindrical lanterns used by coaches, ships, and for street lighting. Metal parts may be of japanned iron, brass or copper, the latter being more desirable. They also vary considerably in technical construction. They range in price from about £10 for a small lantern of simple design and styling, with japanned metal and plain glass sides, £25 — £40 for copper or brass lanterns, to £30 — £60 for ship's navigation lamps in

Highly decorative and desirable lamp with Kosmos burner.

copper and brass with coloured lenses. Plus factors are inscriptions of police forces, civic insignia or the badges of the old railway companies of the pre-grouping era.

Piano Lamps were elegant, small lamps usually fitted with a spring toe for attachment to a sconce or bracket on the piano. They resemble miniaturised table lamps (see below), with cut glass founts, nickel-plated revolving reflector or opal glass Vesta shade. Piano lamps vary greatly in value, beginning with the cheaper moulded or cut glass lamps (£5 — £10), to those with fount and shade in matching styles and colours of fancy glass with silver or silver-plated fittings £10 — £20). Piano lamps with coloured silk shades are unusual and worth a premium. Piano lamps were fitted as pairs but in the intervening years many of them have become split up. Pairs are worth two and a half to three times the price of singles. They were particularly popular from

Duplex burner. An uncommon example with matching globe and chimney.

about 1870 till the First World War, though some lines remained in production till the Thirties. Delicately cut or engraved glass varieties are the earliest, while lamps with brass founts are the latest. An unusual type has a heavy brass base with angled lamp, designed to sit on the piano top, £15 – £30.

Reading Lamps may be divided into two sub-types, according to whether they are portable or table models, and these can generally be distinguished by size. The majority of reading lamps had fixed shades and lamps, but a particularly desirable type is the Queen's reading lamp with an adjustable lamp made of brass mounted on a central pillar with a weighted base; these are in two types, for colza oil or paraffin. A tall cylindrical reservoir was fitted on one side and a burner and domed shade on the other. Large numbers of reading lamps were produced between about 1870 and 1930 and bear such trade names as Kosmos, Wizard and Matador. Small reading lamps with Kosmos burners and revolving conical reflectors were generally nickel-plated up to the First World War (£10 – £20), but those from 1918 onwards were usually chromium-plated and are not so desirable (£5 – £12).

Larger reading lamps, with brass fittings, are now in the price range £20 – £40; those with silver-plated fittings are worth twice as much.

Queen's reading lamps, in working order with reservoir, burner and shade intact, are now worth from £20 upwards, depending on type and quality of shade.

Table Lamps present the greatest scope to the collector, differing widely in decorative appeal and construction. At one extreme are the major rarities of the late 19th century whose decorative qualities are in a class of their own. Etched and enamelled glass lamps with scenic motifs on shade and bowl, are in the price range £500 – £1,200, while those with Tiffany favrile or wisteria shades are now from £2,500 to £4,000. In this category the lamp itself is of comparatively small importance and the type and quality of the glass take over completely.

The common type had ¾ inch or 1 inch Slip burners, flint glass founts and cast iron stands, generally without a globe though sometimes with a lotus chimney with sandblast motifs. These are in the price range £10 to £15. The Duplex burner, invented by Hinks in 1865, has two flat wicks side by side and still is in limited production today. This was the most common burner for table lamps which started with the every-day glass fount type with a cast iron stand (£25 — £35) and comprised a huge variety up to the all cut glass specimens with silver fittings. The common burners had brass winding buttons whereas those of the better ones were of black china bearing the maker's name, the best of all having the two winders in one stem and a weighted extinguisher; frequently this burner had a bayonet catch fitting instead of the thread. The desirable specimens are those with tall Corinthian pillars, cut glass founts and tinted, etched (manography) moons or globes. Price range for Duplex table lamps, £30 — £100. Names to look for on the buttons are Palmers, Hinks, Evereds, Wright & Butlers, Sherwoods.

Early lamps of the pre-paraffin era from 1784 fo the Argand, 1800 to 1840 for the Carcel and 1836 to 1870 for the Moderator, all of which had colza oil for a fuel.

Perfect lamps are hard to find as the burning of colza oil left a hard gum-like deposit resulting in the winders (and in the case of the Moderator, the piston key as well) being forced and broken. Prices from £40 to £100.

Central draught lamps with circular wicks accounted for the luxury end of the table lamp range in both 50 and 100 candle power sizes. Familiar names on the winders were Veritas, Venus, Juno, Court, Sun, Hinks, etc. Where complete with a good etched moon or optic tinted tulip, £35 — £75.

Carcel lamp with clockwork feed.

Franchot's Moderator lamp with spring loaded piston.

Incandescent lamps. The Kronos, Pifco or Candesco burners were sold separately and were interchangeable with Duplex, hence many lamps are found with these mantel burners fitted; this does not affect their value and can in some cases enhance it. Aladdin and Famos were made as mantle lamps and are best fitted with their original fancy opal vesta type shades. The lamps are mainly all metal though pottery vases may be found. The Aladdin start off at their No. 11 made in Britain with a bulge chimney instead of the loxon. Nos. 1 to 10 were made in America and are rare over here, the prototype being the German-made Practicus. There are many clubs in America devoted solely to the collecting of Aladdin lamps. £15 – £50.

Vestibule Lamps or pendant hall lamps were fitted with chains for suspension from the ceiling of hallways. Larger lamps in this category were intended for lighting public halls, churches, railway stations and other public or semi-public places, and they vary enormously in size and construction. The most popular types of suspension lamps were the Veritas, the Monstre and the Union (all British) and the Miller and the Rochester (both imported in large numbers from the United States).

These lamps vary enormously, from plain wrought iron brackets and fittings to quite elaborate brass devices with compensating weights. £20 – £50.

Standard Lamps were fashionable from about 1870 onwards and may be found in many different materials such as wrought iron, wrought iron and copper together, brass, brass and copper. The metal standards were often telescopic or adjustable in some way. Rigid standards of wooden construction were also used. Central draught lamps, similar to those used in suspension lamps, were employed and usually had tulip or moon glassware. Oil standard lamps remained in fashion until the end of the First World War and were widely used in churches; many of them were subsequently converted for electric

Art Nouveau glass table lamp in the Daum style, height 27ins.

light. Brass telescopic standard lamps in original condition are now scarce (£50 − £150), but wrought iron examples are more plentiful (£50 − £100). Plus factors are elaborately engraved or sandblasted shades which can boost the value of quite ordinary wrought iron standards to three figures. The most expensive of all are the Art Nouveau and Tiffany lamps with shades composed of leaded stained or coloured glass, £1,500 − £4,000.

Swing bracket lamps, for use on walls and landings, and also in such vehicles as caravans, are best collected complete with their brackets. The cheaper types in cast iron are often found without their brackets, which were comparatively flimsy. The smaller lamps were fitted with Wizard, Slip and Duplex burners. Larger lamps were produced by Veritas (central draught) and may be found with smoke bells over the top of the chimney to prevent scorching the ceiling. Prices depend largely on the size, type and decorative features of the glass globes. From £7 − £10 for small cast iron lamps to £50+ for large brass lamps with ornamental bracket intact and decorative globe.

Museums
British Museum, London.
Science Museum, London.
London Museum, London.
Victoria and Albert Museum, London.
Art Gallery and Museum, Brighton.
Beamish Museum, Chester-le-Street.
National Museum of Antiquities, Edinburgh.
Royal Scottish Museum, Edinburgh.
City Museum, Hereford.
Museum and Art Gallery, Leicester.
Central Museum and Art Gallery, Northampton.
Blithfield, Rugeley, Staffordshire.
City Museum, Sheffield.
City Museum and Art Gallery, Stoke-on-Trent.
City Museum and Art Gallery, Worcester.
Castle Museum and Strangers' Hall, Norwich.

Reading List
Hughes, Bernard and Therle. Small Antique Furniture. London.
Lindsay, J. Seymour. Iron and Brass Implements of the English House. Medici, 1927.
Meadows, Cecil A. Discovering Oil Lamps. Shire Publications, Tring.

ORMOLU

Term, derived from the French *dorure d'or moulu* (ground gold), denoting a form of gilding on cast bronze or brass objects, mainly used in furniture mounts and small decorative items. Ormolu consisted of an amalgam of gold with mercury which was applied to the surface of the article and then subjected to heat. This drove off the mercury leaving an even gold deposit on the surface. This process was injurious to health and was actually banned in Britain, though it continued to be used on the Continent. Because of the cost of the materials employed and the risk to the gilders, ormolu was always an expensive process. Apart from the handles and mounts on furniture of the highest quality, ormolu may be found on such metal objets d'art as candlesticks, candelabra, inkstands, sconces, brackets, fireside implements, andirons, vases and clock cases. In the last-named the clock itself is usually subsidiary to the ornament which invariably incorporates gilt-bronze figures, reliefs and Neo-Classical decoration. The British use the word ormolu very loosely for castings which are light yellow throughout and much nearer to brass than bronze.

Datelines

Objects of gilt bronze have been made for centuries and prices are widely variable but at a high level.

c.1560-1725 (The end of the Régence)	Ormolu of this period, introduced to France from Italy, is exceedingly rare and most items would now be priced from £1,000 upwards.
1715	Baroque, the style of Louis XIV.
1725-1774	Rococo, which, though declining, overlapped Neo-Classical.

An inkstand (encrier) *of cast and chiselled gilt-bronze in the rococo style. The inkwell with two amorini on the cover set in a Sèvres saucer with a turquoise ground and birds in reserves, flanked by holders for quill pens and pounce. French, c.1765.*

344

1760-1814	Neo-Classical covers the Louis XVI style, 1774-1793, the Directoire 1793-1804, and the Empire 1804-14.
19th century	Limited revival of the Baroque under the names of Louis XIV or Neo-Renaissance.

Prices for the period from 1725.

Clock cases of fine quality up to 18ins. wide, £1,500 – £4,000.

Small clocks up to 9ins. wide of good quality, £200 – £750.

Wall lights c.1760, pair £1,800 – £2,200; single £300 – £600.

Inkstands, £200 – £600.

post-1814   Candlesticks, single £50 – £180; pair £80 – £300.

Candelabra, average price per pair, £150 – £500.

A fine pair complete with marble base and sprays of flowers in the 18th century style could make £900 – £1,400.

The larger the better, 3ft. being a good size for these, though they have been made larger.

Wall sconces, pair £50 – £250.

Clocks, £100 – £500, though up to £3,000 for a large porcelain mounted clock in a garniture with candelabra.

A pair of ormolu candlesticks in the revived rococo style of the 1840s. The drip pans hung with faceted lustres. Perhaps English.

A pair of gilt-bronze curtain holders. French, c.1840.

345

Above: A Chinese porcelain figure of Kuan Tin, made at Tê Hua and decorated in Europe, mounted in gilt-bronze as a two-light candle-holder in the 18th century manner. Marble base.

A five-light candelabrum, one of a pair, in gilded ormolu, cast in sections and assembled. Revived Renaissance style, French, c.1860.

Ormolu mounted porcelain, £100 – £500.
A pair of good Sèvres mounted ewers of large size (about 2ft.) could be in the £800 – £2,000 range.

Points to look for

Ormolu was used less by 1840, when electro-gilding and dipping were more commonly used. Prior to that date various cheaper substitutes were used and should present little problem in identification. True ormolu has softer colouring and a silkier texture than electro-gilding. Gold lacquer was an effective substitute at the time, but has not stood the test of time so well. The lacquer tends to flake and this can be detected by the spots of tarnish which appear on the surface of the metal. Gold-lacquered objects are quite collectable, providing the lacquer is of a good quality and is more or less intact. This process was widely used in Britain. Values of gold-lacquered objects are about half to two-thirds that of comparable articles in true ormolu.

346

Other checks on true ormolu, which help to distinguish it from later and cheaper reproductions, are the quality of the casting, the chasing and other afterwork, the marks of the bronze-founders, stylistic features, such as restrained use of ornament as opposed to the extravagant over-ornamentation which became fashionable in the mid-19th century, and minor technical features, such as the use of hand-made rather than machine-made screws on the base and other detachable parts.

Boulton and Fothergill of Birmingham made high quality ormolu in the 1760- late 1770s period, which is very collectable, but France provided the best makers in the late 18th century and early 19th century. The maker of a clock case could influence the price considerably. Names to look out for are Caffieni and Gouthière.

Pitfalls

All that glisters is not ormolu and even where genuine ormolu gilding has been used, not everything is in the same collectable category. Although this process was applied to cast bronze or brass objects, it is important to note that about 1800 it was also applied to objects produced from cheap mechanical pressings. These objects are much lighter than cast objects and lack the detail and fine chasing of the originals. From 1830 onwards even cheaper substitutes were produced, in zinc, pewter, Britannia metal and spelter. Objects cast in these metals lack the solid, weighty feeling of the earlier bronze or brass articles and do not have the fine crisp finish of the latter. Electrotyped objects were popular in the second half of the 19th century but have a smooth, mechanical appearance and a hollow, tinny sound and bear little resemblance to cast objects.

Museums

British Museum, London.
London Museum, London.
Victoria and Albert Museum, London.
Wallace Collection, London.
Waddesdon Manor, Aylesbury.
Royal Pavilion, Brighton.
Royal Scottish Museum, Edinburgh.
Wernher Collection, Luton Hoo.
Central Museum and Art Gallery, Northampton.
County Museum, Stafford.
Windsor Castle, Windsor.
Blenheim Palace, Woodstock.
Musée des Arts Decoratifs, Paris.

PAPER MONEY

The use of paper instead of precious metals to denote money originated in China during the T'ang Dynasty between 650 and 800 A.D. The earliest block-printed notes were known as *fei-ch'ien* (literally 'flying money') and consisted of paper drafts negotiable in bronze currency. These drafts paved way for the first true paper money, introduced by the Sung Dynasty about 1000 A.D. and redeemable in coin. The proliferation of paper money over the ensuing 270 years led to inflation and helped cause the downfall of the Sung Dynasty. Paper money was also issued far too readily by the Yuan Dynasty. Very few examples of Sung or Yuan notes are in existence today and many of these are in museum collections.

Rather more plentiful are the notes issued by the Ming Dynasty (1368-1644), but even these are rare and fetch between £700 and £1,000 in auctions. The use of paper money in China died out with the collapse of the Mings, but it was adopted in Europe in the late 17th century and arose out of the promissory notes, drafts and bills used by merchants and bankers. The earliest European paper money in the accepted sense were the *kreditivsedlar* (credit notes) issued by the

The West Riding Union Banking Company £5, unissued 18-.
This is a proof of an issued note, printed to show the Directors of the Bank what the final note will look like, also for them to add remarks concerning the design. These early Private bank notes are of great interest to British collectors, especially in issued form.

20/- Note, The East Lothian Banking Company.
This is an unissued note; the issued notes were signed by William Borthwick, who was Chief Cashier of the bank during the 1820s. He eventually absconded with £21,000 of the bank's money and was never caught. The bank collapsed shortly after this.

Stockholm Bank in 1661. None of the first issue has survived, and the few examples of the 1662 and 1663 issues are all in museum collections. The last to appear, dated 1666, is more plentiful and examples are currently in the price range £1,000 to £5,000.

Bank notes in Britain commenced with the Bank of England issues in 1695 and the Bank of Scotland issues a year later. 17th century Bank of England notes, in denominations from £10 to £100 are of the utmost rarity and are now worth from £10,000 upwards.

18th century English and Scottish notes are more plentiful and are in the price range from £50 to £500, depending on date, denomination, bank and condition. 19th century paper money from numerous town and county banks attained its peak in the period 1810 to 1844. Thereafter the number of issuing banks was drastically reduced, as provincial banks lost the right to issue their own notes as they were absorbed by or affiliated with London banks. The last of the independent banks, Fox, Fowler & Co. of Wellington, Somerset, ceased issuing notes in 1921. The value of provincial English and Scottish notes depends on several factors: age, denomination, condition, artistic features and, to a large extent, the location of the bank, since there is now a strong county or regional bias in collecting. £10 – £250.

More recent notes of the major Scottish banks (pound notes only). £5 – £50.

Other denominations, up to £100, are correspondingly more valuable.

Treasury Notes

Emergency paper money introduced at the beginning of the First World War to replace gold coins. These notes were issued by the Treasury and popularly known as Bradburys, after John Bradbury, Secretary to the Treasury, whose signature appeared on them. These notes were issued in denominations of ten shillings and one pound. Numerous variations in date, signature, design and even paper (the first issue was printed on multiple watermarked paper normally used for postage stamps). Treasury notes remained in use after the war, and may be found with the inscriptions 'United Kingdom of Great Britain and Ireland' amended to 'Northern Ireland' in 1927. £10 – £100.

The second issue Bradbury £1 overprinted in Arabic for Dardanelles is worth £1,000.

Later Bank of England Notes

Prior to the bank crisis of 1825 the Bank of England issued few denominations under £5. £1 and £2 notes were issued in 1797 and 1798, £1 notes only in 1801, £1 and £2 notes in 1807 and 1809 to 1821. 1821 notes were re-issued in 1825 and 1826 and then no £1 notes at all were issued until 1928. £200 – £300.

Branch notes, bearing the names of one or other of the thirteen branches in provincial cities are worth at least twice as much as corresponding 'London' notes.

Higher denominations vary considerably in value. £5 notes are the most plentiful, £10 – £450.

£10, £20, £30, £40, £50 notes up to 1829	£300 – £700
£25, £200	£800 – £1,000
£300, £500	£1,500 – £2,500

£1,000 notes were also issued but only about 60 remain unredeemed. £3,500 – £10,000.

Notes bearing the signature of Thomas Rippon (1829-35) are much scarcer and are worth about 30% more than those signed by Henry Hase (1807-29). Notes signed by Matthew Marshall (1835-64) are generally more plentiful and denominations up to £100 are worth about 30% less than Hase notes. Higher denominations are rare and their prices are comparable for Rippon notes of the corresponding denomination. Larger notes are exceedingly complex and their value depends entirely on the particular issue, which can be categorised according to the date and the signatures. Notes were hand-signed by bank staff prior to 1870, and completely printed thereafter. Prices vary considerably, from £100 – £150 for most later 19th century £5 notes to £3,000 – £5,000 for the £1,000 notes of 1870-1943.

The Bank of England took over responsibility for the 10s. and £1 Treasury notes in 1928, and issued their own 10s. notes for the first time, as well as a £1 note. 10s. notes are much scarcer than £1 notes in the first printing. £10 – £15 (10s.). £6 – £10 (£1).

Later issues, up to 1940, 10s. notes worth 10-20% more than £1 notes which are themselves in the price range, £4 – £8.

Later notes are of equal value for 10s. or £1, with the exception of November 1955 issue in which 10s. notes with a prefix of two digit numerals followed by a letter are worth £4 – £5 (the £1 being £3 – £4), while 10s. notes with a prefix of a letter, two numerals and another letter are worth considerably more, £12 – £16.

Overseas Banknotes

This is such a wide range that it would be quite impossible to give more than a very rough guide to values here.

In general, any 19th century note would now be in the price range £1 – £5 minimum. Late 18th century French Revolutionary assignats

Before the French Revolution decided to have his head off, Louis XVI's portrait was used on assignats known to collectors as "Face Royales". Highly prized.

Selection of Paper Money

Confederate States of America, $100; American Military payment certificate; Russian "Babel" note, with political slogans in six languages; British 10 shillings; German Notgeld, City of Emden, 1918; Chinese Sun Yat-Sen Note; Anglo-American invasion money, 1 lira, 1943; Alabama 5-cent note, 1863; Leith Banking Company, £1; Austrian Notgeld 10 heller, Bad Aussee; Mexican Revolution, 2 pesos, 1914; Hungarian hyper-inflation note, 1946; American Military payment certificate.

and mandats range from £2 to £2,000 if genuine, but they were extensively forged at the time by the British authorities. In most cases the forgeries are worth more than the genuine notes, but some reprints designed to deceive collectors are dangerous. The notes of the Confederate States of America, long a drug on the market, are now in great demand and range from £1 for the $10 to £1,200 for the $1,000. Fractional notes (for sums less than a dollar and in some cases as little as 5 cents) are worth £2 – £5. Extensive contemporary forgeries were also made of Confederate notes.

High denomination notes from European countries up to 1900 are in the price range £5 – £5,000. Other countries whose late 19th century notes are highly prized include Australia, Canada, Japan, China, South Africa and Ethiopia.

Early 20th century notes worth collecting include those of Tsarist Russia, Imperial Germany and Mexico prior to the revolution of 1911. £4 – £1,000.

Dominion of Canada $2 — June 23rd, 1923.
Showing a portrait of King Edward VIII (later Duke of Windsor), when he was Prince of Wales, in the uniform of the Welsh Guards, of which regiment he was Colonel-in-Chief. This picture was taken from a painting made before his world tour of the Empire in the 1920s.

South Africa, Orange Free State Republic £5 Note,
issued by the Nationale Bank in 1899.
Notes from South Africa prior to the South African War 1899-1902 are extremely rare in issued form. This note has been split, the two halves being sent separately through the post in case of theft from the old mail coaches, and joined together on reaching its destination. It is understood that the early banks would pay out on half a note, if the other half was lost, i.e. they would have been prepared to pay out £2. 10s. 0d. on this note if only half had arrived.

Banco de Zaragoza 2000 Reales note, dated 14th May, 1857.
An example of an early Spanish note, these notes were numbered but unsigned until issued by the bank tellers across the counter. This note is complete with the counterfoil, which was cut off and kept by the bank as a reference, similar to a cheque stub.

With later notes it is impossible to generalise. Many issues of the 1930s and the Second World War period are of the greatest rarity. At one extreme the Leeward Islands 10s. note of George V (only 6-12 in existence) is worth about £1,200. At the other extreme, however, many low denomination foreign notes, or notes which have been demonetized because of currency reform or inflation, can still be purchased for 10-50p.

Points to look for

Notes should always be collected in crisp, uncirculated condition as far as possible. In many cases, especially with regard to 18th or 19th century issues, circulated condition has to be accepted. In many cases the condition will greatly affect the value of the note. Thus notes which are plentiful in creased or circulated condition, and are in the price range from £10 to £20, might well be worth £400 – £500 in crisp, uncirculated condition.

Apart from the issued notes there are several categories of note which are usually worth more. These include specimen notes (either overprinted SPECIMEN or its equivalent in other languages – Muestra, Muester, Monster, Saggio, etc.) or with zero serial numbers. Printer's

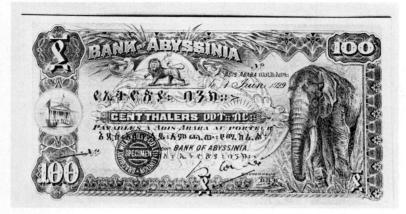

Bank of Abyssinia notes, issued as recently as 1929, very desirable. Bank of Ethiopia notes which followed a year or two later are not so expensive.

specimens may be recognised by zero serial numbers, holes punched in certain places and circular embossed seal marks. Proofs include original art work, uniface notes, colour trials, and finished art work sometimes printed on card or some other material than the normal banknote paper. Stage proofs may take the form of a fragment of the banknote only, with corners deliberately cut off, or even cut in half, as a

Greenland 100 Kroner, Act of 16th January, 1953.
This shows a picture of Knud Rasmussen and a picture of the Thule mountain, with a dog sled and camp. He was an Arctic explorer. This note is valuable because it is a 'Specimen' issued by the Greenland Bank as an example of a new issue to other banks.

1845-1849	Baccarat weights do not have such deeply bulging sides as the other French weights. The flat or slightly concave base is often decorated with a star motif which was distinctive to this factory.
1845-c.1870	English weights manufactured by Whitefriars, Bacchus, Islington, etc. English millefiori canes generally more muted in colour and with a smaller variety of shapes. Associated millefiori articles — inkwells, perfume bottles, doorknobs, etc.
1851-1880	Classic period of American weights. Wide range of types departing from European models. Greater emphasis on floral and fruit weights by the New England Glass Co.,

Left, top: A miniature Clichy swirl weight, set with pink and white threads springing from a central green and white florette. 1-7/8ins.
Bottom: A Baccarat primrose weight, the white ogee petals surrounding the stardust centre, emerald green stalk and six leaves. 2½ins.

Right, top: A Clichy scattered millefiori weight composed of a central cane within a ring of six various canes of usual type and an outer band of eleven further canes, the whole set on a regular white muslin ground. 2-5/8ins.
Bottom: A St. Louis fruit weight of usual type, the pears and cherries set in a white latticinio basket. 2½ins.

	Sandwich, Gillinder, Mount Washington, Millville, etc. Unusual shapes include oblongs and squares, pedestal floral weights and moulded fruit weights on a 'cookie' base.
1850-1920	Green bottle glass weights, associated with Kilner of Wakefield, but also made at Nailsea and in Scotland. Floral motifs created by tiny air bubbles.
1880-1920	Intermittent production of paperweights in America, Belgium, Scandinavia. Complete break with the millefiori tradition of the classic French weights.
1920-onwards	Millefiori weights by Paul Ysart in Scotland. Inter-war and post-war period marked by fine weights by individual craftsmen, mainly in the United States, preceding the more commercial revival of interest in paperweight manufacture in Britain, France, Scandinavia, Italy and Czechoslovakia in the 1960s.

Price Range

The spectrum of antique paperweight prices is very wide, from under £5 for a poor quality Chinese weight of about 1920 with coarse yellowish glass and crude millefiori canes in garish primary colours to the highest price so far paid for any paperweight of £8,500. Only about six weights have made more than £5,000; these are quite exceptional weights of various types, mostly flora and fauna, and so far unique.

£2,000-£5,000	Certain overlays, in particular St. Louis encased overlays and the better Baccarat and Clichy double overlays. Also some Clichy and Baccarat flat bouquets, 'Swan in the pond' weights, insects and birds, salamanders, some snakes and a few rare single flowers.
£1,000-£2,000	Many single flowers, butterflies with flowers, some overlays, carpet grounds. American magnum flat bouquets and Mount Washington rose weights.
£500-£1,000	A lot of single flowers and millefiori weights, particularly mushroom weights, magnum millefiori weights and American pedestal weights.
£150-£500	Virtually any weight which can be classified as French 1845-1870; this includes the more usual sulphide subjects, early Italian or Bohemian weights and the more elaborate English weights.
£50-£150	Early English weights of the millefiori pattern, early Ysart insect weights, very common flowers such as pansies, swirls and colour grounds.

| £25-£60 | Kilner weights, depending on size and complexity of floral decoration. |
| £10-£25 | Virtually any pre-war paperweight, other than the very crude Chinese or Japanese millefiori weights. |

It should be noted that many modern paperweights in current production are in the price range £10 – £20 in unlimited editions, and up to £150 for limited editions, so that age itself is not such an important criterion at the lower end of the value scale.

Points to look for

There may be a wide disparity between the value of two seemingly identical weights and there are several subtle factors which have to be

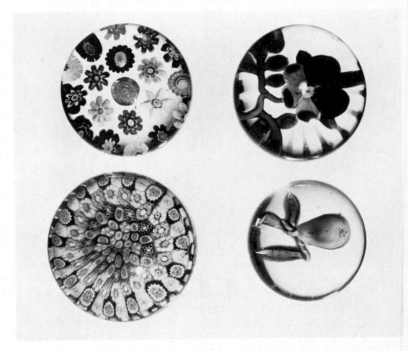

Top left: A Clichy scattered millefiori weight set with a central rose enclosed by two concentric rings of typical canes. 2¾ins.
Top right: A Baccarat pansy weight, the purple and peach petals with stardust centre resting on green petals and stalk. 2¾ins.
Bottom left: A rare Clichy weight composed of a medley of tightly packed canes contained in a green and white basket. 3ins.
Bottom right: A St. Louis or Baccarat pear weight, the ripe fruit with three adherent green leaves set in clear glass. 2½ins.

taken into consideration. Thus, in considering classic French weights, the following criteria are important: the number and variety of silhouette canes in Baccarat or St. Louis weights; the inclusion of initial and/or date canes; the presence of the distinctive Clichy 'rose' in weights of that factory; additional buds in flower weights. The size may also be of importance, miniatures and magnums being much more desirable than standard-sized weights.

Pitfalls

Bearing in mind that paperweights were made by hand at each stage of their production, it is inevitable that the quality of craftsmanship should vary, even within such a well-defined group as the antique French weights. The points which will tend to detract from the desirability of a paperweight are the presence of tiny air bubbles and other minor flaws in the encapsulating glass; dirt specks or other impurities in the surrounding glass; striations and distortions within the dome; mis-alignment of designs within the weight when viewed from above or asymmetrical when seen in profile; irregularities in millefiori canes, including individual canes out of alignment; insect and flower weights with broken or detached components. All these are features in the workmanship which detract from the value.

Condition is of paramount importance, though minor surface scratches are inevitable. Cuts and chips are much more serious and their presence will automatically halve the value of all but the very rarest weights. Scratches can often be polished out without detracting from the appearance or symmetry of a weight. Beware of weights which have been re-ground and the dimensions of the dome reduced thereby; such drastic action may eliminate chips but will invariably result in distortion to the overall appearance and may even bring the canes or underlying motif disastrously close to the surface. Weights with an unnaturally flat dome or uneven diameter should be regarded with suspicion. Chinese and Japanese weights should fool no one, since the millefiori canes are very coarse and garish in colour, and the 'set-up' of the canes is often haphazard. The quality of the glass, however, is an immediate give-away, being yellowish and flawed with bubbles and impurities. More deceptive are the French weights produced by M. Dupont in the early 20th century, often confused with Baccarat weights, though the canes are rather smaller than the originals. A curious mistake in the Dupont weights, however, is the inclusion of canes bearing dates as far back as 1831 — fourteen years earlier than the oldest authentically dated weight! Nevertheless French weights by Dupont (c.1910-34) and Brocart (post-Second World War) are now collected in their own right.

Top, left to right: A St. Louis mushroom weight; a St. Louis dated mushroom weight.
Middle, left to right: A Baccarat shamrock weight; a Clichy faceted swirl weight.
Bottom, left to right: An unusual Clichy initial weight, 3ins; a Clichy patterned millefiori weight, 3ins.

Museums

Victoria and Albert Museum, London. (Not on view)
Art Gallery and Museum, Brighton.
City Museum and Art Gallery, Bristol.
Royal Scottish Museum, Edinburgh.
Willmer House Museum, Farnham.
Littlecote House, Hungerford.
Museum and Art Gallery, Leicester.
Scone Palace, Perth.
Pilkington Glass Museum, St. Helens.
City Museum, Sheffield.
City Museum and Art Gallery, Worcester.
Musée des Arts Decoratifs, Paris.
Art Institute of Chicago.
Francis Fowler Museum, Los Angeles.
Bergstrom Art Centre, Neenah, Wisconsin.
New York Historical Society Museum.

Reading List

Bedford, John. Paperweights. London, 1968.
Bergstrom, Evangeline. Old Glass Paperweights. New York, 1947; London, 1948.
Bozek, Michael. Price Guide Handbook of Glass Paperweights. Hollywood, 1961.
Cloak, Evelyn C. Glass Paperweights. London, New York, 1969.
Elville, E.M. Paperweights and other Glass Curiosities. London, 1954.
Hollister, Paul. The Encyclopedia of Glass Paperweights. New York, 1969.
Imbert, Roger and Amic, Yolande. Les Presse-Papiers Français. Paris, 1948.
Jokelson, Paul. Antique French Glass Paperweights. New York, 1955.
Glass Paperweights and Cameo Heads. New York, 1968.
McCawley, Patricia K. Antique Glass Paperweights from France. London, 1968.
Mackay, James A. Glass Paperweights. London, New York, 1973.
Mannheim, Frank J. A Garland of Weights. New York, 1967.
Melvin, Jean S. American Glass Paperweights and their Makers. New York, 1967.
Smith, Francis Edgar. American Glass Paperweights. Wollaston, Mass., 1939.

PAPIER MACHE

The ancestor of the plastics industry, a technique for making small pieces of furniture, trays, boxes and other articles from a composition of paper pulp containing chalk, size, sand and other stiffeners. Papier mâché originated in the Far East and was introduced to France in the 17th century, hence its French name. It came to Britain about a century later and was used increasingly from 1750 onwards. John Baskerville, the Birmingham printer, was the first to appreciate the commercial application of papier mâché to light surfaces (such as coach panelling) previously made in wood. Henry Clay of Birmingham invented a new technique of manufacture in 1772 using whole sheets of paper glued together and compressed, moulded and baked. Papier mâché of the late 18th century is often referred to as Clay ware. In the early 19th century the process was further improved and costs reduced by compressing a mixture of paper pulp, hemp, flax, tree bark, plant fibres and even mangel-wurzels into moulds under steam pressure. The resulting substance was much lighter than wood and was ideally suited to such decorative treatment as japanning, inlaying with mother-of-pearl or ivory, or painting with flowers, scenery and allegorical compositions. Mid-19th century inlay was often elaborate and extravagant, incorporating gold leaf, tortoiseshell and coloured stones

Jennens and Bettridge papier mâché tray, stamped Jennens and Bettridge, c.1830.

364

as well as mother-of-pearl. Papier mâché was used for furniture of all kinds, though seldom practicable on its own and usually designed to cover wood or metal. It is best known for its application to small tables, writing-cases, desk-tops, trays, pole-screens and small boxes of all kinds.

Date-lines

1750-1780   Relatively heavy, solid appearance, with little gilding or inlay and restrained decoration.

1772-1820   Clay ware of compressed sheets glued together. Increasing use of inlay and painting. Clay ware was comparatively expensive and is thus relatively rare.

Mother-of-pearl inlaid papier mâché writing desk, 1ft. 9ins., mid-19th century.

1825-1864   Main period of Jennens and Bettridge output. Inlay of mother-of-pearl very popular; other materials added later. Articles bear incuse name of manufacturers on the underside.

1864-1900   Later period characterised by over-elaborate decoration. After the death of Jennens in 1864 articles by this firm bore a metal name tag instead of an incuse name and are much less desirable. Hand-painting superseded by transfer printing and other mass-production techniques.

Points to look for

Hand-painted articles were in vogue in the early 19th century and are still undervalued. The corresponding painting, if on canvas, would be worth about 50% more at current market values. These paintings are invariably unsigned, but the distinctive styles of such artists as Edwin Haseler (flowers) and Frederick Newman (peacocks) are readily identifiable and are worth looking for. Topographical subjects were the speciality of Spiers of Oxford (who marked their wares with the firm's trademark) and these are now highly prized.

Clay papier mâché tea caddy. 7½ins. high, inscribed Clay, King Street, Covent Garden, second quarter of 19th century.

Condition is of paramount importance since papier mâché is not a very robust material. Consequently early pieces in fine condion are rare. Small pieces of furniture are of pure papier mâché if they are light for their size and appearance; heavier pieces are papier mâché on a wooden base and are post-1840 and not so desirable. Gilding should be complete and original, and inlay should be intact. Damaged or incomplete items are relatively plentiful and should be priced accordingly. There was a craze for chinoiserie about 1850 and papier mâché articles smothered with mother-of-pearl pagodas and Chinamen are best avoided. Mother-of-pearl inlay was sadly overdone and is not currently a good selling point, unless it is restrained. Scenic motifs in mother-of-pearl, where identifiable, are worth looking for.

Price range

18th century-1830	Pieces of furniture in pure papier mâché, with painted decoration. £100 – £250.
18th century-1825	Articles – trays, pole-screens and work-boxes with hand-painted decoration. £30 – £90.
1825-1850	Inlaid papier mâché trays, work-boxes, writing-cases, blotter covers. £20 – £50. Smaller articles (letter-rack, pen-case, snuffbox). £10 – £25.

| | Chairs and tables from 1825 onwards. £30 – £80. Outstanding examples of chairs and tables. £120 – £150. |
| 1850-1900 | Inlaid articles, especially mother-of-pearl. £15 – £30. Transfer-printed articles. £2 – £10. |

Museums
London Museum, London.
Bethnal Green Museum, London.
British Museum, London.
Victoria and Albert Museum, London.
Royal Scottish Museum, Edinburgh.
City Museum and Art Gallery, Birmingham.
Royal Pavilion, Brighton.
City Museum, Hereford.
Central Museum and Art Gallery, Northampton.
City Museum, Sheffield.

Reading List.
DeVoe, Shirley S. English Papier Mâché of the Georgian and Victorian Periods. London, 1971.
Toller, Jane. Antique Papier Mâché in Great Britain and America. London. 1962.

PATCHWORK

A form of folk art which flourished in Britain and America between the early 18th and late 19th centuries, reaching its zenith in the early 19th century. Quilting was practised from medieval times but the peculiar form using patches of variegated cloth seems to have originated in New England in the late 17th century and to have been introduced to England itself a century later. Scraps of cloth from outworn garments, curtains and loose covers were salvaged, cut into squares or hexagons and tacked to paper templates (often old letters, bills and newspapers), and then sewn together to form a patterned surface. The patchwork was then superimposed on an inner lining and a sheet of backing material and the three layers quilted together. Patchwork reached the height of its popularity in the early 19th century and distinctive regional and district designs were evolved. Thus geometric patterns were favoured in Wales, curvilinear motifs in the north of England and floral, bird and animal motifs in the West Country. American patchwork tended to be much more elaborate, reflecting the greater history of the art there. In particular use was made of appliqué work, in which fancy shapes were cut from cloth and arranged in intricate patterns on a plain or contrasting ground. As in England, there were many different patterns which came to be associated with particular areas. These patterns are known by such fanciful names as 'Birds in Air', 'Drunkard's Path', 'Goose Tracks', 'Moon over the Mountain' and 'Tree of Life'.

The majority of patchwork quilts now in existence belong to the 19th century. Earlier patchworks are rare, but it is difficult to assess date accurately since the materials were often much older than the quilt itself. The presence of scraps of printed cottons, however, would indicate a patchwork no earlier than about 1825 when printed calicos improved enormously in quality and appearance. Machine stitching begins to appear about 1865, though hand-sewn quilts continued to be made in country districts till the 1890s.

Price Range

Cottage patchwork quilts of average size, quality and condition, now range from £10 to £30. Large, elaborate, finely hand-sewn quilts incorporating interesting or unusual motifs, are worth much more and range from £50 to £200.

Appliquéd oak leaf design in red paisley on white ground.

Section of a very fine quilt with patches of less than an inch square.

Good example of English Log Cabin design.

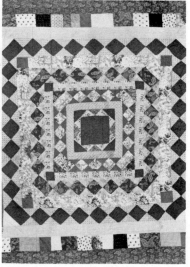

Section of typical 19th century cottage quilt, incorporating dress and furnishing materials.

PEWTER

Left to right: back row
Quart c.1820; pint, mid-Victorian; George IV pint; pint 1780-1800. All marked. Note handle differences as well as body shape. The front row consists of half pints.

An alloy of tin with lead or copper, sometimes containing antimony or bismuth, with a silver appearance when new, shading to grey with the patina of age. Pewter was cast into bowls, vessels and dishes from Roman times, but the bulk of extant pewter dates from the 16th century. Though largely superseded by ceramics in the 18th and electro-plate in the 19th centuries, pewter survived fitfully and even enjoyed something of a revival in the late 19th century and again in the period between 1910 and 1935, though articles made in the latter period may mainly be regarded as reproductions.

Date-lines (according to touch-marks)

1503	Makers' touch-marks became compulsory in England, although in many cases these were applied voluntarily before that date. Usually consisted of initials or simple emblems (the ancestors of trademarks).
1509	Quality marks added by the Pewterers' Guild and consisted of the portcullis and lilypot marks.
c. 1550	Fleur-de-lis mark replaced the lilypot mark. Rose and crown mark applied to wares of the highest quality.
1671	Rose and crown mark extended to all export wares.
1690	Rose and crown mark now used generally on all pewter, in conjunction with maker's mark.

1580 – 1750 Marks simulating the hallmarks of silver sometimes used, despite periodic ordinances forbidding this practice. These pseudo-hallmarks take the form of four small shields incorporating the maker's initials and emblem.

1600 – 1750 Pieces often marked with the initials of the client (house-mark), often simulating a silver hallmark.

Types of Pewter

The value of pewter articles depends largely on the type of object, though age, condition and decorative qualities are also important. The most valuable items are lidded tankards with thumb-pieces, dating from the 16th to the late 17th centuries. Lidded tankards were made right on till the early 19th century, but later types are not so expensive. Stuart tankards are now in the price range £400 – £700.

Late 18th and early 19th century lidded tankards are £70 to £100. Tankards evolved chronologically as follows: straight- sided, slightly tapering upwards; baluster shapes; footed rims, handles projecting from the side; waisted sides; straight sides tapering from top to bottom.

Quart tankards of the early 18th century.

Tankards with open tops were used in ale-houses and continued in service long after pewter had been superseded in private households by pottery or electroplate. Open-top tankards are of relatively little value, though they parallel the shapes of lidded vessels. Thus 18th century tavern mugs with open tops, broad bases and narrow tops now rate £25 – £40; early 19th century mugs with slightly balustroid bodies are from £15 to £30; and later 19th century mugs with bulbous bodies, S-shaped handles and a high foot rim, are in the price range £6 – £12. These styles, or variations of them, have continued to be produced to the present day and examples from 1850 onwards are worth £10 – £20.

Series of baluster wine measures with "double volute" thumb-pieces to their lids. Quart to gill sizes, c.1750. Only the quart is marked.

Measures are often confused with mugs or tankards but can generally be differentiated by their markings, indicating their capacity. Pewter vessels with brass banding were used for measuring dry goods. Similarly mugs with a pouring lip or spout were intended as measures. Measures are rather less popular than tankards and their prices are correspondingly lower: from £10 to £40 is about average for late 18th and 19th century examples, depending on size and styling.

Patens and **chalices** were ecclesiastical plates and vessels respectively, sometimes found in pewter. The earlier patens are relatively small, and increased in size in the 17th century. Price depends on size and decoration, plus features being a high foot rim and a central lobed depression. Prices are from £60 to £100. English pewter chalices are comparatively scarce (£80 – £150); the bulk of those encountered are of European origin and consequently of little value to collectors in Britain.

Pot bellied measures. Left to right: ½ pint with unusual hallmarks on rim, c.1830; ½ gill c.1880; a rare Old English wine pint, c.1800; ½ pint, marks on rim, c.1830.

Alms-dishes were popular in the Presbyterian churches from about 1660 to 1850. Plain examples now rate about £60 to over £80; but those with the name of the church or the denomination (after the Disruption of 1843) are worth considerably more.

Salts. The larger 'cup' salt is c.1760 and stands 3ins. high. The others are about 1800. Sugar sifter in background.

Bowls exist in a wide variety and in different sizes and range from £30 to £75, depending on size, age and decorative features.

Candlesticks follow the same styles and patterns as brass candlesticks (q.v.) of the corresponding period and are in the price range £30 — £120. Matched pairs should rate three times the price of singles.

Small pewter articles include salts, snuff boxes, pounce pots, casters, ink-wells and spoons and the majority belong to the late 17th and 18th centuries. Prices for small pewterware range from £5 to £20, the more ornamental items tending towards the upper end of the price scale.

Points to look for

The biggest headache with pewter is the question of age. A knowledge of the touch-marks is essential (see **Reading List**). A good patina should have a deep, dark lustrous quality and the pewter should 'feel' right, with a surface showing microscopic pitting and the fine marks of scouring acquired with centuries of use. Ornament on English pewter was generally engraved or punched into the surface; examples with cast decoration and wrigglework are worth looking for. Gilding on pewter is unusual though not unknown. It was permitted in England only if goods were expressly intended as gifts; Continental pewter was not so rigorously controlled.

Pitfalls

Two periods in which there was a romantic revival in the popularity of pewter have created problems for the collector and dealer alike. Much pewterware was produced in the 19th century when medievalism was at its height and the Gothic Revival was in full swing. Similarly there was a vogue for reproduction pewterware from about 1910 to 1930 and most of these pieces are now old enough to have acquired a respectable patina, though this differs from the hard scale of oxidation found on genuine antique pewter. Since genuine antique pewter has often been cleaned over-zealously (destroying the original patina) and since fake touch-marks have been noted on reproduction pieces, the collector should be particularly wary of such items as 17th century lidded tankards, Stuart candlesticks, 17th and early 18th century salts, chalices, patens, broad-rimmed plates, lidded wine measures and 15th or 16th century spoons, these being the areas which have particularly attracted the attentions of the faker.

Museums

British Museum, London.
Guildhall Museum, London.
Geffrye Museum, London.
London Museum, London.
Victoria and Albert Museum, London.
Wallace Collection, London.
National Museum of Antiquities, Edinburgh.
Royal Scottish Museum, Edinburgh.
Museum and Art Gallery, Glasgow.
City Museum, Hereford.
Museum and Art Gallery, Leicester.
Central Museum and Art Gallery, Northampton.
Salisbury and South Wiltshire Museum,
Salisbury.
City Museum, Sheffield.
Somerset County Museum, Taunton.
Elizabethan House, Totnes.
City Museum and Art Gallery, Worcester.
The Yorkshire Museum, York.

Plates of 8ins. to 9½ins. diam. Top to bottom: "Triple reeded", hallmarked on rim, c.1680. Narrow rim, c.1690; single reed, c.1710; common plain rim, c.1780. All marked.

Reading List

Bell, Malcolm. Old Pewter. New York, 1905; London, 1913.
Cotterell, Howard H. Old Pewter: its Makers and Marks. London, 1929; Rutland, Vt., 1963.
Graeme, A.V.S. Old British Pewter (1500 – 1800). London, 1952.
Laughlin, L.I. Pewter in America (2 volumes). Boston, Mass., 1940.
Masse, H.J.L.J. Chats on Old Pewter. London, 1949; New York, 1969.
Michaelis, Ronald. Antique Pewter of the British Isles. London, 1955; New York, 1971. British Pewter. London, 1969.
Peal, Christopher A. British Pewter and Britannia Metal. London, 1971.
Ulyett, Kenneth. Pewter Collecting for Amateurs. London, 1967.
Verster, A.J.C. Old European Pewter. London, 1959.
Wood, Lindsay I. Scottish Pewterware and Pewterers. Edinburgh, 1907.

PHOTOGRAPHS

'The process by which natural objects may be made to delineate themselves without the aid of the artist's pencil', as Fox Talbot described his process in 1839, is an apt definition of photography. The principle of the camera obscura, or pin-hole camera, had been known since the 16th century, but no means was devised for fixing the image until 1826, when the Frenchman, Nicephore Niepce, succeeded in fixing the image of his courtyard using pewter plate with a coating of bitumen of Judea dissolved in oil of lavender. This primitive photograph was made directly on to the light-sensitised plate, after an exposure of eight hours. From this primitive beginning developed the science of photography. Prior to about 1865 photography may often have been aesthetically unsatisfactory, but technically of the greatest interest; thereafter as technique became less important, the artistry of the photographer and the subject matter became more important. In the early period the value of photographs depends on the process used, the provenance of the photographer and the subject, the condition and aesthetic appeal. After 1865 the actual process is of lesser importance.

A photogenic drawing — the earliest form of photography.

A photographic glass positive, unusual in showing a working class subject.

Date-lines

1829-1839   Earliest experiments by Niepce and Daguerre using bitumenised pewter plates (Heliotypes) and silver-plated copper coated with silver iodide. Positive images produced direct on to the plates, so each one is unique. These experimental plates are of the greatest rarity and would be worth £1,000+.

David Octavius Hill. Group of fishwives at Newhaven, June 1845.

1839-1860   Daguerreotypes on metal plates, usually ornately framed, housed in leather cases gilt-stamped with the photographer's name, or (in America) housed in union cases. The earliest daguerreotypes, prior to the expiry of Daguerre's patent in 1853, are the most desirable. The process died out by 1860 as it was comparatively expensive and suffered the disadvantage of producing a positive image which could not be copied. £20 – £50 for good examples of unknown sitters; £50 – £100 for identified subjects, though exceptional prices of £1,000 – £4,000 have been paid for stereo daguerreotypes of outstanding interest. Portraits are usually more desirable, though topical views or pictures of important events command a high premium.

1841-1855   Calotypes using paper negatives and positives – the earliest process by which copies could be made of a photograph, invented by Fox Talbot in 1839. Calotypes are seldom signed and identification of photographer is mainly by technique, finish and subject. The earliest were salted-paper prints from paper negatives, whereas later examples were albumen-prints. Salted-paper may be recognised by its matt surface and on early images the outlines are soft and lacking in sharp detail. Later calotypes (especially those by Samuel Smith or Henry Renault) were often very sharp. Albumen-prints can be identified by a microscopic examination of the constant tones which have a slightly mottled effect. Early calotypes are rare, and examples definitely attributed to Fox Talbot range from £120 to £500 depending on subject. Calotypes by Hill and Adamson of Edinburgh range from £100 to £500. Other artists whose work is highly desirable include John Forbes White, Thomas Keith, Joseph Cundell, John Stewart, Samuel Smith, Victor Renault, John McCash. £30 – £100.

An unusual Ambrotype self-portrait by an anonymous photographer.

A quarterplate Ambrotype of the Niagara Falls with six spectators.

1851-1871   Wet Collodion process of Frederick Scott Archer, using glass plate negatives, combined the sharpness of daguerreotypes with the positive/negative advantage of calotypes. Superseded by chemical dry plates in 1871. Used to produce the ambrotype, in which a collodion negative was backed with black paper to create a positive. Ambrotypes are relatively plentiful and the majority of them show insipid poses of unknown people £5 – £10.

Julia Margaret Cameron. A good portrait of Herschel.

Julia Margaret Cameron. A good study.

Ambrotypes of identified sitters range from £30 – £100, depending on the subject and size.

Ambrotypes of historic events and scenes (including the Crimean and American Civil Wars) range from £50 – £200.

Photographs of this period by well-known artists such as Roger Fenton, Julia Margaret Cameron and Lewis Carroll range from £50 (for sentimental poses of unknown sitters) to £500 or more for portraits of their famous contemporaries. The record for a Cameron photograph is £1,500 for a portrait of Virginia Woolf's mother.

1853-1880   Tintypes – earliest metal plates used by street photographers. Comparatively cheap to produce, but usually of very poor quality and the majority are unsigned. Poor quality tintypes were, in fact, still in use until fairly recently and have no market value. Good quality, early tintypes of unusual subjects are rare and may be worth up to £25, depending on the subject.

After 1870 photography became much more popular and the equipment came within the reach of people even of modest means.

Alfred Lord Tennyson photographed by Lewis Carroll, 1857. A celebrity photographed by a celebrity at an early date.

John Thompson and Adolphe Smith: Street Life in London, published 1877.

By the end of the century the rapid strides in the development of cameras (q.v.) meant that photography was commonplace and universal. Photographs from the latter part of the 19th century therefore have little market value, unless the subject is of topical or historic interest.

Points to look for

Early photographs which can be attributed to the leading photographers of the period are worth a high premium. The identification of the sitter will enhance the value of otherwise undistinguished photographs, but only prior to 1870. Post-1870 photographs of other people's ancestors excite relatively little interest unless they had some claim to fame. Portrait studies are more desirable than scenic studies (except where the latter possess topographical interest), and scenes are preferable to 'still life' photographs. The larger the photograph the more desirable it becomes. Topographical albums of some countries, e.g. U.S.A., are very valuable. Attractive mounts or union cases can also boost the value of photographs (usually daguerreotypes or calotypes) considerably.

Francis Frith. Stereoscopic view of the 'Photographer's Headquarters'.

Photograph by Frank Meadow Sutcliffe.

Pitfalls

The value of early photographs lies in the fact that they are demonstrably early — i.e. the paper or metallic plates on which they are printed is contemporary with the photography itself. Early paper positives, for example, can often be identified and dated by the paper watermark, while the characteristics of the various printing processes can be detected with experience. The major problem concerns late prints from early negatives, such as the carbon prints by Jessie Bertram about 1916 from the Hill-Adamson negatives of 1845-8, or late prints by Frith, Bedford, Sutcliffe and other topographical photographers.

Other Types of Photograph

Two other categories of late 19th century photographs worth considering are cartes de visite and stereoscopic photographs. The former are thought to have originated in France in the 1850s, but were widespread by 1860 and remained popular till the First World War. They consisted of small photographs mounted on cards of the then fashionable visiting-card size, permitting a space at the foot for a personal message, and often having an elaborate advertisement for the photographer on the reverse. Cameras were designed to accommodate several carte-de-visite photographs on one plate, thereby cutting the costs of developing and printing considerably. Much more satisfactory than tintypes, they were the first photographs to come within the reach of most people, and the craze for exchanging cartes developed rapidly. Most households eventually had an imposing album containing cartes de visite and these have survived in large numbers to this day. Individual cartes de visite have little market value as yet (50p — £2) but complete albums are now collectable and range from £10 to £50, depending on the interest and diversity of the contents, together with the condition and degree of sumptuousness of the albums themselves. Many of them were handsomely bound in leather, hardwoods, mother-of-pearl or inlaid with ivory or marquetry. There were several attempts to enliven cartes de visite by the adroit use of colouring. At best these coloured cartes come close to the portrait miniatures which they superseded, but the majority consist of inadequate flesh tints on the sepia ground.

Curiously enough, the more famous the sitter the less value is likely to be attached to cartes de visite, since cartes portraying royalty, politicians and contemporary celebrities were sold by the thousand and were the fore-runners of cigarette cards and picture postcards (q.v.) in providing the masses with portraits of their heroes. A much larger version of the carte was the cabinet photograph, which became increasing popular from 1860 onwards. These seem to have less appeal than the cartes, though the quality of photography is often much higher. Cabinet photographs were not used extensively for the portrayal of contemporary celebrities, other than actors and actresses.

The principles of stereoscopy were known to scientists for centuries before Sir Charles Wheatstone invented an optical instrument in 1832 which produced a three-dimensional effect using twin images which were almost but not quite identical. As early as 1846 Roger Fenton and Fox Talbot were applying stereoscopy to photography, using twin-lensed cameras, but it was not until the Great Exhibition of 1851 that the stereoscope caught the popular imagination. The heyday of the stereoscope as a form of home entertainment was from 1860 to 1914

Henry Peach Robinson: A House Party.

and during that period millions of stereoscopes were produced on both sides of the Atlantic. The number of stereographs, as the photographs were called, must have been astronomical. Commercial stereographs were mostly produced by the wet collodion process, though a few daguerreotypes and ambrotypes are known. They may be classified as topographical, news, social scenes and comic situations (in descending order of numerical importance). Prices range from £1 — £5 for individual stereographs; complete sets from £40 to £150.

382

Museums
Kodak Museum, London.
Royal Photographic Society Museum (by appointment only).
The Science Museum, London.
The Victoria and Albert Museum, London.
The National Portrait Gallery, London.
Museum of Science and Technology, Birmingham.
The Royal Scottish Museum, Edinburgh.
The Lewis Carroll Collection, Guildford.
Museum of Science and Technology, Manchester.
Barnes Museum of Cinematography, St. Ives.
The Sutcliffe Gallery, Whitby.

Reading List
Brown, Bryan. The England of Henry Taunt. Victorian Photographer London.
Castle, Peter. Collecting and Valuing Old Photographs. London, 1973.
Coe, Brian. George Eastman and the Early Photographers. London, 1972.
Ford, Colin. The Hill and Adamson Albums. London, 1974.
Gernsheim, Helmut and Alison. The History of Photography, London, 1969.
Howarth-Loomes, B.E.C. Victorian Photography. London, 1975.
Matthews, Oliver. Early Photographs and Early Photographers. London, 1972.
Strong, Roy and Ford, Colin. An Early Victorian Album. London, 1974.
Thomas, Dr. D.B. The Science Museum Photograph Collection. London, 1971.

PICTURE POSTCARDS

Items of postal stationery, intended for transmission through the post without any form of envelope, and bearing some form of pictorial embellishment. Postcards themselves originated in Austria in 1869 and rapidly spread to other parts of Europe the following year. The earliest cards were official postal issues, bearing an impressed stamp, and having the back and front respectively confined to the message and address. From the outset postcards appeared with privately printed matter on them. In Britain this was confined to tradesmen's advertisements which often included some pictorial motif, but in Europe the pictorial element began as a patriotic sentiment during the Franco-Prussian War of 1870-71 and rapidly developed into a popular medium of tourism. In the 1880s and 1890s these souvenir cards took the form of a group of tiny vignettes in the upper and left-hand sides of the 'message' side, with the caption 'Grüss Aus' (German) or 'Souvenir de' (French) followed by the name of the town or locality. Picture cards of this type were not permitted in Britain where the postal regulations were very strict. At first only the officially stamped cards were permitted, but gradually the regulations were relaxed. First adhesive stamps were permitted on non-official cards, then in 1894, a pictorial element was permitted on part of the message side. Gradually the pictorial element became larger, until it all but filled the message side, and left only a broad margin at the foot for this purpose. After 1897 messages could also be written on the address side, but only on internal British postcards as other countries forbade this. Between 1902 and 1905, however, other European countries relaxed this rule, and 'divided backs' then became more widespread.

The heyday of the picture postcard was the period up to 1915. Many of the cards published in Britain were of German manufacture and the supply was exhausted soon after the outbreak of the First World War. Wartime restrictions on paper and printing, followed by a doubling in the postcard rate (1918) and trebling a year later, seriously affected the popularity of the picture postcard, which has never since recovered, although it continued to be a relatively popular expression of tourism till 1940. Thereafter successive increases in postal rates, not to mention the rising costs of producing the cards themselves, have diminished their popularity in current use, though with this has developed their popularity as collectables. The hobby of collecting postcards is now known as deltiology.

Date-lines

1870-1890   Earliest British cards, with imprinted ½d or 1¼d stamps (for inland and foreign rates). Pictorial elements confined to trade advertisements.

1890-1894   Various postal stationery cards with pictorial elements commemorating exhibitions and the Jubilee of Penny Postage. Unused examples relatively plentiful (50p – £2), but those bearing special exhibition postmarks are much scarcer (£5 – £30).

1870-1885   Earliest European picture cards. Most highly prized are the 'patriotics' of the Franco-Prussian War (£10 – £40). Scenic cards, postally used in this period, often published by Alpine hotels, etc. £5 – £25.

1885-1905   Continental postcards with 'Grüss Aus' or 'Souvenir de'. Tiny vignettes on message side. Pictorial postal stationery cards, with impressed stamps and motifs marking exhibitions, jubilees, coronations, etc. £1 – £5 (unused); £3 – £25 (used). Add 50% for special exhibition postmarks.

1894-1902   Earliest British picture cards, known as 'Undivided Backs'; picture and message on one side, and the address on the other. Examples postally used before 1900, 50p – £2; examples used after 1900, 10p – 50p.

1905-1915   'Divided backs', with message and address on one side, and picture occupying the other. Many different types from 5p upwards (see below).

1914-1920   First World War patriotic cards. Patriotic sentimental cards, propaganda cards, and those satirising or lampooning the enemy – in ascending order of desirability. Prices from 20p upwards, depending on card, and such factors as Field Post Office marks, censor marks, etc.

1920-1940   Later period of 'divided backs'. Less variety and artistry than in the Edwardian period. Greater emphasis on static poses (little demand for general views, except from collectors specialising in certain localities). More desirable are comic postcards (Donald McGill, early Bamforth cards, etc.). Most desirable are political propaganda cards of European origin (Nazi, Communist, Fascist etc.).

Types of Postcard

Apart from the very early Continental cards, the bulk of the more collectable varieties belong to the period from 1895 to 1915. Within that period come the styles, designs and individual artists whose work is most highly prized. The criteria which affect the value of a postcard are discussed briefly below. Various detailed priced catalogues now exist (see *Reading List*) but the following notes may be of some use.

Age

Any postally used card of the 19th century, regardless of subject or country of origin, is now worth more than early 20th century examples. British picture postcards for example used in 1894 are now worth £6 − £10; those of 1895, £4 − £7; and those of 1899, £1 − £3. Unused cards are more difficult to date and are not so desirable. Where they can be dated according to subject (particularly true of those recording topical events), the pricing ranges from £4 − £7 (1894) to 50p − £1 (1899). Thereafter age itself is unimportant since postcards of 1900-10 are probably more numerous than those of 1930-40.

Subject

Apart from cards with general scenic views, of interest to collectors of a particular locality, cards can often be categorised according to their subject. There are literally hundreds of subjects, all of which have their following and relative values. Value depends on supply and demand and what was a popular subject in 1910 may not be so fashionable today. Thus the most popular subject in 1910 was actors and actresses, which accounts for the enormous range of this subject now available. But portraits of obscure beauties of the stage are not the most popular subject today, and this is reflected in the prices. Portraits of stage actors and actresses rate 10p − 20p, whereas those of screen actors of the same period rate 20p − 50p. A fear that aerial bombardment might destroy our architectural heritage during the First World War stimulated a craze at that time for cards depicting churches and castles. As a result these cards (mostly unused) are still very common (5p − 10p), whereas views of more prosaic buildings have shot up in price, because of their interest to students of postal or transport history. Thus cards featuring old post offices are worth 30p − £1; and those featuring railway stations are from 40p to £2. Transport in general is a very popular subject, with ships, trains, buses and aircraft in ascending order of desirability, 50p − £10 (unused). Aviation cards bearing the postmarks of aviation meetings, or bearing markings to denote early airmail, range from £4 to £100.

Among the other very desirable subjects may be mentioned the following:

Picture Postcards
Canadian letter card, c.1900; souvenir album Japan-British Exhibition, 1907; Donald McGill comic card; German anti-Scottish card 1914; children's postcard, c.1920; actress postcard, Ellen Terry, c.1905; aviation meeting, French, 1910; Franco-British Exhibition, 1908: advertising card for Moet et Chandon Champagne; card advertising Bovril, 1916; Austrian card by Kolo Moser celebrating the Diamond Jubilee of Kaiser Franz Josef II, 1908.

Cards depicting stamps (50p — £2), coins, especially if embossed in metal foil (£2 — £5), embossed heraldic cards (50p — £2), Boer War subjects (£1 — £10), early motor cars and buses (40p — £1), electioneering and early political cards (30p — £1), flags in full colour (30p — 60p), Irish Home Rule and Easter Rising cards (50p — £3), ethnographical subjects (25p — 50p), First World War 'patriotics' (40p — £2), shipwrecks (50p — £2) and zeppelins (£2 — £10).

Artists

In recent years more attention has been given to artistic cards, ranging from the whimsical and allegorical to the comic. Cards with very pronounced Art Nouveau styling are now worth 50p — £1 irrespective of the designer, but exceptional prices are now paid for cards bearing the signature of the following artists:

Alfons Mucha, £5 — £15.

Raoul Kirchner, £3 — £7.

Louis Wain, £3 — £5.

Lance Thackeray, Tom Browne, Phil May, John Hassall, Dudley Hardy, 60p — £2.

Harry Payne, Donald McGill, 25p — 60p.

Types

There are numerous types of card whose value depends on the method of construction or the inclusion of some gimmick and these may be summarised briefly.

Cards made of unusual materials range from wood, leather and aluminium (50p — £2), to celluloid (£2 — £5) and silver (very rare). Silk postcards, because of their connection with stevengraphs, are even more desirable. Woven silk cards by Stevens are now £20 — £40, similar cards by Grant range from £3 — £5 for scenes, to £10 — £15 for ships. Continental woven silk cards are more plentiful and range from £3 to £7. Embroidered cards were popular in the First World War and may be found with patriotic motifs (£2 — £4) or expressions of love and sentiment (£1 — £3). Others have embroidered flags or regimental insignia. (£1 — £4). Stereoscopic picture postcards were popular up to 1914, (50p — £2). Cards which revealed a secret picture when held to the light (known as 'hold to lights') range from £2 for simple window cards, to £5 for 'metamorphics' which change design. Other desirable types include jigsaw cards (£1.50 — £3), mechanical cards (£2 — £5), fabs (with pieces of fabric on their surface) (£2 — £5), reflectors (which reveal another picture when held at an angle) (£5 — £10), mosaics (50p — £1), composites which consist of cards joining together to form a much larger picture (30p – 50p each card, £2.50 – £5 for the complete set).

Other cards consist of greetings cards (Christmas, New Year, Valentine, birthday cards) and were briefly popular about 1910-1930. 30p – £1.

Points to look for

As yet, the manufacturer of the card is an aspect which has been little studied. With the exception of such examples as Tuck's oilettes and posters (50p – £3) the maker's name tends to have little bearing on value but this situation will not remain for ever. In general, however, the cards to look for (all other points being equal) are those bearing imprints of local stationers, and in particular, imprints showing that the publisher was the local postmaster or postmistress.

The value of an otherwise undistinguished postcard can be enormously enhanced by the stamp or the postmark on it. In the first case, value is less likely to be affected by the stamp, since only the very lowest denominations invariably pre-paid the printed matter and postcard rates. Much more important is the postmark, since postcards attract the attention of postmark collectors and postal historians. An unused view card of the island of Herm, for example, may be worth 10p, while the same card bearing the circular date-stamp of 1925-38 is currently worth about £80.

On British postcards the presence of a Victorian duplex mark (20p – 50p), a skeleton date-stamp (£1 – £3), a village rubber handstamp (50p – £1.50) or an early experimental machine cancellation (£1 – £7) enhances the value considerably. More obvious examples are special postmarks used in connection with fairs and congresses, aviation meetings, field post office marks, paquebot marks, wartime censor marks, or Christmas advance posting marks. The ordinary postmarks of small islands and other remote places are usually worth a high premium. Unofficial cachets of Land's End, John o'Groats, Ben Nevis, etc. enhance the value of a card, but preferably postally used. Similar cachets from Europe (the top of the Eiffel Tower, Swiss Alpine hotels, etc.) have little bearing on the value of a card unless they are pre-1900.

Museums

At one extreme, most local museums have collections of picture postcards relating to their locality. At the other extreme, the British Library (formerly part of the British Museum) has a vast collection of postcards, c.1911-14 in bound volumes available to users of the Reading Room. No museum, as yet, has built up a general comprehensive collection of postcards for display on a permanent basis.

Reading List

Alderson, Frederick. The Comic Postcard in English Life. Newton Abbot, 1970.

Bernard, I. and W. Picture Postcard Catalogue: Germany 1870-1914. London, 1972.

Burdick, J.R. The American Card Catalogue. New York, 1968. Pioneer Postcards (to 1898). New York, 1972.

Butland, A.J. Picture Postcards and All About Them. London, 1959.

Calder-Marshall, Arthur. The Art of Donald McGill. London, 1966.

Carline, Richard. Pictures in the Post. London, 1959.

Guyonnet, Georges. La Carte Postale Illustrée. Paris, 1946.

Hewlett, M.R. Priced Catalogue of British Pictorial Postcards, 1894-1939. Chippenham, 1973.

Hill, C.W. Discovering Picture Postcards. Tring, 1970.

Holt, Toni and Valmai. Picture Postcards of the Golden Age. London, 1971.

Kaduck, J.M. Mail Memories: Pictorial Guide to Postcard Collecting. New York, 1971.

Klamkin, Marian. The Picture Postcard. Newton Abbot, 1974.

Lauterbach & Jakovsky. A Picture Postcard Album. London, 1961.

Lowe, J.L. Standard Post Catalog. Folsom, Pa., 1968.

Scott, W.J. All About Postcards. London, 1903.

Staff, Frank. The Picture Postcard and its Origins. London, 1966.

PIPE STOPPERS

Small seal-like devices, otherwise known as tobacco tampers, which were designed to keep the lit tobacco in the pipe-bowl reasonably compact. Some sort of stopper must have been in use from the early 17th century, when pipe-smoking became fashionable in Britain, and they have continued in use to this day although they declined in popularity from the late 19th century onwards. One of the most 'British' of antiques as the vast majority come from this country followed by Holland and Germany.

Date-lines

The earliest stoppers had a plain top of relatively small diameter, reflecting the very narrow or small size of pipe-bowls at a time when tobacco was very expensive. As tobacco became cheaper, pipe-bowls became broader and deeper and pipe stoppers were accordingly increased in girth.

17th century stoppers are very rare. When they do turn up they are most likely to be brass and medallion or finger-ring shaped though those with longer bases continued through until at least 1710. Medallion stoppers seem to have been popular with the Royalists in the Civil War as several of their commanders appear on these medallions with their arms on the reverse, as well as King Charles with Henrietta Maria on the reverse. Outstanding silver and treen examples exist from this period but are virtually unknown outside important collections.

From the first half of the 18th century onwards they become rapidly more available and variable in quality and material. For instance wood, bone, horn and ivory examples vary from the finest craftsmanship to the obviously homemade figure of perhaps the smoker's favourite dog.

1750-1850. The vast majority are brass but virtually every practical material was used. Wood and bone are often the most individual whereas gold, silver and glass are the more important and valuable. Porcelain are known including figures from Chelsea and Derby.

Smoking was closely associated with drinking and this is reflected by the number of stoppers incorporating the 'barrel/bottle/glass/punchbowl' and the silver combined corkscrew/stopper.

Left to right, top row: good brass tool incorporating pricker c.1800; fine treen figure c.1775; one of a frequent coursing series occurring in wood and ivory and varying quality, usually round 1750-1800, this is a good one c.1770; a fine 18th century ivory bust; good silver multiple tool example c.1800 with tamper, perforated drainer with pricker and silver mouthpiece for a clay pipe, all screwing together, this example is hallmarked on the tamper which is exceptional. Bottom row: simple brass example of barrel bottle glass c.1800; crude Britannia of uncertain date; exceptional leg with fine detail of toes in ivory c.1800; very unusual steel ring example 18th century; standard 19th century booted leg, this one happens to be inscribed as a souvenir made from the wreck of the Royal George thus above average price; 19th century average brass full length figure of Minerva (?).

Types

The commonest type consist of small cast figures: 19th century personalities, characters from Shakespeare's plays, including himself, or Dickens' novels, St. George and Dragon, the Lincoln Imp and similar figures from folklore. These figures have been the subject of modern reproductions, generally of inferior quality both in metal and casting.

Genuine examples from the first half of the 19th century are in the price range £10 to £20.

St. George and dragon and King Charles subjects have been made from the 17th century until the 20th century Wine sales sometimes incorporate corkscrew/stopper examples — good to view but usually exorbitant in price owing to foreign corkscrew collectors.

Stoppers in the shape of legs were very popular in the 19th century. Of these the most popular (and still the commonest) show naked female legs. More desirable examples are clothed in boots or shoes of various kinds. Animal legs (horses' hooves) are much scarcer. Legs range from £4 to £20, a premium being paid for decoration and detail.

Stoppers in the form of hands, with or without pipes (mid-19th century). £5 — £15.

Types in the shape of tools of various trades (popular in the late 18th and early 19th centuries). These stoppers feature hammers, barrels, shoes, poultry, farm-implements, tailor's shears, etc. £10 — £50.

Stoppers incorporating a pricker; double-ended stoppers with a seal engraved at the other end; stoppers mounted on finger rings. £12 — £40.

Elaborate stoppers incorporating moving parts, tiny boxes, domino packs. £15 — £40.

Novelty stoppers with finely chased figures (clowns, dancing girls) incorporating prickers and other objects. £20 — £60.

Stoppers with medals mounted on the end (satirical medalets on stoppers were very fashionable in the late 17th and early 18th centuries). £25 — £75, depending on the medal.

Silver corkscrews start around £25 for plain examples going up to £100 for fine handles, usually Dutch, incorporating animals etc., also occasionally with prickers in the base.

Souvenirs from famous buildings, objects, events or trees, such as the Royal George (ship) say £20. Shakespeare's tree £75, Boscobel Oak £100+.

Barrel/bottle/glass variety varies from the basic solid brass at say £15 to the finer ivory incorporating compartments containing dice, dominoes, miniature drinking utensils, etc., up to £100.

Only the finest silver, gold, treen and, of course, porcelain reach three figures.

Pitfalls

Modern reproductions of the Pickwick and other Dickensian characters are quite common, but the blurred appearance and poor quality of the casting is readily apparent. Cases of broken turned-top

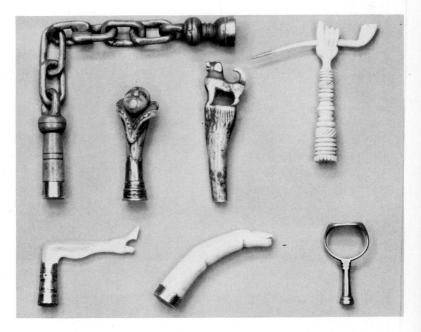

Left to right, top row: an 18th century fine treen chain carved from one piece of boxwood with stopper one end and seal the other; two bone carvings, man's head, 18th century, and a small dog, probably 17th century; hand holding a detachable pipe pricker c.1800. Below: mother-of-pearl leg (note Stuart shoe) 17th century; ivory finger c.1780; brass finger-ring with stopper, 17th century.

spoons being implanted with coins or medals and converted into rare medallion stoppers have been reported. It should be noted that many seals doubled as stoppers. 'Hatching' on a seal therefore does not necessarily exclude it from also being a stopper. Initials on a seal are deep cut and in reverse whereas on a stopper are shallow and straightforward. Seals can be oval or rectangular but to fit the pipe properly a tamper is always round.

PLASTIQUES

'Bandalasta' table lamp with weighted base and tilting dome, c.1927.

Armed with only hammers, chisels and files the plastic toolmakers of the 1920s produced some fine works, of which the Telsen radio illustrated is an excellent example.

Antiques made of plastic substances. At the present time there is little market for articles made of plastic, though the field is enormous and the time-span surprisingly long. Plastiques have only begun to attract the serious attention of collectors since 1962, the year in which the plastics industry celebrated its centenary, and even now it is still possible to pick up small plastic objects of considerable antiquity and interest for little more than a few pence in junk-shops and at jumble sales. This survey of plastiques is included as a guide to collectors looking for a relatively inexpensive subject with tremendous future potential. The major categories of plastic are discussed separately, with an outline of the collectables for which they were employed and the period in which they were used.

Parkesine

Although Henri Bracconot in France and C.F. Schonbein in Germany were independently working on the derivation of substances

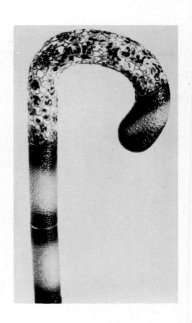

Above: Urea thiourea clock with Smith movement, c.1929.

Right: Celluloid umbrella handle.

from animal and vegetable matter, pride of place in the genesis of plastics is usually given to the Birmingham chemist, Alexander Parkes, inventor of Parkesine. In its original form Parkesine consisted of a mixture of cellulose nitrate and castor oil, but later camphor was substituted for castor oil as the plasticizing agent. Parkesine is the oldest polymer to have been used commercially and made its debut at the Great International Exhibition of 1862 in London where it was displayed in the form of medallions, buttons, combs, knife handles, brush backs and even book-bindings. Most of the surviving examples of Parkesine take the form of small toys and fancy goods. Parkesine is exceedingly rare and the majority of extant items are now in museum collections. Parkesine was produced between 1862 and 1868.

Xylonite and Ivoride

The financial collapse of the Parkesine works in 1868 was caused by technical problems with cellulose nitrate. Daniel Spill took over the enterprise and made improvements in the cellulose nitrate compounds, which were marketed under the names of Xylonite and Ivoride, simulating wood and ivory respectively. Spill was little more successful than Parkes and his products were rapidly superseded by developments in the United States. If anything, Xylonite and Ivoride articles are rarer than those made of Parkesine.

Celluloid

A world shortage of ivory, coupled with rapidly increasing demand, forced up the price of this commodity dramatically in 1863. The American company of Phelan and Collander, manufacturers of billiard balls, offered a prize of $10,000 to anyone who could produce a satisfactory substitute. John Wesley Hyatt and his brother Isaiah spent six years working on this problem before devising a billiard ball coated with a solution of collodion. Subsequent improvements, involving more than 75 separate patents, in the combination of pyroxylin and camphor led to the production of Celluloid, the name being patented in 1871. Initially this substance was used in the manufacture of billiard balls and dental plates. The Hyatts's enterprise was soon renamed the Celanese-Celluloid Corporation and has since become one of the giants of American industry. Subsequently the trade name, spelled with a small 'c', became a generic term for all plastics of the cellulose nitrate and pyroxylin group.

Celluloid was universally used from the 1870s till 1926. Its chief advantages were flexibility and resistance to wear. Its major disadvantages were its high flammability and its susceptibility to discoloration and deterioration in sunlight. It was used in an enormous variety of small articles: buttons, combs, brush handles, spectacle frames, typewriter keys, the heel-covering of ladies' shoes, knobs and dials in early electrical equipment and babies' rattles. It is chiefly associated with gentlemen's collars of the turn of the century. Transparent celluloid was used in the side curtains of early motor cars and eye-shields issued to both horses and men during the First World War. Its most notorious usage was in toys and fancy goods, emanating from Japan in the early 20th century.

Cellulose Acetate or Non-Flam Celluloid

The fire risk of celluloid stimulated the search for safer materials. In 1894 C.F. Cross and E.J. Bevan took out a patent for a process involving high acetyl chloroform and nine years later A. Eichengrun and T. Becker secured a patent for cellulose acetate plastic (the earliest recorded use of this term). Cellulose acetate was exclusively used at first in the film industry, the earlier celluloid having caused a number of disastrous fires in cinema projection rooms. It was not until 1926 that experiments by the Dreyfus brothers and the Celanese-Celluloid Corporation resulted in a form of cellulose acetate which could be given a much wider application. The modern thermoplastics industry began in 1927 with the production of cellulose acetate in sheets and rods. The versatility of this plastic was greatly increased in 1929 by the invention of cellulose acetate powder, coinciding with the injection moulding press. Non-flam celluloid was widely used in the 1930s and 1940s in all kinds of electrical equipment, especially knobs, switches and handles, telephone bases and handles, early microphones and head-sets, tool handles, pen and pencil containers. Its high resistance to impact made it an ideal material for workmen's goggles, lanterns, gas-mask lenses and aircraft parts. During the Second World War non-flam celluloid replaced metal and glass in much lightweight military equipment.

Shellac

Though used for centuries in the Far East as the basis of lacquer ware, shellac as a plastic substance dates from 1868 when John Merrick took out a patent for that purpose. Shellac was relatively little used, however, until 1895 when it was applied by Emile Berliner to the records played on gramophones (q.v.) and this remained its main employment until the advent of long-playing records in the 1950s. From 1900 onwards shellac moulding composition was extensively used in electrical insulators. More rarely, it was used in the ignition systems of the early motor cars, but was soon discarded because of its tendency to distort in heat.

Bakelite

As long ago as 1872 Dr. Adolf von Baeyer discovered the resinous

'Candlestick' telephone with phenolic mouthpiece and ebonite receiver, 1930.

Plastic urea cameo badges moulded in 1936 for the 'coronation that never was'.

properties of phenol combined with aldehydes, but failed to appreciate the implications of his discovery. In 1907 Dr. Leo Baekeland, attempting to find an artificial substitute for shellac, rediscovered phenolic plastic and subsequently evolved the very tough substance known as Bakelite. Following the establishment of the General Bakelite Corporation in 1910 phenolic resins were increasingly used in a wide range of electrical and mechanical fields. Baekeland's patents expired in 1926 and since then phenolic resins have been manufactured by many other companies, though the generic term bakelite has been retained. Its high resistance to heat made it ideal for the handles of cooking utensils. In the more decorative field, bakelite was used for ornamental ashtrays of the Art Deco period.

Casein

Adolf Spitteler and W. Krische secured a patent in 1900 for the manufacture of casein, a hornlike substance produced by uniting sour milk and formaldehyde. Although this is the name by which it is known at the present day, it was marketed in Britain under the name of Erinoid, in France as Galalithe or Nacrolague, and in the United States as Aladdinite. From the collector's viewpoint casein offers considerable scope, since its attractive appearance made it an ideal medium for small decorative articles and fancy goods. It was largely employed in the manufacture of buttons, brooches, hair slides, combs, brush handles, parasol handles, belt buckles for ladies' dresses, pens, knitting needles and crochet hooks, small boxes in mock tortoiseshell, cigarette boxes and lighters and a whole host of ornaments and novelties, mainly dating from between 1920 and 1940. Its poor moisture resistance tended to limit its use to smaller articles, although candlesticks and fruit bowls have been recorded in Erinoid.

Urea Formaldehyde Resins

The plastic property of urea combined with formaldehyde was known as early as 1897, but did not have any significance until after the First World War. In 1920 Hanns John took out patents for transparent urea formaldehyde which could be regarded as unbreakable glass. This substance was marketed in the United States in 1928 under the trade name of Aldur, but was found to be unsatisfactory because of its tendency to crack under certain conditions. The addition of wood flour or bleached pulp corrected this fault and this led the way to a wide range of urea plastics, marketed under such names as Beetle, Scarab, Aldur and Plaskon. These urea plastics possessed numerous advantages — an infinite range of colours, lightness, durability, resistance to heat, light and moisture, absence of taste and odour,

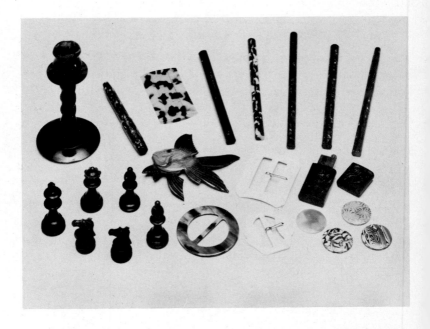

*Early Erinoid items. 1929 candlestick; 1935 pen; pre-1939 comb;
sample rods of c.1935; pre-1939 chessmen; a 1935 fish brooch; buckles
of the 1930s; a 1940 cigarette lighter; circular sheet pattern samples
c.1930.*

dimensional stability and shock resistance. Consequently urea-moulded
plastics were employed from 1930 onwards in lamps and lampshades,
tableware, utensils, piano keys, reflectors, electrical equipment, dress
accessories, toys, novelties and ornaments. Laminated urea sheeting was
used in table tops, door and wall panelling, decorative murals and many
other aspects of architecture and interior decoration.

Polystyrene

Although this substance had been discovered in England in the
1820s, more than a century elapsed before it was given any practical
application. The Dow Chemical Company and the Bakelite Corporation
began producing transparent polystyrene in 1937. It is used nowadays
in its opaque form as an insulating material, but in the immediate
pre-war period it was widely used for transparent dials and indicators in
aircraft and motor cars.

Acrylic Resins

The synthesis and polymerization of acrylic resins was undertaken by the German scientist, Dr. Otto Rohm, as long ago as 1901, but thirty years elapsed before acrylic was marketed commercially under the trade names of Acryloid and Plexigum. Originally these substances were used as unbreakable glass (an improved version being Plexiglas, introduced in 1936), but the crystal clarity and edge-lighted beauty of the acrylic group made them popular in lamps and ornaments of the 1930s. In the more mundane fields acrylics have been employed since the late 1930s in the manufacture of more realistic dentures, highway reflectors, advertising signs, spectacle lenses, surgical instruments and light covers in aircraft.

Other Plastics

The above substances are the ones most likely to be encountered in plastiques. Other plastics, while in existence before the Second World War, have only been commercially developed on a large scale in more recent years and are thus outside the scope of this survey. In particular the Polyvinyl group, ethyl cellulose and lignin have had widespread application in the 1960s and 1970s, replacing wood, glass, metal and ceramic materials in a wide range of products, both functional and decorative. Melamine, in existence in the 1930s, but more expensive than gold at that time, has been widely used in tableware in recent years. Pre-war melamine articles are of the greatest rarity.

Points to look for

The identification of particular plastics is a major problem, especially for the beginner. In most cases, however, articles are impressed with a trade name which provides some key to identification − although there are literally thousands of such trade names. Much research into contemporary trade directories and the registration of trademarks requires to be done. Already the more obvious items of the inter-war period − Art Deco and Art Moderne cocktail shakers, ashtrays, powder compacts, cigarette boxes and lighters − have been eagerly snapped up, but there is much else, both kitsch and everyday utilitarian articles, which are currently disregarded and undervalued.

Museums

Plastics Institute, London.
Science Museum, London.
Museum of the History of Science, Oxford.

PLAYING CARDS

The earliest cards were block-printed and hand-painted and were fashionable in court circles in France and Italy from the late 14th century onwards. The oldest authenticated cards were the Tarocchini or Tarot cards arranged in packs of 78 divided into four suits, plus a number of atouts or trump cards. These cards were often lavishly gilded and decorated in the manner of medieval illuminated manuscripts. Considerable artistry was involved in the production of a single card, and consequently individual items from the 14th to the 16th centuries are usually priced from £1,000 when they appear in the saleroom. At various times government edicts and church regulations tried to stamp out card-playing and for these reasons cards of the 16th century are scarce. Individual prices for hand-painted cards from wood-cut blocks of this period range from £200 to £500 for good average specimens. From a practical viewpoint, however, the cards which are most collectable are those dating from the early 17th century.

Date-lines

1600-1710 Earliest cards printed from copper plates. Size of pack standardised at four suits of 52 cards. Face cards invariably depicted full-length figures. French and Italian cards usually captioned face cards with distinctive names. English face cards seldom bear names. Cards can be dated roughly according to the evolution of the designs on face cards. An important development in England was the establishment in 1628 of the Worshipful Company of Makers of Playing Cards, which required makers to apply their mark to the ace of spades card, and such marks had to be registered with the company.

Complete packs of cards of this period are very rare and would now be priced from £1,000 upwards. Packs of cards inlaid with coloured silks and hand-painted with gilt edges, produced as presents for royalty, are in the price range £3,000 to £5,000.

Individual cards of this period: face cards, £10 − £50; others, £3 − £10.

Cards with pictorial of political motifs (popular from 1680), £15 − £60.

The pitcher goes not so often to y̆ well
but it comes home breake at last

Four of Diamonds. From a pack
of illustrated Proverbs made in
1698.

Ace of Spades. The most elaborate indication of tax on cards
c.1801. Aces were printed at
that time by Somerset House.
Total tax 2s.6d. (12½p) per
pack.

1710-1832	Tax on playing cards indicated from 1710 onwards by the ornate stamp on the ace of spades card. Cards can be dated according to the amount of duty (ranging from 6d in 1710 to 2s. 6d in 1804), the Royal monogram and the maker's name. Plain packs of cards of this period £50 – £200. Many novelty packs produced, with pictures on the front, headed by the card's number and suit and often bearing a caption of four lines underneath. Packs may be found covering a wide range of subjects – social, political, humorous, satirical, educational. Of these, the political packs are the most desirable (£300 – £500). General thematic packs (counties of England, Castles of Europe, Humours of the Age, etc.) range from £150 to £300. Particularly desirable are packs produced at the time of the French Revolution, with royalist or revolutionary themes. £200 – £350.
1790-1800	Packs by Rowley & Co. with cards printed in red, green,

black or yellow according to suit. This experiment was short-lived and such cards are now rare. £200 – £250.

1800-1820   'Transformation' cards, with values of each card indicated by the number of motifs in the picture (e.g. two of hearts – two heart-shaped faces). Best transformation cards produced by Cotta of Württemberg, 1805-11. Cotta sets can be dated since the subjects of the face cards were changed every year. Similar cards published in England by S. & T. Fuller. £100 – £300.

1832-1850   Earliest cards printed by combination of letterpress and lithography by Thomas De La Rue. Designs of the earliest cards continued the traditions of the 18th and early 19th century. £100 – £200.

1850-1900   Two-headed face cards and jokers introduced about 1850. Corners now rounded instead of square. Cards from this period are generally less decorative than before, but thematic sets and political packs continued sporadically till the end of the century. Most desirable

Jack of Clubs. From Rowley's cards of c.1770. An attempt (unsuccessfully) to reform the suits and the court cards. This "Jack of Clover" is a Prussian bodyguard.

Four of Spades. From one of the most famous early English transformation packs by S. & J. Fuller, 1811.

404

Jack of Hearts. This is from the first pack printed in 1832 by Thomas De La Rue who in that year patented a new typographical process of printing.

Jack of Hearts. Double headed court card by Thomas De La Rue, c.1860.

are those advancing the cause of women's suffrage. £25 – £100.

Post 1900   Little interest in packs, other than the political and patriotic packs produced in France, Britain, Germany and the United States during the First World War. 'Democracy' packs produced in America in 1918-20 and in 1933. A few propaganda packs (mainly of Belgian origin) in 1939. £10 – £30.

Points to look for

The leading European manufacturers of 18th and early 19th century cards were Wokaun of Prague and Gobl of Munich (no longer in existence), Piatnik of Vienna and Grimaud of Paris. Packs of these manufacturers are highly desirable. Early packs by De La Rue are also much in demand.

Apart from standard packs of playing cards, there is now rising interest in packs designed for card games of a didactic nature.

Children's playing cards date from the 1830s and originated in the United States. Happy Families is the best known and has gone into innumerable editions over the past 140 years. These packs are comparatively rare if complete and in reasonably good condition.

Standard packs with unusually decorative backs, late 19th century 'pin-up' cards and mid-19th century German heraldic cards are also worth looking for.

Early packs which are still in their original wrappers or cartons are worth a premium.

Pitfalls

Beware of 18th and early 19th century packs composed of miscellaneous cards. This is not always easy to detect, since cards from different editions of the same publishers may have been put together to make up a complete set. Pay particular attention to minor details in the printer's imprint (where it exists). The quality of the printing, sharpness of impression and type of card are other useful factors. Because the copper plates were liable to wear, plates were frequently reworked; it is thus possible to distinguish successive states of the plates.

Museums

British Museum, London.
Guildhall Museum, London.
Victoria and Albert Museum, London.

Reading List

Benham, W.G. Playing Cards. London, 1931.
Hargrave, C.P. A History of Playing Cards. Boston, 1930.
Mann, S. Collecting Playing Cards. London, 1967.
Morley, H.I. Old and Curious Playing Cards. London, 1931.
Tilley, Roger. Playing Cards. London, 1967.

Jack of Clubs. Double headed figure, card showing rounded corners, c.1880.

406

PROPELLING PENCILS

Sampson Mordan patented his 'mechanical pencil' in 1822. A knob moving along a spiral split or groove makes a fine rod push up a thin length of lead, held firmly in a nozzle. This basic principle is still in use today. Slide-up holders for wooden pencils were already in production and Mordan adapted these to contain his new device. Disregarding date, the collector looks for variety in the sheath or holder of the pencil and in the means of freeing the writing end from its protection.

Main Types

Propelling pencils may be divided into six main types:—

1. Early holders are basically cylindrical, with collar, sliding ring or push knob, and knop or seal end. Finials were soon made to pull or screw off, revealing a lead reserve often with a grille. Holders range

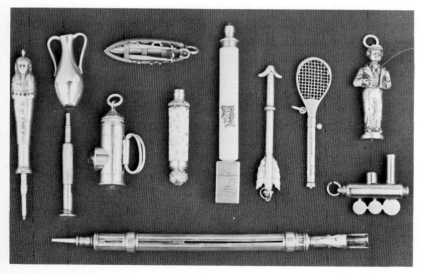

Left to right: Egyptian mummy. Pitcher-case pencil (detached sheath). Boat — (Cambridge oars! Oxford ones and white ones also exist). Bull's eye lantern, 1873. Porcelain casing. Ivory with matching silver lead case, (monogrammed). Arrow, 1844. Tennis racquet, 1878. Victorian railway porter, 1881. Tin railway engine. Georgian pen and pencil, 1824 (with swivel fitting for nib).

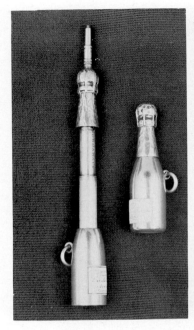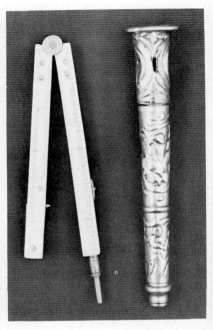

Left: Telescopic. Champagne bottles (open and shut), Mordan c.1870. Right: Propelling pencil combined with useful articles; ivory ruler and sealing-wax holder with seal end.

from plain silver to every kind of engraving, embossing, bright-cutting, etc. Early ones are usually hallmarked, carrying the name of the maker or patentee.

2. The writing end of the pencil is rotated out of the holder.

3. More complex spirals made the writing end emerge by pulling a projection at either end of the pencil.

4. The 'detached sheath' pencil (advertised by Mordan) is one which can be removed entirely from its cover.

5. Telescopic holders may be found incorporated with all the above types.

6. Although some earlier pencils are streamlined, this design only took over finally in the 1920s.

Date Lines

Pencils with all these mechanisms exist in many designs and materials, the greatest variety occurring between 1840 and 1900.

*Left: Novelty case. Cleopatra's Needle c.1878. Centre: Base metal.
Lochaber axe with peepshow of Oban, Iona and Glencoe. Right: Early
cylindrical, Mordan 1826.*

Dating is difficult even up to the present, unless aided by the maker's
name, hallmarks, or a registration mark. Some may be self-dating e.g.
Cleopatra's Needle. Around two hundred and fifty designs have been
noted, but the list continues to grow.

Price Range
   Early holders in silver: run of the mill £6 – £10; Georgian £15 –
£25.
   With working parts of silver or gilt, most often of type three, vast
quantities of pencils have been made with casing in mother-of-pearl,
tiger's eye, ivory, tortoiseshell, piqué, enamel, porcelain, etc.. £7 – £20.
   Also with silver working parts, and very difficult to find, are those
with fantasy cases. Some examples of novelty cases include bottles,
from Champagne to Codd's Wallop, sports gear, birds, animals and

people. Comparatively common are crosses, keys, bottles, owls, pigs and mummies. £10 – £45.

Cheaper, but no less attractive, are pencils with working parts in base metals, and casing of metal, bone, wood, early plastics, or natural objects like shells and nuts. New shapes continually turn up – sports gear, bellows, bottles, limbs, the globe, vegetables, souvenirs of localities and exhibitions and advertisements. They occur in local materials and crafts, such as lava, Mauchline tartan and Tunbridge Wells mosaic. Some include peepshows. £1.50 – £5. Rarer novelties £5 – £15.

An early brass pencil is a good find. In the 1840s Josh Baker made interesting muskets, and Sheldon made pen and pencil-holders, some with calendars, and a rare one containing a tiny letter balance. £5 – £15.

All types of pencil occur in gold, variously embellished. These are really jewellery and are priced accordingly. £10 upwards.

Pencils may be combined with other useful items such as penholders, rulers, bookmarks, whistles, penknives, paperknives, etc. Compendiums exist in many materials with pencils of different colours or several useful articles to be pushed up in turn. Some fantasy ones are highly ingenious. Thornhill made a flat fish, with a pencil in its mouth, a whistle in the tail and a penknife and nail-file folding out of the side.

Base metal working parts. £3 – £7.

Silver working parts. £6 – £10.

Pen and pencil sets. £7.

Georgian. £15 – £25.

Novelties. £20 – £30.

Pitfalls

With no established price structure, prices vary widely from one dealer or locality to another. High prices are paid for rarities at auctions and fairs and finding pencils at the lower figure will depend on luck. Damaged or marred examples are virtually worthless unless they are a particularly interesting rarity.

POTTERY AND PORCELAIN COTTAGES

Small cottages, houses and even castles with crenellated towers, were produced in various forms of pottery or porcelain in the 19th century for a variety of purposes. The great majority of them were intended as pastille burners and were fashionable between 1810 and 1850. Others were probably intended as candlesticks, spill-holders or money-boxes and their intended purpose is self-evident. Finally there were cottages in terracotta or Parian ware, an early speciality of the Goss factory, and these were produced in the 1880s as ornaments for the mantelpiece. Date-lines do not apply in this instance, since the time span was relatively short. The value of these items depends on purpose, form, materials, decorative features and manufacturer (the last being least important since many examples are unmarked). The different types are described in broadly descending order of rarity and value.

Pastille Burners

The earliest and most sought after type of ceramic model architecture consists of pastille burners. The commoner form is a building in which the roof and walls were shaped in a single piece to make a cover which was then superimposed on the rest of the building.

A pottery cottage with a minaret.

A model in the form of a castle.

411

The rarer form has a detachable roof which lifts off like a lid from the walls. In genuine examples the rims of the walls were ground flat and left unglazed to prevent the roofs slipping off and breaking. A very unusual type has tiny pull-out drawers at the side or back to hold spare pastilles. These pastilles comprised small cones of compressed herbs which were placed inside the burner and ignited. They would then burn slowly and diffuse fragrant smoke through chimneys and windows, to cover up the foetid smells so prevalent in an age when personal hygiene was virtually non-existent. The best examples were made of bone china and were encrusted with delicate flowers, moulded and painted individually by hand. The quality of these china cottages varies enormously. About 20 minor potteries are known to have made cottages from 1810 onwards and the majority of these have no markings on them at all. Unmarked cottages range from £25 to £60, depending on the detail and quality of modelling and encrusted floral decoration.

A large group of china cottages are popularly known as Rockingham cottages, from their affinity to the decorative wares of this company. But although Rockingham is known to have made pastille burners in the shape of sea-shells, egg-shells or Grecian vases, no evidence has come to light that Rockingham made burners in the shape of cottages. Nevertheless tradition dies hard, and the term 'Rockingham' is conveniently attached to a number of unmarked cottages distinguished by their exceptionally clear whiteness, matched by precision of finish, and gilding with a coppery tinge. Small summer houses with umbrella roofs now rate from £40 to £80, while medium-sized cottages of this type range from £45 to £100, depending on the complexity of decorative features.

Minton. More positive attribution can be made in the case of Minton which produced large china pastille burners in cottage form, devoid of decoration but for a characteristic goldfinch perched on the roof. £50 − £100.

From 1842 onwards Minton marked their wares with an impressed date symbol − four-line star, triangle, square, etc. (see **Handbook of British Pottery and Porcelain Marks** by Geoffrey Godden for full details). Minton also produced plain cottages and castles with a lavender finish. Cottages of this type are in the range £60 − £120, while the castles range from £120 to £250.

More elaborate Minton castles range from £200 to £500, depending on the number of turrets and unusual architectural features, as well as the intricacy of the floral ornament.

Coalport. Pastille burners were produced by this pottery from about 1819 onwards. They were made of clean white bone china, often with a leadless glaze fired at a low temperature which gave it an exceptional clarity. Coalport cottages and castles were encrusted with more flowers than those from other potteries and characteristic flowers included buttercups, sweet peas and carnations. The earlier, and most sought after, Coalport cottages have the CD or 'C Dale' mark of the Coalbrookdale period (up to 1825). Marked Coalport cottages and castles of the early period are now in the price range £400 to £1,000. Later Coalport pastille burners, with the marks 'Coalport' or 'Coalbrook Dale', range from £250 to £400. After 1830, however, most Coalport flower-encrusted porcelain was unmarked and this tends to affect the price, though fine examples of cottages and castles which can positively be attributed to this pottery are in the range £200 – £350. (see **Pitfalls**).

Worcester. A relatively small number of cottage pastille burners was produced at the Worcester factory during the Barr, Flight & Barr period and, after 1813, in the Flight, Barr & Barr period. Cottages in both periods (1807-13 and 1813-40) are clearly marked on the bases. Worcester cottages were built up from flat slabs of clay and the joints are usually visible. Worcester burners had a distinctive style, in that the walls and roof slid upwards from the box-shaped base. Moreover, the platform on which the pastilles were placed is usually raised on four feet and drilled with eight holes to facilitate combustion. These features apply to the earlier cottages with solid windows, and were made up to about 1825. £350 – £500. Later Worcester cottages had open windows and dispensed with the drill holes in the combustion platform. £200 – £350.
Worcester cottages are much plainer than their Minton or Coalport counterparts, with plain white walls and brickwork pointed in gold. Occasionally flowers are painted on the walls like gold silhouettes, and the roofs are painted to simulate thatch. Worcester also produced conical pastille burners in the 1820s, on a rectangular raised base, with floral or classical allegorical decoration on the sides of the cone.

Spode The rarest of the named pastille burners were those produced by Josiah Spode II. Many of them were unfortunately not marked but a few may be found with the name 'Spode' in red lettering. Between 1833 and 1847 they were sometimes marked 'Copeland & Garrett' in a wreath surmounted by a crown. Spode burners were probably the most rustic of all cottages, with shaggy thatch and craggy stonework and a riot of flowers climbing all over the porch and window frames. The early Spode cottages are now the most expensive of all and range from £600 to £1,200.

Porcelain pastille burner.

An unusual three-tier 'cottage'.

The cottages of the Copeland & Garrett period may be recognised by their bright blue walls and emerald bases and these are much more plentiful. £200 – £450.

Spode also produced four-footed conical burners with rustic decoration. £120 – £200.

Of the unmarked china burners the rarest and most expensive are those resembling churches which now rate £200 to £400. Castles are more plentiful and range from £100 to £250, depending on architectural details, while cottages range from £25 to £60.

Pottery cottages were produced during the first half of the 19th century, either as pastille burners or as night lights. They are much simpler and cruder in appearance and were produced by the Staffordshire potteries. Earthenware cottages are in the price range £20 – £40.

Prattware cottages, used as money-boxes or spill-holders, were made between 1800 and about 1850. Prattware cottages often have two figures, one on either side. Some of the Prattware buildings are inscribed with the name of the owner; others indicate that they represented Wesleyan chapels. These cottages were often decorated in unusual combinations, with green, black and puce predominating. £35 –£80.

Among the earliest wares produced by W.H. Goss (q.v.) were cottages in terracotta or Parian ware. These cottages were solid and intended as ornaments. Their interest lies in the fact that they represented actual buildings. The commonest examples featured Shakespeare's house, Anne Hathaway's cottage or Robert Burns' cottage at Alloway. These smaller pieces are in the price range £35 — £50.

Larger versions were hollow and were intended for use as night lights. £50 — £100.

Among the rarer Goss cottages are the Old Thatched Cottage at Poole, the Tudor House, Southampton, the Old Market House, Ledbury, St. Nicholas Chapel, Ilfracombe and the cottage in Kirriemuir which was immortalised in J.M. Barrie's **A Window in Thrums**. These cottages are in the price range from £100 to £170. Major rarities, such as Isaac Walton's cottage in Shallowford, rate £180 — £250.

Pitfalls

The popularity of cottages and castles with collectors in recent years has led to their reproduction. Probably the most dangerous of these fakes are those which have been produced in Paris since the mid-19th century. The oldest of these imitations are now antiques in their own right and have the appearance of age. Both these French imitations and recent fakes emanating from Portugal, however, are usually in one piece rather than two and the flowers are poorly modelled and painted compared with the originals. A pottery in Devon has recently been producing crude versions of turretted castles. These firms make the crude blunder of marking their wares with Chelsea gold anchors or other famous 18th century marks, which immediately give them away Of a much higher quality are the recent Coalport revivals, made from original moulds, but clearly marked with the name of the design (e.g. The Umbrella House) followed by 'Coalport/Fine Bone China/Made in England'. These marks are printed on the base, but unfortunately they are not impossible to erase, with the result that Coalport modern reproductions have subsequently been marketed as early 19th century originals. A test for this is to examine the glazing on the underside. This should be fully and evenly glazed, and any matt patches should be regarded with suspicion.

POWDER
FLASKS AND HORNS

Receptacles for gunpowder were widely used between the late 14th and mid-19th centuries. One of the simplest devices was a cow-horn with a plug fitted to the wide end, and a cap mounted on the point to control the amount and flow of powder. Throughout the same period, however, flasks of leather, wood or metal were also used and afford an enormous variety of types and patent caps.

Powder-Horns

In its simplest form the powder-horn remained unchanged for 400 years, and the value lies therefore not in the age so much as the decorative features. Powder-horns can be grouped according to their decorative treatment.

Flattened Cow-horn. In this type the horn has been subjected to heat to make it soft and pliable, and then squashed into a flat shape, oblong in section. Metal mounts are fitted at both ends, with a pourer device in the narrower end. The flat surfaces of these horns were invariably decorated by engraving and carving. Horns of this type were particularly popular in the countries of central Europe in the 16th and 17th centuries. Their value depends largely on the quality of the engraving. Average prices for flattened horns with hunting scenes are £100 – £150.

The inclusion of dates and inscriptions enhances the value, especially in good early examples. £200 – £300.

The mounts may be of copper, brass, silver or gilt-metal, and the use of precious metals is a major plus factor.

Military Horns. Cow-horns left in their round, natural state were employed by soldiers in the 18th and early 19th centuries. As a rule the treatment of these horns is fairly basic, with mounts of copper, pewter or brass. In many cases decoration is confined to the regimental number and emblem, either engraved or incised by means of pokerwork. Regimental powder-horns of this type depend on date and the popularity of the particular regiment. £40 – £70.

Towards the end of their career military horns were often engraved with more elaborate decoration. A favourite motif was an engraving of a fortress or fortified town with surrounding landscape, covering the

Top left: A copper and brass pistol flask in two parts. The base unscrews to reveal a cavity for patches, alongside the patent charger for powder is a cavity for a ball. Bottom left: A horn pistol flask in three parts, the base holds patches and the top powder. Centre: A seamed horn flask bound with copper wire stitching. Right: Cow-horn flask with patent charger.

Left: A 17th century German antler flask, 10ins.

entire length of the horn. Inscriptions identifying prominent landmarks are particularly desirable. These horns were mostly produced between 1760 and 1840. £80 – £150.

Oriental Powder-Horns. Various animal horns were used in Asia and have been recorded from the Caucasus to Northern China. The horn itself is usually left undecorated but both ends are fitted with elaborate mounts. The commoner varieties have brass mounts inlaid with silver, but the more sumptuous examples have silver inlaid with gold or enamelling. Many of the extant brass examples (without inlay) were produced in the late 19th century as tourist souvenirs from the North-west Frontier of India, Afghanistan, Persia, Turkestan and Sinkiang and are of relatively little value. £25 – £35.

The more decorative examples, including those with sides inlaid in ivory, and those with mounts inlaid in silver or gold. £50 – £150.

Scrimshaw Horns. Cow-horns were immensely popular in Colonial America as powder containers and by the mid-18th century were providing a ready medium for a form of folk art originally practised by seafarers. Scrimshaw or scrimshander, the nautical art of carving on bone, ivory, tusks or horn, was borrowed by the colonists and developed into a distinctively American skill. The value of these scrimshaw horns depends on the motifs. Floral, hunting and general scenic motifs are relatively plentiful and less sought after. £45 – £100.

Identifiable scenes, especially those of forts along the frontier of the thirteen American Colonies, and bearing inscriptions relating to the Anglo-French colonial wars of the 18th century, are highly prized. £120 – £300.

19th century horns, portraying contemporary political figures, or with scenes illustrating events of the period 1800 to 1860. £60 – £120.

Scrimshaw horns are usually found with brass or copper mounts, but those with silver mounts are worth about 15-20% more.

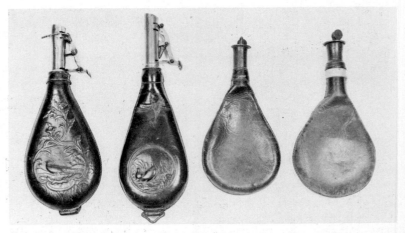

Examples of plain and embossed leather flasks, the smaller examples with scoop chargers.

Antler Horns. Powder-horns were made in Germany and eastern Europe from the part of the antlers where the tines branch out from the central horn. The stag-horn was cut a few inches from the junction and this produced a broadly triangular shape, with stoppers on the end of each section and a cap and pouring device set in the apex of the pyramid. These horns were often intricately carved and engraved, and mounted in brass, silver or silver-gilt. They were fashionable in the 17th and early 18th centuries and their value depends on the quality of the decoration and the type of mount. £200 – £350.

Powder-Flasks

The simplest form of flask was made of wood covered with leather and bound with iron. Because of the perishable nature of the components few of these early leather and wood flasks have survived. They may be recognised by their very tiny nozzles and simple plug stoppers. Flasks of this type were widely used in Europe up to about 1560. For all practical purposes, however, the collectable varieties of flask date from the early 17th century. As with powder-horns it is not often possible to date examples from their materials, decorative features and general appearance. Various refinements, introduced in the 18th and early 19th centuries, included double or treble compartments, central brass chargers and various spring-loaded patent pouring devices. Once adopted, however, these technical features tended to remain in use for very long periods, in many cases surviving until powder-flasks went out of use in the mid-19th century, so that they are only useful as a guide to dating in a negative sense. The value of powder-flasks, as with horns, depends largely on the type, materials used, ornamentation and technical refinements. The principal types are discussed separately below.

Leather Flasks. These were often in the form of a truncated cone or a circular bottle with flattened sides. In the 17th century the earlier leather flasks were substantially modified, with heavy iron or brass base-plate, charger and stopper, and brass reinforcements along the sides. Relatively plain examples of this type are in the price range £50 – £80.

Similar flasks, but with the brass and ironwork chased and engraved with floral ornament and hunting scenes. £150 – £250.

Leather flasks with silver mounts, decorated with niello inlay or enamels. £200 – £400.

Pear-shaped leather flasks with brass chargers, their sides pierced for suspension and with pokerwork or engraved decoration on their sides were popular in North America in the 18th century. £75 – £120.

Pear-shaped Metal Flasks. This is the commonest group and the wide range of metals, styles of decoration and types of charger is reflected in the values. The simplest flasks are of plain brass or copper, without ornament, and with only a simple spring-loaded cap on the nozzle. £15 – £20.

Bristol flasks, usually produced *en suite* with cases of pistols but frequently detached from the original set. Lacquered copper body and

Pear-shaped metal flasks with patent chargers. A copper embossed rope weave example, a brass hunting scene flask by James Dixon and Sons, 7ins., and three small flasks in copper, brass and Britannia metal, 3½ins.

Right: A pear-shaped brass flask showing Colt stand of flags, with plunger-type charger, 7ins.

patent charger. £30 – £80.

Large plain musket flasks, in copper or brass, with plain chargers. £25 – £35.

Decorated copper or brass flasks, with embossed rope weave or fishnet motif covering the whole surface. £30 – £85.

As above, but with the addition of embossed motifs such as a trophy of arms, game or hunting scene. £40 – £90.

Large copper or brass flasks with fluted decoration interspersed by beading. £40 – £90.

Pear-shaped flasks with overall embossing of hunting scenes, trophies of arms, coats of arms. £50 – £100.

Similar flasks, but with the ornament finely engraved overall. £60 – £120.

Die-stamped large flasks, by Batty or Ames, featuring the American eagle, stars and martial emblems. Popularly known as 'Peace' flasks. £45 – £80

Colt's patent brass flasks, decorated with arms ('Stand-of-Arms' type). £70 – £100.

Gunstock Powder-Flasks. This is a comparatively rare type, in which the flask is shaped like a miniature rifle butt and stock terminating in the brass mount and charger. This type seems to have been mainly confined to North America. £35 – £50.

Cylindrical Flasks. Another uncommon type, but usually plain and uninteresting in its decoration. Cylindrical flasks are mainly of European origin. £15 – £25.

As above, but with fish-scale overall decoration, trophies of arms and animal masks. £35 – £45.

An English variant of the cylinder flask is the bag-shaped type, in which the cylinder widens towards the bottom and is rounded. Plain copper or brass. £15 – £20.

Decorated surfaces, £25 – £35.

Curved Flasks. Metal flasks curved and fluted to resemble powder-horns were a speciality of eastern European countries, especially Russia and Turkey. These flasks are usually found in silver, with brass or iron chargers and mounts. Their value depends on the decoration which varies considerably. £60 – £100.

Double-Cavity Flasks. Small flasks, usually 4-5 inches in height, with two compartments and a central brass charger were produced in the

A Scottish engraved powder-horn of flattened form, inscribed '1684' within strapwork and geometrical borders, 12ins. This example has the stopper missing.

early 19th century for use with pistols. The shape varies considerably, but the commonest form is a broad, flattened pear-shape. £35 – £45.

Straight-sided flasks, tapering towards the base; two or three compartments. £40 – £60.

Points to look for

The majority of flasks before 1760 are unmarked, but increasingly from then onwards they may be found with the names of the manufacturers and latterly also patent numbers. Most British flasks were made in Sheffield and the names to look for are Dixon and Sons and W. and J. Hawksley. Of the foreign flasks, the most desirable are those made in the United States. The most sought after are those marked Colt. Other names to look for are N.P. Ames, Batty of Springfield and the American Flask and Cap Company.

Unusual technical features in the mounts and chargers enhance the value of powder-flasks considerably. Types to look for include swivel chargers, sloping chargers, or internal cut-off and long charger. Many of the English patent chargers bear an inscription specifying the amount of powder (in drams) released.

Pitfalls

The only point that requires caution concerns the charger whose spring is frequently broken or missing. Springs are difficult to replace, and flasks which are defective in this way should be heavily discounted, unless the decoration and general design are unusual. There are also an ever increasing number of copies and expert advice is needed in many cases to distinguish the better copy from the original.

Museums and **Reading List** – see *Militaria*
but include:
Riling, R. The Powder Flask Book. New York (undated).

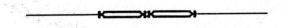

RAILWAY RELICS

Railway Relics. Enamel sign, Caledonian railway, c.1900; Liverpool-Warrington tickets (uncut pair), 1832; Bradshaw's Railway Time Tables, 1839; selection of railway tickets from Germany, Uganda, Egypt, England, Australia and France.

The collecting of items associated with the railways has developed enormously since the major closures began in the 1950s. The so-called 'Beeching axe' not only stimulated a wave of nostalgia for the passing of the old steam trains and the country lines, but also provided the means of satisfying the new-found demand by collectors for relics of a bygone railway age. Although much of the railwayana has now been absorbed into railway museums or has been acquired by the railway preservation societies, many of the smaller and more collectable items have come on to the market.

Date-lines

1804-1825 The earliest steam locomotives by Trevithick (1804), Blenkinsop (1811), Hedley (1813) and Stephenson

423

(1814) were designed to haul coal and other minerals from the mines to the seaports, and were not concerned with passenger traffic. Collectables from this period are virtually unknown.

1825-1921 Beginning with the Stockton-Darlington (1825) and Manchester-Liverpool (1830) lines, numerous railway companies were formed in the United Kingdom. Over a hundred companies operated services at some time or other during this period. The value of identifiable relics associated with them is in inverse ratio to their size and the period during which they were active. Highly prized are items bearing the name or crest of the smaller railway companies which reached their zenith in the 1850s. By 1880 many of the more ephemeral lines had been amalgamated with each other or had been absorbed into the larger companies. By the turn of the century there were still over 40 railway companies operating in the United Kingdom. This is known as the pre-grouping era.

1921-1947 The First World War rationalised the multitude of services and by the Act of 1921 the railways were compelled to amalgamate into four major groups: the London, Midland and Scottish, the London and North-Eastern, the Southern and the Great Western Railways. A few of the smaller lines were jointly owned by the four major groups. The London Underground system was similarly rationalised. Other railways which continued to operate outside the major groups included the Metropolitan Railway and several light railways or narrow gauge lines, such as the Talyllyn, Eskdale, and the Romney, Hythe and Dymchurch. Collectables from the post-grouping era are more plentiful and form the mainstay of the market.

1947-1960 After the Second World War the major railway groups were amalgamated and nationalised to form British Railways. Earlier the London Underground and the Metropolitan Railway had been amalgamated and taken under the aegis of the London Passenger Transport Board (1933). Only a few narrow gauge and light railways remained outside the national network. Many of the latter became defunct in the immediate post-war period, but have mostly been resurrected by preservation societies and — so far as the provision of souvenirs is concerned — play a not inconsiderable part in the market for railway relics. After nationalisation there was a gradual standardisation of equipment. Modernisation, especially the transition from steam to diesel, and latterly from diesel to high-speed electric trains, together with the closure of uneconomic lines in the 1950s and early 1960s, has provided a vast amount of collectable material.

Collectable Material

From the foregoing it will be seen that the value of railway relics depends to a large extent on whether they belong to the pre-grouping, post-grouping or British Railways period. Within these three periods, however, there is a vast range of equipment and material of interest to the collector. One method is to collect everything and anything associated with a particular company, line or period, while the other popular method is to concentrate on a specific type of material, irrespective of the railway line concerned. Below are discussed some sixteen categories of railway relic, in alphabetical order.

Carriage Panel Prints

An important form of interior decoration in railway carriages, these panel prints were widely used between 1850 and 1950. Though they declined thereafter, as carriages were modernised or replaced, they survived in some cases into the early 1960s and are thus not too difficult to find. They took the form of (a) maps of the railway line, (b) advertisements and miniature posters for the railway company and its hotels, and (c) photographs or reproductions of paintings of scenery associated with the railway line. Of these, the most desirable are early route maps and posters, pre-1900. £5 – £10.

Panel prints bearing the names of railways in the pre-grouping era. £2 – £5.

Carriage Destination Boards

Long narrow boards with the names of the termini, and sometimes intermediary points on the line, were affixed below the eaves or rainstrip on carriages. These destination boards vary considerably in size and styling. The larger boards were fixed to the sides of the carriages, while smaller but similar boards were occasionally fixed in brackets either above or between the windows. The most desirable are the hand-painted wooden boards in the colours of the pre-grouping companies, and the tartan boards used by the 'Royal Scot' (Euston to Glasgow) in the L.M.S. period. £10 – £20.

Later boards in the colours of the four major companies, and the square boards used by British Railways to denote both destination and intermediary points. £3 – £10.

Enamel Signs

Signs enamelled on sheet iron are among the most collectable of all railway relics, on account of their compact, two-dimensional form. The most interesting are instructional notices and signs which bear the name, emblem or colours of the pre-grouping lines. The commonest and simplest signs indicate toilet and restaurant facilities and are in the price range from £2 to £5, depending on date and size.

19th century signs tend to be more verbose (e.g. 'Please do not spit in the Carriages. It is offensive to other Passengers and is stated by the Medical Profession to be a source of Serious Disease') and may be worth much more, depending on the inscription. £5 – £30.

Many of the smaller, label-sized signs do not bear any insignia of a particular company, but are still collectable (e.g. 'Please Adjust Your Dress' or 'Mind your head when leaving your seat'). £1 – £3.

Lamps

There are several different types of lamp associated with the railways. The most plentiful, but also the most popular with collectors, is the station hanging oil lamp decorated with the name, initials or badge of the railway company. Such oil lamps in full working order, with copper sheathing and the emblem or name of a pre-grouping line are in the price range £15 – £30.

Lamps of the LMS, LNER, GWR and SR period, painted black or white, with three aspects are more common. £5 – £10.

Early hand lamps with prominent bull's-eye lenses, brass tops and pre-grouping insignia, usually square, more rarely circular in section. Plus factors are brass caps (steel are more common), and small brass safety chains. £10 – £20.

Buffer lamps, with the frontal aspect surrounded by a large disc. Cross handles on inner and outer casing. £5 – £15.

Crossing lamps, up to 2 feet high, with brass and copper mountings, paintwork according to the livery of the company or the region. Four aspects, filtered red at back and front and green at the sides. £15 – £30.

Locomotive head lamps attached to the buffer beam and smoke-box door. A vast range in sizes and types. £15 to £40.

Small battery-operated hand-lamps, increasingly used from 1920 onwards, are worth from £1 to £3, depending on construction details and whether they feature emblems of the post-grouping or BR periods.

Name Plates

Undoubtedly the most popular and most highly prized of all railway relics. The practice of naming locomotives varied from line to line. In general the larger companies restricted this to the larger passenger trains, whereas the smaller lines tended to name every engine, no matter how humble its function. The value of name plates depends on several disparate factors: the glamour surrounding certain outstanding locomotives, the company itself, especially from the pre-grouping era, the method of construction and the aesthetic qualities of the lettering, in descending order of importance.

Name plates from the more famous engines are now very rare and fetch high prices when they come up at auction. £300 – £500.

The name plates of express passenger trains of the second rank, irrespective of age, are more plentiful (sometimes still available from British Rail). £100 – £200.

Name plates from the less important engines of pre-grouping companies. £50 – £150.

Early name plates engraved or incised on brass plates. £75 – £150.

Later name plates cast in brass with raised lettering and rim; sunken areas waxed black or painted in colour. Styles of lettering vary considerably in the latter part of the pre-grouping era and value depends on the amount of florid ornamentation of the letters. £50 – £200.

More prosaic lettering on cast brass plates of the inter-war period. £50 – £100.

Unusual decorative features: the running fox of the 'Hunt' class, the regimental insignia on LMS and 'Peak' class locos, the house flags of the steamship companies on the name plates of the SR 'Merchant Navy' class, etc., are very important plus factors, which enhance the value of a plate by 50-70%.

Several companies are now catering to the demand for name plates by making replicas, either full-size or miniature. Although the manufacturers are quick to stress that the production of these replicas is strictly controlled and that, as they are relatively expensive to make, they will rapidly become 'antiques of the future', one can foresee considerable problems of differentiation for collectors in years to come.

Number Plates

Every engine bears a serial number irrespective of its name, class or line. Two main types were produced, differing in size, and of varying interest to collectors. The more desirable are cabside plates, usually about half the size of name plates, but much larger than the second category, smoke-box number plates. £40 – £60.

Smoke-box plates. £20 – £30.

Other plates, much smaller in size, bear combinations of numerals and letters and show the shed code of the motive power department to which the locomotive is allocated. These shed plates consist of small oval plaques fitted to the smoke-box door. £3 – £7.

Works plates are usually cast in brass with raised lettering and record the maker's name and address, the date of manufacture and the works serial number. The more desirable plates refer to firms which have long ceased to exist. The more elaborate works plates from the pre-grouping era are in the price range £25 – £50.

Post-grouping plates are more functional in appearance and are generally worth £10 – £20.

Plates on modern diesel and electric engines are of brass or aluminium alloy sheet with much shallower die-struck lettering. £2 – £5.

Signal Box Name Boards

The modernisation of the railway system in recent years and the elimination of many of the old-style signal boxes, has brought a large number of their name boards on to the market and also stimulated interest in this hitherto rather neglected field. These name boards range in material and design and are valued accordingly. The earlier types were cast in iron with raised lettering, painted in contrasting colours. £15 – £30.

Painted wooden name boards are less desirable, and their value depends largely on condition and the degree of interest attached to the particular signal box. £7 – £15.

Enamelled sheet metal signs bearing the names of signal boxes are those met with most frequently. The size of tnese name boards varies considerably, from 4 to 15 feet in length. £5 – £10.

Signalling Equipment

The commonest forms of signalling equipment are the signal arms, which differ in shape and colour combination depending on their function. The earlier or lower quadrant type was generally wooden, whereas the later (since about 1930) or upper quadrant type was of metal. More elaborate signal arms have large white metal letters attached to the extremity (e.g. S indicates a shunting signal). Smaller signals were mounted on short poles near ground level and were mainly used in shunting. Signal arms alone are in the price range £3 – £10.

Signal arms, complete with double glass 'spectacles' with coloured filters are worth much more. £7 – £15.

The poles or gantries on which signals were mounted were often capped with a decorative finial. These finials themselves are quite collectable. £5 – £10.

Miscellaneous signalling equipment includes indicators, block instruments, bells and repeaters. With brightly polished brass and wooden cases, these items make attractive ornaments. Prices vary considerably, according to age and technical features. £10 – £30.

Station Furniture and Equipment

This heading covers a multitude of relics, the importance of which depends largely on the crest, insignia or inscriptions found on them. The most collectable items are wall clocks from waiting-rooms and booking-offices, bearing the names of the pre-grouping companies. Examples range from £20 – £50, depending on age and the name of the line. Wrought-iron fenders and other fireside items with railway insignia. £5 – £15.

There is a wide range of miscellaneous office equipment, including rubber stamps, ticket dating machines, staplers, metal punches and high stools, which is difficult to price individually, but is usually in the price range from £1 to £10 if crested or otherwise identifiable.

Window straps, antimacassars and foot warmers are among the items of carriage equipment now in great demand. £2 – £10.

Crockery bearing railway insignia is highly collectable: mainly cups, saucers and various sizes of plate, but also including electroplated serving dishes, bowls and even tureens. The value of such items depends largely on the crest. British Railways items are in the price range 50p to £2.

The inter-war period, £1 to £5.

Pre-grouping items, £3 to £20.

Cutlery bearing the initials or crests of the railway companies is fairly plentiful (much obsolete flatware being retained in service long after the amalgamation had taken place). Both crockery and cutlery (as well as linen) were used not only on the trains and station refreshment rooms, but in the many hotels operated by the railway companies. Since the nationalisation of the Pullman Car Company a vast quantity of crockery and cutlery bearing its elaborate crest has come on to the market, and is consequently of comparatively lower value at present.

Station Name Boards

Many of the original cast metal signs' with raised lettering and protective rim, were retained after 1921 on grounds of economy and incorporated the names, initials or crests of the Caledonian or the Brighton and South Coast railways long after they had been absorbed by LMS and SR respectively. Following nationalisation, however, these old cast metal signs were replaced by plain enamelled sheet metal signs in the standard colours of the British Railways regions. The fact that both pre-grouping and inter-war station name boards were scrapped in the late 1940s before collecting was well established explains their relative scarcity. The main station name boards are often of considerable length and their value depends on age, and the name of the station concerned. Decorative lettering and ornamental features are plus factors. £25 − £60.

Smaller signs, with rounded ends which were attached to lamp-posts and walls, are much more plentiful and more manageable. £5 − £15.

Post-nationalisation enamelled signs became relatively plentiful with the closures of the 1950s and early 1960s and are still available from the British Railways regional sales points. £5 − £10.

Tickets

The most popular form of railway ephemera, tickets vary considerably in value. Unfortunately there is no priced catalogue yet available giving details for the myriads of variations, but the following points may give some guide to relative scarcity and value. Unlike other forms of ephemera, such as stamps or bus tickets, railway tickets have never been plentiful in genuinely used condition, since it has long been normal practice to surrender tickets at the end of a journey, and such tickets are then normally scrapped after a period of time. Over the years, however, collectors have devised various cunning dodges for the retention of tickets but they are nevertheless still relatively elusive. This applies particularly to the tickets relating to the earlier lines, which would have been scrapped long before anyone thought of collecting them. The most desirable tickets relate to long-defunct branch lines and the more ephemeral companies of the late 19th century. Any tickets dating before 1870, irrespective of the company or the stations inscribed on them are highly desirable. The very early tickets, pre-1840, were comparatively large, made of paper and largely hand-written and are in the price range from £10 upwards.

Other very desirable tickets include those produced for special excursions connected with historic events (coronations, jubilees, international fairs and exhibitions). The value of these tickets depends on the interest attached to the event. Tickets may be collected according to their class or purpose (adult, child, cheap-day, half-day, ordinary excursion, workman, forces, schoolchildren, cycles, prams and dogs), according to the company, route or even individual station − bearing in mind that the number of possible combinations of destination and route possible for some of the more important stations would run into thousands at any given time.

Single tickets and intact return tickets are much more desirable than half return tickets. Tickets overprinted 'Specimen' or 'Cancelled' have come on to the market following the closure of a line or station; these are worth much less than genuinely issued tickets (which invariably show the date of issue stamped on the reverse).

Other types include season tickets and platform tickets. The latter are comparatively disregarded, though examples issued at obsolete stations are now beginning to rise in value.

The majority of tickets are of the Edmondson pasteboard type, though they have now been largely superseded by other and usually larger types, with their salient details printed by machine at the time and point of issue. Undoubtedly the many experimental types of paper and thin card tickets of the 1960s and early 1970s will eventually rise in value commensurate with their undoubted scarcity.

Time-tables

These fall into three distinct categories, of varying degrees of interest and value. The most sought after examples are the working time-tables used by the railway personnel themselves, with detailed instructions about speeds over certain stretches of line, signals to be observed and times between certain points. Examples of 19th century working time-tables in good condition are now among the most highly prized railway relics and may be worth £25 − £50 or even more for exceptionally early examples. Later working time-tables, especially those of the amalgamation and nationalisation periods are more plentiful, usually less interesting technically, and in the price range £5 − £10.

Official railway time-tables for the use of the general public vary enormously in size and complexity, from simple pamphlets giving details of only one or two routes, to the bulky volumes giving details of the entire railway network. Their value also depends to a large extent on date, the earlier time-tables being in the range £5 − £20.

Time-tables of the nationalisation period are fairly plentiful and range from £1 to £5, the more expensive ones relating to the defunct services of the 1950s.

Official time-tables produced in connection with exceptional services connected with excursions or additional trains to cope with important national events (e.g. the 1953 Coronation, 1951 Festival of Britain) are worth a handsome premium.

Unofficial time-tables include all those published by commercial undertakings other than the railway companies. The best-known of these are the Bradshaw guides which first appeared in 1838 as a tiny, slim volume including coloured maps of the very few routes then in operation. Early editions of Bradshaw are in the range £20 – £50. The much bulkier volumes of the late 19th century are worth £5 – £15, and early 20th century examples £2 – £5. Time-tables by other publishers are not so desirable and range from £1 to £5 depending on date and size.

Tokens

Discs which appear to all intents and purposes to be like coins, were designed to enable railway employees, public servants and certain other groups to travel by train without the need for an actual cash transaction. These tokens were issued by many railway companies and had a specified cash value, so that they could be exchanged when required for a ticket of the desired amount. These tokens were mainly struck in copper or bronze, though some are known in brass, white metal or pewter. They invariably feature the emblem of the railway company and the value expressed in shillings or pence. The more desirable examples are those which also incorporate a tiny picture of the rolling stock, early locomotives and station facades. Transport tokens of this type belong mainly to the latter half of the 19th century, though some types continued in use until the nationalisation period. Similar tokens were issued by local authorities for use by public employees on buses and tramways. Tokens of this type are in the range 50p – £4.

Track Side Plates

The majority of these signs were intended to guide the engine driver and railway guard and are inscribed with simple instructions, such as 'Whistle', 'Beware of Catch Points' or 'Shut off Steam'. Many others are not inscribed as such, but bear various conventional symbols and figures, indicating distances, gradients and the siting of water troughs, repair huts, telegraph offices, etc.. The value of these track side plates is in the price range from £3 to £10.

Other signs were designed for the instruction of the general public and were usually of cast iron with raised lettering painted to contrast with the background. The majority relate to trespass and the limitations of public access to the track or footbridges restricted to railway personnel. Others mounted on the approach to road bridges over railway lines advised of weight or speed restrictions, or limitations on the type of vehicles permitted. Similar signs were often (and still are) found on the banks of canals controlled by the railway companies. The value of these signs depends on the name of the railway company, the location and the content of the warning. £7 – £20.

432

Uniforms

Complete railway uniforms are of comparatively little interest, and collectors are mainly concerned with ancillary items. Of these the most important are railwaymen's caps, ranging in value from the functional grease-top hats of footplatemen, via the more decorative pill-boxes and peaked caps of porters and signalmen, to the gold-braided caps of ticket collectors and station-masters. These caps should be complete with their badges. Value depends on the insignia, the badges of the pre-grouping era being the most desirable. Prices of caps vary from £1 for BR grease-tops to £10 for late 19th century station-masters' caps.

A wide range of insignia may be found on the buttons of the old railway companies. The buttons worn by railway personnel were in three main sizes and may be found in gilt-bronze, brass, chrome, white metal or plastic – in descending order of value. A plus factor is buttons stamped on the reverse of the rim 'special quality'; such buttons were worn by station-masters and other senior officials. The value of buttons depends mainly, however, on the company whose insignia is depicted: from 10p to £1.50.

Armbands, worn by lookout men, pilotmen, porters and other employees working outside a station area range in value from 50p for relatively plain BR green bands, to £2 – £3 for the more decorative armbands of the early 20th century with the initials or crests of the pre-grouping companies.

Whistles and Rattles

Devices carried by railway guards and platform staff to signal the departure of trains. Whistles in particular may be found in many different sizes and styles. Their value depends, of course, almost entirely on the identification, by means of names, initials or emblems, with particular railway companies or even stations. £1 – £5.

Museums

Science Museum, London.
Pendon Museum, Abingdon.
Museum of Science and Industry, Birmingham.
Tramways Museum, Crich.
Beamish Museum, Chester-le-Street.
Bressingham Hall, Diss.
Museum of Transport, Glasgow.
Museum of Transport and Technology, Leicester.
Science and Engineering Museum, Newcastle-upon-Tyne.
Locomotive Museum, Penrhyn Castle.
Swindon Museum, Swindon.
Railway Museum, York.

Reading List   Smith, Donald J. Discovering Railwayana. Tring, 1971.

ROLLING PINS

Glass rolling pins are known to have been in use from the late 17th century, but early examples were plain, heavy and made of coarse glass. At the end of the 18th century, however, the Nailsea glassworks started a fashion for more decorative pins and they rapidly became popular as a form of love token, often given by sailors to their wives and sweethearts. This nautical connection probably explains the popularity of glass rolling pins among the earlier seaside souvenirs. They attained the height of their popularity during the first railway boom, which opened up the coastal areas to urban holidaymakers, but they declined sharply in popularity after 1860. Attempts have been made in recent years to revive the custom. The hollow rolling pins were often filled with salt and suspended over the hearth to keep the salt dry.

Date-lines

1790-1810　　The earliest Nailsea pins were of deep Bristol blue glass. Though superseded by other colours, this type remained in production till the 1860s. Very early examples, which can be dated by their inscriptions, are rare. £25 − £40.

1810-1830　　Opaque white or bottle green pins predominate in this period. Particularly desirable are examples with blue and white marbled effect. £10 − £30.

1830-1860　　Other colours becoming popular included amethyst, ruby and turquoise. Wide variety of inscriptions which may be grouped into pious mottoes. £7 − £12. 'A gift from . . .' (£10 − £20); commemorative pins with dates of births, betrothals or marriages (£15 − £30).
Very elaborate pins with verses and scenes or pictorial motifs, £20 − £40.

Points to look for

Good, even colouring in the glass, finely lettered inscriptions, enamelled polychrome pictures and dates are all important plus factors. Very elaborate floral decoration is not as desirable as interesting inscriptions, and is generally not rated so highly.

Pitfalls

Decorated glass rolling pins have been 'revived' in recent years. The modern examples lack the naive, primitive charm of the original motifs and the colouring is usually too crisp and bright. The enamel colours on

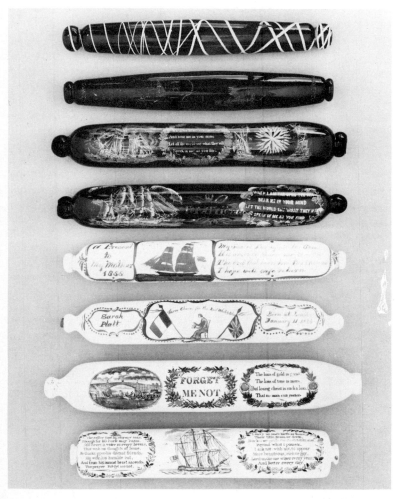

Glass rolling pins. From the top: Nailsea; Sunderland; nautical pin; a gun ship; a pin dated 1858; commemorative portrait pin; pin with print of Sunderland Bridge; rare Staffordshire pottery pin.

the early ones have often rubbed or flaked off, as has the gilding on the examples shown in the photograph, and this would of course affect the price.

Museums and Reading List

Most provincial museums have a few examples, but there are no important collections nor are there any books on the subject.

SAFETY LAMPS

Lamps designed to give illumination in mine-workings without igniting fire-damp and other gases and thereby causing an explosion. The appalling loss of life in the coal-mines of the early 19th century led to experimentation with lamps which could be lit in gaseous atmosphere. Sir Humphrey Davy is credited with the invention of the safety lamp in 1815, based on the principle that a metal gauze cylinder protects a naked flame from igniting gases in the surrounding atmosphere. Other inventors were working on the problem simultaneously and produced their own versions of safety lamps, while subsequent developments in the technology of safe lighting resulted in lamps of other designs and patterns. The rationalisation of the British coal industry in the 1950s and 1960s brought a large number of safety lamps on to the market and because of their decorative appeal (burnished steel, with copper and brass fittings) they have become one of the more desirable aspects of industrial archaeology.

Date-lines

1815   Original Davy lamp, with gauze cylinder. Plain burner at foot, circular metal top with carrying ring. Later models

  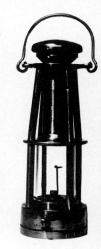

George Stephenson's early lamp with gauze. 1815.

English Mueseler lamp. 1840.

Gray's safety lamp. 1868.

436

	were fitted with metal windshields.
1815	Gauze cylinder lamp by George Stephenson; similar to the Davy lamp but usually more elaborate.
1833	Improved Davy lamp by Upton and Roberts; totally enclosed windshield making for greater safety, but comparatively cumbersome and expensive to produce.
1839	Lamp with glass replacing the lower part of the gauze cylinder and giving out a much better light; patented by Dr. W.R. Clanny.
1840s	Improved Clanny lamp with a metal bonnet surrounding the upper part of the gauze.
1840	Belgian lamp, by J. Mueseler; similar to the Clanny but less liable to smoke, having a wrought iron chimney supported by a gauze diaphragm.
1844	Boty lamp, an improved version of the Clanny, with air entering through rings below the glass.
1846	Elion lamp, based on the Clanny; greater illumination but too easily extinguished.
1868	Gray lamp, also based on the Clanny: bonneted lamp with tubular feed system.
1882	Improved Mueseler lamp by the French inventor, J.B. Marsaut; chimney replaced by two or three gauze caps; air-holes immediately above the glass.

The Improved Davy, the Clanny, the Gray and the Mueseler-Marsaut lamps were widely used until recently, though electric lamps have gradually gained ground since the early 1900s. Mining statistics show that some 677,688 flame safety lamps were in use in Britain in 1907 and close on half a million in 1926, so the basic material for collection should still be relatively plentiful. The majority of lamps now on sale are of relatively recent manufacture and are in the price range £3 – £10. At present these lamps are collected mainly for decorative effect and there is no market for the older and less ornamental varieties. These are undoubtedly rare, and as interest in industrial archaeology develops, the price for early Davy, Clanny and Mueseler lamps must rise.

Museums
Science Museum, London.
Mitchell Museum, Hanbury, Stoke-on-Trent.

Reading List
Mining Association. A Historical Review of Coal Mining. London, 1925.

SCALES & BALANCES

Instruments for weighing date back more than 2,000 years, but for all practical purposes the collectable examples date from the late 17th century when pocket scales of various types came into general use. Among the larger types those designed for use by apothecaries and grocers are the most plentiful. Precision balances for scientific use became widespread in the early 19th century and spring balances, with weights read on a dial, date from the mid-19th century. The different categories of scales and balances are discussed separately.

Apothecaries' Scales

These are among the earliest scales available to the collector, with examples surviving from the 17th century. They consist of two small brass or glass pans, suspended from a beam balanced on a fulcrum mounted on a central brass pillar. The styling of the wooden base varies considerably, from plain solid rectangular stands, to elaborate bases

(a) Folding guinea scales, c.1770. (b) Coin scales, with table of weights, c.1780. (c) Apothecaries' scales, velvet-lined shagreen case, c.1780. (d) Pocket balance for sovereigns and half-sovereigns, c.1840. (e and f) Arc-and-pointer letter balances, late 19th century. (g) Patent letter balance with desk clamp, 1839.

containing tiny drawers for the weights, and having bracket feet at each corner. Apothecaries' scales can usually be dated by the inspector's marks, showing the crown and Royal cypher. The weights themselves often bear the Royal cypher and in some cases even feature the Royal profile. Names of manufacturers are frequently inscribed on the reverse of these early weights, giving a further clue to date.

Good examples of such scales, from 1670 to 1720 are in the price range £100 – £150.

Georgian apothecaries' scales, £50 – £100.

Victorian scales, £30 – £60.

Apart from the standard table models there are apothecaries' scales designed for the pocket. These are fitted into a small shagreen, ebony, oak or mahogany case and consist of folding scales equipped with tiny brass pans, beam, fulcrum and set of weights. The majority of these scales date from the early 18th century. £10 – £40.

Coin Balances

Small pocket or folding balances were indispensable in an age when gold coins were current and it was necessary to check the weight of foreign coins and to guard against the abuse of clipping. This abuse was later checked by the introduction of a grained edge in the mid-17th century, but there was still the problem of counterfeits which could only be checked by accurate weighing. Coin balances fall into two main categories. Early 19th century simple balances made of brass had a fixed weight at one end and two circular indentations at the other, one for sovereigns and the other for half sovereigns. These balances usually bear the crown and cypher marks which enable them to be dated roughly. £6 – £25.

The more elaborate consist of folding balances contained in a small narrow mahogany case. When the lid is released the scales are automatically raised into position. Some even have calibrated beams so as to give the weight of any coin, and are not restricted to sovereigns and half sovereigns. Important plus factors are the inclusion of the original instructions and tables of weights, printed on paper glued to the inner side of the case, and makers' labels. £15 – £35.

Letter Balances

These date from 1840, when the principle of the charge according to weight was adopted. Prior to the introduction of Uniform Penny Postage letters were charged according to the distance carried and the number of sheets (irrespective of the size of the sheets). Anticipating the introduction of these reforms various patent balances were devised.

The most desirable is the small brass balance patented by H. Hooper in 1839. It has a screw clamp for attachment to the edge of a desk or table, a sliding beam calibrated in half ounces (from ½ to 4) and a fixed weight bearing the Royal Arms and inscription 'Post Office Letter Weight' on one side, and a lengthy inscription on the reverse giving details of the Act of Parliament implementing the proposals of Rowland Hill. Examples of these balances are rare and highly prized by philatelists. £40 – £70.

Small household letter scales with circular nest of weights from ½oz. to 2oz. on a walnut base 6½ins. long, brass frame with zinc pans stamped "Registered Criterion Trade mark", c.1910. Unusual type of apothecary scales, steel beam with green silk cords to hang brass bowl-shaped pans which are detachable from lid holder and fold into oak carrying case 7ins. long, c.1840. Small set of apothecary pocket scales of similar type, these were contained in oval Pontypool tin cases in mahogany or oak oblong boxes to slip into the pocket. Pocket sovereign scales contained in their original cardboard box with retailer's label reading "S.W. Fores, Book seller and stationer, 41, Piccadilly"; these were to check the weights of half and full sovereign coins, c.1840. Five graduated brass bell-shaped butcher's weights showing variations in style of handles, the larger the set, the higher the value.

Some later 19th century letter balances consist of a calibrated arc suspended by a ring, with a weight sliding on an arm, and a clip to hold the letter at an angle to the weighted arm. Examples may be found in brass, steel or enamelled metal, with weights in fractions of ounces or in grammes. £5 – £20.

Small tension spring balances date from the end of the 19th century and are still being made. The earlier (and more collectable) varieties can be dated by patent numbers, trade marks, registration marks and occasionally by Royal cyphers. £5 – £15.

Brass letter scales mounted on a wooden base were produced for use on desks and tables. These scales vary in size, number of weights and decorative features (from marquetry banding on the sides of the base to cast brass ornament on the fulcrum of the balance). These features are relatively unimportant, the date of the scales being the chief factor governing value. These letter scales invariably had tables of postal rates engraved on the letter pan or printed on inlaid bone or ivory plaques and the periodic changes in rates enable these scales to be dated fairly accurately. Any reference to parcel rates, for example, places the date after 1883; any reference to printed matter or postcard rates places the date after 1870. Scales showing a minimum letter rate of one penny per half ounce belong to the period before 1871; those showing the minimum rate of one penny per ounce are from 1871 to 1918; those showing 1½ pence per ounce are from 1918 to 1940. A very rare type show the rate as twopence per ounce (1920-1922) – but beware of recent imitations bearing this table of rates. £10 – £35.

Very elaborate examples, decorated with Tunbridge ware (q.v.) £40 – £60.

Butchers' and Grocers' Scales

The earliest form consists of a brass beam and pillar with brass or pottery pans, mounted on a broad wooden base, usually of mahogany. The value of these scales, widely used throughout the 19th and early 20th centuries, depends on their size, ornamental features and the scope of the weights. The latter may either be flat and circular, forming a nest of weights from half an ounce to 4 lb.; or may be upright, waisted, bell-shaped cylindrical weights. In the latter case sometimes special boxes were also provided to house them. These scales and weights can be dated accurately according to the crown and cyphers found on them. £35 – £70.

Even larger grocers' scales exist in which the wooden base is replaced by a heavy circular cast iron or brass foot to the pillar. Value depends on the decorative features found on the pillar and stand. Examples with

Top: 18th century hand-wrought steelyard, a portable type of scale to weigh meat by sliding the pear-shaped weight along the calibrated arm; larger steelyards were used to weigh sacks of corn, 22ins. long. Left: Large set of postal scales in brass with oak base 13ins. long complete with nest of weights from ½oz. to 2lbs., by S. Mordan & Co., of London, c.1890. Right: Very accurate type of brass banker's scales to weigh up to 50oz. troy weight; these were used to weigh silver currency and gold sovereigns in a banking house to save time in counting out the coins. c.1860.

brass pans are in the range from £30 to £60. Similar scales but with enamelled pans or slabs of marble or ceramics, £40 - £60. Makers' trade marks and ornate emblems in underglaze transfer decoration are a good plus factor. Late 19th century grocers' spring balances, by Salter, Avery and other leading manufacturers, may be found with elaborate cast decoration round the dial and the plinth. These scales are in cast iron or brass and are rare in good condition. £50 − £80.

Points to look for

Completeness is very important, and scales with one or more weights missing from the set should be 25% less in price. Scales with no weights at all have even less value unless they possess unusual decorative or historic features. Individual weights, especially the brass bell-shaped butchers' and grocers' weights, are collectable in their own right, and it should be possible to build up sets of weights with matching cyphers. Spring balances invariably feature their patent number and date on the dial. Other balances can usually be dated by the cyphers and inscriptions (see **Letter Scales**, above).

Pitfalls

The more decorative of the smaller balances — letter balances and scales — have been widely forged in recent years, possibly in India. They can be detected easily by the scratched, ultra-bright appearance of the brasswork. Genuine brass scales acquire a patina with age.

Museums
British Museum, London.
London Museum, London.
Pharmaceutical Society Museum, London.
Science Museum, London.
National Postal Museum, London.
Bruce Castle Museum, Haringey, London.
City Museum and Art Gallery, Birmingham.
Fitzwilliam Museum, Cambridge.
National Museum of Wales, Cardiff.
Royal Scottish Museum, Edinburgh.
Museum and Art Gallery, Glasgow.
Museum of the History of Science, Oxford.

Reading List — see **Scientific Instruments**

SCENT BOTTLES

Small bottles intended for scents and perfumes, found in coloured glass or porcelain, with enamel, gold or silver ornament. Small decorative bottles for this purpose were evolved in the late 17th century and remain in use to this day.

Date-lines

1670-1750   Bottles of Continental origin, made in black or deeply coloured glass (France and Germany), or in the styles of Venetian glass of the period (Italy). Enamelled decoration on sides. Caps of gold or silver with repoussé decoration. £40 – £100.

1720-1770   English bottles made in London or Bristol in deep blue glass. Best quality are enamelled and gilded. Price depends on quality and condition of the decoration. £150 – £350.

Fine, clear glass scent bottles of the same period, with little or no decoration are much more plentiful and much less desirable. £20 – £35.

1750-1790   Very flat, thin and elongated oval bottles with small, silver-mounted neck. Very shallow cut over most of their

Art Deco scent bottles. The black bottle was designed by the French decorators Sue et Mare. The others are by Lalique, the two tall ones for Coty, the sea urchin was possibly designed for Worth.

surface, with engraved mottoes (often in French, though of English manufacture). £30 – £50.

Similar bottles incorporating a date are worth more. £40 – £60.

1770-1840   Wider range of coloured glass, including emerald, amber and amethyst. Enamelled or engraved decoration, often combined. Names of scents and toilet waters enamelled or engraved on sides, or engraved on tiny silver labels affixed to the neck of the bottle. Caps of silver, sometimes pierced, fretted or inlaid with gold. £25 – £60.

1750-1800   Bottles in opaque white glass, with overall faceting decorated with gilding in the manner of James Giles. £200 – £400.

Opaque white glass bottles with smooth surface decorated with polychrome enamel motifs (chinoiseries, pastoral scenes, floral subjects). £30 – £80.

1780-1820   Scent bottles made of enamelled copper. Best quality made at Bilston, but most early 19th century examples are of German origin. £20 – £80.

1830-1880   Victorian scent bottles of the horizontal type, with stoppers at both ends. One compartment for perfume, the other for aromatic spices or smelling salts. Faceted coloured glass and silver caps. £15 – £30.

1870-1920   Scent bottles in American art glass, with pressed or moulded decoration and silver mounts. Opaque, rose or amber tints predominant. £15 – £40.

Bottles of opaque glass with tinted overlay, cut cameo fashion. £25 – £50.

1890-1940   Commercial scent bottles commissioned by leading French perfumiers (Coty, Chanel, Lanvin, etc.) from Daum, Gallé and Lalique. Wide variety of forms (animals, birds, human heads, geometric styles) and decorative treatment, moulded, pressed, engraved, acid-etched, frosted surface). Price depends on size, period and decorative qualities. £10 – £60.

Points to look for

Most scent bottles can only be judged on their innate features and qualities. Those which can definitely be attributed to a leading manufacturer or craftsman command a high premium. Condition is very important; decoration, such as gilding or enamelling, should be as near intact as possible; caps, mounts and stoppers should be complete.

Selection of scent bottles showing various styles of manufacture. a: Red overlay glass*; b: Double end ruby*; c: Glass; d: German Nailsea type; e: Blue stopper brass mount; f: Owl; g: Miniature; h: Torpedo; i: Vinaigrette top*; j: Vivid blue Bristol; k: Two ended ruby*; l: Very thin centre, polished; m: Georgian; n: French — metal and enamel*; o: Enamel Birmingham 1904*; p: Artificial ruby; q: Amber glass; r: Finely engraved*. * These items have silver mounts.

Pitfalls

Chief problem concerns porcelain scent bottles, which were made by Chelsea, Bow and Worcester between 1750 and 1770. These porcelain bottles were exceedingly ornate and often modelled in the form of tiny figures, girls, putti, animals, etc. incorporating tiny clock faces, floral encrustation and gilding. Other popular subjects included floral bouquets and chinoiseries. The best porcelain bottles were modelled by Charles Gouyn and Nicholas Sprimont. Chelsea or Bow scent bottles are in the price range £100 — £250; Worcester bottles from £45 to £100.

Both these porcelain bottles and the late 18th century enamel bottles were extensively forged by Samson of Paris in the late 19th century. Although subtle differences in the fake marks distinguish the Samson forgeries from genuine bottles it is advisable to purchase such items only against a guarantee.

Museums

British Museum, London.
Wallace Collection, London.
Victoria and Albert Museum, London.

Harris Museum and Art Gallery, Preston.

Reading List

Foster, Kate. *Scent Bottles*. London, 1966.

SCIENTIFIC INSTRUMENTS

Three universal dials, from left to right, by Newton, Dollard and Elliot Bros.

A bronze quadrant by Roxby, c.1820, with compass and artificial horizon built in.

The following are described under separate entries: Barometers, Cameras, Microscopes, Sextants, Scales and Balances, and Telescopes. For the sake of convenience, however, the Museums and Reading List pertaining to all categories of scientific instrument are given at the end of this entry. Below are details of several minor categories of instruments which have recently become collectable.

Metronomes are instruments for measuring or denoting the speed at which a piece of music should be played. Credit for its invention was formerly given to Johann Nepomuk Maelzel of Ratisbon, though it is now thought that the true inventor was a Dutch musician named Winkler. In its simplest form the metronome consists of a pendulum swung on a pivot. Below the pivot is a fixed weight and above is a sliding weight which controls the velocity of the oscillations. The speed is determined by sliding the weight along the pendulum rod which is calibrated in MM numbers (Maelzel's Metronome). Metronomes date from the early 19th century. Plain metronomes in simple wooden pyramid cases rate £10 − £15 for late 19th century examples. Early 19th century types are worth from £20 to £50 depending on maker's name and styling of the case and pendulum. Decorative features such as inlay or marquetry on the case are highly desirable. Later metronomes of simple construction are of little value at present. The exceptions are those with semi-mechanical features, such as clockwork (£25 − £40) or incorporating a bell mechanism which strikes at the first of a given number of beats (£30 – £60).

Armillary Spheres and Orreries were produced to demonstrate the solar system and the movement of the planets. Armillary spheres consisted of concentric rings or hoops of bronze or brass showing the moon, sun and planets in relation to the earth and its terrestrial features (equator, tropics and poles). Such spheres are known to have been made from the 2nd century, having been devised by Ptolemy the geographer and astronomer. Medieval examples, showing the earth at the centre, are extremely rare. Later examples, dating from the adoption of Copernican theory on the movement of the planets round the sun, were used to demonstrate the solar system and were made up to the mid-19th century. They vary widely in size and decorative appeal, but the most elementary types would now command over £400, and the more complex and attractive 18th century examples would be in the range £500 – £1,200. Orreries serve a similar purpose but are driven by hand or by clockwork to show the actual movement of the planets round the sun. The name is derived from Charles Boyle, fourth Earl of Orrery (1676-1731), soldier, statesman, dramatist and amateur astronomer. The original clockwork device was sold in 1974 for £29,000. Other clockwork orreries of 18th century manufacture would now be in the price range of £8,000 and upwards. Hand-operated orreries would certainly be not less than £1,000 and would rate considerably more depending on complexity and the amount of detail given.

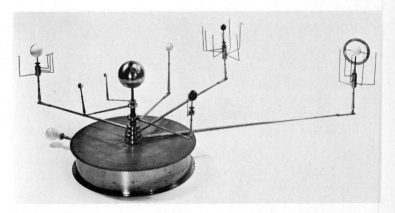

A George III orrery by W. and S. Jones, London, in brass and with ivory and painted solar bodies and silvered scales, the terrestial globe dated 1800.

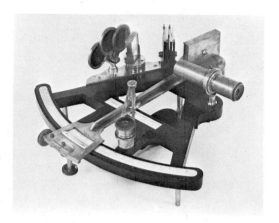

An ebonised and brass mounted octant by Gowlands of South Castle Street, Liverpool.

Magnetic compasses, long regarded as a Chinese invention, are now thought to have originated in Scandinavia in the 12th century and were described by the English writer, Alexander Neckam, about 1160. By the 14th century the use of a magnetised needle, either mounted on a pivot or floated in a bowl of water, to determine the north and south magnetic poles, was widespread in Europe and the Near East. The earliest compasses were no more than magnetised needles, though their mounts, of gold or silver, were often elaborately chased. The earliest compasses in their present form, consisting of needles mounted over a calibrated card or disc, date from the mid-16th century. The finest compasses were produced from about 1670 to 1800. Gold, silver, gilt-metal and ivory were frequently used in their construction and the more sumptuous examples were decorated accordingly. Apart from finely engraved latitude scales and chapter rings with the hour numerals, the most desirable examples had hinged lids or plates giving the latitudes of the more important European cities. Compasses of this period now fetch £300 – £2,000, depending on materials used, decorative and technical features, makers' names, date of manufacture, qualities of craftsmanship and condition. Later compasses (1800-1900) are generally less decorative, but this was the period of the greatest technical advances. Single flat needles were in use from 1766 to 1840, but subsequently groups of four laminated steel needles were used (an invention of the whaling missionary William Scoresby). There were also many improvements in liquid compasses between 1813 and 1866. Dry card compasses became fashionable in the late 19th century, following the invention by Lord Kelvin in 1876. Liquid compasses, modified by Captain L.W.P. Chetwynd, were adopted by the Royal Navy in 1906 and most compasses since then have been variants of this type. There is considerable variety to be found in the different styles of compass cards produced in Britain, Europe and America from 1760 onwards. 19th century compasses are generally in the £10 – £60 range, but are relatively unconsidered and therefore undervalued at present.

Theodolites are surveying instruments whose name is thought to be derived from the mathematician Theodolus. The theodolite consists of two graduated circles at right angles to each other (for measuring horizontal and vertical angles) and an alidade for each circle which carries two or more vernier scales. The instrument is supported on a pedestal resting on adjustable feet used to keep the instrument level. Theodolites in primitive form were used in the 16th century, but did not become precision instruments until the early 18th century when a telescope (q.v.) was incorporated as well as devices for levelling and orientation. From the collector's viewpoint the most attractive theodolites date between about 1730 and 1840 and those signed by one of the leading instrument makers of the period are worth a high premium. Theodolites of the late 18th and early 19th century are in the price range £150 – £400. Later theodolites may be found in many different forms and sizes, incorporating numerous refinements which give more accurate results. In the period from 1840 to 1910 the plus factors are the technical features, but this period has so far attracted little serious attention and theodolites are currently underpriced at £40 to £100.

Waywisers are instruments for measuring distances and came into use in the late 17th century. Stylistically the examples with smaller wheels (up to two feet in diameter) tend to be earlier, while those with larger wheels (about three feet in diameter) date from the mid-18th century. An early 19th century type has two wheels joined at the axle. The wheels are usually of hardwood bound with iron, but are occasionally found in an all-metal or all-wood construction. Mounted on the shaft above the hub of the wheel was a dial which measured the distance covered, and above that was a steering handle, often decorated with fine baluster turning. The dials are usually of brass covered by glass and give measurements in yards, poles, chains, furlongs and miles or their European equivalents. As a rule the maker's name was engraved on the dial; names to look for include Heath and Wing, Fraser and Cole, all of London. Examples bearing an official inscription, especially that of the General Post Office, rate a good premium. Waywisers are in the price range £250 – £450 for 18th century examples, and £120 – £250 for 19th century examples. The majority of extant examples date around the 1820s, when the mileages between post towns were being re-surveyed by the Post Office to determine the scales of postal charges.

The elimination of postal rates computed by distance in 1840 did away with the need for waywisers.

Museums
National Maritime Museum, Greenwich.
Science Museum, London.
Victoria and Albert Museum, London.
City Museum and Art Gallery,
                        Birmingham.
The Whipple, Cambridge.
National Museum of Wales, Cardiff.
Royal Scottish Museum, Edinburgh.
Hunterian Museum, Glasgow.
Museum and Art Gallery, Glasgow.
Gloucester City Museum, Gloucester.
Museum and Art Gallery, Leicester.
History of Science Museum, Oxford.
Ashmolean Museum, Oxford.
City Museum, Sheffield.
County Museum, Stafford.
The Castle Museum, York.
The Museum of Transport, York.

A marine chronometer by William Cozens.

Reading List
Bell, G.H. and E.F. Old English Barometers. Winchester, 1970.
Carpenter. The Microscope and its Revelations. London, 1901.
Cousins, F.W. Sundials. London, 1969.
Daumas, Maurice. Scientific Instruments of the Seventeenth and Eighteenth Centuries and their Makers. London, 1972.
Goodison, Nicholas. English Barometers, 1860-1860. London, 1969.
Gunther, Robert T. The Astrolabes of the World. Oxford, 1932.
Herbert, Sir Alan P. Sundials, Old and New. London, 1967.
Hill, H.O. and Paget-Tomlinson, E.W. Instruments of Navigation. Greenwich, 1958.
Knowles, W.E. Middleton. The History of the Barometer. Baltimore, 1964.
Michel, H. Scientific Instruments in Art and History. Paris, 1966; London, 1967.
Taylor, E.G.R. The Mathematical Practitioners of Hanoverian England. Cambridge, 1966.
Van Henrick. The Microscope. London, 1893.
Wynter, Harriet and Turner, Anthony. Scientific Instruments. London, 1975.

451

SCREENS (Cheval)

Popularly known as fire screens, these screens were fashionable in Europe from the 17th century and reached the zenith of their development in the 18th and early 19th centuries. They consist of light covered frames between two uprights which terminate in pairs of feet, with or without stretchers between them. Many European cheval screens have a solid base. The purpose of such screens was two-fold, to protect people seated round a fire from the excessive heat and diffuse the heat round the room, and to add a decorative touch to the fireplace by concealing the empty grate when the fire was not in use. The extent to which the first of these functions could be fulfilled is questionable since the materials of which most cheval screens are made would not have stood up to excessive exposure to heat.

Date-lines
The finest cheval screens are of 18th century manufacture. The most

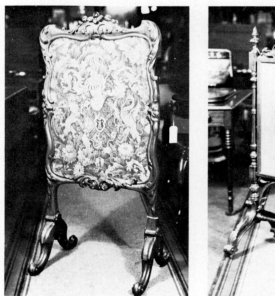

Left: A walnut cheval fire screen, c.1850, with an elaborate wool tapestry screen of heraldic design.
Right: A rosewood cheval fire screen of c.1850 elaborately carved with scroll and leaf forms and attractive floral design.

sumptuous examples have giltwood carving, intricate piercing and silk covers, with extravagant decoration characteristic of the rococo period. Good examples with original gilding and silkwork, of French or Italian origin, would now rate £350 upwards. English cheval screens of the 18th century, with constructional and decorative features of the appropriate period, are scarce and would now be worth from £80 to £150.

1830-1850	Early Victorian cheval screens in rosewood, fruitwoods or mahogany rate £60 to £100, much depending on the quality of the carving and also the decoration of the screen.
1850-1860	Walnut screens of a more naturalistic design, with elaborate wool tapestry screen of floral or heraldic design. £80 – £130.
1870-1910	Late Victorian and Edwardian screens, often characterised by a horizontal openwork panel across the foot. Those with fine decorative embroidery rate £20 – £30, but those with printed cloth panels are in little demand and are worth no more than £5 – £8.

Points to look for

Finely embroidered panels of unusual design rate a premium. Particularly sought after are cheval screens with glass panels decorated with scraps or postage stamps (a craze which was at its height 1845-70). Though possessing few aesthetic qualities, these screens were often broken up on account of the component stamps, and are consequently now scarce. £30 – £60.

(Folding)

Large standing screens, consisting of two, three or four panels, were used from medieval times in Europe, but probably date back much further in China and Japan. In Europe they were used primarily as draught excluders, but in the Far East as room dividers or merely to enhance the decor of rooms. Medieval examples are of the greatest rarity and seldom seen outside museum collections.

Date lines

16th-18th centuries	Heyday of Oriental lacquered screens, a large number of which were exported to Europe. Prices begin at around £300 for small, two-panelled screens and rise to well over £2,500, depending on size, quality of lacquer, decorative inlay and condition.

17th-19th centuries	European folding screens were often japanned in imitation of Oriental lacquer and decorated with chinoiseries. £250 – £700. Leather screens with painted decoration were fashionable in the same period. £100 – £300.
1840-1890	Two- or three-panelled screens with rosewood frames. Each panel divided into smaller compartments containing inset embroidered panels. £80 – £150.
1870-1910	Screens with panelling in beaten metal plaques or 'Aesthetic' tiles were fashionable. £100 – £300 depending on the quality and provenance of the tiles.
1890-1910	Late Victorian and Edwardian folding screens, characterised by the styling of the period (e.g. flattened broken pediments along top of frame) rate £60 to £110 with fine embroidered panels. Similar screens with printed fabric or plain panels are more common. £40 – £70.

Points to look for

As screens of this type were subjected to hard usage, hinges, feet and corners were liable to damage. Examples in exceptionally fine condition are rare and rate a high premium. Victorian nursery screens of leather-covered boards decorated with scraps and varnished for protection are now in great demand and well-decorated examples might rate £140+. But beware of plain screens with decoration of this sort applied relatively recently to meet the demand.

(Pole)

Small screens mounted on a pole, the height of the screen usually being adjustable by means of a small clamp and screw device. Ostensibly pole screens were intended to shield from the heat of a fire, from a draught or, more probably, from strong sunlight. It is doubtful whether pole screens ever served much useful purpose and from their inception in the 18th century they seem to have been regarded as purely decorative items.

Date-lines

1750-1800	The most elegant screens were produced in this period. The stand and tripod should accord with the furniture styles of the period. Finely carved examples with rich gilding are now scarce and would be worth £300+.

A pair of English rosewood pole screens, 4ft. 7ins. mid-19th century.

Less ornate examples, in walnut, mahogany or fruit-woods, with embroidered screens are in the range £70 – £150.

1800-1840 Tripod base, fluted pole, rectangular or circular screen, general styling in the Regency manner, decoration of screen frame comparatively restrained. £35 – £70.

1840-1870 Bases often flat and circular or rectangular. Poles and screen frames much more elaborate. Screen shapes more varied – shield, oval, scalloped and truncated circles now common. Superabundance of scrollwork, spiral twist turning and elaborate finials. £30 – £50.

Examples with finely embroidered panels rate £15 – £20 higher. The majority of the embroidered screens of this period are in Berlin woolwork.

Points to look for

A few pole screens were also made with panels of papier mâché (q.v.), 1830-50. Examples with fine decoration and good inlay work should rate £60 – £80. Early screens bearing the name of the manufacturers, Jennens and Bettridge, are worth rather more.

Pitfalls

As pole screens were unfashionable for a long time many of them were subsequently wired for electricity and converted into standard lamps. Beware of reconversions to the original function, and uneasy marriages of late-Victorian embroidered panels to poles of earlier periods.

SEXTANTS

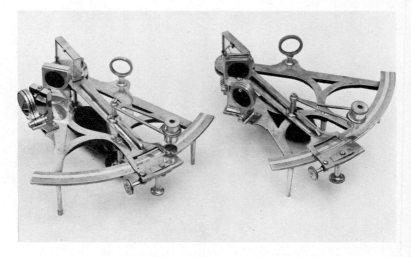

Two 19th century brass sextants.

Navigational instruments for measuring angular distances. The sextant was invented by John Hadley in 1731 and originally consisted of an octant using a graduated arc of one eighth of a circle. Captain Campbell increased the arc to a sixth in 1757 to meet the requirements of navigation, hence the term sextant, meaning a sixth of a circle. Nevertheless octants continued to be widely used for many years after that date. In 1771 the application of Jesse Ramsden's dividing machine enabled finer calibration of sextants. Subsequent types can be dated according to the technical features.

Date-lines

1731-1771	Early quadrants or octants with calibration up to 90 degrees, with an arc up to 20ins. in diameter, of rosewood or lignum vitae. Very rare.
1771-1850	Later octants with finer calibration; arc and index arm more usually made of brass than wood. Plus factors are

smaller size (8-16ins.), ebony or ivory radius, fine engraving on brass parts, especially trophies of war and maritime allegory, indicating use by naval officers. £150 – £400.

1780-1820   Early sextants of the double frame type invented by Edward Troughton (the double frame gives greater rigidity). £200 – £400.

1820-1900   Single frame sextants of brass construction, usually supplied in a mahogany case, complete with shades, mirror and accessories. £100 – £300. Plus factors are vernier scales of silver or, more rarely, platinum.

1900-1920   More utilitarian brass sextants of First World War vintage, with minimum of decoration and simplified technical features. £80 – £120.

Points to look for

Instruments should be in good working order and all parts should be complete and authentic. Plus factors are unusual technical features, fine decoration and the use of more expensive materials (ivory, silver) instead of boxwood and brass. Makers' names to watch for are Berge, Dollond, Bardin, Cary, Jones, B. Martin, Newton and Troughton. Sextants of more recent date are commonplace and of little value to the collector, though bubble sextants (in which a spirit level is reflected into the field of view) used in aerial navigation in the Twenties, are worth looking for. At present they change hands for £12 – £20 but are undervalued.

An early 19th century brass sextant by Cary of London, 8½ins. radius.

SIGNS

Trade signs evolved gradually in the Middle Ages and were produced primarily in an age when illiteracy was rife, in order to identify trades and professions readily. The earliest signs consisted of enlarged replicas of objects associated with a particular trade or vocation and these were suspended from a pole outside the tradesman's shop. Giant emblems became standardised in the 17th century and remained in constant use until the 20th century when various regulations and local bye-laws gradually drove them off the street. A few examples may still be seen *in situ*, but the majority have long disappeared from the high streets of towns and villages. Standing figures are a very important group mostly associated with tobacconists' shops and these flourished from the early 18th to the late 19th centuries, though a few examples are still in actual use. The third major category consists of two-dimensional painted signboards which have long been associated with inns and public houses. At first taverns had standardised signs, a pole surmounted by a crown of ivy and vine leaves, but as the number of pubs increased in the 16th century individual signs were evolved in order to distinguish them. In more recent years metal signs with enamelled decoration have been used, mainly to advertise various branded goods. These four main categories are discussed separately below.

Trade and Shop Emblems

The majority of these signs belong to the early 19th century, though examples are known from about 1670 onwards and a few were still being produced as late as the 1920s. These three-dimensional signs were carved from wood which was then painted or gilded. Certain emblems became the recognised form of identifying the sort of trades which would have existed in every town or village: spectacles (optician), shears (tailor), boot or shoe (cobbler or shoemaker), hat (hatter), pestle and mortar (apothecary or chemist), padlock (locksmith), bull's head, pig's head (beef or pork butcher), loaf of bread (baker), coil of pastry (pastry-cook), and the red and white striped pole (barber). Of these, only the last-named is still ubiquitous. Carved wood and painted signs range from £150 to £400, depending on condition and quality of carving. The addition of dates and inscriptions is an important plus factor.

Similar signs were produced from sheet metal in the late 19th century and are more plentiful. As well as the foregoing, they include the three brass balls emblem of the pawnbroker. £25 − £100.

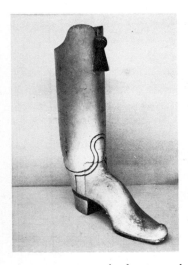

A gargantuan-sized carved wooden hessian boot from a boot and shoe makers covered with original gold leaf, circa 1760. At the top of the boot is a handsome black painted carved wood tassel. Overall height 39½ins. x 25ins. long.

Other trade signs exist, produced in a combination of cast and wrought ironwork. This was a European practice which was not widely adopted in Britain, hence the comparative scarcity of examples. These signs were produced specifically for individual tradesmen and are consequently often more decorative, with gilded scrollwork and scrolled brackets. These signs belong to the mid-18th to late 19th centuries and vary considerably in size, quality and decorative features. £200 – £600.

Tobacconists' Figures

Standing figures which graced the doorways of shops are now associated mainly with tobacconists, though at one time figures of sailors and midshipmen were to be found in the entrances of nautical instrument-makers. The fashion for standing figures, taking snuff or smoking a pipe, was probably established before the end of the 17th century. One tradition gives the credit to David Wishart who kept a tobacco shop in London in the early 18th century and is said to have devised the Highlander figure as a means of attracting the attention of passing Jacobites. This tale can be discounted, however, since the fashion had spread to other towns as well as London, long before the Jacobite Rebellions of 1715 and 1745 glamorised the Highlander in his kilt. Ironically, the Disarming Act of 1747, which made the wearing of the kilt punishable by death in the Highlands, does not seem to have affected the popularity of these wooden store figures. Though commonest in London and the south-east, they eventually spread all over England and even penetrated the lowlands of Scotland where real, live Highlanders were long feared and distrusted.

Perhaps by a similar analogy the idea was extended to other ethnic types — that people who were feared or despised should be regarded as a suitable medium for advertising tobacco. Thus carved wooden figures of Turks, Negroes (known as Blackamoors) and American Indians were popular in this context in the second half of the 18th century. Though the actual production of these figures declined after 1810, they continued to stand in tobacconists' doorways down to the time of the First World War, and not a few have survived in this location to the present day. They vary considerably in size, from life- size up to a giant eight feet tall; but the majority are 2-3½ feet in height.

Their value depends on size and the quality of the carving and decoration. The subject has some bearing on value, with preference being shown for Indians, Highlanders, Negroes and Turks in descending order. Date is not such an important factor, since it is difficult to date these figures accurately. Highlanders alone can be dated reasonably accurately by their dress, and there is a preference for figures in the large kilt of 1710-40, over the later figures based on the Black Watch (originally a military force raised for the policing of the Highlands) dressed in the philibeg or little kilt. Prices range from £100 to £600.

Figures were occasionally made in matched pairs, but these are exceptionally rare and would now be worth from £1,000 upwards. A pair of Indians, c. 1710 made £1,312 at Christie's in May 1975.

Carved wooden tobacconists' figures. Left to right: c.1740, 33ins; c.1740, 34ins; c.1780, 32½ins; c.1780, 37ins; c.1780, 31ins.

Figures portraying recognisable celebrities are very rare and seem to have been mainly produced in the United States in the early 19th century. They include Sir Walter Raleigh, who introduced tobacco to the English-speaking world, and Princess Pocahontas (though this swiftly degenerated into a rather stereotyped squaw figure). Named figures are rare and would be in the price range from £500 to £1,000.

Inn Signs

Decorative wooden signboards became popular outside inns and taverns in the 17th century when the number of ale-houses began to proliferate. The competitive element drove publicans to devise more and more eye-catching signs, matched by colourful names for their hostelries. Historically such signs reached their zenith in post-Restoration England and the plethora of flapping signboards was blamed for fanning the flames of the Great Fire of London in 1666. Thereafter their size was strictly regulated, and various attempts were made to eliminate them altogether. As late as the reign of George III (1760-1820) swinging pub signs were frequently regarded as a nuisance and legislation passed to limit them.

From the collector's viewpoint inn signs are restricted to the period from 1750 onwards. Although earlier signs are still extant, the majority of them would have been replaced fairly frequently as they weathered or split with the action of rain and sunlight. Once in position, a sign might last for a considerable length of time, and it is only within the past decade that wooden painted signs have become available to collectors in any number. This resulted from the disappearance of the old-style independent pubs and the rise of the great multiple brewery chains. As part of their policy of standardisation the breweries, led by

Public house sign.

Public house sign.

461

Whitbread's, began replacing wooden signs in the early 1960s with more enduring metal ones. Many of the wooden signs were subsequently destroyed before their antiquarian interest was fully appreciated and the sudden disappearance of the traditional wooden sign tended to focus attention on them and this promoted them to the status of a collectable subject.

The value of pub signs varies considerably, depending on age, condition, quality of painting, whether uniface or two-sided. At the lower end of the scale come relatively plain signs, simply lettered with the name of the pub, in drab colouring and poor condition. Examples of this type were relatively common in the midlands and north of England and are in the price range £15 − £30.

More elaborate scenic pictures in a solid wooden frame carved in one piece, with motifs on both sides, are in the price range from £70 to £100.

Heraldic wooden inn signs (usually of pubs known as 'The . . . . . Arms') vary enormously in decorative quality but are relatively unconsidered. £60 − £80.

Portrait signs, featuring local or national celebrities. £90 − £120.

Humorous, 'situation' or genre paintings for pubs with whimsical names. £120 − £200.

Pub signs of the late 19th and early 20th centuries were hand-painted on sheet iron or enamelled on tinware and are generally cheaper than their wooden counterparts. £40 − £100.

Enamelled Metal Signs

These date from the mid-19th century when the commercial production of branded goods began to develop rapidly. Within a generation Cadbury's Cocoa, Sunlight Soap, Pears Soap, Wills' Tobacco, Beecham's Pills and many other foodstuffs, patent medicines and consumer goods had become household words largely as a result of a form of outdoor advertising which consisted of enamelled sheet iron signs affixed to walls and the sides of buildings. This form of advertising reached its zenith at the turn of the century, when almost every conceivable square foot of wall space in the commercial sections of most towns was occupied by a rash of metal signs. Greater restraint in public taste, coupled with the rise of more effective advertising media (tabloid newspapers and magazines), led to a decline in the use of outdoor metal signs, although they have continued fitfully to this day. Though largely superseded by the more ephemeral bill-posters occupying large hoardings, the metal signs may still be found on the walls of tobacconists, general stores and petrol filling stations. The present pace of advertising means that brand images and even styles of lettering become quickly out of date, and thus the old-fashioned metal sign is not often suitable. Interest in these commercial metal signs is still relatively slight, and there is no hard and fast market as yet. Prices noted in different parts of the country vary considerably, as and where these signs become available. Signs of the period 1850-1900 are rare and would probably be worth from £10 to £30, depending on size and innate interest. Those belonging to the period 1900-1930, £5 − £10; more recent signs, £2 − £7.

Warrant Holders' Plaques

Circular, shield-shaped or oblong metal plaques bearing the coats of arms of royalty or the nobility are displayed to this day outside the shops of tradesmen who enjoy the patronage of the Queen and other members of the Royal Family. This custom, once widespread all over Europe, is now mainly confined to those countries which still have a monarchical form of government, although examples may also be seen in France and in parts of Germany. The practice dates back to the Middle Ages when shopkeepers would incorporate the insignia of their loftier patrons in their own signs as a mark of approbation by Establishment figures. Thus early painted signs of this type frequently feature the insignia of the local nobleman. By the 18th century, however, this aspect of 'patronage' signs had fallen into disuse and thereafter the practice has been restricted to royalty. The commonest signs are those which depict the arms of the reigning sovereign. Nowadays the display of such signs, or their incorporation in other forms of advertisement, is strictly controlled and limited to holders of Royal Warrants; but the custom seems to have been more widespread in the early 19th century. Relatively common are plaques bearing references to the holder's appointment to Queen Victoria (£50 − £80). Plaques bearing the names of more recent monarchs (usually Edward VII, George V and George VI) are less plentiful (£70 − £100), while those bearing a reference to King Edward VIII are extremely rare, on account of his brief reign of eleven months in 1936. Similar plaques, bearing the arms of Queen Alexandra, the Prince of Wales (either Edward VII or Edward VIII) are not plentiful, but are of lesser interest (£45 − £80). Pre-Victorian signs are rare and highly desirable and date from the early 18th century (George I or George II, £100 − £180). Similar plaques for George III are more plentiful on account of his long reign (£70 − £120). Those inscribed for the Prince Regent (George IV) or the Duke of Clarence (William IV) are comparatively elusive (£100 − £150).

English signs referring to foreign royalty date from the late 19th century and are of lesser value, since they do not have the cachet of a British Royal Warrant. £50 − £75.

Boundary Marks

Small shield-shaped, oval, circular or oblong plaques, cast in iron or lead, were used to delineate the boundaries of parishes or other administrative units of local government, and were affixed to the walls of churches, public buildings and even private houses. The majority of extant examples date from the early 18th century and continued down to the end of the 19th century. In most cases these boundary marks bear a date, indicating when they were erected or boundaries were fixed. In their simplest and commonest form they consist of shields bearing the initials of the parish or ward. This type includes both the earliest and many of the latest types so that date is not important. Prices depend on the decorative styling of the marks and the degree of interest in the parish. £10 – £25.

The more elaborate examples include a date, and their value depends on the period. Dated examples from the early 18th century are scarce (£40 – £80), but not many 19th century examples exist without dates (£15 – £30). In between come the dated specimens from 1760 to 1840, which are in the price range £25 – £50.

Boundary marks which also incorporate a civic or municipal emblem were produced in the late 18th and early 19th centuries. This group includes the largest and most elaborate types, with a full coat of arms, or equestrian figures in relief. £80 – £120.

Most of these heraldic types, however, show a simple civic device flanked by initials or the digits of the date. £40 – £80.

Quite a few of these boundary marks are still *in situ,* and only become available to collectors as buildings are demolished and districts redeveloped.

Fire Insurance Marks

Similar to, but usually much more elaborate than, boundary marks, are the plaques bearing the emblems of insurance companies which organised their own fire brigades for much of the 18th and early 19th centuries. The marks were placed on the walls of buildings by these companies to ensure that their fire brigades only dealt with fires on the premises of their clients. The Royal Exchange Company instituted this practice in 1722 and other companies rapidly followed suit. The various insurance companies pooled their resources in 1833 and, in London, at any rate, responsibility for the fire services was taken over by the Metropolitan Board of Works in 1865. As other cities organised municipal fire brigades the need for these marks fell into disuse. The majority of them thus date between 1722 and 1865, though a few examples continued to be produced down to the end of the 19th century.

Redevelopment in the major cities of Britain, and the subsequent demolition of many older buildings, has brought many of these insurance marks on to the market. The commonest types were cast or embossed in iron, lead, copper, brass, or stamped from sheet iron, copper, zinc or tinware. They were either unpainted, or decorated with enamelling. They feature the arms and emblems of the old insurance companies and vary enormously in their decorative qualities. Metal insurance marks range in value from £5 for a simple, uncoloured embossed copper example, to £25 - £40 for an enamelled sign.

Examples which incorporate the policy number belong to the earlier period (1722-60) and are worth very much more than un-numbered examples. £50 — £100.

Fire insurance marks in other materials — terracotta, pottery or porcelain with polychrome underglaze decoration — are comparatively rare. £60 — £120.

Museums
Victoria and Albert Museum, London.
City Museum, Hereford.
Museum and Art Gallery, Leicester.
City Museum, Sheffield.
City Museum and Art Gallery, Stoke-on-Trent.
Elizabethan House, Totnes.
City Museum and Art Gallery, Worcester.
Castle Museum, York.

Reading List
Christensen, Erwin O. Popular Art in the United States. London, 1948.
Lambert, M. and Marx, E. English Popular Art. London, 1951.
Lillywhite, Bryant. London Inn Signs. London, 1966.
Larwood and Hotten. History of Signboards. London, 1966.
Little, Nina Fletcher. The Abbey Aldrich Rockefeller Folk Art Collection. Williamsburg 1957.
Norman, Philip. London Signs and Inscriptions. London, 1967.
Sanborn, Kate. Hunting Indians in a Taxicab. New York (undated).
Williams, B. British Fire Marks. London, 1934.

SILHOUETTES

Otherwise known as shades or profiles, a form of two-dimensional portraiture in which the outline of the sitter is depicted in black against a white or tinted background. There were several methods of taking a profile. In one the shadow of the sitter was projected by means of lights on to a sheet of white paper, the outline traced and then filled in with black or some other dark colour. Many silhouettists, however, were adept at cutting profiles from black paper, working free-hand, and mounting the cut-out portion on white card. Some drew the profile first and then cut it out. An alternative was to remove the silhouette portion from a piece of white card which could then be mounted on a black background, so that the profile appeared in recess. The time-span of silhouettes was relatively short, from about 1770 to 1840 when they were superseded by photographs (q.v.). The value of silhouettes depends on the artist where known, the identity of the sitter and certain technical features discussed below.

A print entitled 'A sure and convenient machine for drawing silhouettes', showing the artist and sitter in situ.

A nice example by Mrs. Beetham. Her paintings on convex glass fetch more than those on card.

A very charming early Miers c.1785, most saleable at a high price.

A good clean specimen but would not fetch as much as a Miers.

Techniques

Scissor-cuts, as true silhouettes are known, represent the simplest method of production and probably the earliest, since this was a hobby of Etienne de Silhouette, Comptroller General of Louis XV, who has given his name to this art form. This was a relatively restrictive medium, however, and the value depends on how well and cleanly the cutting has been performed. Black paper mounted on white card is the commonest. £10 – £25. Silhouettes cut from white paper and mounted on black card are scarcer. £10 – £40. Cut silhouettes were also revived in the late 19th century, mainly on the Continent, and may be found as full-length figures, or even groups, with background scenery also in black silhouette. Various attempts have been made to revive scissor-cuts in more recent years (especially in France, Germany and America, where cut silhouettes are very popular today). £10 – £50, depending on size and intricacy of the subject.

Painted silhouettes were much more popular and provide the greatest variety of decorative treatments. The commonest were painted in pine soot mixed with beer on white card or paper, from a traced outline taken from a shadow. The earliest examples (1770-85) were mainly amateur productions, but after the publication of Lavater's *Essays on Physiognomy* (1775-8) interest in the human profile rapidly became a professional business. Lavater himself invented a special chair

Celebrities always sell well. This pair by Hamlet of Queen Charlotte and George III are in the top bracket for that artist.

for use in conjunction with candle-light and a projection screen to facilitate the taking of shades, which were then reduced by means of a pantograph.

The most expensive silhouettes at the time, and nowadays the most collectable, are those which were painted on specially prepared plaster or on the reverse side of convex or flat glass. The leading English exponents of this art were John Miers and Isabella Beetham and silhouettes by these artists now command between £60 and £300. Early Miers silhouettes have plain brass frames, but later examples have frames of pearwood or papier mâché. A characteristic of Mier's work is the soft, cloudy grey appearance of the subjects' hair. Mrs. Beetham specialised in silhouettes on the reverse of convex glass set over plaster to give a most unusual shadow effect. Her profiles were bordered with white and gold and then mounted in oval pearwood frames.

Prior to 1800 most silhouettes were executed entirely in monochrome, but after that date tinting and body colour were increasingly used. Bronzing (gold paint) was used more or less judiciously to highlight details of hair, features and dress. One of the best exponents of this form of gilding was John Field, an associate of Miers, but whose work is less delicate. Field often gilded shades first made by Miers and these bear the trade label of Miers on the reverse. Field's silhouettes are in the range £40 − £70.

William Bullock of Liverpool specialised in the use of white ink to highlight details of dress. The quality of his work varies considerably.

His silhouettes were mounted in rectangular wood supports, and had thin brass oval frames. The top of the wooden rectangle usually has a die-struck brass hanger bearing the word 'Museum' — a reference to a museum of profiles which he also operated. £25 — £50.

A notable exception to the use of monochrome in the late 18th century was John Buncombe of the Isle of Wight who specialised in profiles of military gentlemen and painted their uniforms in full colour. John Phelps of London applied the same colourful technique to profiles of ladies whose clothing resembles contemporary fashion plates. Silhouettes by these artists are among the most highly sought after, and are now in the price range £120 — £300.

Other Artists

Profilists almost invariably identified their works by means of printed trade labels affixed to the reverse of the mounts, and details of these artists and their works may be found in books on the subject (see **Reading List**). Among the artists whose work is most highly prized are Francis Torond (painting on card, bust length profiles and family groups, extremely detailed and intricate work). Very scarce and expensive. £200 — £400.

Charles Rosenberg, painter of bold, sharp profiles on glass, using a very dense black paint unrelieved by any attempt at gradations of tone or shade. £40 — £100.

A. Charles, one of the most prolific profilists (claiming to have produced almost 12,000 shades by 1792 alone). Painting on card, with hair tints, etc. £40 — £70.

William Rought, working in the early 19th century. Dense black painting, strongly drawn on card or glass. Fine detail. Single, £50 — £80; groups; £100 — £250.

Augustin Edouart specialised in cut-paper work and always worked in black and white without any colour. One of the most prolific artists in the later period, his average silhouettes are fairly plentiful and are priced from £20 to £40 for unidentified sitters or nonentities, to £60 — £80 for minor celebrities.

Edouart also produced genre cut-outs and family groups, with the black silhouettes mounted on a painted background. £100 — £300.

Other artists whose work is worth looking for include Edward McGauran of Dublin (extremely rare), Hamlet of Bath, J. Spornberg of Bath, Edward Foster of Derby, and Frederick Frith of Dover. Silhouettes by these artists of the second rank are in the price range £50 — £80. Work by later artists, such as W.J. Hubbard, is worth £15 — £40.

An attractive 'verre églomisé' plaque, singed Geddes. British artists rarely used this process, which was a popular technique on the Continent.

Points to look for

The complexities of the trade cards can add considerably to the value of an otherwise run-of-the-mill silhouette. It is possible to date Miers's silhouettes, for example, fairly accurately by the style and wording of his labels, taken in conjunction with the type of frame used. This is an aspect of silhouettes which still remains to be fully explored and would amply repay serious study.

The chief criteria of value are artistic merit, draughtsmanship and condition. Attention should be given to the artist's treatment of hair, details of dress and methods of conveying the character and individuality of the sitter. The outline should be clean, the features uniform and unwavering, whether painted or cut. The dark area of a painted profile should be matt and even, free from brush strokes or other disharmonious touches. Any extraneous detail added by painting or bronzing should be delicate and restrained. Avoid silhouettes whose background paper has become badly foxed or unevenly discoloured or faded.

470

Value is also affected by the subject of a portrait particularly where, as in the case of Dorothy Wordsworth, a silhouette is the only known existing likeness. The type of frame also affects the value; an oval pear wood frame, for example, will generally fetch more than a rectangular papier mâché frame.

Pitfalls

Beware of painted silhouettes in which the paint has flaked off or become blistered, or been touched up (particularly true of profiles on glass or plaster). Examine gilded silhouettes carefully for flaking of the bronzing or tarnishing. Other not uncommon problems include foxing (reddish-brown rust marks due to iron impurities in the paper) and mildew or bloom on plaster or glass caused by long exposure to damp conditions. Dust and loose particles of plaster can be eliminated by carefully removing the backing and frame, but this may require expert assistance. This should never be attempted if damage is likely to the trade label. Once a label is broken or torn it will detract seriously from the value of the silhouette. Scissor-cuts are less prone to deterioration than painted profiles, though mildew may be caused by organic impurities in the fixative.

Museums

British Museum, London.
Victoria and Albert Museum, London.
Fitzwilliam Museum, Cambridge.
City Museum, Hereford.
Temple Newsam House, Leeds.
Museum and Art Gallery, Leicester.
Central Museum and Art Gallery, Northampton.
Elizabethan House, Totnes.

Reading List

Bolton, E.S. Wax Portraits and Silhouettes. London, 1914.
Coke, D. The Art of the Silhouette. London, 1928.
Hickman, Peggy. Silhouettes. London, 1968. Silhouettes, Celebrities in Profile. London, 1971. The British Silhouette Portrait. (H.M.S.O., 1972). Silhouettes A Living Art. Newton Abbot, 1975.
Jackson, E. Nevill. The History of Silhouettes. London, 1911.
Silhouettes: Notes and Dictionary. London, 1938.
Megroz, R.J. Profile Art through the Ages. London (n.d.).
Morgan, L.M. A Master of Silhouettes. London, 1938.
Woodiwiss, John. British Silhouettes. London, 1966.

SNUFFBOXES

Although the habit of sniffing powdered tobacco was established in the early 17th century, and boxes were produced for this purpose, no authentic example of a 17th century snuffbox is known to exist. The earliest tabatières or snuffboxes now extant date from the early 18th century. The earliest boxes were made of gold, silver, brass or pewter, often inset with panels of tortoiseshell, ivory, mother-of-pearl or glass. Date is not such an important criterion since the same materials and techniques were used throughout the two centuries in which these boxes were fashionable. The only technical feature which helps to date a box is the hinge. Those made before about 1740 had a stand-away hinge, whereas those made after that date had an integral hinge. Snuffboxes may best be grouped according to the materials used.

Gold

The finest snuffboxes of the 18th century were made of gold and were elaborately enamelled on the lid and sides with pastoral or classical scenes and often encrusted with precious stones. Gold boxes with enamelled miniature portraits were a popular gift exchanged among royalty and the nobility of Europe. Other snuffboxes of this period had a guilloché pattern worked in gold, then coated with clear enamel to create a brilliant lustrous effect. Gold boxes of the 18th century are extremely rare and costly. £1,500 − £10,000.

Silver

This metal was widely used for snuffboxes throughout the 18th and 19th centuries. Many of the earlier boxes (1730-1760) are of the type with a close-fitting lid which fits all round, and lifts off in use. Boxes of this type are usually oval. £200 − £400.

A more common type has a scalloped edge or an irregular shape. £150 − £300.

18th century hinged boxes may be found with three, five or seven knuckles and lugs, the more knuckles generally the better the box. All silver boxes of this type average from £100 to £250. Boxes can be found outside this price range depending on the type of decoration or if there is something particularly interesting about them.

Late 18th and 19th century boxes are usually rectangular and vary considerably in size. From 1760 onwards the integral hinge became more common. Value depends on size, decoration, maker, condition and the presence or absence of presentation inscriptions (see **Pitfalls**).

London silver boxes of the late 18th century; pictorial, floral or geometric motifs. Often unmarked, usually maker's mark only. £50 – £120.

Later London silver boxes, 1800-1840. Floral, or pictorial overall decoration. £100 – £400.

Good quality engine turning or guilloché pattern overall. £75 – £200.

Large table snuffboxes (5-6 inches in length) with elaborate border decoration, £300 – £500.

A selection of 'Jacobite' pedestal-shaped boxes.

Birmingham snuffboxes, 1800-1830, engine-turned with floral borders, £100 – £150.

Prices vary with the maker; Nathaniel Mills would command a much higher price.

Similar but 1830-1850 and usually somewhat smaller, £80 – £120.

Unusual Shapes in Silver

The majority of the novelty snuffboxes are in the form of ladies' shoes, with a narrow hinged lid in the top. They were made from about 1830 to 1880. £130 – £180.

473

A rare type, made in Birmingham in the 1830s, consists of a fox's mask, with a hinged lid in the top. £350 — £500.

Thumb snuffbox made in the late 18th century. Double box made to fit over the thumb. £500.

Silver Combined with other Materials

The commonest form consists of silver boxes, rectangular or oval, with inset panels of agate, tortoiseshell or mother-of-pearl in the top and bottom. London made, main period of manufacture 1730-1760. £150 — £200. The price of piqué work examples of this period would be affected by the quality.

Later examples, mostly Birmingham made. £50 — £80.

Large cowrie and small nautilus shells were mounted in silver and fitted with a silver lid across the operculum. Made in London, Birmingham or Edinburgh. £50 — £100.

Ram's horn or staghorn snuffboxes and mulls with silver mounts and lids were a Scottish speciality from 1800 onwards. 18th century examples, £35 — £75.

Above left: An oval Swiss gold and enamel snuffbox, the lid decorated with a spray of flowers against a translucent blue ground, the sides and base with further panels of blue enamel over a guilloché ground, the borders decorated with foliage and lozenges, 2¾ins. Above right: Shell of a small tortoise made into a box, 2¾ins.

Other Materials

Enamelled decoration (often coats of arms) on silver boxes, 1750-1800. £100 — £250.

Battersea or Staffordshire enamelled snuffboxes, 1750-1800. £150 — £400.

474

German snuffboxes of rock crystal, often in fantasy shapes. £70 − £200.

Porcelain snuffboxes, made at Meissen, Vienna, Sèvres and other Continental potteries; usually circular with floral decoration and gold mounting. £120 − £250.

German Zellenmosaik boxes, with hardstone panels by Neuber, 1750-1800. £80 − £200.

Silver-plated boxes, made in Sheffield, 1750-1830. £40 − £80.

Wooden Boxes

As the habit of taking snuff spread to the lower classes in the mid-18th century boxes were produced in wood. Plain wooden boxes are the commonest, and are difficult to date, though those with stand-away hinges belong to the earlier period, while those with the integral hinge are later. Plain boxes are in the price range £2 − £5.

Above left: Silver snuffbox decorated with leaf and berry relief sides and engine-turned cover and base, hallmark Birmingham 1838; maker, Joseph Willmore, 2¾ins. Above right: Antique silver gilt snuffbox with repoussé lid, J.L. London 1815, 4.75oz.

Scottish hand-painted boxes, with scenery or animal subjects, date from about 1740. Unidentified scenes rate from £15 to £40; scenes with a caption or commemorative inscription are rare and highly desirable. £30 − £70.

Snuffboxes with transfer-printed motifs (Mauchline ware). £4 − £15.

Boxes with marquetry decoration (first period Tunbridge ware). £5 – £20.

Boxes with wood mosaic decoration (second period Tunbridge ware). £8 – £15.

19th century wooden snuffboxes with incised or carved pictorial motifs. £5 – £10.

Wooden boxes with silver mounts, engraved inscription panels. £4 – £10.

Papier Mache

Boxes in papier mâché or clay ware, with lacquered surface and no decoration. £2 – £4.

Similar boxes with painted floral decoration, chinoiserie motifs and inlaid mother-of-pearl ornament, mainly of London or Birmingham manufacture in the 19th century. £5 – £15.

Points to look for

Because of the long and frequent use to which snuffboxes were subjected, condition is of supreme importance. Hinges should be intact and undamaged, engraving, engine-turning and applied ornament should be crisp, hallmarks should be legible, and the fit of the lid good without any distortion. The presence of damage, signs of wear or poor workmanship in the closure of lids detract heavily from the value. Certain manufacturers produced boxes of superlative quality and these are now worth a handsome premium. Makers' marks to look for on silver boxes include Nathaniel Mills (Birmingham) and William Eley and Edward Edwards (London). Continental boxes with unusual decoration (e.g. Swiss enamelling or Russian niello) are now attracting greater interest and are worth looking for. The majority of snuffboxes are small (2-3 inches in length). Larger boxes for table use, and especially those large enough to serve as cigarette boxes, are highly desirable. More elaborate mounts and bold decoration greatly enhance the value of snuffboxes of any period.

Pitfalls

The chief problem is the vexed question of presentation inscriptions. There are two schools of thought: one holding that inscriptions detract from the value of a box since they do not have a personal interest for the owner or user of the box; the other assessing the value of an inscription according to its historic association or degree of human interest. In the past, undoubtedly the former school of thought prevailed, and this led to the widespread practice of erasing obsolete inscriptions from boxes before they were re-sold. Boxes with erased or partially erased inscriptions should be heavily discounted. Boxes with the original inscription intact are still relatively disregarded unless the inscription relates to a famous person or historic incident. Re-engraved inscriptions covering erasures detract considerably from the value of boxes; examine the engraving carefully for traces of previous lettering.

Museums
British Museum, London.
Victoria and Albert Museum, London.
Wallace Collection, London.
Wellington Museum, London.
Waddesdon Manor, Aylesbury.
City Museum and Art Gallery, Birmingham.
Royal Pavilion, Brighton.
National Museum of Wales, Cardiff.
Royal Scottish Museum, Edinburgh.
City Museum, Hereford.
Temple Newsam House, Leeds.
Museum and Art Gallery, Leicester.
Central Museum and Art Gallery, Northampton.
Ashmolean Museum, Oxford.
Salisbury and South Wiltshire Museum, Salisbury.
City Museum, Sheffield.
City Museum and Art Gallery, Stoke-on-Trent.
Royal Tunbridge Wells Museum and Art Gallery.
Windsor Castle, Windsor.
City Museum and Art Gallery, Worcester.

Reading List

Bramsen, B. Nordiske Snusdäser. Copenhagen, 1965.
Curtis, M.M. The Book of Snuff and Snuff Boxes. London, 1935.
Delieb, Eric. Silver Boxes. London, 1968.
Hughes, G. Bernard. English Snuff-boxes. London, 1971.
Le Corbeiller, Clare. European and American Snuff Boxes. London, 1966.
MacCausland, H. Snuff and Snuff Boxes. London, 1951.
Nocq, Henri. Tabatières, Boites et Etuis. Paris, 1925.
Norton, Richard and Martin. A History of Gold Snuff-boxes. London, 1938.
Snowman, Kenneth. Eighteenth Century Gold Boxes of Europe. London, 1967.

SPOONS (Early)

Principal item of flatware in use in Europe from the Middle Ages. The earliest types were made of horn, bone or wood and spoons made of these materials continued to be produced in less sophisticated areas until the late 19th century. Metal spoons date from the Roman period and were mainly of gold or silver, used by the nobility and higher clergy. Base metal spoons, of latten or pewter, have also been recorded in the same period. Silver spoons were confined to the upper classes of society until the 18th century but because of their comparatively personal nature (each person would have had his own spoon) they have tended to survive in larger numbers than any other form of silver dating before the Restoration in 1660. Fundamentally spoons have been produced in two main forms. The earlier, dating from about 1300 to the late 17th century, had a fig-shaped bowl, narrow stem and terminal knop. The later style, adopted in the late 17th century and continuing to the present day, had a longer, narrower or elliptical bowl, longer and flatter stem terminating in a broad, rounded end. Apart from the assay marks which enable silver spoons to be dated accurately, spoons can be grouped chronologically by shape, ornament and construction. Prior to the 18th century spoons were produced for general purposes in standard sizes, but thereafter a wide variety of sizes and shapes was produced for specific purposes, from diminutive salt spoons and mustard spoons to table spoons and serving spoons. Specialised forms, such as caddy spoons, mote spoons, straining spoons, medicine spoons and salt shovels, are often collected and studied thematically irrespective of period or decorative style. Commemorative spoons date from the accession of William III and Mary in 1689 and form an interesting group. Crested tea spoons and caddy spoons are to flatware what Goss china is to porcelain, but are now highly collectable and include foreign souvenir spoons with enamelled bowls and stems. The remarks that follow pertain to silver spoons, though it should be noted that spoons were also made to some extent in Sheffield plate from about 1770 to 1830 and were extensively electro-plated from about 1850 onwards

Date-lines

In general, the shape of the stem and bowl are guides to date. Early spoons (13th to 16th centuries) have tapering stems and a narrow top and bottom face, the bowl drops away from the stem considerably, and the bowl is usually fig-shaped. Later spoons have little or no tapering of

 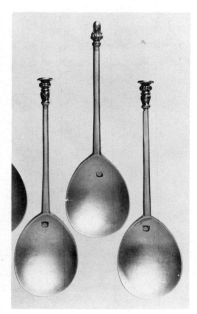

Left: Notice the different proportions of the 13th century acorn knop with the late 17th century seal top. The acorn knop is a superb example and the seal top is in very fine condition.

Right: Pair of Charles I seal tops, London. In the centre a Maidenhead spoon, London, early 17th century, in good condition.

the stem, which usually also has a broad face; the bowl and stem are more or less in line and the bowl becomes less fig-shaped — though it should be noted that some mid-17th century bowls are quite ovoid whereas in some 14th-15th century specimens the bowl is noticeably round.

A more accurate guide to date is the knop, which can be classified chronologically and valued accordingly:

13th — 15th century	Acorn Knop. £300 — £750.
early 14th — mid-15th century	Diamond Point. £250 — £600.
early 14th — mid-17th century	Slip Top (see **Points to look for**). £300 — £750.
15th — early-17th century	Wrythen Knop (spirally fluted). £250 — £1,500.
early-15th — early-17th century	Lion Sejant. £350 — £1,500.

mid-15th — 17th century	Heraldic and Rebus Knops, featuring the emblem of a family or a punning reference to its name, are very rare. £1,000+.
late-15th — mid-17th century	Apostle Spoons (q.v.). £350 — £1,500.
14th — 17th century	Maidenhead, Virgin and Heart, Virgin and Child — knops found on small spoons, possibly intended for children. £450 — £1,000.
1550-1620	Moor's Head (the curly-headed figure may have been a cherub or the Baby Jesus) — found on children's spoons and therefore rare in fine condition. £350 for average specimens.
16th — 17th century	Knops with figures other than the above, including the so-called 'Buddha' knop and female figures like miniature ship's figureheads. £250 — £750.
1500-1580	Baluster Knop. Very rare type. £750 — £1,200.
1550-1570	Seal Top, short baluster, hexagonal seal. £350 — £750.
1570-1600	Seal Top, longer baluster, circular seal. £250 — £600.
1600-1650	Seal Top, acanthus decoration on baluster, circular seal. £140 — £400.

A worn example is indicated by the lower figure and one in superb condition would command the higher figure.

Points to look for

Early spoons bearing an early (15th century) Leopard's Head punch rate a hefty premium. The date letter appears on Slip Top spoons at the top of the stem, quite separate from the maker's mark and Lion Passant which appear at the base. This is a useful guide to genuine Slip Top spoons. Lion Sejant spoons with well-modelled lions rate a premium; later 16th and 17th century examples are not so well-modelled and the space behind the legs is invariably filled in. Plus factors are lions supporting shields with heraldic engraving, or a lion seated sideways (extremely rare). In Seal Tops the engraved initials should be original and care must be taken with examples in which the original initials have been erased and new initials engraved. The early hexagonal seal tops tend to become oval or circular with wear and this detracts considerably from their value. Spoons used by children (usually Maidenhead or Moor's Head spoons) often have the bowl badly worn on one side. Attempts to counteract this by beating up the silver from the other side result in a much thinner bowl all round. Provincial hallmarks of known centres command a good premium, except Exeter which is quite common.

Pitfalls

Outright forgeries consist of spoons cast from an original. Apart from the 'feel' of the article, the tendency is for cast forgeries to be heavier, with thicker bowls than the genuine spoons. The cast bowl in forgeries tends to be quite rigid, whereas a genuine one always has a certain amount of 'give'. The marks, being cast, have a grainy appearance and lack the incuse characteristics of genuine marks. Early silver spoons had the knops gilded, the stems and bowls being left white. Spoons completely gilded may well be suspect, since overall gilding may have been used to conceal faking.

More problematical are spoons of a relatively common type (Seal Top) which have been converted to earlier and rarer types (such as Slip Tops). Genuine Slip Top spoons have the stem tapering in the opposite direction to all other spoons of the comparable period. Seal Tops have also been converted to Apostle or Maidenhead spoons, so caution should be exercised in this respect. Early style spoons with 18th century marks are almost certainly fakes. This applies to some extent to 19th century spoons similarly converted, although genuine copies of early styles were produced quite legitimately in the late 19th century as part of the gothic and medieval revival. Repairs to damaged bowls may have been effected by soldering which should show up as a thin yellowish stain (though this may be disguised by silver-plating). Splits in the stem near the junction with the bowl are likewise repaired by soldering. As stem and knop are much less liable to damage, the appearance of solder lines in these places would probably indicate faking rather than restoration.

See also **Apostle Spoons, Caddy Spoons.**

STOOLS

Rudimentary form of low seating with neither back nor arm-rests, usually on three or four feet. Stools provided the main form of seating in the Middle Ages and continued to do so until well into the 17th century. Thereafter they continued to be useful and convenient types of occasional seating. The early all wood type is often referred to as the joint or joined stool, because of its use of the mortise and tenon joint form of construction. Joint stools were fashionable from the 16th to late 17th centuries and were revived in the 19th century as part of the cult of medievalism. These stools were characterised by plain wooden tops with a simple moulding round the edge, turned legs, braced by stretchers fixed near the bottom of each leg, and by their overall sturdy construction. The zenith of stool-making came in the 18th century, when elegant stools with upholstered seats were carved and decorated in the contemporary furniture styles. Though the four-footed stool remained perennially popular, stools with legs and feet in an X-frame arrangement were fashionable in the mid- to late 18th century and also in the early 19th century. A much wider range of stools was produced

A rare James I oak joint stool with fine carved frieze and well shaped fluted legs. Note the wear on the moulded rails where one would expect to find it.

A stool of about 1680 showing the same curved scrolls and stretchers that one finds on dining chairs (q.v.) of this period. They were usually made in beech, walnut or painted black.

A walnut cabriole leg stool, 1725, with good carving on the knees and a period tapestry seat.

Left: A simple country-made oak stool of the early part of the 18th century. The top, which is in two pieces (a replacement made out of old floorboards?) is nailed on through the legs the rails being pegged.

from the mid-18th century onwards; these included the long, low hearth stool, low round or rectangular foot-stools, round stools for dressing-tables, adjustable piano stools, rectangular stools for window seating, gout stools, with a raked top on which sufferers of this malady could rest their legs, and patent stools which concealed a chamber pot or a spittoon beneath a hinged lid, and box stools, whose upholstered top lifted to reveal a coal-box.

Date-lines

16th-mid-17th century	Oak joint stools, usually in the range 16-20ins. high. Baluster turnings, neat and sturdy and often fluted; small rim of carving below seat typical. Earlier examples have legs at right angles to the seat; later examples have legs slightly splayed. Tudor stools rate from £400 to £1,000 for a really fine specimen; Jacobean £250 − £600 but mostly around the £250 − £350 mark.
1640-1670	So-called Cromwellian oak joint stools: generally plainer, with less elaborate turning on legs and little or no carving on sides. £120 − £250.
1660-1690	Restoration period oak: return to more elaborate turning. Stools often taller. Long low stools are rare and rate a high premium. The wider variety of styles is reflected in the price bracket, from £100 − £225. Joint stools sometimes in walnut or fruitwood, very

elaborate, bobbin, spiral or various forms of cotton reel turning, on legs and stretchers. £200 – £300.

1690-1700 Upholstered tops now the rule, legs either in elongated S-shape scrolls or turned and squared-off or faceted, usually in walnut or fruitwood or beech, with ebonised (blackened) or gilded ornate carved and fretted stretchers on one or more sides. Stools of this period may range from £250 upwards to about £800 depending on decorative features such as carving, and condition. Remember that woodworm love walnut and it rots easily on damp stone floors so that perfect examples should be viewed with great care.

1700-1750 The introduction of the cabriole-leg stool in walnut until late 1730 then dark heavy Spanish mahogany used predominantly. Increasing use of carved decoration, towards the end of the period, for which mahogany was especially suitable. Simple stools in solid walnut, £150 – £250. Walnut rails veneered and with decoration on legs, £300 – £1,000. Mahogany examples £160 – £800. Most pieces around the lower level need to be really exceptional to hit anywhere near four figures.

A mid-Victorian piano stool. Heavily carved and highly functional as the top revolves to make the height of the seat adjustable.

The Victorian love of novelty and 'naturalistic' portrayal is illustrated (parodied?) in this stool/occasional table, which makes use of stuffed emu feet to produce what must be about the ultimate in bad taste (kitsch) and out-of-balance design.

484

1740-1830	Wide variety of ornamental styles corresponding to the patterns in furniture current at different times. Most Georgian and Regency stools are in the price range £100 to £300.
1830-1900	Victorian stools come in different shapes according to their function. Circular music stools have a circular or tripod base and spiral pole for adjusting the height. £30 – £50.
	Numerous 'period' stools, reproducing earlier styles, or concocting neo-medieval styles such as the Dante stool with X-frame, low back and arm-rests (£50 – £80). 'Elizabethan' stools in vogue, 1840-70, with baluster legs and stretchers and needlework upholstery. £35 – £60.
1880-1910	Low stools with canework or straw seating reflect the craze for Japonaiserie at the turn of the century. These are quite common and in little demand. £4 – £10.

Points to look for

Plus factors are original upholstery in fine condition; gilding on 18th century stools; fine complex decoration on 18th century stools and restraint in decoration and balanced lines in late-Victorian examples where decoration tends to be excessive. Most stools are available as individuals, but pairs carry a premium over the combined price of two single examples. For 17th and early 18th century pairs the price may be three or four times that of a single; late 18th and early 19th century pairs rate two to three times that of a single.

Pitfalls

Joint stools continued to be made in country areas well into the 19th century, but can sometimes be recognised by their heavier, larger size and rather flatter turnings. The late Victorian craze for anything medieval led to the production of numerous joint stools in the manner of the 15th-16th centuries; the age of the wood should help to distinguish genuine from reproduction. The pegs often went through the joint and stuck out on the mortise and tenon joint just under the seat, often by half or even an inch. They look seven-sided rather than round and come to a blunt point. Seats were also pegged on but normally (there are few absolute rules with furniture) into the rails not the tops of the legs. This is because pushing a peg lengthways into the grain might act as a wedge and cause it to split.

Watch carefully for new tops added to old bases. There should be no unexplained holes in the top and the unpolished wood underneath should be dry, though the edges, where generations of fingers have lifted the stools, should be darker. Dirt also gathers between the top and the top rail so as to form almost a line.

SUNDIALS

Instruments for measuring time according to the direction of a shadow cast by the sun. The principle of determining the hour of day by means of a standing rod (style or gnomon) was known to the Egyptians and developed by the Greeks and Romans. In the Middle Ages, however, astronomers and mathematicians devised movable sundials which could give accurate readings, by the adjustment of the angle and direction of the gnomon, according to the time of year and the latitude of the sundial. The earliest sundials were fixed, usually engraved stone or metal slabs inset on the walls of buildings or standing on stone plinths in a fixed place. Portable sundials, with adjustable gnomon, dials and compass, were developed in the 15th century and reached their height of accuracy and ingenuity in the 18th century. Thereafter the use of portable sundials declined as pocket watches became more accurate. More recent sundials have consisted mainly of the fixed, ornamental variety. For all practical purposes the collectable

A French Butterfield dial.

A brass and silvered table ring sundial. Invented by George Wright of the Navigation Warehouse.

types of sundial belong mainly to the period from 1500 to 1850 and are described below according to type.

Dieppe sundial, popular in France early in the 17th century. Dials

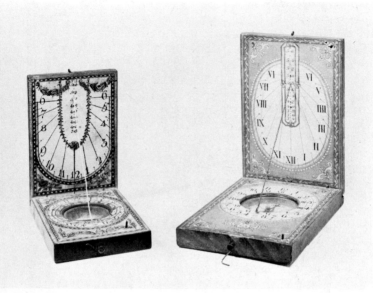

Two examples of diptych sundials of the Nuremberg type.

engraved on two double-sided folding ivory plates and sometimes housed in a rectangular case with a hinged lid. Central needle detachable gnomon. Separate dials include a calendar, hour scale, phases of the moon, tables of latitudes and a compass for correct orientation. The most desirable of these sundials were made by Charles Bloud. £300 — £800.

Butterfield sundial named after Michael Butterfield, instrument maker to King Louis XIV, and produced in France in the late 17th and early 18th centuries. Made of silver with up to four hour scales and usually having the gnomon in some highly decorative shape. The base contains an engraved list, showing the latitudes of the principal European cities, and incorporates a compass for accurate setting. £400 — £800.

Simple pocket magnetic sundial, popular in the 18th and 19th centuries. Usually quite functional in appearance, with card dials and brass fittings. Simple folding gnomon and compass. £50 — £100.

Diptych or Nuremberg sundial, mainly of German manufacture as the name suggests. These were folding wooden sundials with two or more dials, hinged together, with a silk cord gnomon threaded into holes in the lid to correspond to the latitude of the nearest city. The more cities listed the more desirable the sundial (from 12 to 50 are known). Dials often decorated with floral ornament. £40 – £120.

Shepherd's pillar sundial, consisting of a cylinder or polygonal column of wood or ivory, with a metal gnomon (tinned iron or brass). Each face of the pillar is calibrated, and readings are taken by suspending the

A shagreen-cased table sundial. The hour ring is engraved, 'Thos. Rubergall Optn. to their Majesties, 24 Coventry Street, London.'

pillar by a metal ring, with the gnomon horizontal and pointed towards the sun. Primitive timepieces of this type are used in the Pyrenees to this day. £15 – £60.

Ring sundial, in which the sun's rays pass through a tiny hole in a slide and give a reading against the calibrated inner side of the ring. This simple device varies considerably in size and complexity, from simple finger rings, to large instruments with two collapsible rings mounted at right angles to each other. They also vary in the number of cities whose latitudes are engraved on them. The small, simple ring dials range from £25 to £80, but the large multiple ring dials are rare, £200 – £800.

Table sundial, consisting of calibrated rings, movable gnomon, compass, spirit level and adjustable levelling screws. Dials of this type were much favoured by mariners for checking the accuracy of ship's chronometers and were made well into the 19th century. £150 – £400.

An octagonal English, Charles I period, brass horizontal sundial, finely engraved. The outer ring, signed and dated 'R.W. fecit 1643'.

An armorial engraved 15¾in. circular horizontal sundial by Thomas Heath, London.

Gunpowder sundial, designed to detonate a small charge at midday as a form of signal gun. The adjustable ring incorporates an aperture and a magnifying glass which focuses the sun's rays on the touch-hole of the tiny cannon and ignites the gunpowder when the sun reaches midday. The position of the cannon is adjusted by means of calibrated rings, to suit the time of year and the latitude. £200 – £500.

Horizontal garden sundial, intended for use in a fixed spot. Gnomon fixed and the dial (of brass, lead, bronze, slate or stone) is engraved with concentric circles with readings of hours and, or, minutes. Often with a watch fast and slow compensating scale against the days and months of the year for that particular latitude. An infinite variety of decorative styles may be found. These dials are usually engraved with the name or initials of the maker, the date and sometimes with the owner's coat of arms. £30 – £500.

Vertical wall sundial, similar to the above, but usually of incised stone or plate. Many extant examples are still embedded in their original walls. Usually much larger and simpler in design, numerals often gilded to make them more visible from a distance. £100 – £300.

Points to look for

Any unusual or additional technical features are desirable, and the greater the detail and information given on the dials and scales the better. Instruments incorporating silver or even gold components were fashionable in the early 18th century and the presence of precious metal immediately lifts these dials into the upper end of the price range. Finely engraved ornament on brass, wood or ivory plates and dials is an important plus factor. Interesting inscriptions, including dates and mottoes, are also highly desirable.

Museums
British Museum, London.
Guildhall Museum, London.
London Museum, London.
National Maritime Museum, London.
Science Museum, London.
Victoria and Albert Museum, London.
National Museum of Wales, Cardiff.
National Museum of Antiquities, Edinburgh.
Royal Scottish Museum, Edinburgh.
Museum of the History of Science, Oxford.
Elizabethan House, Totnes.
Windsor Castle, Windsor.

A simple south-facing vertical wall sundial, 17ins. by 15ins. Carved of sandstone and dated 1740, has the owner's initials I.R.W. in the form of tulip flowers at the top.

A small 19th century brass cannon sundial by Troughton and Simms.

490

Reading List

Cousins, Frank W. Sundials. London, 1969.

Daumas, M. Scientific Instruments of the 17th and 18th Centuries and their Makers. London, 1972.

Gatty, Mrs. A. The Book of Sundials. London, 1900.

Gaye, Samuel and Michel, Henri. Time and Space. London, 1971.

Herbert, Sir Alan P. Sundials, Old and New. London, 1967.

Horsky, Zdenek and Skiopova, Otilie. Astronomy Gnomonics. Prague, 1968.

Michel, H. Scientific Instruments in Art and History. Paris, 1966; London, 1967.

Taylor, E.G.R. The Mathematical Practitioners of Tudor and Stuart England. Cambridge, 1966. The Mathematical Practitioners of Hanoverian England. Cambridge, 1970.

TEA-CADDIES AND CHESTS

Containers for tea, derived from the Malay word *kati* (a unit of weight slightly more than 1 lb.). The containers were originally known as canisters, and the term caddy does not seem to have become widely accepted until the late 18th century. Caddies were made in a wide variety of materials and this rather than date, governs their value. Nevertheless it is possible to date caddies according to the material used. Early caddies were relatively small, reflecting the high cost of tea, and they were housed in wooden cabinets known as tea-chests, and secured under lock and key. Later caddies became much larger, often holding 1-2lbs., and eventually the role of caddy and tea-chest merged, so that caddies were made of wood, lined with silver foil, and the tea-chests, as such, were dispensed with.

Date-lines

1620-1700   Earliest caddies were made of porcelain and were imported from China. Oblong or octagonal upright form with flat sides and top and a circular hole on a short neck, surmounted by a tight-fitting stopper. Decorated

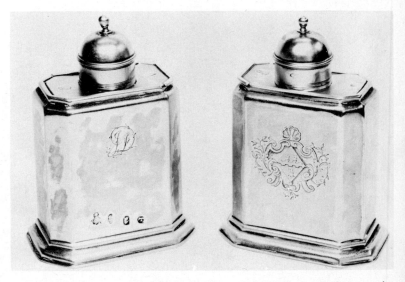

A pair of George I octagonal tea-caddies with sliding tops and measuring cups chased with contemporary armorials, maker's mark Gi star over, Britannia standard silver London 1721, 11.50oz.

A George II oval-shaped silver tea-caddy with beaded edges and urn finial by Augustus Lesage London 1779, 11.50oz.

A fine George III tea-caddy by James Young, London 1791.

according to the prevailing styles of Chinese porcelain. Very rare. £250 – £700.

1680-1740   Earliest silver caddies in the shape of the porcelain caddies. Often fitted with a sliding panel in the base to facilitate filling. No locks on lids and though often produced in pairs, not apparently intended for housing in a tea-chest. £300 – £500 single; £750 – £1,200 matched pair. Decorative features, especially engraved arms, are a plus factor.

1715-1750   Rectangular silver boxes with lids covering the top. Hinged lids preferable to pull-off ones. £500 – £1,000 single; £1,200 – £3,000 matched pairs.

1715-1750   Baluster-shaped silver caddies. Narrow necks less desirable than wide necks. Generally less collectable than box caddies. Value depends on period and decorative style. Early Georgian: £300 – £500; later Georgian with over-ornate rococo decoration: £120 – £200 single; £250 – £450 pairs.

1740-1770   Lavishly decorated box caddies of the rococo period, with embossed motifs and often with four small feet. Often produced in sets. Prices range from £250 – £350 single, £600 – £900 pairs and £900 – £1,500 threes. If equipped with the original tea-chest add 20-25% to value.

1760-1800	Elegant vase-shaped caddies in silver. Wide range of sizes and styles and now produced as individuals in a much larger size. Large singles, £125 – £250.
1770-1820	Silver caddies now fitted with individual locks and generally much larger than previously. Chronologically they range from flat-topped ovals, domed ovals and fluted oblongs to domed ovals with feet. £150 – £500.
1820-1860	Silver caddies, in Victorian style of decoration but no longer fitted with locks as tea was much cheaper by then. £125 – £350.
1760-1840	Caddies made in Sheffield plate. Earliest form was bombé, without any lock and produced often in sets: £70 – £120 single, £200 – £300 pairs, £350 – £500 threes. Later Sheffield plate caddies parallel silver caddies in form and decoration. Prices from £45 to £150.
1770-1810	Glass caddies in square, oblong or cylindrical form, usually in opaque-white glass (Stourbridge, Bristol) with enamelled decoration which often included the name of the tea (Green, Hyson, Bohea, etc.). £150 – £250.
1740-1800	Mahogany tea-chests, often mounted with a silver carrying handle and lock-plate. £80 – £500.
1780-1850	Individual caddies made of wood. Fitted with locks up to c.1820. Fitted with a metal foil (tin, silver or even gold) lining. Box shapes commonest, but fluted oblongs and spherical shapes desirable. £25 – £100 singles; £60 – £275 pairs. Decorative features, such as marquetry, rolled paper-work, needlework panels, boulle work, are important plus factors.
1780-1830	Caddies made of paper mâché with lacquering and mother-of-pearl inlay. £30 – £80 singles; £70 – £150 pairs.
1800-1840	Caddies decorated with Tunbridge ware mosaic (q.v.) £60 – £150.
1850-1900	Later wooden caddies in Victorian style. Often intricately carved. Revival of walnut, maple and other traditional woods. Usually oblong with tapering sides. Brass handles, lock plate and mounts. £15 – £60.
1850-1900	Metal caddies in electroplate, eclectic in style. Often die-stamped and embossed in earlier styles (chinoiseries, rococo, Regency). Very little demand for this type. £5 – £15.

A George III fruitwood tea-caddy, 4¼ins. high.

A rolled paper tea-caddy, early 19th century.

1890-1920   Early tinware caddies, often lacquered and decorated with chinoiserie or japonaiserie. Designed as 'giveaways' by the tea importers. Most desirable kind are those bearing firm's name, advertisement, etc. Later tinware caddies decorated with scenic motifs. Commemorative or patriotic motifs (Diamond Jubilee, Boer War etc.) worth looking for. Average £2 − £10, but up to £30.

Points to look for

Silver caddies should be fully hallmarked (usually one full set of marks on the body and partial marks on the lid). Caddies by the leading silversmiths of the 18th and early 19th centuries are likely to be worth very much more than comparable examples by lesser or unknown smiths.

Wooden tea-chests may be found which, from their external appearance, were intended to house caddies, but which may have been converted to other uses at a subsequent date. Such boxes will depend for their value on the type of wood and quality of the craftsmanship, even though the canisters themselves are missing. The same applies to the 19th century wooden caddies. Those which are intact, and have complete foil lining, are worth a premium.

Pitfalls

The 18th century wooden caddies in the form of spheres or shaped like hollow apples or pears are very popular with collectors, but care must be taken to distinguish between them and late-Victorian 'revivals' or modern copies. The genuine caddies were made of beech, box or

Above: A Sheraton fiddle-back mahogany two-division tea-caddy with inlaid marquetry, 7ins. wide.

Left: A tortoiseshell two-division tea-caddy strung with pewter. 6¼ins. wide.

walnut, had silver stop-hinges and foil lining. The later imitations are often of varnished whitewood, though many Victorian examples were painted to simulate the colour and texture of apples and pears. In the Regency period fruit caddies had brass hinges and locks, whereas the Victorian examples had steel or stamped toleware hinges.

Museums
Geffrye Museum, London.
Sir John Soane's House, London.
Victoria and Albert Museum, London.
Royal Pavilion, Brighton.
Royal Scottish Museum, Edinburgh.
Museum and Art Gallery, Leicester.
Central Museum and Art Gallery, Northampton.
Salisbury and South Wiltshire Museum, Salisbury.
City Museum and Art Gallery, Stoke-on-Trent.
Wedgwood Museum, Stoke-on-Trent.
Elizabethan House, Totnes.

Reading List
Frost, T.W. The Price Guide to Old Sheffield Plate. Woodbridge, 1971.
Harris, Ian. The Price Guide to Antique Silver. Woodbridge, 1969.
Hughes, Bernard and Therle. Small Antique Furniture. London, 1967.

TELESCOPES

Optical instruments for viewing distant objects. There are two basic classes of telescope — refractors and reflectors. The first uses lenses to produce the magnified image, the second uses curved mirrors. Refractors came first and were invented by the Dutch spectacle maker, Hans Lippershay in 1608. He discovered, probably by accident, that if he held a strong convex lens close to his eye, and a weaker one in line with it and further away, it was possible to see an inverted, magnified image of distant objects. About a year later, Galileo, having heard of Lippershay's empirical discovery worked out the optics involved, and concluded that replacing the convex eye lens with a concave one would also result in a telescope, though now the image would be the right way up. This is the Galilean telescope, still with us in the form of opera glasses. It is, however, of inherently limited magnification and field. Lippershay refractors could be made more powerful by making them longer, and for astronomical work, such workers as Christian Huygens and Hevelius produced very long instruments, up to 150 feet from end to end. However, due to the prismatic action of simple lenses, all early refractors produced colour-fringed images, and it was not until the middle of the 18th century that John Dollond produced achromatic telescope lenses which cured this fault.

Reflecting telescopes do not suffer from this drawback, since the rays of light do not have to pass through thicknesses of glass, but are bounced off the mirrored surfaces. James Gregory produced the first Gregorian telescopes in 1663. Isaac Newton designed a reflector with a different arrangement of mirrors in 1668, the Newtonian. The third

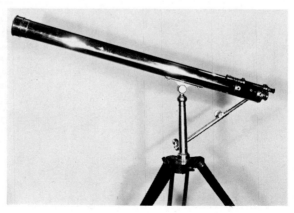

A refractor brass telescope by Bardou of Paris, with mahogany tripod stand and a brass table stand.

type of reflector, with yet another optical arrangement carried the name of its inventor, the Frenchman Cassegrain, and appeared in 1672. These three basic designs are still to be seen in the most modern and powerful telescopes in the world, the giant astronomical instruments.

Datelines

1608-1650 The slender instruments of this period, with tubes of vellum and leather, are seldom seen outside museums. Any examples that do emerge must be considered individually.

1650-1760 For refracting telescopes only. There are some smaller portable instruments, little changed from the earlier period. But the only way a small instrument could be made more powerful was by using more deeply curved convex eye lenses, which resulted in excessive colour fringing. The very long instruments used for astronomy used quite flat lenses, which limited colour fringing, but they are hardly likely to appear in the saleroom. Often they were part of a structure, rather than a discreet instrument. Again a period for individual valuation.

1760-1920 For refracting telescopes only. John Dollond's achromatic lenses, which were well within the capacity of contemporary opticians to make, were compounded of two different glasses, with varying optical characteristics. With no colour fringing (chromatic aberration) to worry about, more powerful compact instruments could be designed in the case of instruments of the basic Lippershay type, and compound (terrestrial) eyepieces could turn the image right way up.

1663-1760 For reflecting telescopes only. These are quite small

Three 18th century tripod-mounted brass telescopes. Rear: Gregorian reflector by Nairne & Blunt, c.1780. Centre: Unique reflector by B. Martin, c.1740. Front: Refractor with four fixed foci by N. Adams, c.1730.

498

instruments, almost always on a table or floor stand. The front end of the tube is quite open, and at the back end is the main mirror, its delicate surface quite unprotected, and therefore very vulnerable. When small achromatic refractors became available, the small reflector became obsolete, and the reflector became purely an observatory instrument. All reflectors should be considered and valued individually.

Price Range

Telescopes made before 1750, refracting or reflecting, are of the greatest rarity and are seldom encountered. Hand-held examples between 1750 and 1800 covered in vellum with brass mounts are now worth from £100 upwards. Plus factors are shagreen casing, silver mounts and the names of the more famous makers (Bradley, Molyneux, Scarlet, Hearn, Dollond). £250 – £1,000.

Late 18th and early 19th century telescopes with long mahogany barrels, sometimes hexagonal with one draw and a shutter at each end. Often highly decorative and usually of great technical interest. £120 – £300.

Floor models, 1790-1830, with tooled leather or shagreen case mounted on a tapering column with cabriole legs. £300 – £1,200, according to maker, decorative features and technical factors.

All-metal (usually brass) table or floor telescopes, 1780-1830. £150 – £400.

All-metal table or floor telescopes with black oxidised body, 1840-1900. £20 – £100.

Plus factors are all-brass casing, decorative stands, or names of leading makers. £80 – £200.

Late 19th and early 20th century military pocket telescopes with leather casing and brass mounts. £10 – £30. These usually bear the WD and arrow device of the War Department. Plus factors are regimental insignia, or plates engraved with the owner's rank, name and regiment.

Points to look for

Telescopes of any period should be in good working order. Care should be taken to see that the lenses are not cracked or damaged and that the case is not dented. Cased sets with matching accessories are rare, and are mainly brass table outfits. Make sure that the accessories actually match. Rare astronomical stand instruments with clockwork for rotating the inclined mount in opposition to the earth's rotation must be valued individually.

For Museums and Reading List see *Scientific Instruments.*

THIMBLES

Small devices for protecting the finger-tip while sewing, thimbles date back to Roman times when they were cast in bronze. Medieval thimbles were often made of leather but understandably few have survived. In the Far East thimbles were carved from ivory, hardstone, bone, mother-of-pearl or hardwoods. In Europe silver and even gold were used in thimbles made from the 15th century onwards. Brass thimbles of utilitarian design began to appear in the 17th century and steel thimbles in the 18th. Steel thimbles with a brass rim or lining were common in the 18th century and throughout the 19th century. Very few examples in precious metals are hallmarked since they were too small to be affected by the various assay acts, and the situation is further confused by the late-Victorian penchant for neo-Gothic or pseudo-medieval styles. Between 1739 and 1790 silver thimbles were exempt from hallmarking and thereafter only those above five pennyweight had to be marked, so that there was seldom any obligation on the silversmith to comply. Only after about 1870 did hallmarking of such small objects become a general practice. The invention of the nose machine in the mid-18th century permitted the indentation of thimbles in regular, spiral patterns and this is a useful guide to dating. Thimbles with indentations punched individually and irregularly are probably pre-1750. Thimbles can be classified according to materials, type and decoration, and are priced accordingly.

Left to right
"Roman" type bronze, said to have been dug up in Chichester, could be any date up to medieval; heavy hammered metal, thought to be 15th or 16th century but very difficult to date; mother-of-pearl, gilt-banded, early 19th century; ivory, with carved floral band; gold, probably French, early 19th century, with cornelian top, and quatre-couleur work border of leaves and flowers, set with turquoises; wood, with cut steel rim and ornament, 19th century; Oriental, bone, made in two pieces, and very difficult to date.

Base Metal Thimbles range from Roman bronze to modern nickel-plated steel. Early bronze examples are cast in thick, heavy metal, with more sloping sides and a domed top. They are relatively rare and are classed as antiquities. £5 − £20.

Brass thimbles with irregular indentation were widely produced in the 16th to mid-18th centuries. Again, most of these are comparatively thick and clumsy, with the traditional high-domed top. They are rare, but not particularly attractive and this has depressed their value. £3 − £10.

Brass thimbles with machined indentation in an overall pattern, with plain rims are plentiful and of little value, since they continued to be made until the end of the 19th century. 25p − £1.

Brass thimbles with some degree of decoration are more desirable. A wide variety of this type were produced in the 19th century, with an infinity of decorative treatments to the rims and sides. At the upper

Left to right
Steel tailor's thimble, brass-lined; 18th century brass, steel-topped; 19th century steel thimble, brass-lined; 19th century brass; late 19th century brass with blue and red enamel bands.

end of the scale are those brass thimbles with a decorated top, floral piercing replacing the more functional indentations. 50p − £2.

Steel thimbles lined or rimmed with brass date from the mid-18th century. 25p − 50p.

Styles range from a complete steel shell to those with only a steel cap on a brass body. £1 − £2.

The plainer varieties are relatively common.

19th and early 20th century steel thimbles with inscriptions on the rim are worth more, depending on the inscription. A popular type in the 1920s was produced as an advertising gimmick and bore the name and trademark of various household goods. Plus factors are the inclusion of a slogan or a small pictorial motif. £1 − £4.

Steel or brass thimbles with patent devices are much sought after. The simpler types are those with an inscription denoting that they are patent non-slip or ventilated. The more elaborate types incorporate wire needle threaders or cutters attached to the side. £1 − £5.

Left to right
Dorcas thimble; patent ventilated thimble; patent non-slip thimble; brass thimble with wire needle threader attached; brass thimble with an unworkable gadget thought by some experts to be a cutter, by others to be a different type of needle threader. These all date from the late 19th century.

Other base metals are sometimes encountered, but they are relatively scarce. They include pewter, zinc and enamelled steel. £1 – £2.

Decorative steel thimbles were a rare French speciality of the 19th century and these occur with many different motifs of an artistic nature. £2 – £8.

Silver thimbles begin with the Dorcas thimble, consisting of a steel shell with a silver lining and a decorative silver cap. This type often has the trade name 'Dorcas' impressed near the rim and was a mid-Victorian attempt at combining functionalism with ornament. They were immensely popular and continued to be made well into the 20th century. £1 – £2.

More expensive, and of earlier vintage (18th-early 19th centuries) is the steel-topped silver thimble, with a predominantly silver body and a steel cap for greater durability. £3 – £5.

Pure silver thimbles are recorded from the Middle Ages, but early examples which can definitely be dated are rare and would be in the

Left to right
Victorian silver, "Windsor Castle"; silver, Great Exhibition, "Hyde Park, 1851". There are several versions of this thimble, this particular one being foreign made; 1911, silver, commemorating the coronation of George V and Queen Mary; silver, commemorating the end of the First World War; very plain silver, commemorating the coronation of George VI.

502

Left to right
Early Victorian silver, with applied band (note the seamline); later 19th century fleur de lys band; silver, hallmarked Chester 1897; child's Victorian silver; Victorian silver, "From a Friend"; silver finger protector, 19th century, to wear on the opposite hand from that which has the ordinary thimble; different shape finger protector, 19th century.

price range £10+, (late-17th century to 1740). Pre-1660 silver thimbles are virtually non-existent outside museum collections. As befitted the use of precious metal, the most elaborate decoration is to be found on silver thimbles. Good 18th and early 19th century examples. £4 – £10.

Silver thimbles may also be found with scenery or landmarks round the sides. At the lower end of the scale are 'town' thimbles, with the names of places inscribed rather plainly round the rim. £2 – £5.

Scenic thimbles of a general landscape or landmark. £3 – £8.

Commemorative thimbles were popular throughout the 19th century and survived spasmodically up to the Second World War, and a few are still produced to celebrate important events. They celebrate royal events (jubilees, coronations, weddings, births) and national or international events, from the Great Exhibition of 1851 to the Armistice of 1918. £10 – £25.

Silver thimbles inlaid with gold are rare and would be priced from £10 upwards.

Silver thimbles decorated with semi-precious stones are more frequently met with and date from the late 17th century, though the majority were probably produced between 1850 and 1900. The rims are inset with small hardstones, such as amethyst, greenstone, lapis lazuli, cornelian and moonstone. £8 – £30.

Beware of modern silver thimbles of European manufacture with what purport to be semi-precious stones. These are invariably of glass paste or even plastic, and are produced as cheap tourist souvenirs in France, Spain, Italy, etc.

Gold thimbles are now exceedingly expensive on account of their bullion content. The plainest 19th century examples are now in the range of £30 – £40, but the price rises steeply for earlier examples or thimbles with fine decoration. Particularly prized are gold thimbles

Left to right
Porcelain, early 19th century, hand-painted with pink flowers and green and blue ornament; bone china, late 19th century, hand-painted with bluebird, no mark; very small bone china, decorated with gilding and pink enamel, beginning of this century, no mark; Royal Worcester, hand-painted with a thrush, 1927.

Left to right:
Royal Worcester, hand-painted redstart, 1929; Royal Worcester, hand-painted chaffinch, 1932; Royal Worcester, modern, hand-painted violets.

incorporating four-colour work, a late 18th century speciality.

Enamelled thimbles were among the objects of vertu produced by the enamellers of Bilston, Battersea and Limoges. As a rule the enamelling is on copper, but silver is occasionally met with. These 18th century trifles are now rare and expensive and the starting price is around £80, though fine examples are worth very much more.

Continental enamelled thimbles are still produced as tourist souvenirs and have charming scenic decoration round the sides. These have been fashionable from about 1870 and are now in the price range £5 – £15, depending on age and quality.

Porcelain thimbles with hand-painted designs have been produced since the mid-18th century and continue to be made to this day as elegant trifles. The modern thimbles are now made by six or seven English firms, some selling for less than £2. Earlier 20th century examples are usually Worcester and cost from £10 upwards. At the other extreme Meissen thimbles of the early 18th century have passed the £1,000 mark at auction. In between come the vast range of 19th century porcelain thimbles, in many different decorative styles and representing the majority of the porcelain factories of the period. Marked examples are relatively scarce and are worth a high premium. From £30. Unmarked thimbles are more plentiful but vary enormously in quality. From £15.

Thimbles in ivory, £8 upwards.

Bone thimbles. From £5 for plain examples.

Vegetable ivory thimbles. £8.

Mother-of-pearl. From £15.

Tortoiseshell thimbles, very rare. From £20.

Carved or inlaid hardwood, hardstone and even glass (a speciality of the Venetian, Bohemian and Silesian glasshouses) are regarded as objects of vertu and were not intended for actual use. They are comparatively rare. £20 – £50.

Apart from the thimbles themselves, the cases are collectable. From about 1780 to 1850 thimble cases were made in silver, gold, enamels or hardwood or bound in shagreen or leather and these are highly desirable. In the 19th century thimble cases were made in Mauchline ware (q.v.) in wood, ivory or porcelain. These cases are usually barrel- or acorn-shaped and unscrew to reveal the thimble inside. Some of the more elaborate examples also have compartments for needles and pins. Novelty thimble cases, in the form of castles, windmills, lighthouses, human figures, etc. are worth looking for. There is no hard and fast market in thimble cases as yet, but as a rough guide expect to pay roughly twice as much for the case as the thimble it contains, but rarities, such as 18th century precious metal cases, or 19th century novelty shapes, would be worth more.

TIE - PINS

Otherwise known as stick pins, these articles of male adornment date from the early 19th century when cravats superseded stocks as neckwear. They died out gradually in the early years of this century when neckties became narrower, though they have survived fitfully to this day and have enjoyed periodic revival in the intervening years. Apart from the comments made below, these pins would be impossible to date, since the same types remained popular throughout the period in which pins were fashionable. Their value depends primarily on materials — gold, silver, silver-plated brass, blued steel, mild steel or enamelled steel — and the decorative treatment of the heads. As with all antiques, quality and rarity have a great influence on today's prices, e.g. a finely carved mother-of-pearl cameo will make more than a pressed-out 18ct. one. Condition is of great importance. Stick pins are sometimes hallmarked fully, or carry a carat stamping. It is worth noting that any pin stamped 9ct. cannot be earlier than 1854, when 9ct. was introduced; also that from 1854 until 1932, 12ct. and 15ct. were legal as well as 18ct. and 22ct.

The most expensive are those featuring precious stones — diamonds, rubies, emeralds or sapphires. The value of these will depend on the setting and the size of the stones. Usually the only precious stones left in stick pins are quite small, as most of the finest diamond ones have been converted into rings etc. long ago. £15 – £100. Pins with semi-precious stones offer a much wider field: garnet, beryl, amethyst, opal, onyx or chrysoberyl. Prices range from £6 to £25 depending on setting. Pins with pearls, semi-precious stones and enamelling, a speciality of Peter Carl Fabergé, would be in the price range £40 – £75. The price of articles from the Fabergé, workshops is rising all the time and examples in good condition rarely come on to the market below £150. The Fabergé, style was widely imitated and pins with decoration in this manner range from £10 to £30. to £30.

Intaglio gemstones, carved cameos and similar decoration range from £45 to £100, depending on the materials and the fineness of the engraving or carving. Intaglios and cameos in stones are more sought after than the same thing in shell. Signed ones are most desirable and condition is very important here. Intaglio carved crystals, painted so that the motif stands out in a three-dimensional effect, were popular at the turn of the century, with human or animal portraits. £5 – £15. For reverse intaglio painted crystals, also stone cameos, from £60.

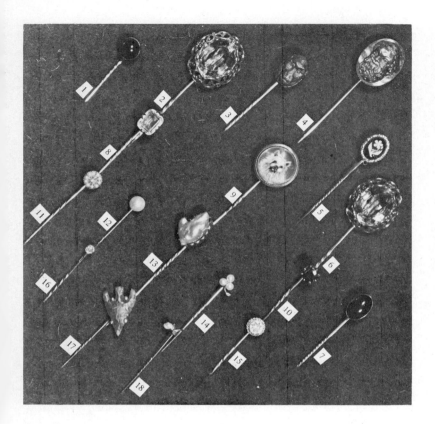

Tie Pins

1. *Cabochon garnet in enclosed setting.* 2. & 6. *Large citrines in hand-pierced silver setting.* 3. *Labradorite, carved cameo, (Canadian) in enclosed setting, of a monkey's face.* 4. *A labradorite cameo, of a bearded man, set in heavy, hallmarked 18ct. gold.* 5. *Black and white onyx cameo of a small flower.* 7. *A foil-backed cabochon garnet.* 8. *Green beryl, similar in colour to an aquamarine.* 9. *This pin was produced by intaglio carving into the back of a piece of domed crystal, then by painting the motif.* 10. *Reconstructed ruby, in gold coronet setting.* 11. *Small diamond in raised rubbed-over setting.* 12. *Single round pearl, on gold pin.* 13. *Baroque pearl.* 14. *Three tiny pearls forming a trefoil with a rose diamond set into the stem.* 15. *Diamond set in bloomed gold with star effect and fine rope surround.* 16. *Quarter carat diamond in coronet setting. The head of this pin unscrews and can be worn as a stud.* 17. *Flint arrow of unknown origin.* 18. *White opal bud with rose diamond in stem.*

507

TILES

Earthenware slabs have been produced since the Middle Ages for interior decoration. They were used as wall or ceiling decoration, as panels of various sizes, either alone or in multiples, in place of wall hangings or pictures, as ornament on stoves and as decoration on screens or pieces of furniture. Although tiles may be broadly categorised according to date, the country of origin and the style of decoration are also important. We are here concerned with tiles in the modern sense, covering the period of the last eight centuries. Tiles exist from much earlier periods, but these are now so rare that they are not collected on the same lines as more recent examples. Individual tiles of a decorative nature date back as far as the Minoan civilisation in Crete, almost 4,000 years ago, and examples from Greece, Rome and Egypt are not unknown.

Date-lines

12th-16th centuries	Persian tiles produced at Kashan and Kubaki. Brilliant blue lustre glazes with non-figurative motifs, often incorporating Arabic script. Tiles of this type were widely used in mosques and public buildings. Examples are now rare and are in the price range £120 – £400.
16th-18th centuries	Persian tiles decorated with enamelled portraits on a tin-glazed ground, reflecting the influence of European fashions. Also greater use of natural motifs, flowers, leaves, etc. £50 – £90.
15th-18th centuries	Syrian tiles, made mainly in the Damascus region, painted on the biscuit in underglaze blue and fired with a thin white glaze. Hexagonal shapes common, decorated with flowers, grasses and animals in dark blue on grey slip. Turquoise, sage-green, blue and purple also characteristic. £50 – £100.
15th-18th centuries	Turkish tiles, primarily from Isnik, made of rather coarse, greyish earthenware covered with very white tin-glaze slip brightened with tin oxide. Much bolder and more imaginative colouring and use of natural motifs. Later 16th and 17th century tiles often include red enamelling. Isnik tiles often produced in multiples, for panels up to 12 feet across. Individual tiles vary greatly in size, up to a foot square. The dramatic quality of their

Turkish (Isnik) tile made in the late 16th century. The colours on a brilliant white ground include blue, turquoise, and a thick red like sealing-wax. Rare and highly desirable.

A 17th century Dutch tile painted in polychrome with a bird.

colouring compensates for a certain mechanical feeling in design. Isnik tiles reached their zenith in the late 16th century. £200 – £450. Later Turkish tiles are more plentiful and of lower quality. £80 – £150.

16th-18th centuries
Tin-glazed earthenware tiles spread to Spain from the Moorish countries of North Africa. The best-known are the *cuenca* (hollow) or moulded tiles, formed by pressing a mould into the soft clay to produce ridges which separated the coloured parts and prevented them from running together when fired. Enamel colours are predominantly green, white, purple and yellow, with geometric motifs. These tiles are generally much thinner than Islamic tiles. These designs remained popular for centuries and were widely used in both interior and exterior decoration. £10 – £30.

16th-18th centuries
Italian tiles of the same period were produced in tin-glazed maiolica, sometimes imitating Hispano-Moresque styles, but also reviving classical imagery from Ancient Rome. These neo-classical tiles are very rare in complete panels. Subsequently, however, single tiles were designed with religious, historical or allegorical motifs. The more secular designs were fashionable in the 18th century and were intricately painted by such artists as Lolli, Gentili, Terchi and the Grue family of Castelli.

511

Majolica panels and tiles were made at Faenza and Siena and elsewhere in northern Italy as well as in Sicily. Although not rare, these pictorial panels are immensely popular and this is reflected in their prices, from £200 to £1,200.

Value Points

Castelli plaques bearing a signature, e.g. one of the Grue family, will increase by up to 50% in value. In general, classical or contemporary subjects are more popular and desirable than religious subjects. Early plaques and tiles are always expensive. The cruder late 16th and 17th century examples from Sicily and southern Italy are less desirable.

16th-18th centuries

Tile-making was established in the Netherlands, primarily in Antwerp, Amsterdam, Delft and Haarlem, though by the 17th century most tiles were produced in the Rotterdam district. Dutch tiles fall into two distinct groups. The earlier tiles (up to 1630) were polychrome with complex floral motifs and may be found in various sizes and shapes. Most popular subjects are birds and animals, with flowers and fruit second and formal motifs third. The earliest square tiles with geometric motifs are scarce (£120 – £180), but early 17th century square tiles with floral motifs are more plentiful. £50 – £100. After 1630 the typical blue and white tiles, with their wide range of floral, animal and scenic designs, became very popular and were also exported in vast quantities. Complete panels of different scenes are rare, but individual tiles are plentiful in the range from £2 to £20. These are very desirable, particularly polychrome examples with birds (e.g. parrots) and animals – cats, dogs or horses. Cows are more common. In the 18th century there was a revival of polychrome tiles, used to form composite panels of bird and flower pictures. Dutch tiles can be dated by the body: thickish red clay in the earlier period and thinner buff-coloured clay in the later period.

17th-18th centuries

Delftware tiles of the Dutch pattern were made in England, chiefly in London and, to a lesser extent, in Bristol and Liverpool. The tiles of the 17th century are apt to be confused with their Dutch counterparts. Prices are similar to, or slightly higher than, those for Dutch

512

tiles of the same period. 18th century English tiles, however, became much more imaginative and distinctive styles began to emerge, such as the landscape tiles of Bristol, sometimes with powdered manganese grounds, and the chinoiserie tiles from Liverpool. Bird tiles were very popular, with blue or polychrome borders, £40 – £50, or white decoration on a pale blue ground, 'bianco-sopra-bianco'. Tiles of these types are in the price range £10 – £60. Blue and white tiles approximately £5 – £10 each. Landscape tiles £15 – £20. Tiles with painted subjects after the manner of Boucher and Watteau were fashionable in the 1760s, but these are scarce. £100 – £150.

1750-1850 Transfer-printed tiles, pioneered by Sadler and Green of Liverpool, superseded hand-painted tiles. A wide variety of subjects may be found, ranging from Shakespearean characters and Aesop's Fables to landscapes and scenes of courtship, chinoiseries and sporting subjects. Popular are rare signed prints or amusing subjects (e.g. Fortune-Teller or Itinerant Tooth Puller). Neo-classical subjects, such as urns are less desirable. These tiles, often reproducing line engravings from book illustrations, were printed in blue, black, sepia, maroon, green and other colours. They are still relatively common and are in the range from £20 to £70, depending on the subject. Those

A signed Sadler earthenware tile made in Liverpool around 1756 with a scene of courtship. About 3/8th in. thick, 5ins. square.

A Sadler tile showing the fable of the Fox, the Dog, the Sheep, the Vulture and the Kite, from Aesop. About ⅜in. thick, 5ins. square.

513

tiles bearing Sadler's signature (1757-61) are highly prized and are worth much more. £30 − £100+.

1850-1914   Several new types of tile became fashionable in this period. Majolica was used for relief tiles with green, yellow or brown glazes, and these featured a wide variety of motifs, often derived from the Renaissance or Gothic periods. £2 − £10.

Press-moulded tiles, made from compressed dust, were mass-produced on both sides of the Atlantic. They had a keyed back to facilitate cementing and this usually bears the name of the maker. Late 19th century tiles can be dated by the lozenge registration mark. £1 − £5.

Polychrome tiles were revived from 1860 onwards, and given fresh impetus by the Aesthetic Movement, and, latterly, by William Morris and the Arts and Crafts Movement. These tiles may be found in an infinite variety: sets featuring the Seasons, Japonaiserie, Shakespearean characters, floral or geometric motifs, allegorical groups, etc. The value of these tiles varies enormously. Mass-produced tiles by such firms as Maw, Doulton, Simpson or Pilkington range from £2 to £10. The more artistic tiles produced by Minton, or Beete of Birmingham, range from £4 to £25, depending on the design and whether they can be ascribed to such artists as Moyr Smith or Kate Greenaway. Tiles using the Spanish *cuenca* style were designed by Walter Crane for Pilkington at the turn of the century and these are in great demand. Tiles by Crane are now in the price range from £10 to £50.

The most sought after of late Victorian tiles were those hand-produced by William De Morgan, using brilliant enamel colours and lustre. The early De Morgan tiles show a strong Islamic influence; later tiles had geometric patterns or flowers in strong polychrome enamels on a white ground. De Morgan polychrome tiles are from £30 to £80; lustre tiles are scarcer and rate £50 to £100.

Majolica or polychrome tiles with strong Art Nouveau motifs are common, but because of the revival of interest in this fashion they rate £2 to £15.

1914-1940   Mass-produced tiles of this period are both plentiful and cheap and occur in an enormous range of styles and patterns, often derived from earlier patterns. They can

514

Autumn, designed by Kate Green-away, April 1883. Transfer-printed tile made by Beete of Birmingham; 6 inches square, the most popular size.

Tile panel produced by the Morris firm, about 1872. Figure painted in blue on white in the medieval style.

Right: One of a series of tiles designed by Walter Crane for Pilkington's in 1920, in the cuenca method.

usually be identified by markings on the back. Prices are from 50p to £2, depending on the subject.

Hand-made tiles were produced intermittently in this period and names to watch for include the Omega workshop (tiles painted by Duncan Grant, Vanessa Bell) and the tiles from studio potters like Bernard Leach and Dora Billington, styles being influenced by the Bauhaus, Japonaiserie and Cubism. Art Deco and Art Moderne

515

hand-painted tiles by artist-potters are now in demand and rate from £5 to £30.

Mass-produced tiles with Art Deco themes are plentiful and rate £1 — £5. Many excellent hand-painted tiles of European origin were produced in the same period, but these are currently undervalued and little hard and fast market exists for them as yet. In both these categories famous names are very much at a premium. Prices generally from £1 to £5.

Points to look for

In the early period of English and European tiles (16th-17th century) tiles decorated with coats of arms and mottoes were used by apothecaries as pill slabs. Although most of them were rectangular, some may be found in octagonal or shield form and as a rule they are pierced with holes for suspension from a hook when not in use. Such items were made up to about 1700 and they are now much sought after by collectors of medical antiques. Prices range from £250 to £600, according to condition.

Museums

British Museum, London.

Geffrye Museum, London.

Guildhall Museum, London.

Victoria and Albert Museum, London.

City Museum and Art Gallery, Birmingham.

Museum and Art Gallery, Brighton.

Royal Scottish Museum, Edinburgh.

City Museum, Hereford.

Museum and Art Gallery, Leicester.

Central Museum and Art Gallery, Northampton.

Salisbury and South Wiltshire Museum, Salisbury.

City Museum, Sheffield.

City Museum and Art Gallery, Stoke-on-Trent.

Dyson Perrins Museum, Worcester.

Reading List

Barnard, Julian. Victorian Ceramic Tiles. London, 1972.

Berendson, Anne. Tiles, a General History. London, 1967.

Jonge, C.H. de. Dutch Tiles. London, 1970.

Korf, Dingman. Dutch Tiles. New York, 1964.

Lane, Arthur. Guide to the Collection of Tiles: Victoria and Albert Museum. London, 1960.

Ray, Anthony. English Delftware Tiles. Faber, London, 1972.

TINS

Containers for perishables and foodstuffs, such as biscuits and confectionery, tobacco, matches, beef cubes, patent medicines and many other small articles. Tins provide a valuable insight into packaging techniques and the development of graphic design over the past century or so. Among the earliest, and certainly the best known and now most desirable of tins, were those produced by Huntley and Palmer of Reading to package their biscuits. Thomas Huntley purveyed biscuits to passengers on the West Country stagecoach which passed his shop in Reading, and sold them in airtight tins, hand-made by his brother Joseph who ran an ironmonger's shop. The early hand-made tins were relatively plain in design but are now highly desirable and would be worth up to £50.

Date-lines

1850-1860   Hand-made tins, with paper covers intricately decorated. Very rare in fine condition as the tins tended to rust and this corroded the paper. £40 – £60.

1860-1880   Earliest machine-made tins, surfaces decorated by transfer printing (patented by Benjamin George about 1860). £25 – £50.

1880-1888   Decoration applied by offset-lithography; surfaces still relatively plain. Pictorial motifs now more complex and detailed. £15 – £40.

'Log cabin' biscuit tin by S. Henderson and Sons, 1910.

A small chocolate tin exported to South Africa during the Boer War, complete with a New Year greeting from the Queen.

1888-1920   First 'shaped' tins, by a process which allowed embossing and shaping after the motif had been printed. Shaping restrained, with lids scrolled, fluted and gilded to simulate picture frames round reproductions of late Victorian narrative paintings. £10 – £30.

1900-1920   Technical improvements in manufacture resulted in tins of many shapes, from the bizarre and whimsical to the highly imaginative. The most desirable tins are those which resemble other materials (leather, wickerwork) and assume the least likely shapes (books, clocks, coaches, golf-clubs). £15 – £40.

1920-1939   In this period the most unusual novelties were produced, and these included tins which also served as toys (shooting galleries, coconut shies, toy prams, coaches, aeroplanes, etc.). £20 – £50.

Throughout the period from 1870 to 1920 less decorative tins were produced for sweets, chocolates, tobacco, matches, patent medicines, etc. Not only are these tins less ornamental, but the same design tended to be retained for many years. 50p – £2.

Commemorative tins, celebrating coronations (1902, 1911, 1937, 1953) and jubilees (1887, 1897, 1935) were given to schoolchildren and form a large group. – £5.

Points to look for

Transfer-printed tins are elusive in really fine condition, and care must be taken not to damage the delicate surface decoration. On no account should they be washed, since they bloom very badly. At best they can only be carefully wiped with a slightly damp and very soft cloth, but if in doubt leave well alone. Lithographically-printed tins can be cleaned, but this must also be done very gently, with damp cotton wool. They can be dried in an oven with a low heat until thoroughly dry and then lightly coated with clear white wax and polished lightly when dry. Novelty tins with moving parts (wheels, windmill sails, etc.) should be complete with hinges and catches intact. Avoid tins with bad dents or scratched surfaces.

Reading List

Corley, T.A.B. Huntley and Palmer's of Reading. London, 1972.
Davies, Alex. Package and Print. London, 1967.

Left: 'Book' biscuit tins, Huntley and Palmers, 1920. Right: 'Literature',
Huntley and Palmers, 1901.

TOBY JUGS

Left to right: A Toby jug with manganese tricorn hat, waistcoat and shoes, blue coat and green breeches, a jug of ale supported tenderly on his ample knee. 10ins.; a Ralph Wood Toby jug of usual type, the man with fuddled leer on his warty face, with pale greyish coat, manganese breeches, black shoes and tricorn hat, seated in a green high-backed chair extending into the handle. 10ins.; a rare Welsh country gentleman Toby jug, the adipose fellow seated in a high-backed chair grasping a brim-full jug close to his button-bursting belly, wearing a manganese coat, hat, breeches and shoes and blue striped stockings. 8½ins.; a Leeds Toby jug, the seated toper wearing a muddy green tricorn hat, blue spotted coat and ochre breeches and is clutching a frothing jug of ale. 10ins. Note the finer glazing and crisper modelling of the Ralph Wood example.

Character jugs originating in the late 18th century and based on a popular character of the period named Toby Fillpot, created by the Rev. Francis Hawkes in a translation of the poem 'Metamorphosis' by Geronimo Amalteo. The character of the hearty toper inspired a popular drawing by Robert Dighton, subsequently published as a print by Carrington Bowles and this in turn inspired the pottery jugs produced by Ralph Wood I about 1761. The seated figure of the rotund Toby, clutching a foaming tankard and wearing a tricorn hat, has remained popular to this day. Inevitably other potters were quick to imitate the Toby jug and before the end of the 18th century other characters were modelled as jugs in the same fashion. The modern counterpart of this was the series of Toby jugs portraying Allied war leaders during the First World War, and, more recently, the jugs featuring the late Sir Winston Churchill.

Date-lines
1761-1772   Earliest Toby jugs made by Ralph Wood I. Thinly potted

520

in greyish creamware, with low bases, usually unglazed. Colours: muted shades with brown, purple, greyish-blue and green predominant. Variants show Toby clutching his mug or jug in both hands, or holding a pipe or glass in his right hand and the beer jug in the left. Fine modelling. Some examples marked RW but often unmarked. £400 – £700.

1772-1780   Early Toby jugs made by Ralph Wood II. More thickly potted in paler creamware and raised on higher bases; colouring as before. Some examples marked 'Ra. Wood Burslem'. £150 – £300.

1780-1797   Later Toby jugs by Ralph Wood II. Potting and designs as 1772-80 but much brighter enamel colours, with orange, black, blue and green predominant. £150 – £250.

1770-1790   So-called 'Astbury-Whieldon' Toby jugs. Decorated with the mottled glazes characteristic of this ware. Very rare. £600 – £1,000.

1790-1846   Enoch Wood Toby jugs. Enoch Wood, cousin and originally partner of Ralph Wood II, but subsequently in business on his own account. The majority of early 19th century Toby jugs were produced by him and may be found (in chronological order) with the markings E. WOOD, ENOCH WOOD, WOOD & CALDWELL (1790-1819), or ENOCH WOOD & SONS surrounding a shield motif (1819-46). Bright enamel colours; many different styles of Toby, including the comparatively scarce standing Toby. £50 – £150, but not more.

1780-1820   Prattware Toby jugs. Generally rather smaller, with sponging round the base. Characteristic colours: brown, ochre, black and blue. No marks, £50 – £150.

1790-1850   Staffordshire Toby jugs. Closer to the Ralph Wood originals than the Prattware examples (characteristic stare and toothy leer) but both modelling and colouring relatively crude. Staffordshire Tobies were fitted with covers, but these are often missing. With cover, £60 – £90. Without cover, £30 – £60.

1790-1850   Toby jugs by other potters, notably S. Hollins (1790-1820), Neale and Co. (1790-1801) or Wilson (1795-1850). More stereotyped than the Woods, though better modelling and colouring than Staffordshire. £40 – £80.

1850-1914   'Late Victorian' Toby jugs. Numerous but poorly modelled with syrupy glaze and exaggerated signs of 'running', e.g. from Brameld. Not really worth collecting, though examples are now in the price range £3 to £10.

During the same period some porcelain Tobies were made by Spode. These are scarce, but do not command the same interest as the earthenware jugs, £40 – £80.

All these categories, however, unless marked, are very hard to distinguish from one another, and consequently price ranges are very loose and overlap.

Other kinds of Toby jug

The above remarks concern the jugs depicting Toby Fillpot or close variants of the subject. Jugs were also modelled on other characters and these are invariably rarer and more valuable than their Toby counterparts. A taller and more elegant version, modelled by Ralph Wood, c.1770-1780, is known as the Thin Man. Others in this category are the Snuff-taker, the Planter, the Squire, the Parson and the Sailor. All of these are rare and in the price range £400 – £800. The Night Watchman jug, modelled by Enoch Wood is much rarer than his Tobies, £100 – £250. Religious figures (such as John Wesley) or naval heroes (Lord Howe, Lord Rodney, Sir Edward Vernon) were produced as Toby jugs from 1780 to 1820. £150 – £400. Martha Gunn (gin-seller and bathing attendant at Brighton) and Bluff King Hal (Prinny in fancy dress and identifiable by the Prince of Wales' feathers in the hat). £250

Left: A latish example but quite desirable because of the lively modelling and detailed decoration.

Right: Rare model of "Thin Man", good tortoiseshell glazes and modelling.

− £600. Toby jugs in silver or gold lustre are unusual. £70 − £120. Late 19th century Toby jugs featuring political figures (Disraeli, Gladstone). £35 − £70. First World War Toby jugs by Carruthers Gould featuring Allied leaders. £40 − £80.

Pitfalls

Reproductions of Toby jugs abound and are mostly of late 19th or early 20th century manufacture. They were not intended to deceive the collector into thinking they were Ralph Wood originals, since there was little demand for 18th century pottery jugs at that time, but were merely a late-Victorian interpretation of a perennially popular subject. Many of them are unmarked, but their poor modelling, crude colouring and coarse glazes should not deceive anyone. Later 20th century Toby jugs are more finely modelled and their enamel colouring is good. Fakes often have an imitation crackle glaze and good early examples should not have crackled glazes. Toby jugs have fallen considerably in popularity over the last five years or so, and only the very finest examples make the high prices quoted. Standard examples are common and therefore not so desirable. Modern Tobies are invariably marked by the pottery.

Museums

British Museum, London.
Imperial War Museum, London.
National Maritime Museum, Greenwich.
Victoria and Albert Museum, London.
Museum and Art Gallery, Brighton.
City Museum and Art Gallery, Birmingham.
National Museum of Wales, Cardiff.
Royal Scottish Museum, Edinburgh.
Ashmolean Museum, Oxford.
Central Museum and Art Gallery, Northampton.
Salisbury and South Wiltshire Museum, Salisbury.
City Museum, Sheffield.
City Museum and Art Gallery, Stoke-on-Trent.

Reading List

Bedford, John. Toby Jugs. London, 1968.
Eyles, Desmond. Good Sir Toby: The Story of Toby Jugs through the Ages. London, 1955.
Price, R.K. Astbury, Whieldon and Ralph Wood Figures and Toby Jugs. London, 1922.
Mount, Sally. Price Guide to 18th Century English Pottery. Woodbridge, 1972.

TONGS

Small domestic implements used in the handling of various foodstuffs. Tongs of silver or Sheffield plate were produced in the 18th and early 19th centuries for handling sugar or asparagus. The different functions of these tongs can be recognised by the shape of the arms and their ends. Sugar tongs are generally smaller than asparagus tongs and have rounded spade ends, whereas asparagus tongs have longer arms and terminate in flat ends marked with a large number of small ridges.

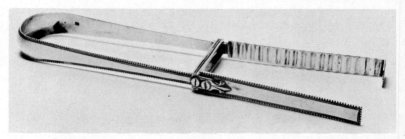

Asparagus tongs, 1790-1820, bow sprung type with a bracket to keep the shafts from straining apart.

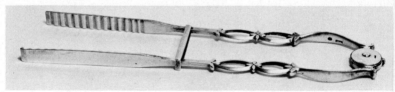

18th century asparagus tongs.

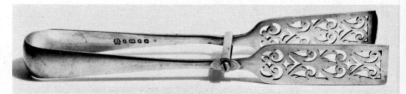

Silver plated asparagus tongs.

Asparagus Tongs

These may be found in four principal types, according to date, as follows:

1750-1770   Scissors type, with 'blades' ending in serrated flat ends. Sides of the finger guards, pivot and arms of the tongs

	often decorated with simple bright-cutting. Very rarely fully hallmarked. £80 – £120.
1760-1780	More ornate examples, with rocaille motifs, leaf patterns, etc. Arms usually much wider and often pierced and fretted. £80 – £150.
1770-1790	Sprung type, with a pivot at the end where the two arms are joined, with a spring mounted in the pivot to keep the arms open. The arms have a broader or thicker portion halfway down, where pressure could be brought to bear. Terminals flat and serrated as before. Examples after 1782 usually fully marked. Wide variety of decoration on arms and pivot. £45 – £70 for relatively plain examples; £65 – £90 for more decorative types.
1790-1820	Bow-sprung type, distinguished by the bow-spring extending from one arm to the other roughly halfway down. Usually with a plain rounded end. Less decorative than the preceding type. The more complex examples have a retaining clip or bracket to keep the shafts from springing apart. £20 – £40.
1800-1830	Bow-sprung type, but rendered in Sheffield plate. Very rare but exciting little interest. £25 – £40.

Sugar Tongs

These are of much greater antiquity, and in their earlier forms resembled the much larger tongs used by blacksmiths or as fireside implements.

1675-1720	Long-handled tongs, with two separately cast arms, pinned together. Balustroid finial, balustroid or spiral arms, terminating in shallow spade ends. Rarely fully hallmarked. Very rare. £100 – £200.
1700-1730	Tongs of silver wire continuous from one end to the other. Silver shaped so as to form a spring near the finial. Deeper ends, resembling shallow spoons or bowls. Relatively plain arms, with engraved ornament. Seldom fully hallmarked. £70 – £150.
1725-1750	Scissors type, often erroneously known as sugar nips. Very wide variety of sizes and shapes. Later examples often highly ornate. £40 – £80.
1750-1770	Large pivot at top containing a spring. Arms generally straight, but more elaborately decorated with chasing and pierced ornament. £30 – £60.

Left to right: Maker's mark F.P., S.C., Exeter, c.1800; maker's mark T.S., London, 1809; maker's mark William John Fisher, 1795; plain Old English by Joseph Kinsleagh, Cork, c.1800.

1770-1790   Cast tongs, with the highly ornamental arms joined by a bridge or arch. Bowls usually decorative (scallop shells, acanthus leaves, etc.), and arms in many different forms, with floral or plant patterns, tiny human figures, etc. £20 – £45.

1780-1800   'Bow' tongs made of continuous flattened silver wire with simple bowl ends. Generally much larger than the earlier types and relying on the tensile strength of the metal itself for its springiness. Plain examples £8 – £12; more decorative ones £10 – £15.

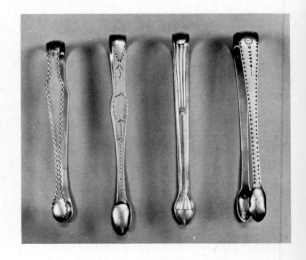

Left to right: By George Benson, London, c.1780; by Dorothy Langdons, Newcastle, c.1790; 'Adam' type by P.W. and A. Bateman, 1803; by William Hall, London, 1795-6.

1800-1820   Similar tongs, decorated in the Regency style. Bright-cut ornament on arms and restrained decoration on bowls. £8 – £15.

1820-1850   Similar tongs, but rather fussy decoration in mid-Victorian style. £5 – £12.

Sugar tongs in Sheffield plate were made in the 'bow' style and parallel the decoration found on silver tongs of the same period. £7 – £15.

Points to look for

Full hallmarking on examples before about 1790 is rare and highly desirable. Tongs made by the more renowned silversmiths are much sought after as minor examples of their work, and the presence of their

Left to right: Old English thread pattern by Thomas Northcote, 1795; variety of Old English thread pattern by Nathaniel Smith, Sheffield, 1789; fiddle, thread and shell pattern by T.B., 1813; fiddle pattern by S.B.I.B., 1810; variety of fiddle pattern by T.T., Dublin, 1821, notice the repair.

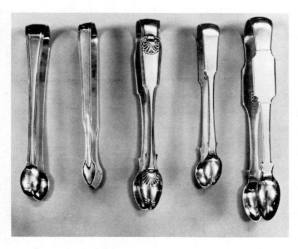

marks adds 50-75% to the value of tongs. Storr marked examples would increase the value three or four-fold.

Pitfalls

Many examples suffer metal fatigue with constant use and will have been repaired. With the earlier tongs, look for mends halfway down the arms, at the top and at the pivot. Often the design is so finely balanced that careless mending would destroy the symmetry. Later 'cast' or 'bow' tongs are also subject to breakage and mends can usually be detected near the tops of the arms. Beware of examples whose broken arches have been clumsily repaired with additional strips of silver wire. Asparagus tongs with metal springs concealed inside them are extremely difficult to repair once broken. For repaired tongs deduct 50% for neat mends, 70% for clumsy repairs.

TREEN

Generic term for anything made of wood, though usually confined to smaller articles. From the collector's viewpoint it is a convenient term for miscellaneous objects whose common denominator is the material of which they are largely or wholly constructed. Treen was formerly used extensively in the kitchen and the home. Wooden measures, trenchers, platters, bowls and utensils, spoons and spirtles were commonplace in the homes of the lower classes up to the middle of the 18th century, when cheap earthenware crockery and pewter flatware gradually superseded it. Nevertheless wood remained the most popular medium for the manufacture of countless other objects in everyday use, from knitting needles to stay busks. Boxes of all sizes were popular as food containers until recently, while kitchen articles, such as bread or cheeseboards, butter pats and biscuit moulds, continue to be produced to this day. There was a revival in the use of wood for utensils in the late 19th century, and this form of treen also survives to the present time, in salad bowls, fruit bowls, biscuit barrels and cake stands.

Selection of collectable treen items.

Irish lhamhog carved from solid willow 17th century. 7ins. high.

Goblet, early 18th century, marked W.S. on base, in fruit-wood. 17½ins. high.

Date-lines

For all practical purposes the treen available to the collector dates from the late 17th century. Good examples of turned goblets of that century are now scarce, and it is very difficult to distinguish original beakers and mugs of 1650 from more recent reproductions. As a rule, 17th century drinking vessels and wassail cups follow the contemporary pewter styles, tapered beakers with small handles on one side being the most popular design. Although turning was in use, many of the earlier utensils were hollowed by hand from a block of wood, and show evidence of gouge marks in the interior. The most popular wood for drinking vessels and food containers was beech, though chestnut and elm were also used extensively. Other woods which may also be found in late 17th century wares are alder, walnut, poplar, pearwood, yew, apple, lime and sycamore.

Although imported woods were being used in the late 17th century, the majority of articles in these timbers belong to the 18th century. Among the earlier imported woods to be used were pine, boxwood and maple; from 1720 onwards more exotic timbers, such as lignum vitae, ebony, mahogany and teak, were very popular. This is a rough guide only, since isolated, though well-documented examples of

Left to right: Oak goblet, 5ins. high; olive wood goblet, 6¼ins. high; fruitwood drinking cup, 5¼ins. high.

these rarer imported woods used in England are known from the 1530s. The zenith of treen vessels (including bowls and vases) was the period from 1720 to 1780, when the most elegant examples were finely turned in walnut, maple, mahogany and lignum vitae. The main problem confronting the collector is how to distinguish fine 18th century examples from the late 19th century revivals. In general 18th century examples were produced from a finer quality of timber — beautifully figured burr maple or glossy dark mahogany — and the quality of turning is more delicate. Late Victorian treen tended to use the lighter and cheaper mahogany and the turning is relatively coarse and clumsy, with thicker walls and stems. Victorian revivals tend also to be larger, measure for measure, than their 18th century counterparts.

Patination is an important factor, though this can be faked to a large extent and should not be regarded as an infallible guide in itself. There is an indefinable quality about genuine old treen, with a rich patina compounded of sunlight and atmospheric exposure, together with a lustrous polish worn smooth by age.

Points to look for

Treen articles are very seldom marked in any way to indicate the maker or date of manufacture. To a great extent, therefore, these factors are much less important than the type and quality of wood and

Mid-19th century quaich, a two-handled drinking cup.

the degree of skill and artistry evident in its production. Fine carving and intricate turning are plus factors in treen of any period. Most objects were produced as functional items and are devoid of ornament, relying simply on the natural grain of the wood and the style of the object itself. However, the addition of carved decoration on the rims of plates and goblets, greatly enhances the value. Especially prized are drinking vessels made from coconut shells with lightly engraved scenes and mottoes on their sides. Beware of genuine, but plain articles, which have been carved or engraved long after the date of manufacture, unless the reason for this late addition is self-evident (e.g. a presentation inscription). The decoration found on the rims of bowls and platters consists of sets of initials and dates (betrothals, marriages), mottoes or biblical quotations ('Give us this day our daily bread', etc.), simple floral emblems and geometric patterns. Similar forms of embellishment may also be found in pokerwork.

Kinds of Treen

Drinking vessels are the commonest, and also the most popular with collectors. They range from rather crudely gouged beakers (popular in Ireland and Scotland), to elegantly turned goblets and chalices. £5 – £40.

The most highly prized are coconut cups. Plain, polished coconut cups on turned stems and bases range from £30 to £60. Those with engraved motifs on the sides £50 – £100. Examples with silver mounts are very rare and are priced from £200 upwards.

At the other extreme egg-cups in treen have been in use from the 16th century to the present day and may range from 50p to £5, depending on age, quality and type of wood. Bowls form a large group, and include all manner of utensil, both useful and decorative. At one extreme are mazers, almost invariably turned from bird's-eye maple and belonging mainly to the 16th and 17th centuries. Relatively plain examples are £60 – £150, but those with additional carved ornament or silver foot rim or edge are £300 – £1,000. Quaichs are shallow

Scottish drinking vessels with one or two 'lugs' at right angles to the rim of the vessel, usually carved from a single piece of wood. Unfortunately quaichs were much reproduced in the 19th century and the majority of extant examples are of this period. Plain turned wooden quaichs are from £5 to £25. Those with silver mounts are from £20 to £50. Also worth looking for are quaichs composed of staves in contrasting colours of wood, thus producing a striped or diced pattern. This type is also being reproduced at the present day, though the quality is excellent. Shallow bowls for fruit, bread, cakes, etc. make elegant sideboard ornaments. Plain ones are difficult to date and are still being produced. £2 – £10. Decorative examples, especially those with dates, may be worth much more, if genuine.

Urns and vases in treen are relatively rare, though mainly produced in the late 18th century. Little demand for these larger items is reflected in their prices. £30 – £70. Miscellaneous kitchen treen includes rolling-pins, lemon-squeezers, potato-mashers, mincers, coffee-grinders, ladles, skimmers, salt-boxes, gingerbread, pastry and biscuit moulds, butter-pats, bread-boards and cheese-boards. There is no hard and fast market for this type of treen as yet, though these items are now very popular. Price should reflect quality, condition, type of wood and any decorative features.

Other types of treen worth considering include wooden boxes of all kinds designed for specific purposes (from church collecting-boxes to Victorian letter-boxes); wooden rulers and ferrules, yardsticks and folding rules; agricultural implements; clappers, rattles and knockers

Victorian letter box in finely grained Cuban mahogany inlaid with brass.

(used as bird-scarers); pipe-racks and letter-racks.

For specific types of decorative treen, see *Mauchline Ware, Tunbridge Ware.*

Museums
Bethnal Green Museum, London.
British Museum, London.
Guildhall Museum, London.
Victoria and Albert Museum, London.
Waddesdon Manor, Aylesbury.
Museum of Welsh Antiquities, Bangor.
Bowes Museum, Barnard Castle.
Ulster Folk Museum, Craigavad, Belfast.
City Museum and Art Gallery (Pinto Collection), Birmingham.
Blaise Castle Folk Museum, Henbury, Bristol.
Beamish Museum, Chester le Street.
National Museum of Antiquities, Edinburgh.
National Museum of Wales, Cardiff.
Royal Scottish Museum, Edinburgh.
Art Gallery and Museum, Glasgow.
Central Museum and Art Gallery, Northampton.
Museum of English Country Life, Reading.
Salisbury and South Wiltshire Museum, Salisbury.
Elizabethan House, Totnes.
Royal Tunbridge Wells Museum and Art Gallery, Tunbridge Wells.
Windsor Castle, Windsor.
Castle Museum, York.

Reading List
Buist, John S. Mauchline Ware. Edinburgh, 1974.
Gould, M.E. American Wooden Ware. Springfield, Mass. 1942. Household Life in America, 1620-1850. Rutland, Vt. 1965.
Pinto, Edward H. Treen, or Small Woodware through the Ages. London, 1949. Encyclopaedia and Social History of Treen and other Wooden Bygones. London 1969. Tunbridge and Scottish Souvenir Woodware. London, 1970.

TSUBA

A rare 17th century Higo tsuba, pierced with open fans.

Signed Toshinaga, late 17th-early 18th century. The signature is a gimei (false signature) but the guard is of good quality.

Japanese sword guards consisting of small flat plates, usually of more or less circular, oval or quatrefoil shape, though square, lozenge or completely irregular outlines are not unknown. The centre is pierced by an elongated slot to receive the nakago (tang) of the sword. The ha-machi is the notch at the base of the blade, on the edge, opposite the notch on the back (mune-machi). Tsuba may often be found with smaller slots to left and right of the main one, and these would have accommodated the blades of small knives carried *en suite* with the sword. Tsuba were originally produced by the swordsmiths and this established the tradition of using iron. Later, however, tsuba were mainly produced by armourers and at this point the more decorative styles began to emerge, and other metals were used instead of, or in conjunction with, iron.

Date-lines

The form of the Japanese sword was established by the 12th century and tsuba in their present guise had begun to emerge. Early tsuba are often extremely well forged from thin discs of iron. Ornament was confined to simple outlines, such as stars, within a circular frame. These discs were relatively large and relieved only by simple, stylised piercing.

14th-15th centuries	More decorative tsuba, with low relief landscapes.
15th-16th centuries	Heraldic emblems fashionable, with flowers and plant motifs in positive silhouette covering most of the plate.
16th century	Emergence of inlay work of bronze, silver or gold.

A superb guard.

Shakudo-nanako guard (cockerel and drum).

Unsigned, possibly of the Hamano School.

535

Late 19th century, shaped as a Buddhist gong with a woman holding a hossu and a girl with a sharito.

Reverse of a tsuba with signed untraced seal.

1570-1850	Very elaborate styles (*mukade* and *shingen* tsuba) involving wires of silver or copper woven on to iron plates, sometimes studded with silver or bronze nails. *Namban* tsuba characterised by beaded decoration (17th century).
1650-1850	Enamelling and coloured relief found on the more decorative court tsuba. Sword guards in general became more ornate in the late 18th and early 19th centuries.
19th century	Highpoint of the elaborately pierced tsuba (trees, flowers, outline animals) which, though very attractive, could not have been practical as sword guards.
1850-1900	Renaissance of earlier, more austere styles, coinciding with the revival of Bushido and traditional military values.

Points to look for

The quality of tsuba is of paramount importance. The forging should be even and flawless; watch for blow holes and pitting indicating poor or hurried forging. The quality of alloys may be determined by colour and patina. Thus *shakudo* and *shibuichi* (alloys of copper, silver and gold) should be rich lustrous violet-black and silver grey (but occasionally a deep greyish olive green) respectively. The greatest imponderable is craftsmanship, reflected in mastery of forging, inlay, carving, incision, piercing, enamelling and other metalwork techniques. Not only should these skills be handled competently, but they should be regarded in the context of the motif or design featured. Composition and balance are also important, though this is more subjective and tastes vary considerably. In general the more restrained decoration of the 17th century (and its late 19th century revival) will score heavily over the more flamboyant styles of the 18th and early 19th centuries (when the elaborate court ritual of the Shogunate was at its height).

The condition of tsuba is also extremely important. Much of the appeal of early tsuba lies in their subtle patination achieved by a variety of pickling processes. Plus factors are rich and unusual patina. Inlay work or enamelling should be intact: check high points of relief designs, or areas near the rim, for signs of wear and loss of inlay.

Pitfalls

Beware of tsuba which have become rusted or corroded through exposure to damp. Avoid examples of unnaturally bright appearance —

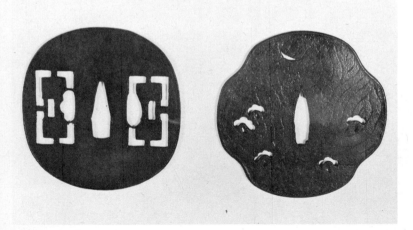

Two examples of rather poor quality. The left-hand example has an ill-formed hitsuana and that on the right, pierced with pines by moonlight, appears to have poor iron.

evidence of rust having been removed by burnishing. The Japanese attach great importance to the surface colour, quality and feel of old iron but it is essential that every trace of oil, wax and rust is removed before judging. Tsuba may only be rubbed with a cotton cloth.

Price Range

The value of tsuba is determined by quality, craftsmanship, unusual patina, decorative effects, subject matter and the school or individual maker. Age itself is not an important criterion, since many early, but relatively plain, tsuba are still in the range £25 – £50, whereas some late 19th century examples have passed £800 in auction.

Pierced openwork tsuba of the 18th-19th centuries, £60 – £100.

Plain surface tsuba with chiselled decoration, £50 – £80.

Tsuba with alloy inlays: simple brass strips, £50 – £80, gold, silver or enamels, £100 – £800.

Animals, battle scenes, human figures in whimsical situations, £150 – £800.

Museums

British Museum, London.
Bethnal Green Museum, London.
Royal Scottish Museum, Edinburgh.
City Museum and Art Gallery, Birmingham.
Chiddingstone Castle, Edenbridge, Kent.
City Museum and Art Gallery, Glasgow.
City of Liverpool Museum.
Museum and Art Gallery, Maidstone.
Whitworth Art Gallery, Manchester.
Museo Orientale, Venice.
Tokyo National Museum.
Field Museum of National History, Chicago.
Metropolitan Museum of Art, New York.

Reading List

Anderson, L.J. Japanese Armour. London, 1969.
Joly, H.L. Japanese Sword Mounts. London, 1910.
Robinson, Basil W. The Arts of the Japanese Sword. London, 1961.
Robinson, H. Russell. Oriental Armour. London, 1967. Japanese Arms and Armour. London, 1968.
Sasano, Masayuki. Sukaski Tsuba.
Yumoto, J.M. The Samurai Sword. London, 1958.

TUNBRIDGE WARE

Group of Tunbridge Ware boxes
Left to right, top row: Geometric top with mosaic sides; mosaic top with plain sides. Bottom row: Mosaic top, imitation stamp and plain sides (real Penny Red: add 20%); mosaic profile of Queen Victoria and mosaic sides; floral mosaic top and mosaic sides.

Name popularly given to small decorative woodware with a distinctive wood mosaic pattern. The name also applies, however, to decorative woodware made in the Tunbridge Wells and Tonbridge area from about 1660, covered with marquetry in deeply contrasting colours of wood. There are numerous contemporary references to 'Tunbridge ware' from the late 17th century onward, though the characteristic wood mosaic was not produced before 1820. The mosaic was composed of thin rods of wood of different types and colours, glued together to make a picture when viewed in section, and then cut into thin slices which could be affixed to the surface of boxes and other useful articles in the same manner as marquetry veneers.

Date-lines

1660-1700	Earliest Tunbridge ware consisted of small boxes decorated with floral marquetry, using veneers of holly, cherry, plum, yew and sycamore. Such boxes often additionally decorated with paint. £20 – £50.
1700-1730	As above, but arabesque marquetry and oyster-shell veneering. The more expensive boxes made of yew (£20 – £40); cheaper lines made of white wood, decorated with simple paint lines (£10 – £20).
1720-1750	Small boxes decorated with lacquer and inlaid with mother-of-pearl or ivory. Chinoiserie motifs popular. £15 – £40.
1750-1820	Much wider range of articles, including writing-sets, cribbage-boards, spill vases, napkin-rings, inlaid in the Sheraton style. Also used veneers treated to resemble tortoiseshell. £15 – £50 depending on size.
1790-1830	Cheaper, painted decorated woodware of natural wood, clear polished or varnished and decorated with oil paint, red, green and black predominating. Boxes, games boards, cup and ball sets, watch-stands and ring-holders known with a label inscribed 'A Trifle' or 'A Present from . . .' Examples recorded from South Coast resorts as well as Tunbridge Wells. £5 – £15.
1827-1887	Earliest mosaic ware produced by James Burrows whose first effort was a necklace for which he was paid two guineas. Enormous range of articles decorated with wood mosaic, from tiny rouge pots to Nye's chromatrope table (decorated with 129,540 tesserae and awarded a medal in the 1851 Exhibition). Most articles can be dated by the gummed label on the base giving the makers' addresses in The Parade (renamed The Pantiles in 1887). The dates of opening and closure of the various companies, and changes of partnership are given in Pinto's book (see **Reading List)** and enable more accurate dating. Prices for 'first period' wood mosaic articles are as follows:

Stamp boxes with tesserae profile of Queen Victoria, £10 – £15.

Stamp boxes with Penny Red stamp inlaid in geometric mosaic, £6 – £10.

Small boxes with geometric pattern, £5 – £8.

Small boxes with floral pattern or pictorial motif, £8 – £12

Other small decorative articles (napkin-rings), paper-knives, pin-cushions, needle-cases, etc.), £8 – £15.

Larger articles – inkstands, work-boxes, pencil-cases, picture-frames and large boxes – range from £30 to £200, depending on number of tesserae, intricacy of pattern and date.

Large boxes with a pictorial mosaic panel showing scenery or landmarks belong to the latter half of the 19th century. £70 – £150.

Exceptionally large items – chairs, tables, cabinets – are known, but are of the greatest rarity and now mostly in museum collections. £300 – £600.

1887-1910	'Second period' wood mosaic, using same 'end of grain' technique, but greater reliance on geometric motifs and fewer floral or scenic patterns. Mostly confined to small boxes, spill-holders, paper-knives and napkin-rings. Objects dated by their labels. £5 – £10.
1931-1940	Late revival of wood mosaic by Thomas Green. Small boxes with simple geometric designs, predominantly cube pattern. Boxes have their purpose lettered in mosaic on the lid (e.g. 'matches', 'pins', 'needles'). £2 – £5.

Points to look for

The greater number of tesserae involved, the more valuable the piece, is a useful rule of thumb. Portraits, identifiable views, birds and animals, floral subjects, butterflies and children are the more desirable subjects, in descending order. Objects composed of delicately lathe-turned stickware, decorated with wood mosaic (watch-stands, pen-stands, thimble boxes and napkin-rings, are more desirable than small boxes of comparable decoration and period. Unusual objects, such as puzzle boxes and dial-operated sovereign cases, are worth a good premium.

Pitfalls

A fair proportion of wood mosaic items are not marked by any label, and most of the earlier marquetry ware is not marked in any way at all. These articles must be judged solely on the quality of construction and the detail of their decoration. Watch for missing or damaged tesserae, particularly on lathe-turned stickware or the corners of boxes. Damage may have been caused by mis-handling, exposure to strong sunlight, heat or damp (which would warp thin veneers), or dropped carelessly. As it is virtually impossible to repair wood mosaic, such articles should not be purchased unless they are rare or unusual, or have rare motifs (birds or butterflies). A scratched surface is not so important if the mosaic is otherwise undamaged. The original varnish and french polish can be stripped and replaced.

Museums
Victoria and Albert Museum, London.
Birmingham Museum and Art Gallery (Pinto Collection).
Museum and Art Gallery, Brighton.
City Museum, Hereford.
Central Museum and Art Gallery, Northampton.
Salisbury and South Wiltshire Museum, Salisbury.
Royal Tunbridge Wells Museum and Art Gallery.

Reading List
Pinto, Edward H. and Eva R. Tunbridge and Scottish Souvenir Woodware. London, 1970.

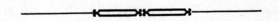

TYPEWRITERS

Writing machines have exercised the mind of man since the early 18th century, when Henry Mill took out a patent for an appliance 'for the impressing or inscribing of letters, singly or progressively, one after the other as in writing'. Mill's machine was clumsy and impractical and more than a century elapsed before further attempts were made to devise a writing machine. Patents were taken out by W.A. Burt in the United States (1829), Progrin in France (1833) and Thurber in the United States (1843) without practical success. In 1868 C. Latham Sholes, Samuel W. Soule and Carlos Glidden of Milwaukee took out a patent for a writing machine which they perfected over the ensuing five years. The first practical Sholes-Glidden machines were sold commercially in 1873. All the basic features of the modern typewriter were incorporated in the Sholes-Glidden machine: the QWERTY keyboard arrangement, a wooden spacer bar, vulcanised india rubber platen, shift mechanism and type-bars grouped in a semi-circle, so that the depression of a key brought the type face down on to an inked ribbon. The Sholes-Glidden machines were manufactured by E. Remington and Sons of Ilion, N.Y. and this company purchased the sole rights to the typewriters in 1878.

Date-lines do not apply to this subject, since the period in which the collectable varieties was produced is very brief, from 1873 to 1914. Typewriters were an instant success and by 1880 vast numbers were being produced in the United States by more than a dozen major companies. They were exported in large numbers to Europe, though indigenous manufacture began there in the early 1880s. Because of the Remington patents, the early rivals in this field had to devise their own systems and this explains the multiplicity of designs in the first quarter century. The various types of machine are discussed according to their principal technical features.

Keyboard and Type-bar Machines

The machines in this group are by far the most numerous, and include all typewriters in which impressions are made by type carried at the ends of levers or type-bars which strike the paper when the keys are depressed. The earliest Remingtons had one key for each character and these are the most desirable in this group. £50 – £80.

Other early keyboard and type-bar machines with single-character keys include the Fitch (with key-bank mounted behind the platen), the New Century Calligraph and the Yost (with eight banks of keys – the largest number produced in one machine). £40 – £70.

Two-character keys on Remington machines, 1890-1910, are still fairly plentiful and such machines are of relatively little value. A small premium for machines with early dates (1890-1900) on their patent plates. £20 – £30.

The other early type-bar machines may be further categorised according to their inking device. Those using an inking pad, brought in contact with the key before it is struck, are relatively scarce. Machines in this group include the Williams (with two key banks, in front of and behind the platen) and the Yost already mentioned. £40 – £75.

Type-bar machines using an inked ribbon, drawn along by the action of the machine between the type-face and the paper, are more common. Of these, the more conventional in appearance include the Empire, Densmore, Fay-Sho and the Smith Premier. £30 – £45.

More elaborate machines in this group include the Bar-Lock, with vertical keys in a semi-circle and unusual keyboard arrangements. £40 – £60.

The Oliver typewriters had the type-bars grouped in two banks, mounted to the left and right of the platen. Machines of this design were still being marketed down to about 1920 and are by no means rare, but their bizarre appearance enhances their value. £25 – £35.

The heavy table model of typewriter on the Remington pattern became standardised about 1920, when the original Remington patents expired. Machines after this date are of little interest to collectors and can usually be picked up in the second-hand market for £5 – £15.

Keyboard and Type-cylinder Machines

In the cylindrical machines the characters are mounted on a cylinder or sleeve and the striking of a key produces a combined lateral and rotary motion for bringing the particular type-face to the printing

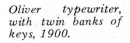

Oliver typewriter, with twin banks of keys, 1900.

Blickensderfer
"Service Blick"
typewriter, 1892.

point. For every separate impression the entire cylinder has usually to make two movements of variable length. These instruments were much noisier and slower than the type-bar machines, and rapidly died out after 1900. Nevertheless the cylinder system is the direct forebear of the modern electronic typewriter with its 'golf-ball' type head. Like the modern electronic machines, the cylindrical machines possessed two important advantages: the type was variable in size (giving more space to broad letters), and different type-faces could be used by changing the cylinders. Machines of this type include the Chicago, the Crandall, the Blick (or Blickensderfer) and the Hammond. £40 − £75.

Wheel Machines

Typewriters of this design had the characters placed at the periphery of a large wheel by the manual rotation of which any desired type-face could be brought into position for printing. Once the wheel was set, a hammer device punched the impression on to the paper. Wheel machines had the advantage of being very much cheaper than keyboard machines, and had the advantages of variable spacing and interchangeability possessed by the cylinder machines. But their chief drawback was their inordinate slowness − much slower than cursive handwriting and attaining barely a tenth of the speed which could be achieved on the Remington machines. It is difficult to appreciate what purpose the wheel machines achieved, except that by 1890 a typewritten letter was coming to be regarded as much more professional than a handwritten one, in business circles at least. Wheel machines were usually equipped with a dial and pointer so that the user could see which type-face was in position.

Wheel machines were produced mainly by the Columbia Typewriter Company and of these the machines of 1886-1890 are the most collectable. £50 − £75.

A Lambert typewriter by the Gramophone & Typewriter Co. Ltd., c.1903, with instruction book.

Later Columbia machines, and those produced by the Lambert Company. £35 − £50.

Points to look for

The great majority of typewriters can easily be dated by means of a small plate, or inscription (usually at the back of the machine) giving patent numbers and dates, always bearing in mind that the actual year of manufacture may be some time after the latest date shown on the patent plate. In the highly competitive world of the typewriter industry at the turn of the century, however, improvements and modifications were made at frequent intervals and it is fairly safe to say that the date of manufacture will be soon after the latest date shown on the plate. Machines should be in good working condition and such defects as missing or broken keys, broken springs and the absence of ribbon spools of the correct type detract from the value of machines in the period 1885-1910 by 20-30%. Machines before 1885 are rare in any condition. The smaller machines, such as the Empire and the Blickensderfer, were intended as portables and are worth a good premium if still intact with their original wooden carrying cases and bases. Decorative features, including transfer-printed motifs, gilding and enamelling, enhance the value of early machines, but make sure that the paintwork is original and in reasonably good condition. Metal parts were usually of nickel-plated steel. The nickelling is frequently found to be defective as a result either of wear or of exposure to damp conditions. Re-nickelling is expensive, and machines with plating in poor condition should be heavily discounted.

Museums

Science Museum, London.
British Typewriter Museum, Bournemouth.(by appointment only).

Beamish Museum, Chester le Street.
Museum of the History of Science, Oxford.

VALENTINES

The custom of exchanging tokens of affection on St. Valentine's Day, 14th February, dates back to the Middle Ages, but the practice of sending a *billet doux* inscribed with amatory verses dates from the late 17th century. The custom was not commercialised until the early 19th century and was slow to catch on, because of the relatively high costs of postage which treated envelopes as 'additional sheets' chargeable at double the normal rates of postage. With the introduction of cheap postage in 1840 the custom spread rapidly, attaining its zenith about 1870. Thereafter it declined, reaching its nadir at the turn of the century when the satirical or derogatory Valentines were fashionable and almost totally eliminated the sentimental nature of the custom. The practice of sending Valentines died out during the First World War but revived in the 1920s and reached its peak in the late 1950s. Since then rising postal charges and the costs of producing lavish cards have led to a marked decline again.

Date-lines

1815-1840   First period of commercial Valentines. Tasteful motifs copper-plate engraved and hand-coloured. Borders of

Left: Valentine with slightly tinselled lace work, and a tape near the top which when pulled forward, exposes a poem.
Right: Friendship valentine c.1845-1850. Brightly coloured, hand painted in an ornate paper lace setting.

	cards and matching envelopes embossed in albino floral decoration. £10 – £20 (without envelope); £25 – £100 if complete with envelope, depending on postal markings.
1840-1870	Cards becoming increasingly ornate, with embossed, fretted and pierced 'lacy' borders. Increasing use of chromo-lithography for the pictorial centre-piece. £3 – £10 (without envelope); £20 – £50 (with envelope).
1855-1875	Cards mounted with scraps and overlays of lacy paper. £3 – £8.
1860-1875	Cards decorated with pressed flowers, ferns, real lace, feathers, glass paste jewels. £10 – £30 (without envelope); £25 – £70 (with envelope).
1870-1890	Novelty Valentines (folding paper fans, pop-up cards or animated cards, unusual shapes, cobweb designs). £8 – £20; add 100% if complete with envelope in postally used condition.
1880-1900	Plainer Valentines with satirical messages. Fold-over type £2 – £5; add 50% if complete with postally used envelope.
1900-1914	Valentine postcards: sentimental type 50p – £1.50; satirical £1 – £3.
1920-1940	Inter-war period: sentimental postcard type 20 – 50p postally used. Unused postcard types 10 – 20p. Fold-over types have little market value as yet unless they have a pronounced Art Deco flavour.

Points to look for

Early examples of cruel or malicious cards of the fold-over variety, outwardly following the fashion of the lacy cards, are worth looking for. They were certainly being produced by 1860, but few of the early examples were considered worth preserving by their unfortunate recipients. Apart from the very ornate sentimental cards of 1860-75, the most desirable cards are those with a military, naval or patriotic theme woven into the Valentine message. Especially prized by American collectors are cards of 1861-65 with allusions to the Civil War. Cards with a musical motif and those resembling miniature sheets of music are worth a good premium. Sentimental cards produced as parodies of postal stationery postcards or even banknotes are now highly prized.

Pitfalls

The collage cards of the 1860s are difficult to find in really fine condition, since many of the components were perishable or extremely

Left: Valentine c.1870, paper lace on thick pink velvet, with a poem inside.
Right:A Victorian valentine decorated with floral motifs, cherubs and motto "Constant to Thee", within a lacework border.

fragile. Beware of relatively plain, embossed-edged cards which have had lace, feathers, flowers, ferns, shells etc. added to them long after the actual period of manufacture.

Museums
British Museum, London.
National Postal Museum, London.
Victoria and Albert Museum, London.
Beamish Museum, Chester le Street.
City Museum and Art Gallery, Birmingham.
City Museum, Hereford.
Museum and Art Gallery, Leicester.
Central Museum and Art Gallery, Northampton.
Salisbury and South Wiltshire Museum, Salisbury.
City Museum, Sheffield.
Blithfield House, Rugeley.
Elizabethan House, Totnes.
Royal Tunbridge Wells Museum and Art Gallery.
City Museum and Art Gallery, Worcester.
Castle Museum, York.

Reading List
Lee, Ruth W. A History of Valentines. London, 1953.
Staff, Frank. The Valentine and its Origins. London, 1969.

VESTA BOXES

Small boxes used as containers for vestas or wax matches, popular in the latter part of the 19th century. Vestas came into use in the 1830s but distinctive cases for them did not develop until a generation later, and their heyday was the period from 1880 to the First World War. Vesta boxes were made of silver, silver-plated metal, wood, ivory, vulcanite, mother-of-pearl and even pottery and porcelain. A few rare examples are known in gold and semi-precious stones. Silver boxes usually have gilding on the inner side to prevent the sulphur in the match heads acting chemically with the silver.

Date-lines

1835-1854	The earliest boxes were converted from other small boxes, such as vinaigrettes or snuffboxes. These 'snuffbox' types are usually beautifully engraved and engine-turned and were mainly produced in London. £20 – £50.
1854-1868	Boxes made specifically for matches, but still following the format of the earlier snuffboxes, with the lid along the top of the box. £15 – £30.
1868-1890	Earliest boxes with the lid set in the end or one side. Boxes also being made with rounded corners. Still predominantly London, though now also being made in Birmingham. Common rectangular or oval shapes from £6 to £12.

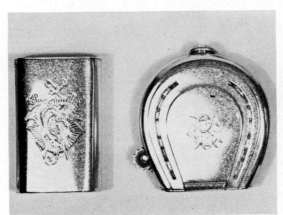

Left: Early end-opening box. Right: Interesting example with enclosed wick.

1890-1914   Majority of silver boxes now made in Birmingham; London markings are rare. Period during which most of the novelty shapes and combination boxes (see below) were produced, as well as those in other materials. Vesta boxes died out during the First World War, when ordinary match-boxes and petrol lighters superseded them. Rare examples are known with hallmarks as late as 1923. Silver boxes with engraved floral or leaf decoration. £5 – £12.

Silver-plated boxes and boxes in other materials. £4 – £8.

Early snuffbox types.

Other Types and Shapes

The details given above relate only to the normal rectangular or oval shapes with plain interiors. Variety may be found, however, in shape and construction. Unusual shapes include completely circular, heart, shield, peardrop, kidney. £12 – £20 for silver; two-thirds these prices for silver-plate.

Novelty boxes, in the shape of musical instruments, bottles, flasks, animals, horseshoes, champagne corks, boots, etc. are in great demand. £10 – £30.

Enamelled boxes in the form of miniature sentry boxes are rare. £25 – £40+.

Vesta boxes were often produced in the shape of books, with a striker down the fore-edge. The majority of these are in white metal or silver-plate. £7 – £12.

Examples in wood or vulcanite are scarce and rate from £12 to £20. Books in silver are rare. £25 – £50.

A very rare type resembles a visiting card and was made in Sheffield. £25 – £40.

Boxes of a commemorative nature may be found with relief portraits of royalty. £15 – £30.

Other boxes with pictorial motifs – landmarks, scenery, animals and birds. £15 – £25.

Novelty boxes, mostly base metal.

Vesta boxes were sometimes fitted with compartments for other purposes, or with gadgets associated with smoking. In the first group come book-shaped boxes with a compartment in the back for sovereigns (usually a spring-loaded circular platform) or stamps (look for the tell-tale ridge dividing the shallow compartment into two stamp-sized spaces). Vesta boxes with stamp or coin compartments are worth from £15 to £30; those incorporating both features are rare and rate £35 – £50.

Boxes with a miniature compass inset or a whistle rate from £15 to £30.

A few early boxes incorporated a wick or taper and these can be identified by a narrow wick compartment and a serrated wheel by which the wick was raised and lowered. These cases were mainly produced in London. £30 – £50.

Book vesta boxes.

Boxes combining penknives, tooth-picks, button-hooks and pencils were produced in the 1880s, but are very rare. £40 — £60.

Boxes with secret opening devices or trick catches are among the earliest produced and are also rare. £35 — £60.

Points to look for

Unusual treatment, or personalised inscriptions (especially with dates) add considerably to the value of boxes. Silver boxes should be fully hallmarked on the bezel, and have a pair of matching marks on the inside of the lid.

Pitfalls

The serious collecting of vesta boxes is too recent, and the material still reasonably plentiful, for it to have become worthwhile producing modern imitations. The only problem centres on the conversion of boxes to form vesta cases, by the addition of the serrated metal striker. Examine the edge bearing the striker and determine whether the decoration continues behind it, or terminates at the edge of it. The presence of hallmarks on the striker, or decorative features not in accordance with the overall pattern of the box, would also indicate that the striker was an afterthought. However, it should be borne in mind that the earliest boxes were snuffboxes or vinaigrettes converted to the purpose, and in these cases it will be obvious that the strikers were later additions.

Museums

London Museum, London.
Art Gallery and Museum, Brighton.
City Museum, Hereford.
Museum and Art Gallery, Leicester.
Central Museum and Art Gallery, Northampton.
Salisbury and South Wiltshire Museum, Salisbury.
Royal Tunbridge Wells Museum and Art Gallery.
City Museum and Art Gallery, Worcester.

Reading List

Bedford, John. All Kinds of Small Boxes. London, 1964.
Delieb, Eric. Silver Boxes. London, 1968.

VINAIGRETTES

Small silver boxes, devised to hold small sponges soaked in acetic acid and aromatic spices as an antidote to contagious diseases and pestilence. In practice, however, the strongly smelling acid and spices would have counteracted the foetid stench in an age when personal hygiene was virtually non-existent. Vinaigrettes became popular in the 1780s, largely as a result of a series of lectures by Dr. William Henry on the subject of prophylaxis. These boxes can easily be identified by their heavily gilded interiors (to prevent corrosion from the vinegar) and the presence of a perforated inner lid, designed to hold the sponge in place. Vinaigrettes were largely superseded by 1860, when the double-ended scent bottle became fashionable, though isolated examples are known bearing hallmarks down to the end of the 19th century.

Various types of vinaigrettes.

Date-lines

1780-1820   Small rectangular boxes; earliest relatively plain externally, though grille perforated in an elaborate geometric or floral pattern. The larger ones are seldom hallmarked fully before 1790, while the smallest (and commonest) type of this period was invariably exempt from hallmarking on grounds of size. £30 – £60.

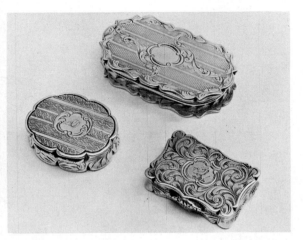

Typical Victorian Cases with shaped outlines. Left to right: by Francis Clark, Birmingham 1847; an oval by Edward Smith, Birmingham 1855; a rectangular form, maker D.P., Birmingham 1815.

Circular or polygonal vinaigrettes of the same period. £40 – £100.

Novelty shapes (fishes, crowns, animals, purses, scallop shells, eggs, flower baskets, etc.). £50 – £500.

Silver vinaigrettes with agate, tortoiseshell or mother-of-pearl panelling are relatively uncommon, but not particularly desirable. £25 – £40.

Gold vinaigrettes are rare before 1820. £160 – £250.

1820-1840   Increasing use of floral and foliate ornament on the cover. The introduction of machine embossing resulted in highly ornate patterns but these are fairly plentiful. £30 – £75.

1830-1860   Zenith of the pictorial vinaigrette. Mainly rectangular, with panels worked in high relief, depicting castles, cathedrals and prominent landmarks. £120 – £250.

1800-1840   Portrait vinaigrettes, especially those showing Lord Nelson, produced by die-stamping or acid etching. £250 – £400.

1840-1860   Continental vinaigrettes in enamelled silver, silver-gilt or porcelain (Vienna, Limoges, Meissen). £30 – £80.

Points to look for

The most highly prized examples are those bearing the marks of the following makers: Samuel Pemberton, Matthew Linwood, Nathaniel Mills, Joseph Willmore and Joseph Taylor, all working in the Birmingham area. Birmingham vinaigrettes, when hallmarked, bear the anchor mark, while those of London have the leopard's head mark. The most desirable vinaigrettes are the novelty, scenic and portrait types, in ascending order.

555

Left to right: 19th century Viennese vinaigrette on silver chain; vinaigrette in the form of a gold ring engraved with a floral design; gold vinaigrette on a watch type chain. The last two are quite rare but being unmarked would not reach their true value.

Pitfalls

Vinaigrettes should be complete, with the inner perforated grille intact. Many examples were subsequently converted to pill boxes, comfit boxes or lockets by the removal of the grille; such hybrids are best left alone. Beware of new grilles and the later engraving of plain examples with interesting scenes.

Museums

British Museum, London.
Victoria and Albert Museum, London.
City Museum and Art Gallery, Birmingham.
Royal Scottish Museum, Edinburgh.
Museum and Art Gallery, Leicester.
City Museum, Sheffield.
City Museum and Art Gallery, Stoke-on-Trent.
Elizabethan House, Totnes.
Windsor Castle, Windsor.
City Museum and Art Gallery, Worcester.

Reading List

Delieb, Eric. Silver Boxes. London, 1968.
Ellenbogen, Eileen. English Vinaigrettes. Cambridge, 1956.

WALKING STICKS

Sticks and canes developed out of the stout staves carried by travellers in the Middle Ages. These sticks were intended mainly for defence and were therefore undecorated. Shorter and more elegant sticks became fashionable in Europe in the late 15th century and the fashion spread to England, developing during the reigns of Henry VII and Henry VIII. Thereafter canes and walking sticks became increasingly important dress accessories. With the decline in the formality of men's wear since the end of the First World War the carrying of walking sticks has gradually decreased in popularity, being largely superseded by the rolled umbrella.

Date-lines

1660-1700	The earliest sticks were fairly short, but became progressively longer in the 1680s. Sticks made of native woods, topped by an ornamental head of silver or ivory, often festooned with ribbons. £20 – £40.
1700-1730	Sticks either quite short or very long, made of malacca, bamboo, myrtle, kingwood, with a silver ferrule (tip) and very elaborate heads of gold, silver, agate or clouded amber. In the most elaborate types the heads unscrew to reveal a tiny mirror or pot of scent or snuff. Those with intricately carved heads are worth a high premium. £25 – £100+.
1730-1750	Temporary fashion for very heavy clubs and cudgels, emulating the lower classes, but surmounted by large

Left to right: Whistle; pencil; dice; lady's pill box; lady's powder box; elegant pencil, all common examples.

Left to right: Smokers' canes, cigarettes emerging from shaft (known only by patent — 1928); vesta box, silver, late 19th century, cigarettes in cane, both commonly found.

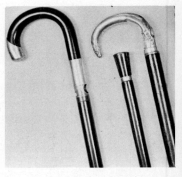

Left to right: Walking sticks with lights. Light below handle; light in amber handle; light in silver crutch.

	wooden heads carved in grotesque or fantastic styles — 'great heads and ugly faces thereon' (1739). £20 — £40.
1750-1800	Taper switches — short, whippy lengths of cane tapering to a point, with a very elaborate head, usually carved in ivory or cast in silver. £25 — £50.
1760-1790	Excessively long sticks (up to 6 feet in length), usually of hardwood, with a silver or gold top. £35 — £100+.
1770-1830	Heyday of the stick with a porcelain handle. Numerous styles and shapes (round or elongated knobs, T-shape, curved handles), often modelled in human or animal form or lavishly decorated with underglaze polychrome motifs. Similar handles used in canes and ladies' parasols. Value depends largely on factory and decorative appeal. £50 — £170.
	Meissen example, £500+.
1750-1800	Sticks with handles of Staffordshire enamel. Truncated cones or spheres with typical Bilston or Birmingham enamel motifs. £60 — £120.
1800-1840	Vogue for sticks with very elaborately carved heads and handles, decorated with human or animal figures. £30 — £70.
1840-1920	Plain sticks of malacca or plain hardwood, decorated with a simple gold or silver band (to conceal the join) and topped by a small gold or silver cap. Ornament reduced to

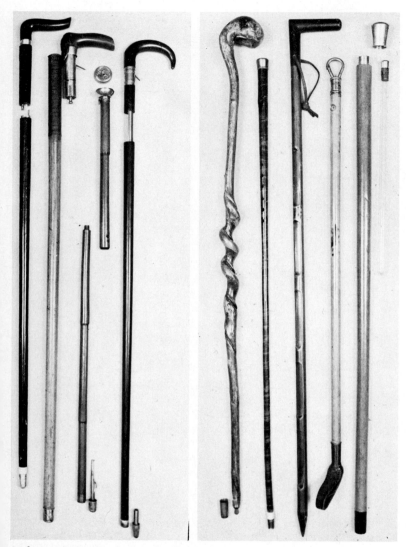

Left to right: Two-shot pistol, French patent, rare; revolver, identical but different cane presentation; blow gun, patented 1876, rare; shotgun, very common.

Various canes. Long pipe, rare example. Flute; wheat tester; with hook for bridle and watch on side of cane; riding whip, signed Dupuy in Paris, common examples. Crystal flask and silver tumbler make the far right example an outstanding piece and highly desirable.

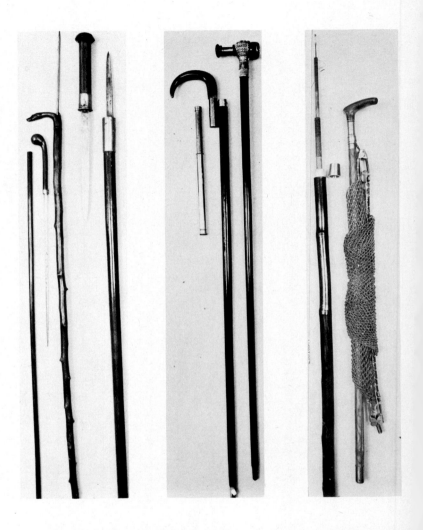

Left to right: Ladies' dagger, 19th century, rare; dagger flips out of handle, head of dog, metal, common; two hands stick, turn of the century, very rare.

Optical canes. Small telescope inside cane, common 19th century; rare opera glass, early 19th century and expensive because of the gilded bronze gauntlet holding the lens.

Fishermen's canes. Cane telescopes by a throwing movement; rare fishing net.

560

	a minimum — the owner's monogram, coat of arms or regimental insignia. £10 – £40.
1870-1910	Long canes of ebony, surmounted by extravagant decoration: either carved ivory or silver. Silver ball or truncated cone decorated with repoussé figures, or cast in unusual shapes (horses' heads, dancing girls, etc.). Silver-topped sticks with Art Nouveau motifs very desirable. £25 – £80.
1880-1920	Sticks provided with curved cane handles. Sticks usually of cherry or ash; handles occasionally leather-covered. £5 – £15.
1890-1910	Revival of canes with porcelain crutch handles, mostly by Continental potteries. The porcelain marks are a useful guide in distinguishing these late 19th century canes from those of 1770-1830. £30 – £60.
1880-1900	Ornamental walking sticks made of coloured glass; purely for decoration and impractical for outdoor use. £10 – £20. Superior coloured twisted glass (red/blue/green/yellow). £20 – £55.

Points to look for

Walking sticks which incorporate other devices are worth a good premium. The commonest is the sword-stick, introduced about 1780, when the wearing of swords went out of fashion. The majority of sword-sticks have malacca cases, gold or silver tops and mounts and blades of Toledo steel, the best being made with Solingen (German) blades. Antique sword-sticks of this type are in the price range £30 – £60. Sword-sticks of ebony with silver handles are slightly less desirable (£25 – £40), while those in cherry or ash are of more recent vintage (£20 – £30).

Beware of black ebony sticks with "Lion" pommels and "Judia" on the blades; these are reproductions produced in the early 1900s. Sticks may be found concealing air canes (an early form of air gun), favoured by poachers in the mid-19th century. Uncased, £30 – £50; with case and accessories, £100 – £250.

A few walking sticks conceal a pistol in the handle, and were produced mainly in the early 19th century. Uncased, £40 – £100; with case and accessories, £100 – £250.

Other objects concealed in walking stick handles include spirit flasks, measuring yards, telescopes, saw-blades, silver/gold snuffboxes, compasses, sovereign cases, watches or fishing lines. £30 – £100 depending on technical features. With a good gold watch top, c.1850, up to £300+.

Bludgeoning sticks. These are fairly common, especially those with lead-weighted handles.

Pitfalls

Silver tops or handles are difficult to date before about 1790, since few of them were marked prior to that date, except for the maker's mark. A major problem therefore is the verification that the top and stick match each other chronologically. Handles themselves are quite collectable in their own right. Condition of sticks is relatively unimportant, except for sword-sticks or other hollow types concealing gadgets. Beware of examples of these sticks in which the cases show signs of splitting.

Museums

London Museum, London.
Victoria and Albert Museum, London.
Art Gallery and Museum, Brighton.
National Museum of Wales, Cardiff.
Royal Scottish Museum, Edinburgh.
Windsor Castle, Windsor.
York Castle Museum, York.

Reading List

Boothroyd, A.E. Fascinating Walking Sticks. London, 1973.

WATCH STANDS

Holders for pocket watches when not carried on the person, often designed to convert the watch into a miniature clock for the table or mantelpiece. Watch stands date from the 17th century and were produced in various materials, notably porcelain, pottery, wood, glass, silver and brass. They continued to be produced until about 1920, when the wrist watch superseded the pocket watch in general use, and such stands were no longer required to any extent. Date-lines are not as important as the material and type of stand. Generally speaking, the porcelain stands resembling contemporary mantel and bracket clocks, belong to the 18th century, though examples were still being made as late as 1860; Staffordshire pottery stands date from the early 1800s to about 1880; wooden stands became popular about 1800 and remained fashionable till the First World War, and the various cased or travelling watch stands date from the second half of the 19th century. Glass and gilt metal stands, often decorated with scenic vignettes, belong mainly to the late 19th and early 20th centuries.

Types of Watch Stand
Stands resembling clock cases were modelled in porcelain from the late 1740s onward. The earlier examples, by Meissen, Sèvres, Chelsea and other leading factories of the mid-18th century, were in the prevailing rococo fashion, lavishly decorated with asymmetrical scrollwork, putti, allegorical figures, birds, animals and flowers, richly painted and gilded. The value of these elaborate stands depends largely on the manufacturer and the period. A mid-18th century example like the Meissen vase-longcase dedicated to Handel, 1759, is now in excess of £1,000, but late 18th and early 19th century examples are usually in the price range £50 – £100. French faience longcases with delicately painted vignettes, £100 – £160.
Stands in the form of miniature longcase clocks, with a circular recess to hold the watch, were an English speciality of the early 19th century, and were usually more simply decorated, though often incorporating a pair of tiny figures on either side. The 'longcase' variety was also modelled in Prattware. £100 – £250.
Staffordshire Pottery Stands consist mainly of flatback figure groups incorporating a circular frame to contain the watch. The more colourful examples belong to the first half of the 19th century, whereas the groups from the latter half of the century tend to have rather more

Tyrolean type travelling watch stands. Top row: simplest types without applied ornaments. Bottom left: probably Austrian. Bottom right: from Ragaz, Switzerland.

the Continent in the late 19th and early 20th centuries and may be found in many different types of wood, with inlaid or painted motifs relating to tourist resorts. £10 – £30.

Pull-out Holders constitute an important variant of the last type, deriving their name from the fact that the solid wood holder slides forward from inside and turns back on pin hinges to rest on the back part at an angle. Again, a very popular form of 19th century tourist souvenir from the Holy Land to the Black Forest, and also found in Mauchline or Tunbridge ware. £15 – £40.

Tyrolean Stands were a speciality of Austria, Switzerland and southern Germany. Superficially these ornately carved stands resemble the belly of a violin or a balloon clockcase. These cases are hinged at the foot and when opened one side is turned back on the other to form the stand. They are characterised by elaborate fluting and carving and remained popular until the early 1920s. £7 – £15.

Glass and Metal Stands consist of a glass frame for the watch itself, supported on a metal stand. Many rather whimsical designs, including chairs, mirrors and gong-stands, often decorated with cast or embossed metal ornament. Found in gilt brass, German silver or electroplate and apparently popular at the turn of the century. £10 – £20.

Travelling watch holders with hinged lids. Left: olive with ebony corners, lid with marquetry roundel, sides with strips and mosaics, holder supported by brass strut and stepped ratchet, Sorrento ware. Centre: walnut veneer overlaid by cut-out brass patterns pinned with china balls, holder similarly decorated, first half 19th century, English. Right: rosewood, lid inlaid with brass, ivory and burr-wood, sides with ivory lines and edges gadrooned, Regency.

Glass Stands were made in France and the Low Countries mainly and consisted of thick, bevelled glass reinforced by gilt-metal and often embellished with photographic scenes pasted to the reverse of the glass. £5 – £15.

Box Holders are hinged wooden boxes of various designs which, when opened, enable the watch stand to rise up on springs. Yet another popular souvenir type with many different styles of decoration. £20 – £50.

Ivory or Bone Stands of the single pillar, double pillar or wellhead type, mainly produced in India and Persia in the late 19th century. Often very elaborately fretted and carved, or decorated with sadeli mosaic and inlay. £50 – £120.

Cast brass was used early in the 18th century with rococo and costume characteristics, and motifs taken from agriculture and the Gothic arts. Some of these designs were copied in iron, particularly in the period of the romantic revival.

WEAPONS Bayonets

Edged weapons used by infantry to convert their muskets into pikes. The name is thought to be derived from the French town of Bayonne. In their earliest form, dating from the late 17th century, bayonets were simply long knives with a plug handle which was rammed into the muzzle of the musket after it had been discharged and close quarter fighting was inevitable. Subsequently various methods of attaching the bayonet to the musket were evolved, permitting the weapon to be fired even when the bayonet was fixed. The styling and method of fixing bayonets has changed gradually over the past 250 years, reflecting changes in infantry tactics. Although modern warfare is faster and with much greater emphasis on fire power, the bayonet is still standard equipment in most armies and a wide variety of types may be found at the present day.

Date-lines
1670-1730   Plug bayonets, tapering wooden handles, blades short and broad at the base. £75 – £300. In 1975 a really fine silver-mounted specimen realised £550.

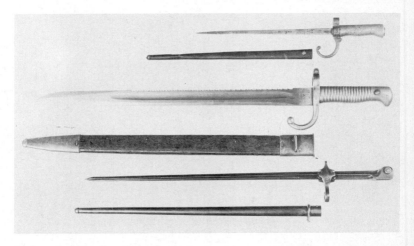

Top to bottom:
A miniature epée bayonet styled on the French M1886; a rare Belgian M.1888 brass-hilted sawback sword bayonet; a rare Swiss Model 1892 all-steel bayonet with cruicform section blade.

1730-1840	Socket bayonets, plug superseded by a fitting ring attached to the grip, to fit over the muzzle. Blades gradually becoming longer and slimmer. £10 – £40.
1840-1900	Slot and spring device for fixing bayonets on to a boss on the underside of the muzzle. Hey-day of the sword-bayonet, with blades up to 21 inches in length. Handles longer and more complex, resembling contemporary swords. Very wide variety of styles. £10 – £50.
1900-1940	Slot and spring device as before, but bayonets becoming shorter and handles streamlined. Blades pointed, with one or two cutting edges, occasionally saw-toothed. £5 – £25.
1940-1960	Bayonets attained their greatest simplicity, with blades shortened to as little as 7 inches. Introduction of spike bayonet. £1 – £10.

Price Range

There is a fairly broad spectrum of prices according to period, but values depend largely on individual make and country of origin, and in some cases on subtle variations. Below are given some typical prices for relatively modern bayonets. **British WWI** 22in. £4 – £6; Bowie-bladed No. 7 13in. £5 – £15; British spike Mark I, 1939 £5 – £7; spike Mark II, 1940 £1 – £2.50; spike 'Victory' model £6 – £8.

German Mauser M-98 £3 – £5; Nazi K98s £5 – £7; Nazi naval dress bayonet £15 – £20.

Italian Storm troop dagger bayonet £5 – £8; Steyr-Snyder 24in., 1886 £6 – £10.

Japanese Arisaka 20in. £5 – £8.

Russian Cropatschek £8 – £12; Mosin-Nagant £4 – £6; folding knife-bayonet £8 – £10.

French Lebel £6 – £8.

American M-3 knife bayonet £8 – £10; M-4 £5 – £8; M-5 £5 – £6.

Portuguese Guedes £5 – £8; **Finnish** Mauser £4 – £6.

Points to look for

Bayonets should be complete with original scabbards and be in good condition with handles, fitting rings, sockets, etc. in complete and working order. Bayonets can usually be identified and dated fairly accurately by manufacturers' and armoury marks punched or engraved on the blade near the hilt. Markings are sometimes found also on handles and scabbards. Bayonets with unusual features are in great demand, e.g. the American 'trowel' bayonet with very broad blade (£20 – £25) or the Armalite AR 10 bayonet whose hilt contains a knife, penknife, corkscrew and screw-driver! (£10 – £15).

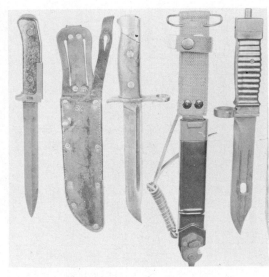

*Left to right:
A Czechoslovakian
M 1 9 5 8 knife
bayonet; a rare
Finnish M1939
Moisin Nagant
knife bayonet; a
rare experimental
wire - cutter
bayonet for the
German Heckler
and Koch G3 rifle.*

Museums — see *Militaria*

Reading List

Atwood, James P. The Daggers and Edged Weapons of Hitler's Germany. Berlin, 1965.

Bozich, Stan. German Relics, 1929-1945. Detroit, 1967.

Carter, J. Anthony. Allied Bayonets of World War II. London, 1969.

Cole, Howard M. U.S. Military Knives. Montgomery, Alabama, 1968.

ffoulkes, Charles and Hopkinson, E.C. Sword, Lance and Bayonet. London, 1967.

Hardin, Albert N. The American Bayonet, 1776-1964. Pennsylvania, 1964.

Mäurer, Hermann A. Military Edged Weapons of the World. New York, 1968.

Rollin, R.V. U.S. Sword Bayonets, 1847-1865. Pittsburgh, 1962.

Stephens, Frederick J. A Guide to Nazi Daggers, Swords and Bayonets. Bury, 1965. Bayonets — an illustrated History and Reference Guide. London, 1968. The Collector's Pictorial Book of Bayonets. London, 1971.

Walter, John D. and Hughes Gordon A. A Primer of World Bayonets. (2 vols.) Brighton, 1969.

Webster, Donald B. American Socket Bayonets, 1717-1873. Toronto, 1964.

Wilkinson-Latham, Robert J. British Military Bayonets, 1700-1945. London, 1967.

Daggers

Term denoting any form of fighting knife with a sharp point and usually two cutting edges. What distinguishes the dagger from the knife (q.v.) is its aggressive character as a cutting, slashing and stabbing weapon. Short edged weapons of this type have been in existence since time immemorial and are to be found all over the world. From a practical standpoint, however, they are limited to daggers dating from the end of the Middle Ages and are described below according to type and locality.

Ballock-knife, kidney dagger or dudgeon dagger. In use from about 1300 to 1700 in western Europe, especially Britain and the Low Countries. It derives its name from the spherical lobes at the base of the hilt. These daggers had long, straight blades tapering to a narrow point and had wooden handles of box or some other close-grained hardwood, terminating in a brass tang. £300 – £600.

Ear dagger or **Poignard à Creilles,** used in Spain and Italy in the 14th to 16th centuries. The name is derived from the twin splayed ends of the pommel. £300 to over £1,000.

Rondei Dagger. A dagger with solid disc guard and often disc pommel as well. Used by medieval knights, but beware of 19th century reproductions. £300 – £1,000.

Quillon dagger, the modern term for any dagger with a cruciform hilt, the quillons straight across or curving alternately upwards or downwards. £100 – £750.

Main Gauche or left-hand dagger, often made en suite with rapiers and used as a left-handed parrying weapon while the rapier was held in the right hand. Straight stiff blade, tapering to a point. Characteristic features are the side-ring at the base of the blade, and strongly arched quillons designed to tangle with the opponent's rapier. £70 – £300.

Stiletto. A small cross-hilted dagger with stiff blade triangular or square in section. Cutting edge or edges may be rudimentary. Stilettos were designed for stabbing and mostly made in Italy in the 16th and 17th centuries. £50 – £300.

Bris-épée or **Sword-breaker,** a modern term used for a left-handed dagger which has a blade divided longitudinally so that, by releasing a spring, it flies open and presents three prongs to entangle the opponent's sword blade. The name is also given to daggers whose blades are notched or hooked for the same purpose. £150 – £500.

Swiss dagger, characterised by a strong hilt, shaped like the letter I, mounted on a short, shaped blade. Famous for its highly ornate sheath of gilt-bronze or silver, elaborately pierced and fretted, and mounted with cast ornament. Price depends on the type and intricacy of the decoration. £300 to over £1,000.

Dirk or all-purpose Highland knife, probably developed out of the universal ballock-knife, and in its earlier form has similar spherical excrescences on the hilt. Generally broad-bladed, with a false back edge often heavily serrated. Handles of black wood, often delicately carved with Celtic ornament. The black leather scabbard was often mounted with silver ornament, and incorporated smaller sheaths containing a knife and two-pronged fork. The addition of these 'eating irons' denotes a dirk of the 18th century. Genuine Highland dirks of the 17th and 18th centuries are rare and are in the price range £100 – £500.

The majority of dirks are 19th century in origin and became increasingly decorative as the century advanced. The inclusion of cairngorms indicates dirks made after about 1830.

Naval dirks were introduced mainly for midshipmen in the late 18th century. They have straight or curved blades and are worn suspended from a short hanger. Price ranges from £25 – £100.

Ornamental dirks were also much favoured by Nazi Germany and (to a lesser extent) by Fascist Italy in the 1930s. Though of recent origin these dirks are highly sought after by collectors of Nazi militaria. They may be found with the emblems of the armed forces youth movements and numerous paramilitary units. Value depends on insignia and decorative features (ivory handles, silver badges). £30 – £150.

Jambiya or Arab curved dagger. Hilt of wood, horn or silver.

Left to right: Naval Dirk c.1800, blade 16ins. A Scottish Dress Dirk of the Gordon Highlanders by Kirkwood of Edinburgh.

Scabbard of wood, often covered with cloth or velvet studded with brass or silver ornament. £15 — £150.

Katar, a highly distinctive Indian weapon. Short, broad blade, often with ribbed reinforcements, joined to a broad handle with parallel bars, with one or more transverse bars forming an H. The hand grips the transverse bar so that the entire weight of the body can be placed behind the thrust. £15 — £100.

Unusual examples are known with a small pistol incorporated in the handle. £200 — £300.

Kris, a dagger found in the South Sea Islands and characterised by its wavy blade of watered steel. Handle often at an angle, so that it could be thrust from the shoulder. £25 — £100.

Kindjal, or broad-bladed Caucasian dagger. I-shaped handle usually with horn grips and inscribed silver. Wide range of styles and value depends on the amount of decoration etched on the blade and the ornament on the handle and scabbard. £20 — £150.

Bade-bade, a large curved dagger of South-east Asia. Usually has a 'walking stick' handle. Curved blade often inlaid, damascened or etched with Arabic inscriptions. Ornament in brass or silver. £30 — £100.

Khanjar. An Indian dagger with a short, curved blade, the hilt curved to continue the arc of the blade. Hilt of stone or ivory usually ending in a scrolled knob, carved or inset with stones. £20 — £500.

Kukri, the famous broad-bladed curved fighting knife of the Gurkhas. The distinctive blade broadens in the middle. Hilt of metal or bone with brass mounts on the grips. Scabbard of wood, sometimes covered with velvet, and containing a skinning knife in a side sheath. £10 — £100.

Kris with accompanying sheath.

Indian Khanjar dagger.

Museums
Imperial War Museum, London.
National Army Museum, London.
Victoria and Albert Museum, London.
British Museum (Ethnography) London.
The Tower of London.
Royal Scottish Museum, Edinburgh.
Scottish United Services Museum, Edinburgh Castle.
Art Gallery and Museum, Glasgow.
Wallace Collection, London.

Reading List
Atwood, J. The Daggers and Edged Weapons of Hitler's Germany. Berlin, 1965.
Blair. European and American Arms. 1962.
Dean, B. Catalogue of European Daggers. New York, 1929.
German, M.C. A Guide to Oriental Daggers and Swords. London, 1967.
Hayward, John F. Swords and Daggers. London, 1951.
Mollo, A. Daggers of the Third German Reich. London, 1967.
Peterson, H.L. Daggers and Fighting Knives of the Western World. London, 1968.
Wallace, John. Scottish Swords and Dirks. London, 1970.
Wilkinson, Frederick. Swords and Daggers. London, 1967.

Swords

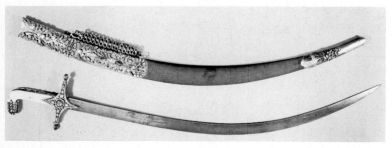

A Persian presentation scimitar, mounted in gold and set with precious stones.

For more than 3,000 years the principal edged weapon used by military and naval forces and within the past 250 years also used extensively as a dress weapon by gentlemen of quality. As the tactical qualities of swords have diminished over the past century, their aesthetic qualities have increased. Since 1914 swords have had little more than ceremonial functions. This is a very large subject which cannot adequately be condensed here and only general pointers to value can be given. The factors which govern value are age, condition, the purpose for which the sword was produced, whether for officers or other ranks, the regiment or unit concerned (indicated by insignia on the pommel or guard), whether for ceremonial or combat, unusual decorative features, country of origin and maker's name. These factors are of varying importance. Thus a 17th century sword would be greatly enhanced in value if the blade bore the authentic mark of Andrea Ferrara (though forgeries abound), but 19th century officers' swords by Wilkinson, Wheeler or Gill are not necessarily more desirable merely on that account, although these were the leading makers of that period and produced the best quality blades. The usual criteria of date-lines are difficult to apply to swords, since styles of earlier periods were copied extensively in the 19th century and European swords of that era frequently borrowed design features from other areas. For example, the curved blade ·and Mameluke handle found on Turkish swords were popular features of presentation weapons and general officers' swords from 1810 onwards.

The picture is further confused by the prevalence of theatrical, masonic and court swords, which frequently deceive both collectors and dealers, and are frequently offered at prices far in excess of their real value. A close examination, however, will reveal that theatrical weapons are usually poorly constructed and rather gaudily finished, with an excess of gilding and decoration on the pommel and guard.

Masonic swords (including society weapons for the Knights of Columbus, etc.) usually have a cross hilt based on those of medieval knights, ornate pommels and engraved blades. Though not in great demand, some masonic and society swords are expensive on account of their decoration with precious metals, enamelling and gilding. Good 19th century examples now fetch from £40 to £90, depending on decorative features and the society associated with them.

Court swords are generally light, very elegant and extravagantly decorated. Often the styling of the decoration is a guide to age in 17th and 18th century examples, while hallmarks on pommels, guards and precious metal mountings on scabbards should make precise dating possible. At the upper end of the scale, elaborate court weapons with a well-established pedigree may fetch more than £100. At the other end of the scale, however, mid- and late Victorian court swords with gilt-metal decoration and no particular redeeming features are in the price range £15 — £40. European court swords, often featuring the insignia of foreign royalty, may be worth from £20 to £60.

Dress swords, Rapiers and **Hangers** worn by gentlemen evolved out of the personal arms carried by persons of quality in medieval times. These weapons may be generally classed as small-swords and have slim tapering blades, with no cutting edge and a pointed tip. Small-swords of the late 17th century, with cruciform quillions, £55 — £120.

Spanish rapiers of this period, renowned for their fine steel blades, £150 — £220.

More elaborate rapiers, with swept hilts, and occasionally also with narrow knuckle guards, £100 — £250.

Later 18th century small-swords are in the price range £40 — £80, though silver-hilted weapons are now from £150 to £300.

Georgian dress swords range from £30 to £70, depending on decorative features.

Mourning swords of the late 18th century (with blackened metal parts), £40 — £80.

The wearing of swords by gentlemen declined in the late 18th century in Britain, though it survived in other parts of Europe as late as 1850. European small-swords of the early 19th century are in the price range £25 — £50.

Ceremonial dress swords of more recent vintage are worn by diplomats, lords-lieutenant and other dignitaries and officials on most ceremonial occasions. Often found with blades which unscrew from the handle, instead of running right through the sword-grip to the tang-end and

Left: A late 19th century naval officer's sword, brass hilt, with braid knot, etched blade. Right: An early 20th century naval officer's sword, brass hilt with braid knot, 3 1½ins. etched blade. Note the difference between Victorian Crown (St. Edward's) and 'modern' Crown (Tudor).

pommel. Value depends on decorative quality, but prices are from £15 to £30 in most cases.

Hunting short-swords were fashionable in Europe in the 18th and 19th centuries and were intended for administering the *coup de grâce* to wounded animals. Blades are usually relatively short, either straight or tapered, with one or two cutting edges, and often furnished *en suite* with a knife or dagger with handle matching that of the sword. Hunting swords are mostly of French, German, Austrian or eastern European manufacture. Hilts are usually more ornate and less protective than in military weapons and are seldom provided with a knuckle guard. 'Working' examples are in the price range £40 – £90, but the more elaborate 'dress' swords (with silver hilts and/or ivory handles) may be worth up to £200.

Presentation Swords form the élite of military edged weapons and may be worth £1,000+ if they were produced individually, with unique decorative features on handle and blade and are associated with a specific individual. These swords were awarded by cities and institutions to famous admirals. Lower down the scale, however, are the patriotic fund swords presented by Lloyds and other organisations to naval and military officers in the Napoleonic wars. Different qualities of sword (priced at the time of issue at £100, £50 or £30) were awarded from patriotic funds to officers in recognition of their gallantry. In addition it was not unusual for a ship's captain to reward gallantry in his junior officers by giving them presentation swords. The latter are generally less ornate than the patriotic fund swords, but this is balanced by the fact that they were usually 'one off' and their value will depend on provenance and association. Prices for patriotic fund swords are £1,500 – £2,000, £3,000 – £4,000 and £3,500 – £5,500. 'Private' presentation swords, £200 – £500.

Presentation swords exist for other periods than the Napoleonic Wars, and of course are by no means confined to the United Kingdom. The value of presentation weapons from other campaigns and countries will depend largely on intrinsic qualities and the circumstances of the issue. In general presentation swords of Germany (including the Nazi period) are the most highly prized, with France and the United States trailing behind. Thus German presentation swords of the 1864, 1866, 1870-1 and 1914 campaigns are in the price range £300 – £500; those of the Nazi period from £150 to £400.

Broadswords, with relatively plain hilts, were the standard European edged weapon from the 17th century onwards. Examples from the 17th and 18th centuries are still plentiful and rate £40 – £100 for good average specimens. More ornate forms, or swords with blades by leading Continental makers, are worth much more. £150 – £400.

Scottish basket-hilted broadswords (sometimes, though erroneously, called claymores) are found from the 17th century (£150 – £300), though 18th century examples are more common (£80 – £130). This distinctive type was also used by Scottish regiments (see below).

Regimental swords date from the Napoleonic Wars and offer considerable scope, with a wide range of values. Prices depend on many factors, including date, whether cavalry, infantry or other formations, whether officers' or other ranks', condition and maker's marks (the last being not as important as regimental markings). Below are given some typical prices:

Army officer's sword, early 19th century, £100 – £300.
Army officer's sword, late 19th century, £50 – £100.

Left: Scottish or English cavalry officer's broadsword c.1760. Right: 18th century Scottish officer's basket-hilted broadsword.

Sergeant's sword, early 19th century, £80 – £150.
Other ranks' cavalry sabre, 1900, £20 – £60.
Mid-Victorian Scottish officer's broadsword, £60 – £120.
Naval officer's sword, early 19th century, £100 – £250.
Naval warrant officer's sword, mid-19th century, £50 – £80.
Naval officer's sword, late 19th century, £50 – £90.
Naval petty officer's sword, mid-19th century, £40 – £70.

Points to look for

Regimental markings, on 19th and 20th century swords, may add considerably to the value, depending on the unit or formation, with preference in descending order to the Household Cavalry, the Brigade of Guards, other cavalry units, infantry regiments, specialist formations (Engineers, Signals), Volunteer and Militia units, non-combatant formations. Inscriptions on swords are important plus factors. In addition to presentation swords for gallantry in action (see above) are weapons presented to officers on retirement. These are not as desirable as weapons presented in recognition of heroic deeds, but their value depends on the person and circumstances of the award. The same applies to regimental awards and 'swords of honour' to prize-winning officer cadets (£50 – £100), though such swords will be worth much more if the recipient rose to high rank subsequently or had an otherwise notable service career.

Pitfalls

Beware of swords with commemorative or presentation inscriptions engraved on the blades when the hilt and scabbard are comparatively plain. The conversion of plain, standard weapons to something desirable has been widely practised in the past. More problematic are blades engraved with such names as Ferrara and Sahagun, in an attempt to pass them off as the work of the great Toledo bladesmiths. The collector will also encounter swords with replaced blades, or with broken sword blades filed down to convert them to dirks. Both practices have actually been known to occur quite genuinely.

Museums

Imperial War Museum, London.
National Army Museum, London.
Victoria and Albert Museum, London.
The Tower of London.
Royal Scottish Museum, Edinburgh.
Scottish United Services Museum, Edinburgh Castle.

The Art Gallery and Museum, Glasgow.

The Castle Museum, York.

Regimental Museums (a detailed list appears as an appendix in *Militaria* by Frederick Wilkinson, 1969).

Reading List

Angolia, J. Swords of Hitler's Third Reich. Leigh-on-Sea, 1969.

Annis, P.G.W. Naval Swords. London, 1970.

Aylward, J.D. The Small-sword in England. London, 1960.

Blair, Claude. European and American Arms. London, 1962.

Bosanquet, H.T.A. The Naval Officer's Sword. London, 1955.

ffoulkes, Charles and Hopkinson E.C. Sword, Lance and Bayonet. London, 1967.

Latham, J. Wilkinson. British Military Swords.

May, W.E. and Annis, P.G.W. Swords for Sea Service. London, 1970.

May, W.E. and Kennard, A.N. Naval Swords and Firearms. London, 1968.

Mollo, E. Russian Military Swords 1801-1917. London, 1969.

Norman, A.V.B. Small-swords and Military Swords. London, 1967.

Oakeshott, R.E. The Sword in the Age of Chivalry. London, 1964.

Peterson, H.L. The American Sword. Philadelphia, 1965.

Wallace, J. Scottish Swords and Dirks. London, 1970.

Wilkinson, Frederick. Swords and Daggers, London, 1968. Militaria. London, 1969. Edged Weapons. London, 1970. Antique Arms and Armour. London, 1972.

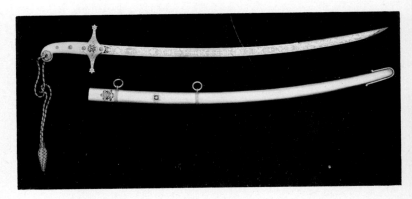

A fine presentation sword with 9ct. gold and ivory hilt — of Mameluke type in silver scabbard.

Tipstaves and Truncheons

Weapons issued to law enforcement officers from the Middle Ages onwards, serving the double purpose of indicating rank and authority. The dual role of tipstaves is indicated by the fact that, from an early age, they were frequently ornamented with coats of arms, civil or municipal emblems, mottoes and names or initials of towns, parishes, districts, counties or other divisions of local government. The earliest examples are difficult to date since they seldom include a date in their inscription, but those featuring the Royal arms (an increasingly common feature from the early 18th century) can be dated fairly accurately by minor details in the arms.

Date-lines

1700-1792   Tipstaves of ebony mounted with brass or silver, with a threaded crown at one end. Usually solid, but sometimes having a small compartment revealed when the crown is unscrewed. Decoration on the staff usually hand-painted, though transfer-printed arms are known from about 1760. £10 − £40. Particularly finely decorated examples might be slightly more.

1792-1830   Tipstaves generally less decorative. Increasing use of transfer-printing for the coat of arms. On the organisation of the London police into eight stations in 1792 tipstaves were issued to the constables inscribed with the name or initials of these stations. Numerous tipstaves bearing the initials or names of county or civic authorities, Bank of England, Overseers of the Poor, Surveyors of the Highways, etc. £5 − £15.

A George III painted truncheon, the body with Royal cypher, dated 1781 and decorated with the Royal coat of arms against a dark ground, 17¾ins., 1781.

A William IV painted truncheon by Parker, Holborn decorated with the crowned Royal coat of arms above WR cypher against a black painted ground, turned wood handle, 18¾ins., 1830-1837.

1830-1870	Tipstaves replaced by shorter truncheons. Similar decoration of Royal arms, county or civic emblems. Great variety of shapes, from straight narrow sticks to thick, balustroid bludgeons. Most desirable type is pivoted at the centre to form a vicious flail. £4 – £12.
1870-1920	Later truncheons devoid of decoration, except occasionally a small engraved or pokerwork crown and Royal monogram, or initials of the police constabulary. Sometimes found with a matching tubular leather case. £3 – £10.

A William IV truncheon by Parker, Holborn with turned wood handle, the black painted body with crowned Royal cypher and inscribed 'Special Constable', 18¾ins., 1830-1837.

Points to look for

The value of tipstaves and truncheons depends on the amount of decoration, especially if it is hand-painted. Condition is very important since, by the nature of these weapons, wear or damage is frequently encountered. The early truncheons of the London police offices which were the precursor of the Metropolitan Police in 1829, are particularly desirable since only a limited number of these weapons were issued in each case. Many truncheons bear a tiny brass plate giving the name and address of the manufacturer. Names to look for are William Parker or Parker Field.

Pitfalls

Interest in this field has encouraged the reproduction of tipstaves and truncheons in recent years. These replicas are almost always decorated with transfer-prints of the Royal coat of arms and can usually be distinguished from genuine transfer-printed truncheons by their bright colouring and fresh appearance.

Museums

Metropolitan Police Museum, London.
The Police College, Bramshill.
The Castle Museum, York.
Most regional and civic museums include tipstaves and truncheons of local interest.

Reading List

Clark, E.F. Truncheons, Their Romance and Reality. London, 1935.
Dicken, E.R.H. Truncheons, Their History. North Devon, 1952.

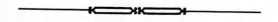

WINE LABELS

Originally known as bottle tickets, these discs or tags bearing the names of wines and spirits came into use in the mid-18th century, replacing the parchment or card labels and superseding the engraved inscriptions on decanters when a change of fashion introduced decanters with an over-all cut glass pattern c.1770. The earliest dateable labels seem to have been made about 1735. A major problem is the fact that many silver labels are unmarked since this was not required by law until the 1790s though some have makers' marks. Labels may also be found in Sheffield plate (up to 1850), electro-plate (from 1840), in enamelled metal or even in porcelain, ivory, mother-of-pearl, bone or tortoiseshell.

Date-lines

1740-1760	Earliest labels often escutcheon or shield shaped. Plus factors are decorative flourishes and the names of unusual or long-forgotten wines. £20 – £30 for unmarked labels; £25 – £50 for hallmarked examples (usually lion passant only), though this figure may rise sharply if one of the notable smiths (such as Sandylands Drinkwater) can be identified. £80 – £100.
1740-1750	Earliest 'broad rectangular' labels, with chamfered ends and occasionally incorporating a tiny medallion above centre. £15 – £25 unmarked; occasionally hallmarked with lion passant. £20 – £40.
1750-1800	Crescent-shaped labels. Earliest examples (1750-60) with plain or bright-cut edges. £25 – £85. Later ones sometimes more elaborate, with floral engraving flanking the inscription. £12 – £20. Hester Bateman. £100+

Top row left to right: Red Port, dome fret top by Hester Bateman; interesting sauce name Elder Vr.; Port, round shape is rare. 2nd row left to right: Bronti, common shape, very rare name; Calcavella, good name combined with rare armorial; Vino de pasto, good name, beautiful bright-cut border. 3rd row left to right: Port, eye shape with typical fine pierced border by Susannah Barker; Mountain, good name, fine scroll by Hester Bateman; Lisbon, another example by Susannah Barker. 4th row left to right: Madeira, feather edged crescent; S, very unusual single letter, fine workmanship; Port, by Hester Bateman with zig-zag border. 5th row left to right: Claret, early, shows good quality of plain escutcheon; Sherry, good late workmanship; Lisbon, early Old Sheffield plate copper

1790-1849	Heyday of the broad rectangular label. Less decorative than the earliest examples and invariably hallmarked. £12 — £20 for average specimens; more for unusual wines, or important names. Those by Hester Bateman, for example, are now in the price range £60 — £80.
1770-1790	Eye-shaped, plain or reed borders. Those with fret edges usually attributable to Susannah Barker. £30 — £80.
1770-1800	Oval labels with reeded edges are comparatively scarce. £20 — £40 for plain ones; £30 — £60 for those with ornament round edges.
1750-1800	Enamel labels, mainly produced in Staffordshire, though also briefly produced at Battersea, 1753-6. Battersea examples shield-shaped and decorated with fauns and putti (£100 — £200); Bilston and later Staffordshire labels £50 — £100.
1760-1780	Escutcheon labels in Sheffield plate with copper backs. £20 — £30.
1780-1800	Crescent-shaped labels in Sheffield plate. £15 — £30.
1790-1800	Circular collars (neck rings) of Sheffield plate. £10 — £20.
1790-1810	Circular collars of silver. £50 — £90.
1800-1840	Broad rectangular in Sheffield plate. £5 — £15.
1800-1820	Crescent in Old Sheffield plate with circular area completely filled by a vine motif (not found in silver). £10 — £20.
1800-1810	Crescent in Old Sheffield plate with angular outer edges. £10 — £20.
1820-1860	Fancy shapes — animals, vine-leaves (relatively common), vine and tendril (especially by Emes & Barnard). £30 — £100.

Left to right: A Staffordshire wine label, late 18th century. A Battersea enamel wine label designed by James Gawin, c.1755. Staffordshire enamel wine label late 18th century.

1840-1900	Victorian silver labels; often a revival of earlier types (including the escutcheon) but generally of much poorer quality. £10 – £25.
1850-1900	Electro-plate wine labels. Commonest type, but of little value. £2 – £5.

Points to look for

Unusual shapes or decorative features in any of the above types are an important plus factor. Silver-gilt labels, especially those by the leading silver-smiths, are highly desirable but very rare. Labels by Paul Storr, for example, have now topped the £200-mark. While labels with standard names (Madeira, Sherry, Whisky, etc.) have a perennial useful function, the labels which are most keenly sought after are those with quaint or unusual names, such as Parsnip, Mountain or Bounce. Ancient spellings or mis-spellings are also highly regarded.

Calcavella. This heavy type neck ring with pendant label is not very common, made by J. Tayleur, 1792.

Pitfalls

Relatively few, since wine labels are so insignificant compared with other forms of silver that they have escaped the attention of the forger to a great extent. Beware, however, of labels which have been removed from larger pieces of silver, such as wine jugs, coolers and épergnes, and then engraved with names of obscure wines. Also avoid labels which have been heavily soldered and are generally in poor condition, or have had the name changed at some stage in their history. A modern chain will detract from the value.

Typical Old Sheffield plate copper back escutcheons.

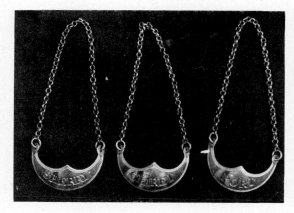

Very unusual shape of crescent.

Museums
Victoria and Albert Museum, London.
National Museum of Wales, Cardiff.
Royal Scottish Museum, Edinburgh.
Central Museum and Art Gallery, Northampton.
City Museum, Sheffield.
Wedgwood Museum, Stoke on Trent.
City Museum and Art Gallery, Worcester.
Yorkshire Museum, York.

Reading List
Cropper, P.J. Bottle Labels. London, 1924.
Penzer, Nicholas M. The Book of the Wine Label. London, 1947.
Whitworth, E.W. Wine Labels. London, 1966.

General Reading List

Amaya, Mario. Art Nouveau. London, New York, 1966.

Angus, Ian. Collecting Antiques. London, 1972.

Battersby, Martin. The World of Art Nouveau. London, 1968. Art Nouveau. London, 1969. The Decorative Twenties. London, 1969.

Bedford, John. The Collecting Man. London, 1968.

Boger, Louise A. and H.B. The Dictionary of Antiques and the Decorative Arts. London, 1969.

Butler, Joseph T. American Antiques, 1800-1900. New York, 1965.

Cameron, Ian and Kingsley-Rowe, Elizabeth (eds.). Collins Encyclopedia of Antiques. London, 1973.

Chu, Arthur and Grace. Oriental Antiques and Collectibles. New York, 1973.

Comstock, H. The Concise Encyclopaedia of American Antiques. (2 vols.). London, 1958.

Davidson, Marshall B. The American Heritage History of Antiques. New York, 1969.

Field, June. Collecting Georgian and Victorian Crafts. London, 1973.

Fletcher, Edward. Digging Up Antiques. London, 1975.

Garner, Philippe. The World of Edwardiana. London, 1974.

Hamlyn, Paul (ed.). The Antique Collector's Illustrated Dictionary. London, 1975.

Hayward, Charles. Antique or Fake? London, 1970.

Harris, N. Victorian Antiques. London, 1975.

Hillier, Bevis. Art Deco. London, 1968. Austerity Binge. London, 1975.

Hughes, G. Bernard. Collecting Antiques. London, 1961. More About Collecting Antiques. London, 1962. The Country Life Collector's Pocket Book. London, 1963.

Hughes, Therle. Small Antiques for the Collector. London, 1964. Small Decorative Antiques. London, 1959. More Small Decorative Antiques. London, 1962. Cottage Antiques. London, 1967.

Kelley, Austin P. The Anatomy of Antiques. London, 1974.

Latham, Jean. Miniature Antiques. London, 1972.

Laver, James. Victoriana. London, 1966.

Lichten, Frances. Decorative Art of Victoria's Era. New York, 1960.

Lesieutre, Alain. The Spirit and Splendour of Art Deco. London, 1974.

McClinton, Katherine M. Art Deco: A Guide for Collectors. New York, 1972.

Mackay, James A. An Introduction to Small Antiques. London, 1970. Antiques of the Future. London, 1970. The Dictionary of Turn of the Century Antiques. London, 1974. The Encyclopaedia of Small Antiques. London, 1975.

Madsen, Tschudi. Sources of Art Nouveau. New York, 1957. Art Nouveau. London, 1967.

Mebane, John. New Horizons in Collecting. London, New York, 1967. The Coming Collecting Boom. London, 1968.

Norwak, Mary, Kitchen Antiques. London, 1975.

Peter, N. Collecting Victoriana. London, 1965.

Ramsay, L.G.C. (ed.) The Concise Encyclopaedia of Antiques (5 vols.). London, 1955-60.

Reade, B. Regency Antiques. London, 1953.

Rheims, Maurice. The Age of Art Nouveau. London, 1966. The Antique Collector's Handbook. London, 1959.

Savage, George. Dictionary of Antiques. London, 1970.

Schmutzler, Robert. Art Nouveau. London, New York, 1964.

Speck, G.E. and Sutherland, Euan. English Antiques. London, 1969.

Toller, Jane. Living with Antiques. London, 1969. Regency and Victorian Crafts. London, 1969.

Wardell-Yerburgh, J.C. The Pleasure of Antiques. London, 1974.

Wenham, Edward. Antiques A-Z. London, 1968.

Whittington, Peter. Undiscovered Antiques. London, 1972.

Wills, Geoffrey. Antiques. London, 1961.

Woodhouse, C.P. Investment in Antiques and Art. London, 1969.

Wood, Violet. Victoriana: A Collector's Guide. London, 1968.